AF884882

GUIDE TO THE CALIFORNIA RULES OF PROFESSIONAL CONDUCT FOR ESTATE PLANNING, TRUST AND PROBATE COUNSEL

FOURTH EDITION

The Executive Committee of the Trusts and Estates Section
of the California Lawyers Association

Thomas W. Shaver, Editor

Guide to the California Rules of Professional Conduct for Estate Planning, Trust and Probate Counsel: Fourth Edition

Copyright © 2020 by The California Lawyers Association. All rights reserved.

No parts of this book may be used or reproduced in any form or by any electronic or mechanical means, including information storage and retrieval systems, without written permission, except for the use of brief quotations in a book review.

CLA books may be purchased for educational, business, or sales promotional use. For information, please contact: info@calawyers.org.

The Executive Committee of the Trusts and Estates Section
400 Capitol Mall, Suite 650
Sacramento, CA 95814
calawyers.org

Fourth Edition
Paperback ISBN: 978-1-7359074-0-6
e-book ISBN: 978-1-7359074-1-3

Each of the following contributors informed and enriched this fourth edition with comments on current ethical issues, the experience of their practice, and thoughtful review of the text and annotations.

CALIFORNIA LAWYERS ASSOCIATION, TRUSTS AND ESTATES SECTION EXECUTIVE COMMITTEE

Agnieszka K. Adams

John M. Andersen

Yvonne A. Ascher

Robert C. Barton

Mason L. Brawley

Cynthia F. Catalino

Elizabeth M. Engh

Ryka Farotte

Cheryl A. Forbes

Judith P. Hehir

Ralph E. Hughes

Melissa R. Karlsten

Howard A. Kipnis

Gina L. Lera

Ellen McKissock

Matthew W. McMurtrey

Erin A. Norcia

Ciarán A. O'Sullivan

Joy J. Paeske

Stella Pantazis

DeAnne E. Parker

Mark S. Poochigian

Michael J. Rosen-Prinz

Thomas W. Shaver

Daniel I. Spector

Herbert A. Stroh

Carlena L. Tapella

Nicholas J. Van Brunt

Carol Elias Zolla

ORANGE COUNTY BAR ASSOCIATION, ETHICS AND PROFESSIONALISM COMMITTEE

Kristin Yokomoto

CALIFORNIA LAWYERS ASSOCIATION, ETHICS COMMITTEE

Neil J Wertlieb

ACKNOWLEDGEMENTS

This fourth edition of the Ethics Guide for Trusts and Estates Practitioners ("Guide") is the culmination of two years of work analyzing the current California Rules of Professional Conduct, relevant cases, ethics opinions, and articles that inform the ethical duties of a trusts and estates practitioner. It is truly the work of the entire Executive Committee of the Trusts and Estates Section of the California Lawyers Association ("Committee"). The members of the Committee brought the experience of their collective practices to this Guide, and devoted many hours to discussing ethical issues and submitting research and writing from that practice. The title page to this edition is a testimony to the many minds and hands that contributed to the completion of this edition.

The Ethics Committee for the California Lawyers Association was formed in October 2019. The members of that committee have a broad range of experience in analyzing the Rules of Professional Conduct and commenting on published ethics opinions. We are grateful to Neil J. Wertlieb for his extensive review and comments on a final draft of the Guide.

We gratefully acknowledge the permission from The American College of Trust and Estate Counsel to reprint from the fifth edition of *The American College of Trust and Estate Counsel, Commentaries on the Model Rules of Professional Conduct* and the third edition of *ACTEC Engagement Letters*. Greater congruity with the American Bar Association Model Rules of Professional Conduct heightens the relevance of the Commentaries to the interpretation of and practice under the revised Rules of Professional Conduct.

Special thanks to Kristin Yokomoto for volunteering with the Committee through this entire process and for her substantial authorship of chapter 10 of this Guide, Ethics and Technology. That chapter takes a systematic look at the ethical duties that may arise in integrating current and emerging technologies into a trusts and estates practice.

The Committee recognizes Ian R. Friedman who acted as the research assistant for most of the two-year process. This edition of the Guide is more thoughtful and comprehensive because of his efforts. The depth of research on current ethics cases, opinions, and other authorities is largely attributable to his diligent efforts on behalf of this edition of the Guide. Ian also contributed written analysis on ethical questions posed to him and guidance from his own practice. Special thanks also to Sophia Cizmark for the painstaking and invaluable work she gave in reviewing the final draft of this Guide.

Thomas W. Shaver, Editor

TABLE OF CONTENTS

CHAPTER 1 INTRODUCTION

The California Rules of Professional Conduct, originally adopted in 1928, were revised by order of the Supreme Court of California effective November 1, 2018. The State Bar Board of Trustees proposed 70 new and amended rules with the goal of bringing the California ethical rules into greater congruity with the Model Rules of Professional Conduct that the American Bar Association ("ABA") promulgated in 1983. The Supreme Court approved 27 rules as submitted, approved another 42 rules as modified by the court, and denied approving one proposed rule, increasing the number of ethical rules by 50%, from 46 rules to 69. The court also adopted a numbering and organizational system based on the Model Rules. The third edition of this Guide noted the differences between the Rules of Professional Conduct and the Model Rules, and many of those differences have now been harmonized.

The one rule that the Supreme Court declined to approve was a proposed exception to the duty of confidentiality that would have allowed lawyers to disclose client confidences when a client is physically or mentally incapacitated and at risk of significant harm from physical or financial abuse. The Rules of Professional Conduct maintain the strict duty of confidentiality as set forth in the State Bar Act, Business and Professions Code section 6068, subdivision (e). "It is the duty of an attorney: . . . [t]o maintain inviolate the confidence, and at every peril to himself or herself to preserve the secrets, of his or her client." This edition of the Guide notes how the statutory duty of confidentiality informs the Rules of Professional Conduct and continues to depart from the Model Rules.

Organization of Materials. The primary goal of this Guide is to assist the trusts and estates practitioner in navigating through the recent changes to the Rules of Professional Conduct and incorporating the ethical duties embodied in those rules to develop a more thoughtful and effective practice that protects the practitioner, law firm, clients, and the public. To that end, each chapter of this Guide is organized, as applicable, in the following format:

- Statement of the California Rule of Professional Conduct
- Discussion of the rule and the practical effects of its ethical requirements
- Comments on the rule from the State Bar of California
- Commentary on the related model rule from The American College of Trust and Estate Counsel and the American Bar Association
- Statement of the related former rule of the Rules of Professional Conduct
- State Bar Act, Evidence Code, and other statutes that inform the ethical rule
- Case studies for discussion
- Case law interpreting the rule and its ethical requirements
- Ethic opinions from the State Bar of California, local bar associations, and the ABA
- Articles on ethical issues
- Sample documents

This Guide quotes frequently from the comments on the Rules of Professional Conduct because they place the ethical rules in the context of evolving California case law. "The comments are not a basis for imposing discipline but are intended only to provide guidance for interpreting and practicing in compliance with the rules." Rules Prof. Conduct, rule 1.0(c). This Guide also includes citations to the case law of legal malpractice where the cited decisions help inform the reader of the conduct that violates the rules of ethical conduct and the practical consequences that may flow from a violation of one or more ethical duties.

Greater congruity with the Model Rules heightens the relevance of The American College Trust and Estate Counsel ("ACTEC") and ABA Commentaries to the interpretation of the Rules of Professional Conduct and practice under those ethical rules. The ACTEC Commentaries on the Model Rules provide specific advice on common ethical issues that frequently arise in a trusts and estates practice.

For ease of reference, this edition of the Guide reprints a prior rule of the Rules of Professional Conduct when significantly changed. The reader can compare the prior and current rules to understand the textual discussion of the changes in the ethical rules. Restatement of the prior rules also assists in reviewing existing case law and ethics opinions that were based on those prior rules.

The case studies in this Guide draw fact patterns from current cases and ethics opinions. The reader is invited to reflect on and discuss how a practitioner might best address the ethical issues presented by those facts. The case citation and holding of the court is given at the end of the study for comparison.

Sample documents are offered to show how to incorporate thoughtful ethical compliance into communications with clients and third parties.

Governing Principles. The Rules of Professional Conduct "are intended to regulate professional conduct of lawyers through discipline." They have been adopted "to protect the public, the courts and the legal profession; protect the integrity of the legal system; and to promote the administration of justice and confidence in the legal profession." Rules Prof. Conduct, rule 1.0. The prohibition against certain conduct in the Rules is not exclusive. Lawyers are also bound by all applicable statutory law, including the State Bar Act (Business and Professions Code sections 6000 et seq.) and opinions of California courts.

Although not binding, opinions of ethics committees in California should be consulted by lawyers for guidance on proper professional conduct. A lawyer may also consider ethics opinions issued, and rules and standards promulgated, by other jurisdictions. Rules Prof. Conduct, rule 1.0, com. [4].

The State Bar of California Committee on Professional Responsibility and Conduct, in its Formal Opinion Number 2019-197, issued guidance that encourages lawyers to seek advice on their ethical obligations. In a thoughtful analysis, the opinion concludes that seeking legal advice concerning ethical obligations owed to a client by itself does not create a conflict of interest between the lawyer and client. When a lawyer becomes aware that the lawyer has committed an error that could prejudice the client, the lawyer may ethically seek legal advice concerning obligations to the client and compliance with the ethical rules, including those rules governing required disclosures to clients. The lawyer is protected in seeking legal advice on ethical rules whether the lawyer seeks that advice from a lawyer outside of the firm or in-house counsel. Consistent with the spirit of Opinion Number 2019-197, this Guide is meant to provide resources that lawyers may use to understand the Rules of Professional Conduct and encourage thoughtful compliance with those rules.

The Rules of Professional Conduct also discuss the special responsibilities of a lawyer for the quality of justice. The California Supreme Court added comment [5] to rule 1.0 of the Rules of Professional Conduct to describe this aspect of a lawyer's professional obligations:

> [5] The disciplinary standards created by these rules are not intended to address all aspects of a lawyer's professional obligations. A lawyer, as a member of the legal profession, is a representative and advisor of clients, an officer of the legal system and a public citizen having special responsibilities for the quality of justice. A lawyer should be aware of deficiencies in the administration of justice and of the fact that the poor, and sometimes persons* who are not poor cannot afford adequate legal assistance. Therefore, all lawyers are encouraged to devote professional time and resources and use civic influence to ensure equal access to the system of justice for those who because of economic or social barriers cannot afford or secure adequate legal counsel. In meeting this responsibility of the profession, every lawyer should aspire to render at least fifty hours of pro bono publico legal services per year. The lawyer should aim to provide a substantial* majority of such hours to indigent individuals or to nonprofit organizations with a primary purpose of providing services to the poor or on behalf of the poor or disadvantaged. Lawyers may also provide financial support to organizations providing free legal services. (See Bus. and Prof. Code, sec. 6073.)

Ethical Violations and Actions for Legal Malpractice. The Rules of Professional Conduct do not create new civil causes of action. "A violation of a rule does not itself give rise to a cause of action for damages caused by failure to comply with the rule. Nothing in these rules or the Comments to the rules is intended to enlarge or to restrict the law regarding the liability of lawyers to others." Rules Prof. Conduct, rule 1.0(b)(3).

Nevertheless, the following comments to rule 1.0 review existing California case law holding that the violation of an ethical rule may be evidence of a breach of fiduciary duty or of professional negligence:

> [1] The Rules of Professional Conduct are intended to establish the standards for lawyers for purposes of discipline. (See *Ames v. State Bar* (1973) 8 Cal.3d 910, 917 [106 Cal.Rptr. 489].) Therefore, failure to comply with an obligation or prohibition imposed by a rule is a basis for invoking the disciplinary process. Because the rules are not designed to be a basis for civil liability, a violation of a rule does not itself give rise to a cause of action for enforcement of a rule or for damages caused by failure to comply with the rule. (*Stanley v. Richmond* (1995) 35 Cal.App.4th 1070, 1097 [41 Cal.Rptr.2d 768].) Nevertheless, a lawyer's violation of a rule may be

evidence of breach of a lawyer's fiduciary or other substantive legal duty in a non-disciplinary context. (*Ibid.*; see also *Mirabito v. Liccardo* (1992) 4 Cal.App.4th 41, 44 [5 Cal.Rptr.2d 571].) A violation of a rule may have other non-disciplinary consequences. (See, e.g., *Fletcher v. Davis* (2004) 33 Cal.4th 61, 71-72 14 Cal.Rptr.3d 58] [enforcement of attorney's lien]; *Chambers v. Kay* (2002) 29 Cal.4th 142, 161 [126 Cal.Rptr.2d 536] [enforcement of fee sharing agreement].)

[2] While the rules are intended to regulate professional conduct of lawyers, a violation of a rule can occur when a lawyer is not practicing law or acting in a professional capacity.

[3] A willful violation of a rule does not require that the lawyer intend to violate the rule. (*Phillips v. State Bar* (1989) 49 Cal.3d 944, 952 [264 Cal.Rptr. 346]; and see Bus. and Prof. Code, sec. 6077.)

The discussion of the Rules of Professional Conduct in the Guide should not be viewed as establishing a standard of care for the lawyer engaged in a trusts and estates practice. Other facts and circumstances may direct or constrain lawyers in making ethical decisions including possible malpractice exposure; the potential for the lawyer to be called as a witness; and the lawyer's exercise of sound, well-informed judgment. The use of the words "should," "it is ethically required," "it is good practice," or words of similar import are not intended to mean that such requirements or practices are the standard for purposes of establishing an ethical violation or civil liability.

Ethical Rules Specific to a Field of Practice. The Rules of Professional Conduct apply generally to all lawyers without regard to the lawyer's field of practice, specialty, or concentration. ACTEC recognizes that neither the Model Rules of Professional Conduct nor the comments to them provide adequate guidance to the professional responsibilities of lawyers practicing estate planning, trust, and probate law. The ACTEC Commentaries on the Model Rules of Professional Conduct respond to this concern, and this edition of the Guide includes commentary from the most recent fifth edition published in 2016. The ACTEC Commentaries are an invaluable resource of practical guidance, including analysis of specific model rules, coordination between different ethical rules, and application of the rules to hypothetical fact patterns. The Guide adopts that approach and is offered by the Trusts and Estates Section of the California Lawyers Association to provide both general and fact-specific guidance to estates and trusts lawyers facing both common and unusual ethical issues.

The focus of the Guide is the day-to-day practice of the trusts and estates lawyer. It is intended to assist the practitioner in navigating through the Rules of Professional Conduct and understanding the manner and timing in which ethical issues may arise. Sample letters are offered that a lawyer can thoughtfully adapt to the procedures of a particular law practice and the facts of an individual representation. Case studies drawn from recent ethics opinions and court cases can be used to generate discussion and to focus attention on the application of ethical rules to specific facts and circumstances. The Guide includes a new chapter dedicated to the ethical issues of a litigation practice and an expanded chapter on ethics and technology. As in prior editions of this Guide, annotations to the discussion of each ethical issue guide the practitioner to updated statutory and case law, ethics opinions, and other primary sources for further study. We trust that the Guide will find a home on the bookshelf or desk in your office, and that you will turn to it to inform your judgment and continue your practice in accordance with the highest ethical standards.

CHAPTER 2 TERMINOLOGY

2.1 Introduction

Rule 1.0.1 of the Rules of Professional Conduct sets forth defined terms that appear throughout the ethical rules. Understanding those definitions will usually be the starting point for an analysis of the applicable ethical issues. This chapter reviews the defined terms set forth in rule 1.0.1 and offers specific examples of how those terms apply in the context of other rules in the Rules of Professional Conduct. Comments, statutes, and opinions are offered for further context.

The Supreme Court of California adopted the current Rules of Professional Conduct in its Administrative Order 2018-05-09 filed on May 10, 2018. In that Order, the court used an asterisk (*) to identify a word or phrase that is defined in rule 1.0.1 wherever it later appears in a specific rule. This Guide adopts that convention whenever a rule is quoted. An index to each identified use of a defined term in the Rules is included in the Appendix to this Guide.

Rule 1.0.1 of the Rules of Professional Conduct expands upon the five definitions provided in former rule 1-100(B) and adds new defined terms to clarify and assist in the interpretation of the Rules of Professional Conduct.

Former California Rules of Professional Conduct, Rule 1-100(B) – Definitions

> (1) "Law Firm" means: (a) two or more lawyers whose activities constitute the practice of law, and who share its profits, expenses, and liabilities; or (b) a law corporation which employs more than one lawyer; or (c) a division, department, office, or group within a business entity, which includes more than one lawyer who performs legal services for the business entity; or (d) a publicly funded entity which employs more than one lawyer to perform legal services.
>
> (2) "Member" means a member of the State Bar of California.
>
> (3) "Lawyer" means a member of the State Bar of California or a person who is admitted in good standing of and eligible to practice before the bar of any United States court or the highest court of the District of Columbia or any state, territory, or insular possession of the United States, or is licensed to practice law in, or is admitted in good standing and eligible to practice before the bar of the highest court of, a foreign country or any political subdivision thereof.
>
> (4) "Associate" means an employee or fellow employee who is employed as a lawyer.
>
> (5) "Shareholder" means a shareholder in a professional corporation pursuant to Business and Professions Code secs. 6160 et seq.

2.2 Belief

California Rules of Professional Conduct, Rule 1.0.1(a)

> (a) "Belief" or "believes" means that the person* involved actually supposes the fact in question to be true. A person's* belief may be inferred from circumstances.

Examples

California Rules of Professional Conduct, Rule 1.6(b)

> (b) A lawyer may, but is not required to, reveal information protected by Business and Professions Code section 6068, subdivision (e)(1) to the extent that the lawyer reasonably believes* the disclosure is necessary to prevent a criminal act that the lawyer reasonably believes* is likely to result in death of, or substantial* bodily harm to, an individual, as provided in paragraph (c).

California Rules of Professional Conduct, Rule 1.7

> (a) A lawyer shall not, without informed written consent* from each client and compliance with paragraph (d), represent a client if the representation is directly adverse to another client in the same or a separate matter.
>
> (b) A lawyer shall not, without informed written consent* from each affected client and compliance with paragraph (d), represent a client if there is a significant risk the lawyer's representation of the client will be materially limited by the lawyer's responsibilities to or relationships with another client, a former client or a third person,* or by the lawyer's own interests.
>
> (c) Even when a significant risk requiring a lawyer to comply with paragraph (b) is not present, a lawyer shall not represent a client without written* disclosure of the relationship to the client and compliance with paragraph (d) where:
>
>> (1) the lawyer has, or knows* that another lawyer in the lawyer's firm* has, a legal, business, financial, professional, or personal relationship with or responsibility to a party or witness in the same matter; or
>>
>> (2) the lawyer knows* or reasonably should know* that another party's lawyer is a spouse, parent, child, or sibling of the lawyer, lives with the lawyer, is a client of the lawyer or another lawyer in the lawyer's firm,* or has an intimate personal relationship with the lawyer.
>
> (d) Representation is permitted under this rule only if the lawyer complies with paragraphs (a), (b), and (c), and:
>
>> (1) the lawyer reasonably believes* that the lawyer will be able to provide competent and diligent representation to each affected client;

(2) the representation is not prohibited by law; and

(3) the representation does not involve the assertion of a claim by one client against another client represented by the lawyer in the same litigation or other proceeding before a tribunal.

. . .

California Rules of Professional Conduct, Rule 3.6(c)

(c) Notwithstanding paragraph (a), a lawyer may make a statement that a reasonable* lawyer would believe* is required to protect a client from the substantial* undue prejudicial effect of recent publicity not initiated by the lawyer or the lawyer's client. A statement made pursuant to this paragraph shall be limited to such information as is necessary to mitigate the recent adverse publicity.

California Rules of Professional Conduct, rule 1.0.1(b) is reserved.

2.3 Firm

California Rules of Professional Conduct, Rule 1.0.1(c)

(c) "Firm" or "law firm" means a law partnership; a professional law corporation; a lawyer acting as a sole proprietorship; an association authorized to practice law; or lawyers employed in a legal services organization or in the legal department, division or office of a corporation, of a government organization, or of another organization.

Comment on California Rules of Professional Conduct, Rule 1.0.1(c)

[1] Practitioners who share office space and occasionally consult or assist each other ordinarily would not be regarded as constituting a law firm.* However, if they present themselves to the public in a way that suggests that they are a law firm* or conduct themselves as a law firm,* they may be regarded as a law firm* for purposes of these rules. The terms of any formal agreement between associated lawyers are relevant in determining whether they are a firm,* as is the fact that they have mutual access to information concerning the clients they serve.

[2] The term "of counsel" implies that the lawyer so designated has a relationship with the law firm,* other than as a partner* or associate, or officer or shareholder, that is close, personal, continuous, and regular. Whether a lawyer who is denominated as "of counsel" or by a similar term should be deemed a member of a law firm* for purposes of these rules will also depend on the specific facts. (Compare *People ex rel. Department of Corporations v. Speedee Oil Change Systems, Inc.* (1999) 20 Cal.4th 1135 [86 Cal.Rptr.2d 816] with *Chambers v. Kay* (2002) 29 Cal.4th 142 [126 Cal.Rptr.2d 536]).

Examples

California Rules of Professional Conduct, Rule 5.1(a)

> (a) A lawyer who individually or together with other lawyers possesses managerial authority in a law firm,* shall make reasonable* efforts to ensure that the firm* has in effect measures giving reasonable* assurance that all lawyers in the firm* comply with these rules and the State Bar Act.
>
> . . .

California Rules of Professional Conduct, Rule 7.5

> (a) A lawyer shall not use a firm* name, trade name or other professional designation that violates rule 7.1.
>
> (b) A lawyer in private practice shall not use a firm* name, trade name or other professional designation that states or implies a relationship with a government agency or with a public or charitable legal services organization, or otherwise violates rule 7.1.
>
> (c) A lawyer shall not state or imply that the lawyer practices in or has a professional relationship with a law firm* or other organization unless that is the fact.

2.4 Fraud

California Rules of Professional Conduct, Rule 1.0.1(d)

> (d) "Fraud" or "fraudulent" means conduct that is fraudulent under the law of the applicable jurisdiction and has a purpose to deceive.

Comment on California Rules of Professional Conduct, Rule 1.0.1(d)

> [3] When the terms "fraud"* or "fraudulent"* are used in these rules, it is not necessary that anyone has suffered damages or relied on the misrepresentation or failure to inform because requiring the proof of those elements of fraud* would impede the purpose of certain rules to prevent fraud* or avoid a lawyer assisting in the perpetration of a fraud,* or otherwise frustrate the imposition of discipline on lawyers who engage in fraudulent* conduct. The term "fraud"* or "fraudulent"* when used in these rules does not include merely negligent misrepresentation or negligent failure to apprise another of relevant information.

Examples

California Rules of Professional Conduct, Rule 1.5(b)

> (b) Unconscionability of a fee shall be determined on the basis of all the facts and circumstances existing at the time the agreement is entered into except where the parties contemplate that the fee will be affected by later events. The factors to be

considered in determining the unconscionability of a fee include without limitation the following:

(1) whether the lawyer engaged in fraud* or overreaching in negotiating or setting the fee;

. . .

California Rules of Professional Conduct, Rule 8.4(c):

It is professional misconduct for a lawyer to:

. . .

(c) engage in conduct involving dishonesty, fraud,* deceit, or reckless or intentional misrepresentation;

. . .

2.5 Informed Consent

California Rules of Professional Conduct, Rule 1.0.1(e)

(e) "Informed consent" means a person's* agreement to a proposed course of conduct after the lawyer has communicated and explained (i) the relevant circumstances and (ii) the material risks, including any actual and reasonably* foreseeable adverse consequences of the proposed course of conduct.

California Rules of Professional Conduct, Rule 1.0.1(e-1)

(e-1) "Informed written consent" means that the disclosures and the consent required by paragraph (e) must be in writing.*

Comment on California Rules of Professional Conduct, Rule 1.0.1(e-1)

[4] The communication necessary to obtain informed consent* or informed written consent* will vary according to the rule involved and the circumstances giving rise to the need to obtain consent.

Examples

California Rules of Professional Conduct, Rule 1.4

(a) A lawyer shall:

(1) promptly inform the client of any decision or circumstance with respect to which disclosure or the client's informed consent* is required by these rules or the State Bar Act;

. . .

California Rules of Professional Conduct, Rule 1.8.2

> A lawyer shall not use a client's information protected by Business and Professions Code section 6068, subdivision (e)(1) to the disadvantage of the client unless the client gives informed consent,* except as permitted by these rules or the State Bar Act.

California Rules of Professional Conduct, Rule 3.7(a)

> (a) A lawyer shall not act as an advocate in a trial in which the lawyer is likely to be a witness unless:
>
> > (1) the lawyer's testimony relates to an uncontested issue or matter;
> >
> > (2) the lawyer's testimony relates to the nature and value of legal services rendered in the case; or
> >
> > (3) the lawyer has obtained informed written consent* from the client. If the lawyer represents the People or a governmental entity, the consent shall be obtained from the head of the office or a designee of the head of the office by which the lawyer is employed.

2.6 Knowledge

California Rules of Professional Conduct, Rule 1.0.1(f)

> (f) "Knowingly," "known," or "knows" means actual knowledge of the fact in question. A person's* knowledge may be inferred from circumstances.

Examples

California Rules of Professional Conduct, Rule 1.9(c)

> (c) A lawyer who has formerly represented a client in a matter or whose present or former firm* has formerly represented a client in a matter shall not thereafter:
>
> > (1) use information protected by Business and Professions Code section 6068, subdivision (e) and rule 1.6 acquired by virtue of the representation of the former client to the disadvantage of the former client except as these rules or the State Bar Act would permit with respect to a current client, or when the information has become generally known;* . . .

Ethics Opinions

Information is "generally known" if it is widely recognized by members of the public in the area. Publicly available information is not necessarily generally known. Unless information has become widely recognized by the public or within an industry, profession, or trade, the fact that the information may have been discussed in open court, or may be available in court records or in other public repositories does not, standing alone, mean that the information is generally known. ABA Com. on Ethics and Prof. Resp., formal opn. No. 2017-479 (discussing ABA model rule 1.9).

A lawyer represented a hedge fund manager defending against a fraud claim brought by several investors. After settling the case and terminating the representation, the lawyer wrote a letter to the Wall Street Journal discussing the lawsuit, including the settlement. In the course of the investigation, the lawyer also learned information about the hedge fund manager from a former investor, and the lawyer commented on allegations posed by that former investor in the letter to the Wall Street Journal. The disclosures in the lawyer's letter violated the ethical duty of confidentiality because they were detrimental or embarrassing to the client. The ethical duty of confidentiality applied even though the hedge fund manager was a former client, and even though the allegations were publicized either in the court proceedings or on a blog posted by the former investor. State Bar of Cal. Com. on Prof. Resp. and Conduct, formal opn. No. 2016-195.

Cases

The fact that information can be discovered in a public record does not, by itself, render that information generally known under rule 1.9(c)(1) of the Rules of Professional Conduct. *In the Matter of Johnson* (Review Dept. 2000) 4 Cal. State Bar Ct. Rptr. 179.

2.7 Partner

California Rules of Professional Conduct, Rule 1.0.1(g)

> (g) "Partner" means a member of a partnership, a shareholder in a law firm* organized as a professional corporation, or a member of an association authorized to practice law.

Examples

California Rules of Professional Conduct, Rule 5.4(a)

> (a) A lawyer or law firm* shall not share legal fees directly or indirectly with a nonlawyer or with an organization that is not authorized to practice law, except that:
>
> > (1) an agreement by a lawyer with the lawyer's firm,* partner,* or associate may provide for the payment of money or other consideration over a reasonable* period of time after the lawyer's death, to the lawyer's estate or to one or more specified persons;*

. . .

2.8 Person

California Rules of Professional Conduct, Rule 1.0.1(g-1)

(g-1) "Person" has the meaning stated in Evidence Code section 175.

Statute

California Evidence Code section 175

"Person" includes a natural person, firm, association, organization, partnership, business trust, corporation, limited liability company, or public entity.

Examples

California Rules of Professional Conduct, Rule 1.8.3

(a) A lawyer shall not:

(1) solicit a client to make a substantial* gift, including a testamentary gift, to the lawyer or a person* related to the lawyer, unless the lawyer or other recipient of the gift is related to the client, or

(2) prepare on behalf of a client an instrument giving the lawyer or a person* related to the lawyer any substantial* gift, unless (i) the lawyer or other recipient of the gift is related to the client, or (ii) the client has been advised by an independent lawyer who has provided a certificate of independent review that complies with the requirements of Probate Code section 21384.

(b) For purposes of this rule, related persons* include a person* who is "related by blood or affinity" as that term is defined in California Probate Code section 21374, subdivision (a).

California Rules of Professional Conduct, Rule 4.3

(a) In communicating on behalf of a client with a person* who is not represented by counsel, a lawyer shall not state or imply that the lawyer is disinterested. When the lawyer knows* or reasonably should know* that the unrepresented person* incorrectly believes* the lawyer is disinterested in the matter, the lawyer shall make reasonable* efforts to correct the misunderstanding. If the lawyer knows* or reasonably should know* that the interests of the unrepresented person* are in conflict with the interests of the client, the lawyer shall not give legal advice to that person,* except that the lawyer may, but is not required to, advise the person* to secure counsel.

(b) In communicating on behalf of a client with a person* who is not represented by counsel, a lawyer shall not seek to obtain privileged or other confidential information the lawyer knows* or reasonably should know* the person* may not reveal without violating a duty to another or which the lawyer is not otherwise entitled to receive.

California Rules of Professional Conduct, Rule 7.3

(a) A lawyer shall not by in-person, live telephone or real-time electronic contact solicit professional employment when a significant motive for doing so is the lawyer's pecuniary gain, unless the person* contacted:

(1) is a lawyer; or

(2) has a family, close personal, or prior professional relationship with the lawyer.

(b) A lawyer shall not solicit professional employment by written,* recorded or electronic communication or by in-person, telephone or real-time electronic contact even when not otherwise prohibited by paragraph (a), if:

(1) the person* being solicited has made known* to the lawyer a desire not to be solicited by the lawyer; or

(2) the solicitation is transmitted in any manner which involves intrusion, coercion, duress or harassment.

(c) Every written,* recorded or electronic communication from a lawyer soliciting professional employment from any person* known* to be in need of legal services in a particular matter shall include the word "Advertisement" or words of similar import on the outside envelope, if any, and at the beginning and ending of any recorded or electronic communication, unless the recipient of the communication is a person* specified in paragraphs (a)(1) or (a)(2), or unless it is apparent from the context that the communication is an advertisement.

(d) Notwithstanding the prohibitions in paragraph (a), a lawyer may participate with a prepaid or group legal service plan operated by an organization not owned or directed by the lawyer that uses in-person, live telephone or real-time electronic contact to solicit memberships or subscriptions for the plan from persons* who are not known* to need legal services in a particular matter covered by the plan.

(e) As used in this rule, the terms "solicitation" and "solicit" refer to an oral or written* targeted communication initiated by or on behalf of the lawyer that is directed to a specific person* and that offers to provide, or can reasonably* be understood as offering to provide, legal services.

2.9 Reasonable

California Rules of Professional Conduct, Rule 1.0.1(h)

(h) "Reasonable" or "reasonably" when used in relation to conduct by a lawyer means the conduct of a reasonably prudent and competent lawyer.

California Rules of Professional Conduct, Rule 1.0.1(i)

(i) "Reasonable belief" or "reasonably believes" when used in reference to a lawyer means that the lawyer believes the matter in question and that the circumstances are such that the belief is reasonable.

California Rules of Professional Conduct, Rule 1.0.1(j)

(j) "Reasonably should know" when used in reference to a lawyer means that a lawyer of reasonable prudence and competence would ascertain the matter in question.

Examples

California Rules of Professional Conduct, Rule 1.13(b)

(b) If a lawyer representing an organization knows* that a constituent is acting, intends to act or refuses to act in a matter related to the representation in a manner that the lawyer knows* or reasonably should know* is (i) a violation of a legal obligation to the organization or a violation of law reasonably* imputable to the organization, and (ii) likely to result in substantial* injury to the organization, the lawyer shall proceed as is reasonably* necessary in the best lawful interest of the organization. Unless the lawyer reasonably believes* that it is not necessary in the best lawful interest of the organization to do so, the lawyer shall refer the matter to higher authority in the organization, including, if warranted by the circumstances, to the highest authority that can act on behalf of the organization as determined by applicable law.

California Rules of Professional Conduct, Rule 3.6(c)

(c) Notwithstanding paragraph (a), a lawyer may make a statement that a reasonable* lawyer would believe* is required to protect a client from the substantial* undue prejudicial effect of recent publicity not initiated by the lawyer or the lawyer's client. A statement made pursuant to this paragraph shall be limited to such information as is necessary to mitigate the recent adverse publicity.

2.10 Screening

California Rules of Professional Conduct, Rule 1.0.1(k)

(k) "Screened" means the isolation of a lawyer from any participation in a matter, including the timely imposition of procedures within a law firm* that are adequate under the circumstances (i) to protect information that the isolated lawyer is obligated to protect under these rules or other law; and (ii) to protect against other law firm* lawyers and nonlawyer personnel communicating with the lawyer with respect to the matter.

Comment on California Rules of Professional Conduct, Rule 1.0.1(k)

[5] The purpose of screening* is to assure the affected client, former client, or prospective client that confidential information known* by the personally prohibited lawyer is neither disclosed to other law firm* lawyers or nonlawyer personnel nor used to the detriment of the person* to whom the duty of confidentiality is owed. The personally prohibited lawyer shall acknowledge the obligation not to communicate with any of the other lawyers and nonlawyer personnel in the law firm* with respect to the matter. Similarly, other lawyers and nonlawyer personnel in the law firm* who are working on the matter promptly shall be informed that the screening* is in place and that they may not communicate with the personally prohibited lawyer with respect to the matter. Additional screening* measures that are appropriate for the particular matter will depend on the circumstances. To implement, reinforce and remind all affected law firm* personnel of the presence of the screening,* it may be appropriate for the law firm* to undertake such procedures as a written* undertaking by the personally prohibited lawyer to avoid any communication with other law firm* personnel and any contact with any law firm* files or other materials relating to the matter, written* notice and instructions to all other law firm* personnel forbidding any communication with the personally prohibited lawyer relating to the matter, denial of access by that lawyer to law firm* files or other materials relating to the matter, and periodic reminders of the screen* to the personally prohibited lawyer and all other law firm* personnel.

[6] In order to be effective, screening* measures must be implemented as soon as practical after a lawyer or law firm* knows* or reasonably should know* that there is a need for screening.*

Examples

California Rules of Professional Conduct, Rule 1.10(a)

(a) While lawyers are associated in a firm,* none of them shall knowingly* represent a client when any one of them practicing alone would be prohibited from doing so by rules 1.7 or 1.9, unless

(1) the prohibition is based on a personal interest of the prohibited lawyer and does not present a significant risk of materially limiting the representation of the client by the remaining lawyers in the firm;* or

(2) the prohibition is based upon rule 1.9(a) or (b) and arises out of the prohibited lawyer's association with a prior firm,* and

(i) the prohibited lawyer did not substantially participate in the same or a substantially related matter;

(ii) the prohibited lawyer is timely screened* from any participation in the matter and is apportioned no part of the fee therefrom; and

(iii) written* notice is promptly given to any affected former client to enable the former client to ascertain compliance with the provisions of this rule, which shall include a description of the screening* procedures employed; and an agreement by the firm* to respond promptly to any written* inquiries or objections by the former client about the screening* procedures.

California Rules of Professional Conduct, Rule 1.18(d)

(d) When the lawyer has received information that prohibits representation as provided in paragraph (c), representation of the affected client is permissible if:

(1) both the affected client and the prospective client have given informed written consent,* or

(2) the lawyer who received the information took reasonable* measures to avoid exposure to more information than was reasonably* necessary to determine whether to represent the prospective client; and

(i) the prohibited lawyer is timely screened* from any participation in the matter and is apportioned no part of the fee therefrom; and

(ii) written* notice is promptly given to the prospective client to enable the prospective client to ascertain compliance with the provisions of this rule.

Cases

"Once the moving party in a motion for disqualification has established that an attorney is tainted with confidential information, a rebuttable presumption arises that the attorney shared that information with the attorney's law firm. The burden then shifts to the challenged law firm to establish 'that the practical effect of formal screening has been achieved. The showing must satisfy the trial court that the [tainted attorney] has not had and will not have any involvement with the litigation, or any communication with attorneys or [ ]employees concerning the litigation, that would support a reasonable inference that the information has been used or disclosed.'" *Kirk v. First American Title Ins. Co.* (2010) 183 Cal.App.4th 776, 809–810 (quoting *In re Complex Asbestos Litigation* (1991) 232 Cal.App.3d 572, 596).

"The specific elements of an effective screen will vary from case to case, although two elements are necessary: First, the screen must be timely imposed; a firm must impose screening measures when the conflict first arises. It is not sufficient to wait until the trial court imposes screening measures as part of its order on the disqualification motion." *Kirk v. First American Title Ins. Co., supra,* 183 Cal.App.4th at p. 810. "[T]he second factor—prohibitions against the discussion of confidential information. Such a prohibition is the primary goal of any ethical wall. In all but the most unusual case, it would be necessary for the challenged law firm to establish express prohibitions against the discussion of confidential information as part of its ethical wall. The purpose of an ethical wall is prophylactic; it seeks to prevent the sharing of client confidences which is otherwise assumed when attorneys are practicing together. An express prohibition against discussing the information which must not be discussed is a basic first step toward establishing this goal." *Id.* at pp. 811–812. "The third factor—established rules and procedures preventing access to confidential information and files—focuses on additional ways to prevent the accidental disclosure of confidential information. Files may be stored in a separate location to which the tainted attorney has no access." *Id.* at p. 812. "The fourth factor is the establishment of procedures preventing a disqualified attorney from sharing in the profits from the representation." *Id.* "An additional element favorably acknowledged in caselaw is that the disqualified attorney have no supervisory powers over the attorneys involved in the litigation, and vice-versa." *Id.* at p. 813.

"Each of these elements need not necessarily be present for an ethical wall to be sufficient to rebut the presumption of imputed knowledge. Any ethical wall must ultimately be judged by whether it is sufficient to meet its purpose: satisfying the trial court that the tainted attorney has not had and will not have any involvement with, or communication concerning, the litigation that would support a reasonable inference that confidential information was or will be disclosed." *Kirk v. First American Title Ins. Co., supra,* 183 Cal.App.4th at p. 814; see *O'Gara Coach Co., LLC v. Ra* (2019) 30 Cal.App.5th 1115, 1132 (law firm operated by defendants' former president who left and became a lawyer was properly disqualified because firm failed to introduce any evidence the former president was screened from litigation against a former company); *Cal. Self-Insurers' Security Fund v. Super. Ct.* (2018) 19 Cal.App.5th 1065, 1077 ("the trial court must perform an analysis regarding whether confidential information was, indeed, transmitted from" the conflicted lawyer to the lawyer's firm).

The court appeared to use the terms "screening" and "ethical wall" interchangeably. Screening is the operative term in the current Rules of Professional Conduct.

In an alternative line of cases, courts did not allow screening to avoid disqualification. "Disqualification of both the individual attorney and his or her firm is required where the attorney has been privy to confidences of a litigant while acting as a neutral mediator.... Where a judicial officer has presided over settlement conferences which included ex parte communication, we presume the revelation of confidences relating to the merits of a litigant's case." *Cho v. Super. Ct.* (1995) 39 Cal.App.4th 113, 125. *Cho* has been extended requiring disqualification of the law firms of all non-judicial settlement officers involved in settlement discussion. *Castaneda v. Super.*

Ct. (2015) 237 Cal.App.4th 1434, 1450. Of counsel lawyers are treated as members of the firm for purposes of the vicarious disqualification analysis. *People ex rel. Dept. of Corporations v. SpeeDee Oil Change Systems, Inc.* (1999) 20 Cal.4th 1135, 1156.

2.11 Substantial

California Rules of Professional Conduct, Rule 1.0.1(l)

> (l) "Substantial" when used in reference to degree or extent means a material matter of clear and weighty importance.

Examples

California Rules of Professional Conduct, Rule 1.6(b)

> (b) A lawyer may, but is not required to, reveal information protected by Business and Professions Code section 6068, subdivision (e)(1) to the extent that the lawyer reasonably believes* the disclosure is necessary to prevent a criminal act that the lawyer reasonably believes* is likely to result in death of, or substantial* bodily harm to, an individual, as provided in paragraph (c).

California Rules of Professional Conduct, Rule 1.12(a)

> (a) Except as stated in paragraph (d), a lawyer shall not represent anyone in connection with a matter in which the lawyer participated personally and substantially as a judge or other adjudicative officer, judicial staff attorney or law clerk to such a person* or as an arbitrator, mediator, or other third-party neutral, unless all parties to the proceeding give informed written consent.*

2.12 Tribunal

California Rules of Professional Conduct, Rule 1.0.1(m)

> (m) "Tribunal" means: (i) a court, an arbitrator, an administrative law judge, or an administrative body acting in an adjudicative capacity and authorized to make a decision that can be binding on the parties involved; or (ii) a special master or other person* to whom a court refers one or more issues and whose decision or recommendation can be binding on the parties if approved by the court.

Examples

California Rules of Professional Conduct, Rule 3.3(a)

> (a) A lawyer shall not:

(1) knowingly* make a false statement of fact or law to a tribunal* or fail to correct a false statement of material fact or law previously made to the tribunal* by the lawyer;

(2) fail to disclose to the tribunal* legal authority in the controlling jurisdiction known* to the lawyer to be directly adverse to the position of the client and not disclosed by opposing counsel, or knowingly* misquote to a tribunal* the language of a book, statute, decision or other authority; or

(3) offer evidence that the lawyer knows* to be false. If a lawyer, the lawyer's client, or a witness called by the lawyer, has offered material evidence, and the lawyer comes to know* of its falsity, the lawyer shall take reasonable* remedial measures, including, if necessary, disclosure to the tribunal,* unless disclosure is prohibited by Business and Professions Code section 6068, subdivision (e) and rule 1.6. A lawyer may refuse to offer evidence, other than the testimony of a defendant in a criminal matter, that the lawyer reasonably believes* is false.

California Rules of Professional Conduct, Rule 3.5(a)

(a) Except as permitted by statute, an applicable code of judicial ethics or code of judicial conduct, or standards governing employees of a tribunal,* a lawyer shall not directly or indirectly give or lend anything of value to a judge, official, or employee of a tribunal.* This rule does not prohibit a lawyer from contributing to the campaign fund of a judge or judicial officer running for election or confirmation pursuant to applicable law pertaining to such contributions.

2.13 Writing

California Rules of Professional Conduct, Rule 1.0.1(n)

(n) "Writing" or "written" has the meaning stated in Evidence Code section 250. A "signed" writing includes an electronic sound, symbol, or process attached to or logically associated with a writing and executed, inserted, or adopted by or at the direction of a person* with the intent to sign the writing.

Statute

California Evidence Code section 250

"Writing" means handwriting, typewriting, printing, photostating, photographing, photocopying, transmitting by electronic mail or facsimile, and every other means of recording upon any tangible thing, any form of communication or representation, including letters, words, pictures, sounds, or symbols, or combinations thereof, and any record thereby created, regardless of the manner in which the record has been stored.

Examples

California Rules of Professional Conduct, Rule 1.7(a)-(c)

> (a) A lawyer shall not, without informed written consent* from each client and compliance with paragraph (d), represent a client if the representation is directly adverse to another client in the same or a separate matter.
>
> (b) A lawyer shall not, without informed written consent* from each affected client and compliance with paragraph (d), represent a client if there is a significant risk the lawyer's representation of the client will be materially limited by the lawyer's responsibilities to or relationships with another client, a former client or a third person,* or by the lawyer's own interests.
>
> (c) Even when a significant risk requiring a lawyer to comply with paragraph (b) is not present, a lawyer shall not represent a client without written* disclosure of the relationship to the client and compliance with paragraph (d) where:
>
> > (1) the lawyer has, or knows* that another lawyer in the lawyer's firm* has, a legal, business, financial, professional, or personal relationship with or responsibility to a party or witness in the same matter; or
> >
> > (2) the lawyer knows* or reasonably should know* that another party's lawyer is a spouse, parent, child, or sibling of the lawyer, lives with the lawyer, is a client of the lawyer or another lawyer in the lawyer's firm,* or has an intimate personal relationship with the lawyer.

California Rules of Professional Conduct, Rule 4.4

> Where it is reasonably* apparent to a lawyer who receives a writing* relating to a lawyer's representation of a client that the writing* was inadvertently sent or produced, and the lawyer knows* or reasonably should know* that the writing* is privileged or subject to the work product doctrine, the lawyer shall:
>
> > (a) refrain from examining the writing* any more than is necessary to determine that it is privileged or subject to the work product doctrine, and
> >
> > (b) promptly notify the sender.

CHAPTER 3 COMPETENCE AND DILIGENCE

California Rules of Professional Conduct, Rule 1.1 - Competence

(a) A lawyer shall not intentionally, recklessly, with gross negligence, or repeatedly fail to perform legal services with competence.

(b) For purposes of this rule, "competence" in any legal service shall mean to apply the (i) learning and skill, and (ii) mental, emotional, and physical ability reasonably* necessary for the performance of such service.

(c) If a lawyer does not have sufficient learning and skill when the legal services are undertaken, the lawyer nonetheless may provide competent representation by

(i) associating with or, where appropriate, professionally consulting another lawyer whom the lawyer reasonably believes* to be competent,

(ii) acquiring sufficient learning and skill before performance is required, or

(iii) referring the matter to another lawyer whom the lawyer reasonably believes* to be competent.

(d) In an emergency a lawyer may give advice or assistance in a matter in which the lawyer does not have the skill ordinarily required if referral to, or association or consultation with, another lawyer would be impractical. Assistance in an emergency must be limited to that reasonably* necessary in the circumstances.

California Rules of Professional Conduct, Rule 1.3 - Diligence

(a) A lawyer shall not intentionally, repeatedly, recklessly or with gross negligence fail to act with reasonable diligence in representing a client.

(b) For purposes of this rule, "reasonable diligence" shall mean that a lawyer acts with commitment and dedication to the interests of the client and does not neglect or disregard, or unduly delay a legal matter entrusted to the lawyer.

An asterisk (*) identifies a defined term in rule 1.0.1 of the Rules of Professional Conduct. For further discussion of a defined term, see chapter 2 of this Guide, Terminology.

3.1 Introduction

Competent representation begins with the lawyer's initial communication with the client, during which time the lawyer determines the client's needs and goals and, if appropriate, defines the scope of representation. Rules 1.2 and 1.4 of the Rules of Professional Conduct direct a lawyer to abide by the client's decisions concerning the goals of the representation and to consult with the client as to the means by which those goals are pursued.

At the initial consultation, the lawyer can realistically determine the scope of services, and communicate to the client which services fall within the lawyer's competence. A lawyer may place reasonable limitations on the scope of representation with the client's informed consent. Rules Prof. Conduct, rule 1.2(b). For a further discussion of the initial engagement of a client, see chapter 4 of this Guide, Identifying the Client and the Scope of Representation. For example, the representation of a trustee in a post-death trust administration may exclude the preparation of fiduciary income tax returns. A lawyer with a trust administration practice may advise a client as part of the initial engagement that, in the event of a formal dispute between the trustee and a beneficiary, the lawyer will not undertake the trust-related litigation. In connection with a trust or estate administration, a lawyer may appropriately decline to advise the client on the disposition of property governed by the laws of another state or jurisdiction. Although an exhaustive list of exclusions is neither possible nor expressly required by the ethical rules, the lawyer would advisedly list any excluded services in the engagement letter to avoid client misunderstandings.

As a representation proceeds, the lawyer may identify legal issues that fall outside the lawyer's competence. For example, a trustee-client discovers after the death of the settlor that real property held in the trust may be contaminated with hazardous waste. Another example would be a client who engages the lawyer to represent the client's interest in a specified litigation, and the initial lawsuit is amended to add new claims that are outside the lawyer's expertise. A change in the initial scope of representation is nonetheless subject to the client's informed consent under rule 1.2(b) of the Rules of Professional Conduct. The lawyer should notify the client in writing of the limitation on the representation arising from unforeseen circumstances and preferably obtain a written acknowledgement of that notification from the client. The lawyer's ethical duties require that the lawyer notify the client in sufficient time to allow the client to preserve available rights and remedies.

As a threshold matter, the lawyer should identify the client and potential conflicts that may prevent effective representation. Those conflicts may arise from joint clients' relationship to each other such as with the representation of spouses in preparing a common estate plan. Conflicts may also arise from a lawyer's relationships either through imputation of conflicts of interest within a firm or with a prior client, or business or personal interests that may hinder the lawyer's independent judgment. For a further discussion of these ethical duties, see chapter 5 of this Guide, Conflicts of Interest.

Lawyers with managerial or supervisory authority are responsible for ensuring that all lawyers in a firm practice in accordance with applicable ethical duties, including competence and diligence. A supervising lawyer is responsible for another lawyer's violation of ethical rules if the lawyer knows of the violation at a time when its consequences can be avoided or mitigated but fails to take reasonable remedial action. Rules Prof. Conduct, rule 5.1(c). See also section 3.9 of this chapter regarding Staff Training and Oversight.

Former California Rules of Professional Conduct, Rule 3-110 - Failing to Act Competently

> (A) A member shall not intentionally, recklessly, or repeatedly fail to perform legal services with competence.
>
> (B) For purposes of this rule, "competence" in any legal service shall mean to apply the (1) diligence, (2) learning and skill, and (3) mental, emotional and physical ability reasonably necessary for the performance of such service.
>
> (C) If a member does not have sufficient learning and skill when the legal service is undertaken, the member may nonetheless perform such services competently by 1) associating with or, where appropriate, professionally consulting another lawyer reasonably believed to be competent; or 2) by acquiring sufficient learning and skill before performance is required.

The ethical duty of diligence was subsumed within the definition of competence in former rule 3-110(B).

Case Study

Lawyer drafted Decedent's will and had possession of it. After Decedent's death Lawyer undertook to arrange distribution of her estate. The will named Son from a prior marriage as executor. The will provided for small personal property gifts, a trust for the support of the Decedent's Husband during his lifetime, a specific gift of stocks and bonds to Decedent's son-in-law, and the residue to the Decedent's two children of a prior marriage equally.

Decedent's Husband and Son met with Lawyer, and told Lawyer that Decedent left a home in joint tenancy with Husband, a savings account held jointly with Son, and two credit union accounts held jointly with Son and Decedent's Daughter. Lawyer prepared inheritance tax forms for Husband's signature, stating the values of the home and the accounts. Lawyer also prepared an affidavit of surviving joint tenant. Lawyer stated that unless there were other assets not held in joint tenancy, a probate proceeding might not be necessary.

Although Son and Daughter had difficulty communicating with Lawyer during this period, they ultimately spoke with Lawyer on several occasions. At one point, Lawyer told each of them that the estate was in probate and proceeding satisfactorily. Husband had suffered a stroke several years earlier making it difficult for him to talk, and Lawyer did not speak with him after the initial meeting.

Son called Lawyer on several occasions, leaving a phone number with an answering service, but received no return calls. Son also wrote to Lawyer, asking whether Lawyer had time to devote to the case and whether Son should secure other counsel. Receiving no response, Son wrote again three weeks later, stating that unless Lawyer responded within ten days Son would retrieve all documents relevant to the estate and hire another lawyer. Again, Lawyer did not respond.

Son then retained another lawyer who wrote three letters to Lawyer asking for the will and any other relevant documents, providing Son's authorization in those letters. Lawyer remained uncooperative, and Son brought a proceeding to compel Lawyer to produce the will. A day before the scheduled hearing, Lawyer delivered the will to the clerk of the court. Lawyer continued to delay matters in the proceeding to prove the will. The probate estate, which totaled about $40,000, included two accounts that Lawyer had treated as joint tenancy accounts, another bank account, and other property. Husband died prior to distribution of the estate.

What ethical issues arise from this set of facts and how should Lawyer have addressed them?

One of the first duties of a lawyer retained to settle an estate is to identify the Decedent's assets and to determine the procedures required to complete the transfer of those assets. In this case, Lawyer failed to investigate the Decedent's assets adequately. Husband and Son had not reported to Lawyer assets specifically identified in the decedent's will. Minimal inquiry would have disclosed accounts, stocks, and bonds in Decedent's name alone.

While a lawyer may rely upon statements made by the client, circumstances known to the lawyer may require an investigation. When advised that all known assets were held jointly, Lawyer must have been aware that, if all of Decedent's assets were in fact held in joint tenancy, the dispositions of assets identified in Decedent's will would be defeated. Lawyer made no effort to check the title to the savings and credit union accounts to confirm how title was held.

The ethical duties of competence and diligence require a lawyer's best efforts to accomplish the goals of a client representation with reasonable speed. In this case, Lawyer failed to communicate with Son as the named executor in the will, failed to communicate and cooperate with the Son's lawyer, knowingly misrepresented that the estate was proceeding satisfactorily in probate, and improperly prolonged the estate proceeding.

Lawyer challenged the findings of failure to communicate with Son and failure to cooperate in the probate proceeding on the ground that Lawyer had no duty to Son because Husband was the client. However, Son was the named executor in the will, and according to Lawyer's understanding, was a joint tenant in the savings and credit union accounts. In stating that no probate was necessary, Lawyer undertook to advise Son in the potential capacity of executor. To the extent Lawyer undertook to administer the claimed joint tenancy accounts, Lawyer was acting in Son's interest who Lawyer believed to be a surviving joint tenant.

The court upheld the findings of the Review Department of the State Bar that Lawyer led Son reasonably to believe Lawyer was representing him, that it must have been clear to Lawyer that Son was led to so believe, and that Lawyer did not advise Son that he was not a client. A lawyer's duty to communicate with a client includes the duty to communicate to persons who reasonably believe they are clients to the lawyer's knowledge, at least to the extent of advising them that they are not clients. The contention that Lawyer was retained by Husband and not by Son was irrelevant because Lawyer did not perform the necessary probate work whoever the client was, and Lawyer led Son to believe that Lawyer represented him without ever advising Son otherwise. *Butler v. State Bar* (1986) 42 Cal.3d 323.

Husband, the supposed client in this case, had difficulty talking with Lawyer due to a prior stroke. For a discussion of the ethical duties owed to a client with diminished capacity, see section 3.13 of this chapter and chapter 7 of this Guide, Communication, section 7.6.

Cases

California Rules of Court, rule 2.30(b) authorizes sanctions for "failure without good cause" to comply with the Rules of Court. Those sanctions may also apply in probate proceedings. The court in this case cited rule 2.30(a), that specifically provides: "This sanctions rule applies to the rules in the California Rules of Court relating to general civil cases, unlawful detainer cases, *probate proceedings*, civil proceedings in the appellate division of the superior court, and small claims cases." *In re Marriage of Bianco* (2013) 221 Cal.App.4th 826 (emphasis supplied).

The hearing judge found that a lawyer failed to perform competently in violation of former rule 3-110(A) of the Rules of Professional Conduct because the lawyer provided no service of value to the clients, and failed to return unearned fees in violation of former rule 3–700(D)(2) of the Rules of Professional Conduct. *In the Matter of Seltzer* (Review Dept. 2013) 5 Cal. State Bar Ct. Rptr. 263.

A lawyer was privately reprimanded for repeated failures to advise the client of state inheritance tax owed with respect to estate administration handled by the lawyer. *Matter of Respondent G* (Review Dept. 1992) 2 Cal. State Bar Ct. Rptr. 175.

A lawyer-executor was disciplined for mismanaging the estate and failing to communicate with the client. *Ridge v. State Bar* (1989) 47 Cal.3d 952.

In a case involving a defectively drafted marital deduction trust, the court observed:

> We are not aware of any cases or guidelines establishing in a civil case a standard for the reasonable, diligent and competent assistance of a lawyer engaged in estate planning and preparing a trust with a marital deduction provision. We merely hold that the potential tax problems of general powers of appointment in inter vivos or testamentary marital deduction trusts were within the ambit of a reasonably competent and diligent practitioner from 1961 to the present [1976].

Bucquet v. Livingston (1976) 57 Cal.App.3d 914, 925.

Ethics Opinion

Lawyers at times may seek legal advice concerning their ethical and other obligations to clients. This advice may be provided by, among others, outside counsel or a lawyer within the law firm serving as in-house counsel. The act of seeking legal advice concerning ethical obligations owed to a client by itself does not create a conflict with the client. Once a lawyer becomes aware of an error that could prejudice the client, the lawyer ethically may seek legal advice concerning obligations to the client and options available, but must comply with the rules governing disclosure to the client and the ethical rules governing conflicts of interest. State Bar of Cal. Com. on Prof. Resp. and Conduct, formal opn. No. 2019-197.

Articles

Andersen, *Informed Decision Making in an Office Practice* (Mar. 1987) 28 Boston College L.Rev., Issue 2, 225-264.

Brown & Brown, *What Counsels the Counselor? The Code of Professional Responsibility's Ethical Considerations - A Preventive Law Analysis*, 10 Valparaiso L.Rev. 453, 476 (1976) ("We view the advisor's aspirations of competence as including the knowledge and skill to grasp the client's goals, to reframe them if necessary, to initiate discussion of alternative courses of conduct and, along with the client, to be creative regarding the uses of the law.").

3.2 Importance of Facts

Many trusts and estates lawyers have developed a questionnaire for the use of their firm in collecting the facts for an estate plan or an estate or trust administration. The questionnaire serves the dual purpose of eliciting the facts the lawyer needs to prepare a comprehensive plan or pursue a complete administration, and alerting the client to additional issues that need to be addressed.

When planning for a married person in California, the lawyer should request information relevant to the classification of the couple's property interests as community, quasi-community, or separate, as well as copies of any pre-nuptial, post-nuptial, or other marital agreement which may affect a future division or distribution of assets upon divorce or death. In assessing property interests the lawyer should also consider issues arising by reason of a client's relationship with a registered domestic partner.

ACTEC Commentaries on Model Rules of Professional Conduct, Model Rule 1.1

> A lawyer who is engaged by a client in an estate planning matter should inform the client of the importance of giving the lawyer complete and accurate information regarding relevant matters such as the ownership and value of assets and the state of beneficiary designations under life insurance policies and employee benefit plans. Having so cautioned a client, the lawyer is generally entitled to rely upon information supplied by the client, unless the circumstances indicate that the information should be verified. For a client who already has an estate plan, it is a good practice, where appropriate, to obtain the client's documents from the previous lawyer. If that is not possible, it is good practice to ask the client to supply originals or copies of signed originals of the most recent documents on which the client is seeking advice or work. These practices reduce the risk of the client inadvertently supplying incomplete or inaccurate information. The lawyer should verify the information provided by the client if the client appears to be uncertain about it or if other circumstances create doubts about its accuracy.

3.3 Mistaken Judgment Does Not Necessarily Reflect Lack of Competence

A mistake in judgment or in the analysis of a legal problem is not, in itself, a failure to act competently. While a lawyer must give sound advice, the lawyer does not have a duty to advise a client on all possible alternatives no matter how remote or tenuous. Nevertheless, when giving advice in a field where the state of the law is uncertain, a lawyer does have a duty to undertake sufficient research to enable the lawyer to make informed and intelligent judgments on the client's behalf. Furthermore, it may be prudent for the lawyer to explain the existence of the uncertainty when advising the client, thereby enabling the client in assessing the risks and not proceeding with the erroneous perception that the proper course of action is clear.

ACTEC Commentaries on Model Rules of Professional Conduct, Model Rule 1.1

> The fact that a lawyer does not precisely assess the tax or substantive law consequences of a particular transaction does not necessarily reflect a lack of competence. In some instances, the facts are unclear or disputed, while in others the state of the law is unsettled. In addition, some applications of law and determinations of facts made by courts or administrative agencies are not reasonably foreseeable. In other instances the complexity of a transaction or its unusual nature generates uncertainties regarding the manner in which it will be treated for tax or substantive law purposes and may prevent an otherwise thoroughly competent lawyer from accurately assessing how the transaction would be treated for tax or substantive law purposes.

Cases

A lawyer who rendered an incorrect opinion was nevertheless absolved from malpractice liability because, although mistaken, that opinion "represented a reasoned exercise of an informed judgment grounded upon a professional evaluation of applicable legal principles.... [Thus] respondent's error in judgment on a question of law [was] immune from a claim of professional negligence." The court further held that merely because the state of the law is unsettled at the time a lawyer's advice is rendered, the lawyer is under no duty to advise the client on all possible alternatives, "no matter how remote or tenuous," to permit an informed choice. *Davis v. Damrell* (1981) 119 Cal.App.3d 883, 889.

A lawyer may be held liable in malpractice for rendering an incorrect opinion on an unsettled legal issue arrived at without the benefit of research. The court observed, "[e]ven as to doubtful matters a lawyer is expected to perform sufficient research to enable him to make an informed and intelligent judgment on behalf of his client." *Smith v. Lewis* (1975) 13 Cal.3d 349, 360, disapproved on other grounds in *In re Marriage of Brown* (1976) 15 Cal.3d 838.

3.4 Special Skills

Rule 1.1 of the Rules of Professional Conduct anticipates that a lawyer may initially lack the knowledge or experience to meet the needs of a particular client. A lawyer may overcome that deficiency through additional research and study before performance is required. A lawyer without the requisite experience may associate another lawyer with the specific skills and knowledge necessary to address the client's case competently or refer the matter to such a lawyer. Rule 1.1 of the Rules of Professional Conduct provides a range of options to avoid getting in over one's head.

Since 1991 the State Bar of California Board of Legal Specialization has certified legal specialists in the practice areas of Estate Planning, Probate and Trust Law, and Taxation, recognizing lawyers who bring special expertise and experience to these fields. In the estate planning and probate field, the less-experienced practitioner may seek advice from lawyers who are more experienced and adept in areas such as tax, litigation, creditor protection, or elder law. For a discussion of the ethical duties regarding communication of specialization, see rule 7.4 of the Rules of Professional Conduct and chapter 10 of this Guide, Ethics and Technology, section 10.9.

When special skills are required to address the client's needs, the lawyer has a duty either to associate or consult with a specialist or to acquire the special skills necessary to address the issues presented. Absent such an association or consultation, the lawyer may be held to the standard of care applicable to a specialist. Any association with another lawyer should be undertaken with due regard to client confidentiality and consent, and informed discussion with the client about the costs of the additional representation.

ACTEC Commentaries on Model Rules of Professional Conduct, Model Rule 1.1

> The lawyer should be candid with the client regarding the lawyer's level of competence and need for additional research and preparation, which should be taken into account in determining the amount of the lawyer's fee.

Cases

A lawyer was suspended from practice after negligently and improperly conducting estate administration; with no probate experience the lawyer failed to associate or consult with experienced counsel. *Lewis*

State Bar (1981) 28 Cal.3d 683.

A lawyer was held liable for defective drafting of "Clifford" trust that failed to obtain intended tax benefits; the court upheld jury instructions that a general practitioner has a duty to refer the client to a specialist or recommend the assistance of a specialist if a reasonably careful and skillful general practitioner would do so. *Horne v. Peckham* (1979) 97 Cal.App.3d 404, disapproved on other grounds in *ITT Small Business Finance Corp. v. Niles* (1994) 9 Cal.4th 245.

Ethics Opinion

There is nothing inherently unethical with a client or lawyer hiring another lawyer—often a contract lawyer—to ghostwrite a document to be submitted to court, without identifying or disclosing the involvement of the contract lawyer. Only when the client or lawyer seeks to recover fees must the contract lawyer's role be disclosed to the court. If, however, the involvement of the contract lawyer constitutes a significant development, then the contract lawyer's involvement must be disclosed to the client. Both lawyers must comply with their ethical obligations, including the duty of competence. If the contract lawyer is not admitted to practice in California, both lawyers must guard against the potential unauthorized practice of law. Orange County Bar Assn., Ethics opn. No. 2014-1.

3.5 Competence with Technology

Notwithstanding the honored traditions of trusts and estates law, lawyers in this field live and practice in the digital age. The ethical duty of competence includes a working knowledge of the uses of technology in a law practice, and its pitfalls. At the time of publication of this edition of the Guide, the State Bar of California had proposed adding the following comment [1] to rule 1.1 of the Rules of Professional Conduct: "The duties set forth in this rule include the duty to keep abreast of the changes in the law and its practice, *including the benefits and risks associated with relevant technology*" (emphasis added). A lawyer should assume that competent practice includes undertaking the necessary research to understand the uses of technology consistent with ethical rules and applicable law before performance is required, and associating with knowledgeable professionals who can provide technical expertise as needed. For a detailed discussion of the duty of competence and other ethical duties related to the use of technology, see chapter 10 of this Guide, Ethics and Technology. That chapter surveys the current law and other authority regarding the ethical duties raised by practice and planning in an age of technological innovation.

ABA Commentaries on Model Rules of Professional Conduct, Model Rule 1.1

> [8] To maintain the requisite knowledge and skill, a lawyer should keep abreast of changes in the law and its practice, including the benefits and risks associated with relevant technology, engage in continuing study and education and comply with all continuing legal education requirements to which the lawyer is subject.

ACTEC Commentaries on Model Rules of Professional Conduct, Model Rule 1.1

> A lawyer who uses technology to transmit or store client documents or communicates electronically with a client regarding the drafting of documents must be aware of the potential effects of such use of technology on client confidentiality and preservation of client information. A lawyer must stay reasonably informed about developments in technology used in client communications and document storage, including improvements, discoveries of risks and best practices.

Ethics Opinions

This opinion focuses on a lawyer's ethical obligations after a data breach, and it addresses only data breaches that involve information relating to the representation of a client. A data breach for the purposes of this opinion means a data event where material client confidential information is misappropriated, destroyed, or otherwise compromised, or where a lawyer's ability to perform the legal services for which the lawyer is hired is significantly impaired by the breach. Compliance with the obligations imposed by the Model Rules of Professional Conduct depends on the nature of the breach, the ability of the lawyer to know about the facts and circumstances surrounding the breach, and the lawyer's roles, level of authority, and responsibility in the law firm's operations. ABA Com. on Ethics and Prof. Resp., formal opn. No. 2018-483.

As it pertains to the use of technology, the Business and Professions Code, and the Rules of Professional Conduct do not impose greater or different duties upon a virtual law office (VLO) practitioner operating in the cloud than they do upon a lawyer practicing in a traditional law office. While a lawyer may maintain a VLO in the cloud—where communications with the client, and storage of and access to all information about the client's matter, are conducted solely through the internet using a third-party's secure servers—the lawyer may be required to take additional steps to confirm compliance with a lawyer's ethical obligations due to distinct issues raised by a VLO and its operation. Failure of the lawyer to comply with all ethical obligations relevant to these issues will preclude the operation of a VLO in the cloud. State Bar of Cal. Com. on Prof. Resp. and Conduct, formal opn. No. 2012-184.

For a discussion of technology competence in connection with e-discovery, including the discovery of electronically stored information, see chapter 9 of this Guide, Ethics and Litigation, section 9.11.

3.6 Mental, Emotional, and Physical Ability

A lawyer's mental, emotional, and physical ability to handle a client's case may be affected by a variety of circumstances, including workload. If a lawyer knows that the lawyer will not have sufficient time to devote proper attention to a client's matter, the lawyer should not accept employment in the first instance. If the lawyer has accepted the employment, the lawyer may be required to discontinue the representation, inform the client of the lawyer's inability to continue, and assist the client in obtaining new counsel. Financial and domestic difficulties, physical handicaps, health issues, and substance abuse may also compromise a lawyer's ability to perform competently.

Ethics Opinions

The following opinions reflect an analysis of the ABA Model Rules of Professional Conduct that has not been applied in California. At the time of publication of this edition of the Guide, the State Bar of California Committee on Professional Responsibility and Conduct had invited public comment on Formal Opinion Interim Number 14-0001. That Interim Opinion provides guidance on the ethical obligations of subordinates, supervisors, and other colleagues who know that a lawyer, due to diminution of mental capacity, may not competently and ethically perform legal services as required under the Rules of Professional Conduct and the State Bar Act.

"If a lawyer's mental impairment is known to partners in a law firm or a lawyer having direct supervisory authority over the impaired lawyer, steps must be taken that are designed to give reasonable assurance that such impairment will not result in breaches of the Model Rules. If the mental impairment of a lawyer has resulted in a violation of the Model Rules, an obligation may exist to report the violation to the appropriate professional authority. If the firm removes the impaired lawyer in a matter, it may have an obligation to discuss with the client the circumstances surrounding the change of responsibility. If the impaired lawyer resigns or is removed from the firm, the firm may have disclosure obligations to clients who are considering whether to continue to use the firm or shift their relationship to the departed lawyer, but must be careful to limit any statements made to ones for which there is a factual foundation. The obligation to report a violation of the Model Rules by an impaired lawyer is not eliminated by departure of the impaired lawyer." ABA Com. on Ethics and Prof. Resp., formal opn. No. 2003-429.

"A lawyer who believes that another lawyer's known violations of disciplinary rules raise substantial questions about her fitness to practice law must report those violations to the appropriate professional authority. A lawyer who believes that another lawyer's mental condition materially impairs her ability to represent clients, and who knows that that lawyer continues to do so, must report that lawyer's consequent violation of Rule 1.16(a)(2), which requires that she withdraw from the representation of clients." ABA Com. on Ethics and Prof. Resp., formal opn. No. 2003-431.

3.7 Supervising Execution of Documents

The lawyer who prepares the client's estate planning documents should supervise their execution or, if that is not possible, arrange for another lawyer to supervise their execution. If personal supervision by the lawyer is not practical, the lawyer may deliver documents to the clients with written instructions regarding the procedures for valid execution. This course of action should be taken only if the lawyer reasonably believes that the client is sufficiently sophisticated and reliable to follow the instructions.

When cost is a concern to a client, a lawyer may have a paralegal or other trained assistant supervise the execution of estate planning documents; however, such paralegal or assistant must not provide legal advice to the client. The lawyer still has the primary ethical duty of competence, which in that case is to ensure that the paralegal or assistant is appropriately trained, and to review the documents after execution. See section 3.9 of this chapter, Staff Training and Oversight. The task assigned to the paralegal or assistant should be limited to the identification of the signers and formalities of execution, without comment on the substance of the estate planning documents.

ACTEC Commentaries on Model Rules of Professional Conduct, Model Rule 1.1

> *Supervising Execution of Documents.* Generally, the lawyer who prepares estate planning documents for a client should supervise their execution. In doing so, it is advisable for the lawyer to develop a procedure for execution that is complete and adequate to meet the requirements of the jurisdiction where the document is to be executed, and to follow that procedure consistently whenever a document of that sort is executed. Of course, he or she may arrange for another lawyer to do so. If it is not practical for a lawyer to supervise the execution or if the client so requests, the lawyer may arrange for the documents to be delivered to the client with written instructions regarding the manner in which they should be executed. The lawyer should do so only if the lawyer reasonably believes that the client is sufficiently sophisticated and reliable to follow the instructions and that there are no present concerns about potential challenges. The lawyer who sends estate planning documents to the client for signing outside of the lawyer's office should request original signed documents be returned for the lawyer's review. If the lawyer determines the documents were signed improperly, the lawyer should resend the estate planning documents for the client to sign. Note that in some jurisdictions the

supervision of the execution of estate planning documents constitutes the practice of law, which a lawyer may not delegate to a member of the lawyer's staff who is not a lawyer.

3.8 Sample Client Letter – Instructions on Will Execution

This sample letter can be adapted to an estate planning representation when it is impracticable for the client to execute estate planning documents in the lawyer's office. It is intended to guide the client though all the usual procedures to create valid estate planning documents. The lawyer should adapt it thoughtfully to the lawyer's customary practice and the needs of a particular client representation.

Dear [Client],

We prefer that you sign your estate planning documents in our office to ensure that they are executed in compliance with California law. A lawyer who witnesses you signing your estate planning documents can later testify as to the circumstances surrounding their execution. Signing outside of our office may make a challenge to the validity of your will harder to defend.

If an office appointment is not feasible, please follow these instructions:

1. Ask two friends or neighbors to be present when you sign your will. No beneficiary under the will should act as a witness.

2. Declare to the witnesses that the document is your will. The witnesses do not need to read the will or know its contents.

3. Ask the witnesses to read the affidavit attached to the back of the will.

4. Sign the will in the presence of the witnesses. The witnesses should sign the affidavit in your presence and in the presence of each other.

5. Ask the witnesses to print their names and provide an address.

Please provide us with a copy of the completely signed will for our records. We will review it for any errors in execution that appear on the face of the document.

Sincerely,

[Lawyer]

3.9 Staff Training and Oversight

Rule 5.1 of the Rules of Professional Conduct places an ethical duty on a lawyer with managerial and supervisory responsibility to provide adequate training, supervision, and oversight of the legal and non-legal staff employees. Lawyers may properly delegate work to paralegals and other trained assistants, where appropriate. The amount of responsibility that may be delegated is dependent upon the level of education, experience, and judgment of the individual. The exercise of legal judgment must not be delegated.

Rule 5.3 of the Rules of Professional Conduct requires that the conduct of nonlawyer staff be compatible with the professional obligations of the lawyer, including the duty of competence. The lawyer must inform staff members who may not have legal training of those obligations, and the lawyer's experience in complying with them. Proper oversight requires that paralegals complete the minimum qualifications and continuing education requirements in Business and Professions Code section 6450. The lawyer may also need to certify the qualifications of the paralegal to obtain court approval of extraordinary compensation for the paralegal's services. See Chapter 8 of this Guide, Compensation, section 8.5.

The ACTEC Commentaries on model rule 5.3 extend the duty to exercise supervisory responsibility to other nonlawyers assisting with the work of a law firm, including outside accounting firms, investigators, appraisers, estate liquidators, business managers, real estate managers, copying services, and data storage providers. Occasionally a trusts and estates lawyer will need to retain a qualified professional to assess the competency of a client or to opine on the competency of a decedent in the event of a will contest. "Even such ostensibly benign use of nonlawyer assistance such as trash removal, computer and/or photocopier maintenance can pose serious risks for confidentiality and need to be carried out with attention to the lawyer's professional responsibilities."

California Rules of Court, rule 7.703(e) sets forth specific educational and supervisory requirements that must be met as a prerequisite to the award of paralegal fees in the performance of extraordinary services. Those requirements also provide guidance on the specific components of using paralegal services in compliance with the ethical duty of competence.

ACTEC Commentaries on Model Rules of Professional Conduct, Model Rule 5.3

> Virtually any kind of preparatory work can be delegated to nonlawyer assistants if the lawyer has reasonable and well-founded confidence in the nonlawyer, has given appropriate instruction to the nonlawyer, exercises appropriate supervision and takes responsibility for reviewing and correcting the final product or services performed. While easily stated, implementation of these duties is often difficult. The ability to assess the competence and professional responsibility of nonlawyers, and the possibility of appropriate instruction and supervision will vary greatly depending on the kind of task delegated and on whether the nonlawyer is inside or outside one's law firm. Thus, nonlawyers may be assigned to collect information from or on behalf of clients, may be asked to draft legal documents for a client, and may be directed to communicate with and/or file appropriate documents with courts and other agencies, public or private. Similarly, lawyers may utilize the services of outside nonlawyer vendors to do this work if they have exercised the due diligence necessary to have reasonable assurance that those nonlawyers will behave in conformity to the lawyer's professional duties and can maintain the requisite supervisorial responsibility. Regardless of what tasks have been assigned to nonlawyers, however, ultimately a lawyer must be responsible for the exercise of

legal judgment required. A lawyer who delegates work and fails to exercise an appropriate level of review over the work product violates a lawyer's ethical duties, regardless of whether the client is injured.

Cases

The hearing judge recommended suspension for two years from practice for failing to properly supervise non-lawyers in a high-volume practice. The lawyer violated loan modification laws, allowed nonlawyers to give legal advice, and failed to perform competently. *In re Huang* (Review Dept. 2014) 5 Cal. State Bar Ct. Rptr. 296.

A paralegal's mistake was attributable to the lawyer responsible for supervising the paralegal. Even though a lawyer cannot be held responsible for every detail of office procedure, the lawyer must accept responsibility to supervise the work of the lawyer's staff. *Hu v. Fang* (2002) 104 Cal.App.4th 61.

3.10 Trust Mills

The State Bar of California Committee on Professional Responsibility and Conduct issued Formal Opinion Number 1997-148, finding that a lawyer who works in conjunction with a marketer of living trusts violates former rules 3-110 and 1-600(A) of the Rules of Professional Conduct. Such a relationship interferes with duty of loyalty to the client when the lawyer relies on the information supplied by the marketer, does not directly counsel the client regarding all the estate planning options and their advantages and disadvantages, and does not exercise the lawyer's independent judgment.

In the hypothetical facts of this opinion, a marketer of living trusts holds seminars and urges those attending to engage a lawyer supplied by the marketer to prepare a living trust. The marketer collects the personal information of the participants on a fact-gathering sheet and forwards it to the lawyer. Based on the questionnaire answers, the lawyer prepares a living trust for the client and sends it to the client. The lawyer conducts no personal interview with the client and has no discussion with the client of the alternatives to the living trust or the advantages and disadvantages of the various alternatives. Fees are paid sometimes to the marketer and sometimes to the lawyer.

Formal Opinion Number 1997-148 finds such activity by the lawyer to be in violation of several ethical duties. A lawyer-client relationship likely exists between the lawyer and the seminar attendee, and also between the lawyer and the marketer. Since the seminar attendee and the marketer may have potentially adverse interests, the lawyer is in violation of the duty to avoid conflicts (former rule 3-310 of the Rules of Professional Conduct) absent the informed written consent of both clients. The opinion, in footnote 11, further suggests that even written consent may not be sufficient because the lawyer will still be unable to represent the seminar attendee competently because of the lawyer's business and professional relationship with the marketer. Communication of information to either the attendee or the marketer may also violate the lawyer's ethical duty to preserve a client's confidences.

Ethics Opinion

To the extent that lawyers sell form-based solutions, they must either provide an electronic form that the customer customizes without recommendations or they must form a lawyer-client relationship. A lawyer may offer a form product without creating a lawyer-client relationship so long as the lawyer provides no advice, including which form to use or how to complete it. San Diego County Bar Assn, Ethics opn. No. 2019-1.

3.11 Diligence

Diligence in estate planning matters often contends with the reluctant or procrastinating client. At the initial meeting the lawyer should establish a realistic time frame to produce draft documents, once the client provides all needed information. The lawyer may also consider a series of follow-up letters to a client who has received draft documents for review. Terminating the representation if a client does not respond within a reasonable time, leaving open the possibility of a new engagement, may limit the lawyer's possible exposure to liability.

Establishing appropriate timetables to complete necessary various tasks in probate and trust administration matters is of primary importance. In addition to court hearing dates, the lawyer should track administration and tax filing deadlines to allow sufficient time to consult with the client and address the needed legal work. In a probate administration, the Probate Code sets statutory dates for filing an inventory, sending notice to creditors, reporting to the court, and filing a petition for final distribution. In a trust administration, important deadlines include disclaimers and estate tax reporting, filing fiduciary income tax returns, and tax elections that must be made on the fiduciary, partnership, or S Corporation income tax returns filed after the date of death.

The death of the owner of an interest in a business entity may trigger a change of ownership of real estate owned by the entity. Revenue and Taxation Code section 480.2 requires that a Notice of Change of Ownership regarding the entity must be filed within ninety days of the event that results in the change. A prospective client may present this issue to the lawyer when the reporting period has almost run. The lawyer should identify and alert the client to this issue as soon as it is presented.

Lawyers with managerial and supervisory responsibility need to establish proper calendaring systems and ensure diligent staff monitoring of those systems. Computerized calendaring programs can assist with tracking the critical dates in probate or trust administration. Those programs can trigger automatic notifications at specified deadlines with reminders in advance of those deadlines. For a discussion of the use of technology to assist in law firm case monitoring and management, see chapter 10 of this Guide, Ethics and Technology, section 10.3.

ACTEC Commentaries on Model Rules of Professional Conduct, Model Rule 1.3

> Insofar as consistent with providing the client with competent representation, the lawyer should adhere to the established schedule and inform the client of any

revisions that are required, whether attributable to the lawyer or to circumstances beyond the lawyer's control. Many clients engaged in estate planning are elderly or are facing medical emergencies. There is thus an enhanced risk that the client might die or otherwise become incapable of completing an estate plan if the estate planner takes more time than is reasonable under the circumstances to do the work requested. In such cases the client may be harmed and intended beneficiaries may not receive the benefits the client intended them to have.

The lawyer and the fiduciary should plan the administration of an estate or trust in light of the fiduciary's obligations to the courts, tax authorities, creditors and beneficiaries. The lawyer and fiduciary may subsequently decide to accelerate or delay some planned payments or distributions in order to improve the tax position of the fiduciary estate or of its beneficiaries. The lawyer's obligation to be diligent includes the duty to advise the fiduciary competently regarding the tax and non-tax impact of sales, distributions and other administrative actions, as well as to take reasonable steps to ensure that the fiduciary completes administration of the estate in a timely manner. In connection with the administration of an estate or trust, it is appropriate for the lawyer and the fiduciary to consider the circumstances of the beneficiaries and to communicate with them regarding the fiduciary estate.

Cases

When preparing a will or other testamentary instrument giving property to a beneficiary who, under applicable state law, is presumptively disqualified from receiving such a gift, the testator's lawyer owed a duty of care to the nonclient intended beneficiary. In this case, the disqualified beneficiary was the testator's caregiver, and the lawyer should have advised the testator to obtain a certificate of independent review from a disinterested and independent lawyer. Without that certificate, the gift failed. The certificate would have evidenced what the testator-client intended, and that the testator had not been unduly influenced to make the gift, and avoided the legal presumption that the caregiver unduly influenced the testator, which could now only be rebutted by clear and convincing evidence. *Osornio v. Weingarten* (2004) 124 Cal.App.4th 304.

One of a lawyer's basic functions is to advise. Not only should a lawyer furnish advice when requested, but the lawyer should also volunteer opinions when necessary to further the client's objectives. *Nichols v. Keller* (1993) 15 Cal.App.4th 1672.

The court held that the intended beneficiaries of a law firm's estate planning services rendered for the beneficiaries' father suffered "actual injury" (lawyers' fees and litigation expenses) in defending a lawsuit by the surviving spouse's conservator. The plaintiffs alleged that the lawsuit would not have been filed but for the law firm's failure to obtain a waiver of community property rights from the allegedly willing spouse when the spouse was competent. *Sindell v. Gibson, Dunn & Crutcher* (1997) 54 Cal.App.4th 1457.

The lawyer was not liable for malpractice, having drafted a will for a client whom the lawyer knew to be terminally ill and failing to follow up with the decedent for over two months. The client died with the will unexecuted. The court held that the beneficiary of an unexecuted will must prove facts that "manifest a commitment by the decedent to benefit" the beneficiary for the deceased client's lawyer to owe a duty to that beneficiary. Although the client was aware of her cancer, no evidence showed that the client believed death so imminent as to leave no opportunity for further thought on the will that the lawyer drafted. The client expressed an intention to discuss the draft with her sister, and the court inferred that the client could reasonably have expected her sister to try to change her mind. *Radovich v. Locke-Paddon* (1995) 35 Cal.App.4th 946.

A lawyer was suspended for unreasonable delay in closing an estate administration while serving as executor and intentionally and recklessly failing to perform legal services competently, thus violating former rule 3-110 of the Rules of Professional Conduct. *Layton v. State Bar* (1990) 50 Cal.3d 889.

3.12 Communication with the Client

Diligent representation begins with the lawyer's communication with client. Rules 1.2 and 1.4 of the Rules of Professional Conduct direct a lawyer to keep the client reasonably informed about significant developments relating to the representation, including promptly complying with reasonable requests for information and copies of significant documents when necessary to keep the client informed. The lawyer must abide by the client's decisions concerning the goals of the representation and the means by which those goals are pursued. For a detailed discussion of the ethical duties regarding client communications, see chapter 7 of this Guide, Communication.

Statute

California Business and Professions Code section 6068, subdivision (m)

> It is the duty of an attorney to do all of the following:
>
> . . .
>
> (m) To respond promptly to reasonable status inquiries of clients and to keep clients reasonably informed of significant developments in matters with regard to which the attorney has agreed to provide legal services.

Cases

A lawyer-executor was disciplined for mismanaging the estate and failing to communicate with the client. *Ridge v. State Bar* (1989) 47 Cal.3d 952.

Mrs. Brandlin, a client for whom Belcher had previously drawn a will and trust, discussed with a trust officer changing the trust to add other children as beneficiaries. The trust officer conveyed this possibility to Belcher, who said he would have to hear from his client. Belcher was sued for negligence by Brandlin's children. The court affirmed a summary judgment in his favor, observing, "Belcher fully discharged whatever duty his prior representation imposed by his request through the intermediary that the client communicate with him personally. Belcher's conduct satisfied rather than violated his duty as a lawyer. It was designed to assure that the personal nature of the attorney-client relationship was protected." *Brandlin v. Belcher* (1977) 67 Cal.App.3d 997.

3.13 Client with Diminished Capacity

Rule 1.4 of the Rules of Professional Conduct allows no exception regarding a lawyer's duty to communicate with a client, if that client becomes incapacitated during the representation. The duty of client communication applies even if the client has difficulty understanding or retaining the lawyer's communications or articulating the client's wishes regarding the goals of the representation or the steps required to accomplish those goals. The duties to the client are absolute, and the lawyer may not substitute the lawyer's judgment for the wishes of the client, however well intentioned. If difficulties in communication prevent effective representation of the client, the lawyer should consider withdrawing from the representation consistent with the procedures set forth in rule 1.16 of the Rules of Professional Conduct.

The role of a guardian ad litem differs from the role of a lawyer, whether or not appointed by the court. A guardian ad litem is a representative of the court with specific authority to report to the court on actions that may benefit a protected person. The duty of diligent representation and the duty to avoid conflicts of interest prevent a lawyer from seeking the appointment of a guardian ad litem for a client.

Cases

An estate planning lawyer, at the direction of a third party and without meeting or speaking to the client, prepared a will and a "confirmation of gift" for a terminally ill individual. The "gift" was to the third party. When the testator signed the documents, testator was lethargic, hallucinating, and in great pain. The testator died three days later. The testator's children contested the will and the gift, and the third party settled by receiving a token amount of cash, but the estate was left with a debt related to the gift. In the subsequent malpractice action, the trial court found in favor of the children against the lawyer. The Court of Appeal reversed, stating:

> Although a lawyer retained to provide testamentary legal services to a testator may also have a duty to act with due care for the interests of an intended third-party beneficiary, the lawyer's primary duty is owed to his client and his primary obligation is to serve and carry out the client's intentions. Where, as here, there is a question about whether the third-party beneficiary was, in fact, the decedent's *intended* beneficiary, and the beneficiary's claim is that the lawyer failed to adequately ascertain the testator's intent or capacity, the lawyer will not be held accountable to the beneficiary—because any other conclusion would place the lawyer in an untenable position of divided loyalty.

Boranian v. Clark (2004) 123 Cal.App.4th 1012, 1014 (italics in original).

Disappointed heirs brought a malpractice claim against the estate planning lawyers claiming that the testator lacked testamentary capacity at the time the estate plan amendments were executed, that the lawyers should have known that the testator's testamentary capacity was questionable, and that the lawyers acted negligently in failing to assure, confirm, and document the testator's capacity to execute the governing will and trust amendments. The Court of Appeal upheld the trial court's grant of a demurrer dismissing the claim without leave to amend. The court found that the lawyer's duty of loyalty to the client may be compromised by imposing a duty to nonclient beneficiaries on issues of determining incapacity. The court cited favorably rule 1.14(a) of the Model Rules of Professional Conduct: "When a client's ability to make adequately considered decisions in connection with the representation is impaired, whether because of minority, mental disability or for some other reason, the lawyer shall, as far as reasonably possible, maintain a normal client-lawyer relationship with the client." None of the authorities imposing a duty upon the lawyer to assess the capacity of the testator indicate that such duty would run to beneficiaries rather than solely to the testator. *Moore v. Anderson Zeigler Disharoon Gallagher & Gray* (2003) 109 Cal.App.4th 1287, 1306.

Citing *Linsk v. Linsk* (1969) 70 Cal.2d 272, 276, the court in this case held: "An attorney is not authorized, however, merely by virtue of his retention in litigation, to 'impair the client's substantial rights or the cause of action itself.'" *Blanton v. Womancare, Inc.* (1985) 38 Cal.3d 396, 404-405. The court distinguished decisions related to settlement or entry of a default judgment from routine procedural and tactical decisions, both in the degree to which they affect the client's interest, and in the degree to which they involve matters of judgment which extend beyond technical competence so that any client would be expected to share in the making of them.

Article

Rudolph & Hughes, *A Lawyer is a Lawyer is a Lawyer* (2019) 25 Cal. Trust and Estates Q., Issue 1.

3.14 Time Constraints Imposed by Client

A lawyer may be called on to work quickly to address an emergency situation, such as an estate planning project for a client whose death appears imminent. The speed of the work should be tempered with due consideration of the legal and ethical problems presented. If possible, the lawyer should advise the client, preferably in writing, of the risks involved and the ethical issues presented in any project undertaken on an emergency basis. The lawyer should keep in mind that the timetable imposed may affect the lawyer's ability to acquire sufficient learning and skill before performance is required. A lawyer owes no duty to a person who is not the lawyer's client and should consider declining to prepare "the deathbed will."

Often the person seeking legal assistance on an expedited basis will be a relative or friend of a current client of the lawyer. In this case, the lawyer must take special note of the ethical issues arising from the potential conflicts of interest between the existing and prospective client.

ACTEC Commentaries on Model Rules of Professional Conduct, Model Rule 1.3

> The lawyer should not agree to the imposition of time limits that may prevent the lawyer from consulting fully with the client or giving a matter the time and attention, it should receive. The lawyer should caution the client regarding the risks that arise if a matter is pursued on an abbreviated time schedule that deprives the lawyer of the opportunity fully to fulfill the lawyer's role. A lawyer who agrees to pursue a matter on such a schedule acts properly if adherence to the agreed schedule is reasonable under the circumstances.

3.15 Planning for Lawyer's Disability, Retirement, or Death

The ABA Committee on Ethics and Professional Responsibility, in its Formal Opinion Number 1992-369, states:

> To fulfill the obligation to protect client files and property, a lawyer should prepare a future plan providing for the maintenance and protection of those client interests in the event of the lawyer's death. Such a plan should, at a minimum, include the designation of another lawyer who would have the authority to review client files and make determinations as to which files need immediate attention, and who would notify the clients of their lawyer's death.

Lawyers practicing in a firm should also ensure that client affairs are not compromised by the death, disability, or retirement of a lawyer associated with that firm. California practitioners should consult Business and Professions Code sections 6180 to 6180.14 for detailed statutory procedures governing the lawyer's cessation of practice.

The State Bar of California has published a detailed sample Agreement to Close Law Practice in the Future, available at:

> https://www.calbar.ca.gov/Portals/0/documents/forms/AGREEMENT_TO_CLOSE_LAW_PRACTICE_IN_THE_FUTURE_REVISED_08-1-2011.pdf

The sample agreement is drawn between an estate planning lawyer and a nominated practice administrator. It becomes operative upon the incapacity or death of the planning lawyer. A current review of the agreement provisions would be helpful in understanding the range of tasks, duties, and responsibilities that the practice administrator may need to undertake in winding down a practice, and the authority that the practice administrator will need to perform those tasks competently.

ACTEC Commentaries on Model Rules of Professional Conduct, Model Rule 1.3

> As stated in Comment (5) to Model Rule of Professional Conduct 1.3, to prevent neglect of client matters in the event of a sole practitioner's death or disability, the duty of diligence may require that each sole practitioner prepare a plan, in conformity with applicable rules, that designates another competent lawyer to review client files, notify each client of the lawyer's death or disability, and determine whether there is a need for immediate protective action. The obligation to assure that clients are represented on an uninterrupted basis should also extend to lawyers who practice in firms.

CHAPTER 4 IDENTIFYING THE CLIENT AND THE SCOPE OF THE REPRESENTATION

California Rules of Professional Conduct, Rule 1.2 - Scope of Representation and Allocation of Authority

> (a) Subject to rule 1.2.1, a lawyer shall abide by a client's decisions concerning the objectives of representation and, as required by rule 1.4, shall reasonably* consult with the client as to the means by which they are to be pursued. Subject to Business and Professions Code section 6068, subdivision (e)(1) and rule 1.6, a lawyer may take such action on behalf of the client as is impliedly authorized to carry out the representation. A lawyer shall abide by a client's decision whether to settle a matter. Except as otherwise provided by law in a criminal case, the lawyer shall abide by the client's decision, after consultation with the lawyer, as to a plea to be entered, whether to waive jury trial and whether the client will testify.
>
> (b) A lawyer may limit the scope of the representation if the limitation is reasonable* under the circumstances, is not otherwise prohibited by law, and the client gives informed consent.*

California Rules of Professional Conduct, Rule 1.2.1 - Advising or Assisting the Violation of Law

> (a) A lawyer shall not counsel a client to engage, or assist a client in conduct that the lawyer knows* is criminal, fraudulent,* or a violation of any law, rule, or ruling of a tribunal.*
>
> (b) Notwithstanding paragraph (a), a lawyer may:
>
> > (1) discuss the legal consequences of any proposed course of conduct with a client; and
> >
> > (2) counsel or assist a client to make a good faith effort to determine the validity, scope, meaning, or application of a law, rule, or ruling of a tribunal.*

An asterisk (*) identifies a defined term in rule 1.0.1 of the Rules of Professional Conduct. For further discussion of a defined term, see chapter 2 of this Guide, Terminology.

4.1 Introduction

Under rule 1.2 of the Rules of Professional Conduct, the client directs the goals of the representation and the means of reaching those goals. The lawyer must keep the client informed about significant developments relating to the representation, including promptly complying with reasonable requests for information and providing copies of significant documents to the client. Rules Prof. Conduct, rule 1.4. The lawyer must defer to the client on all substantive decisions regarding the representation.

The ethical duties arising from a representation require that the lawyer identify the client and any fiduciary, beneficiary, or other specific role the client may have that is related to the matter. The initial engagement letter should specify the client, the client's role if applicable, and the scope of the representation. Identifying the client and the scope of the representation in the engagement letter will assist the lawyer in analyzing the ethical duties that the lawyer owes to the client.

A lawyer must not agree to represent two current clients that have directly adverse interests without the informed written consent of each of them. Rules Prof. Conduct, rule 1.7. When the lawyer has identified the client and the client has accepted the representation, the lawyer must keep the confidences of that client inviolate. Bus. & Prof. Code sec. 6068, subd. (e). The subjects of conflicts of interest and confidentiality of information are discussed separately and in detail in chapters 5 and 6, respectively, of this Guide. Apart from looking at those rules in depth, the lawyer should understand the context in which those duties arise so that potential conflicts in ethical duties can be foreseen and avoided.

Identifying and documenting the client and the scope of the representation at the outset will help the lawyer follow the professional duties owed to a client in the following circumstances:

1. When the lawyer undertakes a matter for new client and the new client has an interest adverse to a current client, or a former client in a substantially related matter, or when the lawyer's ethical duties to a current or former client may compromise the lawyer's loyalty or independent judgment. Rules Prof. Conduct, rules 1.7 and 1.9;
2. When the lawyer undertakes to represent a new client and the lawyer obtained confidential information from a current or former client that is material to the new representation. Rules Prof. Conduct, rules 1.6 and 1.9;
3. When the lawyer undertakes to represent joint clients whose representation may raise questions of conflict of interest or confidentiality—for example, spouses wishing to prepare a joint estate plan, multiple generations seeking to coordinate estate planning, a business entity or its members, or both, or clients who are beneficiaries of the same trust or will; or
4. When the lawyer undertakes to represent a fiduciary in a trust or estate matter, and either beneficiaries may have a mistaken expectation that the lawyer represents their interests, or the lawyer's client is both a fiduciary and a beneficiary.

Comment on California Rules of Professional Conduct, Rule 1.2

> [1] Paragraph (a) confers upon the client the ultimate authority to determine the purposes to be served by legal representation, within the limits imposed by law and the lawyer's professional obligations. (See, e.g., Cal. Const., art. I, sec. 16; Pen. Code, sec. 1018.) A lawyer retained to represent a client is authorized to act on behalf of the client, such as in procedural matters and in making certain tactical decisions. A lawyer is not authorized merely by virtue of the lawyer's retention to impair the client's substantive rights or the client's claim itself. *Blanton v. Womancare, Inc.* (1985) 38 Cal.3d 396,404.

[2] At the outset of, or during a representation, the client may authorize the lawyer to take specific action on the client's behalf without further consultation. Absent a material change in circumstances and subject to rule 1.4, a lawyer may rely on such an advance authorization. The client may revoke such authority at any time.

ACTEC Commentaries on Model Rules of Professional Conduct, Model Rule 1.2

Avoiding Misunderstandings as to Scope of Representation. The risk that a client will misunderstand the scope or duration of a representation can be substantially reduced or eliminated if the lawyer sends the client an appropriate engagement letter at the outset of the representation. If a lawyer is retained by a new client with respect to a single matter, the representation may terminate when the work on the matter is completed; on the other hand, the representation may become dormant. See the discussion of a dormant representation in the ACTEC Commentary on MRPC 1.4 (Communication). Where the lawyer has served a client in a variety of matters, the client may reasonably assume that the representation is active or that the client may reactivate the representation at any time. A lawyer in these circumstances should clarify with the client the scope of the representation and the expectations of the client. A client may terminate a representation at any time, and, subject to the requirements of MRPC 1.16 (Declining or Terminating Representation), a lawyer may also terminate a representation at any time.

Disagreement Between Lawyer and Client as to Means for Accomplishing Client's Objectives. If an adequately informed client directs the lawyer to take action contrary to the lawyer's advice, and the action is neither illegal nor unethical, the lawyer should generally follow the client's direction. See MRPCs 1.4(a)(5) and 1.4(b) (Communication), and 1.16(b) (Declining or Terminating Representation). A client might insist, for example, that a "simple" will alone is all that is needed to accomplish the client's estate planning objectives. The lawyer, however, might disagree, concluding, in the lawyer's professional opinion, that a revocable inter vivos trust and a pour-over will would better achieve those objectives. Provided the lawyer obtains the client's informed consent, the lawyer may proceed against the lawyer's better professional judgment to prepare the "simple" will. See ACTEC Commentary on MRPC 1.0(e) (Terminology) (defining informed consent). If a client insists on an action that the lawyer believes will be ineffective, such as inclusion of a provision that the lawyer believes will not be enforced by a court, the lawyer should inform the client of that risk and may refuse the request if the lawyer believes complying with it would violate the duty of competence under MRPC 1.1.

For a discussion of the ethical duties owed to a client after a representation terminates, see chapter 7 of this Guide, Communication, section 7.7.

Cases

A client did not consent to pay a lawyer's invoice for services rendered under a fee agreement with client's late husband that was never signed, as required by California Business and Professions Code section 6148. The client filed an objection to the lawyer's request to withdraw from limited scope representation. The client followed that objection with an email to the lawyer requesting more information and stating she would make future payments only "provided I understand and approve what it is I am paying for." *Leighton v. Forster* (2017) 8 Cal.App.5th 467.

A minor in a juvenile proceeding, through his lawyer, petitioned the court for the appointment of a psychologist as a defense expert. The psychologist stated that she would respect the lawyer-client privilege and the lawyer's duty of confidentiality, and would not report client information concerning child abuse or neglect. The trial court denied the minor's petition, and the Court of Appeal reversed on a writ of mandate. The Court of Appeal held that a minor subject to a juvenile wardship petition has the right not only to counsel but also to necessary ancillary defense services, and the right to protect communications with both counsel and experts engaged to assist counsel from disclosure. The psychologist was willing to safeguard the confidentiality of the minor's communications at the risk of personal liability that communications to the minor's lawyer might not comply with the mandatory reporting requirements for child abuse and neglect. The lawyer was not a mandated reporter. *Elijah W. v. Super. Ct. of L.A.* (2013) 216 Cal.App.4th 140.

Ethics Opinion

A lawyer must make clear who is the client, disclose any potential conflicts in writing, and obtain any required consents before undertaking to represent a client in drafting a testamentary document when the lawyer has first or simultaneously been contacted by the client's child who will be the beneficiary in the client's testamentary document. San Diego County Bar Assn., Ethics opn. No. 1990-3. See also chapter 5 of this Guide, Conflicts of Interest, section 5.13.

Article

Wertlieb, *The Importance of Knowing Who Is, and Who Is Not, My Client* (Sept. 3, 2019) Cal. Lawyers Assn.

4.2 Sample Engagement Letter – Estate Planning

The following sample letter could be adapted to send to a single client who engages the lawyer for estate planning. The lawyer should adapt it thoughtfully to the lawyer's customary practice and the needs of a particular client representation.

Dear [Client]:

Thank you for your confidence in selecting our firm to represent you in connection with your estate planning.

Scope of the Engagement. We will provide legal services in connection with preparing, reviewing, and executing your estate plan including a revocable trust, last will, durable power of attorney, health care directive, and such other and supplemental documents as you may request or we may deem appropriate for a complete estate plan.

Identification of the Client. You will be our client. As your lawyers, we have a professional obligation to preserve any confidential information we receive from you unless you authorize us to disclose such information. We advocate for your personal interests and give you totally independent advice. We have a duty to act solely in your best interest as our client, without being influenced by conflicting personal interests of any other client or third party. These professional obligations ensure the preservation of your confidences and the elimination of any conflicts of interest between you and any other person as related to this representation.

Fees and Billing Arrangements. [See chapter 8 of this Guide, Compensation]

Resolution of Disputes. [See chapter 8 of this Guide, Compensation]

Termination of Engagement. The execution of your estate planning documents will conclude our representation. We will be happy to provide additional or continuing services, but unless such arrangements are made and agreed upon in writing, we will not undertake to advise you regarding future or ongoing legal issues affecting your estate plan, or to notify you of changes in the laws or the necessity to review your estate planning documents periodically.

Sincerely,
[Lawyer]

For a further discussion of the ethical duties to a client after a representation terminates, see chapter 7 of this Guide, Communication, section 7.7.

4.3 Joint Representation

A trusts and estates lawyer commonly represents multiple parties in an estate planning context, whether they are spouses, registered domestic partners, other family members, or business partners or a family business itself. Unless otherwise explicitly agreed, a lawyer who represents multiple clients in related legal matters is presumed to represent them jointly. Assuming that no actual adversity exists, multiple parties in a legal matter often are better served by joint representation that achieves a coordinated result at a lower cost than if each party were individually represented by a different lawyer.

Even if the estate planning or other goals of the clients are not entirely consistent, the estate planning lawyer is not necessarily precluded from representing parties jointly. If the differences are identified and agreed upon, the estate planning lawyer may still be able to advise joint clients who have somewhat different objectives, and the lawyer's advice and counsel may be consistent with their common interests and the estate planning lawyer's traditional role as the lawyer for the family. However, transfers of property ownership may give rise to a direct conflict in the clients' interests, and an estate planning lawyer generally should not engage in advising or completing transfers of property between joint clients, including transmutations of property from separate to community or the reverse.

In a joint representation information will be shared among the clients with respect to the stated scope of the representation, and confidentiality will be maintained as to all other matters. The engagement letter that defines the scope of representation may also limit the lawyer's duty of confidentiality. The information imparted by one joint client to the lawyer is not protected from disclosure to the other joint client or clients. In the event of litigation between the parties to a joint representation, Evidence Code section 962 prohibits all parties and their successors in interest from claiming the lawyer-client privilege with respect to confidential information related to the representation. For a further discussion of the lawyer-client privilege in litigation, see Chapter 6 this Guide, Confidentiality of Information, section 6.13.

Statute

California Evidence Code section 962

> Where two or more clients have retained or consulted a lawyer upon a matter of common interest, none of them, nor the successor in interest of any of them, may claim a privilege under this article as to a communication made in the course of that relationship when such communication is offered in a civil proceeding between one of such clients (or his successor in interest) and another of such clients (or his successor in interest).

4.4 Sample Engagement Letter – Joint Representation of Spouses

A letter similar in substance to the following sample could be adapted for sending to spouses who consent to joint representation notwithstanding actual or potential adverse interests. Rules Prof. Conduct, rule 1.7 and chapter 5 of this Guide, Conflicts of Interest. The lawyer should adapt it thoughtfully to the lawyer's customary practice and the needs of a particular client representation.

Dear [Clients]:

Thank you for your confidence in selecting our firm to represent you in connection with your estate planning. This letter will confirm the terms of our agreement to represent you jointly in preparing your estate plan.

Scope of the Engagement. We will provide legal services in connection with preparing, reviewing, and executing your estate plan including a joint revocable trust, last wills, durable powers of attorney, and health care directives for each of you, and such other and supplemental documents as you may request and that we agree to prepare, or that we may deem appropriate for your estate plan.

Fees for Legal Services and Costs. [See chapter 8 of this Guide, Compensation]

Confidentiality. It is common for spouses to employ the same law firm to assist them in their estate planning. With few exceptions under the law, communications among us are protected by the lawyer's duty of confidentiality. In this joint representation, you have given your consent to disclose all information about your estate planning to each other, and we will disclose any communications either of you has with us regarding your estate planning to the other. The lawyer's ethical duty of confidentiality would still apply to third parties, but not between the two of you. If instead you were each represented by your own lawyer, communications with your lawyer would be privileged and not subject to disclosure to the other of you.

In addition, if a third party whom we do not represent, such as a family member or financial planner, is included in a meeting or is copied on correspondence, then confidentiality may be lost as to that communication. Confidentiality may also be lost if we communicate using email to which others have access. Please notify us immediately if you become aware of any hacking into your email account or other access by another person. Please also notify us, in writing, if you do not want us to send communications to you through email or other electronic means.

[See chapter 10 of this Guide, Ethics and Technology, section 10.8 for sample disclosures of the risks of electronic communications.]

Conflicts of Interest. Spouses can have differing, and sometimes conflicting, interests and objectives regarding their estate planning. For example, they may have different views regarding their respective property rights or interests or how their property should pass after the death of one or both of them. If you each had a separate lawyer, you would each have an advocate for your position and would receive totally independent advice. If we undertake to represent both of you, we cannot advocate the interest of one of you against the other. If you ask us to continue to serve you jointly, our efforts will be to assist in developing a coordinated overall plan and to encourage the resolution of differing interests in an equitable manner and in the best interests of your marriage.

[See chapter 5 of this Guide, Conflicts of Interest, section 5.4 for a sample disclosure of potential conflicts of interest to spouses seeking joint representation.]

We do not expect conflicts to arise in this joint representation that would prevent us from representing both of you as our clients in accordance with our professional obligations. However, if an irreconcilable conflict of interest arises between you that, in our judgment, makes it impossible for us to fulfill our ethical duties to both of you as clients, we will withdraw as your joint lawyer and advise each of you to seek other legal counsel. By signing this letter, you agree that we can represent the two of you together notwithstanding the conflicts of interest that may arise by virtue of the proposed joint representation.

Conclusion of Representation. The execution of your estate planning documents will conclude our representation. Our professional obligations to preserve confidential information and avoid conflicts of interest will continue to apply to you as former clients. We will be happy to provide additional or continuing legal services, but unless such arrangements are made and agreed upon in writing, we will not undertake to advise you regarding future or ongoing legal issues affecting your joint estate plan, or to notify you of changes in the laws or the necessity to review your estate planning documents periodically.

If you consent to our representation of both of you on these terms, please sign and return the enclosed copy of this letter. If you have any questions about this letter or the proposed terms of the representation, I encourage you to consult another lawyer about this letter before signing it.

Sincerely,

[Lawyer]

CONSENT

We have each reviewed the foregoing letter. Each of us understands the terms of the joint representation set forth in this letter and has had an opportunity to review the letter with independent legal counsel. With that understanding, we both agree to be represented jointly by Lawyer notwithstanding the potential or actual conflicts of interest between us. Each of us also understands and agrees that all communications and information Lawyer receives from either of us relating to these matters may be shared with the other.

Dated: ________________   ______________________________

[Client 1]

Dated: ________________ ______________________________
[Client 2]

4.5 Sample Engagement Letters – Representation of Family Members

The following pair of sample engagement letters reflect two approaches in agreeing to represent multiple family members regarding a coordinated estate plan. Both letters include the disclosures needed to obtain the informed written consent of the prospective clients to joint or concurrent representation notwithstanding direct or potential adverse interests. Rules Prof. Conduct, rule 1.7 and chapter 5 of this Guide, Conflicts of Interest, section 5.5..

The first letter assumes waiver of the lawyer's ethical duty of confidentiality by the joint clients and the resulting full disclosure of all client confidential information between them. The second assumes preservation of the confidences from all family members, with a potential conflict in the duty of loyalty that the lawyer owes to both clients, as discussed in chapter 6 of this Guide, Confidentiality of Information, section 6.9. The lawyer should determine the most appropriate approach, and review and adapt the corresponding letter appropriately for the circumstances of the lawyer's practice and a particular representation.

For a sample disclosure to a former client when later undertaking to represent another family member, see chapter 6 of this Guide, Confidentiality of Information, section 6.10.

A. Consent to Joint Representation of Family Members

Dear [Client 1] and [Client 2]:

As we discussed, I currently represent [Client 1] for estate planning and have also been asked to represent [Client 2] who is the (parent/child/sibling) of [Client 1], regarding estate planning. You have both expressed similar goals and would like me to share information with both of you related to each of your individual estate plans.

While I am happy to represent both of you, and believe that I can provide competent and diligent representation to each of you, before I can do so, I need to disclose to each of you the potential and actual conflicts of interest that are presented by this "joint representation" and obtain your informed written consent to the representation notwithstanding such conflicts. That disclosure and consent is the purpose of this letter.

It is in your interest, and my own ethical obligation to each of you requires, that you fully understand the considerations involved in my joint representation. You should understand that each of you are free to name anyone as the beneficiary of your own estate and that you can each name anyone you choose as your personal representative. You do not have control over each other's decisions related to your estate planning.

Nonetheless, you may disagree with each other's estate planning wishes. For example, [Client 2] may be disappointed if [Client 1] disinherits or substantially reduces the share that [Client 2] might receive from [Client 1]'s estate. Also, [Client 2] may not agree with [Client 1]'s choice of who to name as the personal representative of their estate. Or [Client 2] may disagree with how [Client 1] decides to structure a gift to a beneficiary. In addition, [Client 2] could convert a gift from [Client 1] from separate property to community property with [Client 2]'s spouse and thereby upset [Client 1].

I can document what the two of you agree to, and can identify and provide potential solutions to issues that might arise during my representation. However, if you disagree on an estate planning matter, you will need to work it out yourselves. I will not advise either of you on the resolution of a disputed matter. If you reach an impasse, I may be required to withdraw from the representation, and each of you would be required to obtain independent legal counsel to represent your interests.

If each of you had your own lawyer, you would each have an advocate for your position and receive totally independent advice. This is not the case when you are represented by the same lawyer. Also, generally information given to your own lawyer is confidential and cannot be obtained without your consent.

However, if I represent both of you, you would lose some protection of the lawyer's duty of confidentiality that you would normally have. For example, if you were each represented by your own legal counsel, communications with your lawyer would not subject to disclosure to the other party. In this instance, however, since you both consent to disclose any and all information about your estate planning to each other, any communications you have with me regarding your estate planning would be disclosed to the other party. The duty of confidentiality would still apply to third parties (such as contingent beneficiaries) but not between the two of you. Therefore, for example, if [Client 1] were to ask me about a conversation that I had with [Client 2] related to estate planning, I would have to disclose that conversation to [Client 1].

On a related issue, if a dispute ever arises between the two of you related to your estate planning, I could be called as a witness and neither of you would be entitled to claim the lawyer-client privilege in order to prevent our communications from being disclosed in any proceeding brought as the result of such dispute.

If after reviewing and understanding the foregoing, you each agree to allow me to represent you related to your estate planning notwithstanding the actual and potential conflicts of interest, please indicate by your signatures below. Your signatures acknowledge your understanding of the disadvantages of the proposed joint representation and your informed consent to that representation. If you prefer to retain your own separate legal counsel to represent you related to this matter, rather than having me provide representation, then you are certainly free to do so now, or at any time in the future if you later determine that my representation is no longer desirable. You can also consult with separate counsel on the proposed terms of engagement in this letter. You certainly have the right to decline the representation because of the conflicts disclosed in this letter. I would not be offended in any way.

Thank you for your attention to this matter. Please contact me if you have any questions concerning this letter.

Sincerely,

[Lawyer]

CONSENT

We have each reviewed the foregoing letter. Each of us understands the terms of joint representation set forth in this letter and has had an opportunity to review the foregoing letter with independent legal counsel. With that understanding, we both agree to be represented by Lawyer concurrently notwithstanding the direct or potential conflicts of interest between us. Each of us also understands and agrees that communications and information Lawyer receives from either of us relating to the subject matter of the representation may be shared with the other.

Dated: ________________ ________________________
[Client 1]

Dated: ________________ ________________________
[Client 2]

B. Consent to Separate Representation of Family Members

Dear [Client 1] and [Client 2]:

I currently represent [Client 1] regarding estate planning and have been asked to also represent [Client 2] who is the (parent/child/sibling) of [Client 1], related to a separate estate plan. While I am happy to represent the both of you, and believe that I can provide competent and diligent representation to each of you, before I can do so, I need to disclose to each of you the potential and actual conflicts of interest that are presented by my representation of both of you and obtain your informed written consent to the representation notwithstanding such conflicts. That disclosure and consent is the purpose of this letter.

It is in your interest, and my own ethical obligation to each of you requires, that you fully understand the considerations involved in my separate representation of both of you. You should understand that each of you are free to name anyone as the beneficiary of your own estate and that you can each name anyone you choose as your personal representative. You do not have control over each other's decisions related to your estate planning.

Nonetheless, you may disagree with each other's estate planning wishes. For example, [Client 2] may be disappointed if [Client 1] disinherits or substantially reduces the share that [Client 2] might should receive from [Client 1]'s estate. Also, [Client 2] may not agree with who [Client 1]'s choses to nominate as the personal representative of their estate plan. Or [Client 2] may disagree with how [Client 1] decides to structure a gift to a beneficiary. In addition, [Client 2] could convert a gift from [Client 1] from separate property to community property with [Client 2]'s spouse and thereby upset [Client 1].

If you disagree on an estate planning matter, you will need to work it out yourselves. I will not advise either of you on the resolution of a disputed matter. If you reach an impasse, I may be required to withdraw from the representation, and each of you would be required to obtain independent legal counsel to represent your interests.

If each of you had your own lawyer, you would each have an advocate for your position and receive totally independent advice. This is not the case when you are represented by the same lawyer. I cannot represent one of you against the other.

Since you have not consented to share information between the two of you, I will not disclose information that one of you provides to me related to your individual estate plan with the other.

If after reviewing and understanding the foregoing, you each agree to allow me to represent you related to your estate planning notwithstanding the actual and potential conflicts of interest, please indicate by your signatures below. Your signatures acknowledge your understanding of the disadvantages of the proposed concurrent representation and your informed consent to that representation. If you prefer to retain your own separate legal counsel to represent you related to this matter, rather than having me provide representation, then you are certainly free to do so now, or at any time in the future if you later determine that my representation is no longer desirable. You can also consult with separate counsel on the proposed terms of engagement in this letter. You certainly have the right to decline the representation because of the conflicts disclosed in this letter. I would not be offended in any way.

Thank you for your attention to this matter. Please contact me if you have any questions concerning this letter.

Sincerely,

[Lawyer]

CONSENT

We have each reviewed the foregoing letter. Each of us understands the terms of separate and concurrent representation set forth in this letter and has had an opportunity to review the foregoing letter with independent legal counsel. With that understanding, we both agree to be represented by Lawyer concurrently notwithstanding the potential or actual conflicts of interest between us.

Dated: ________________ ________________________
[Client 1]

Dated: ________________ ________________________
[Client 2]

4.6 Fiduciaries and Beneficiaries

Identifying the client and defining the scope of the representation in undertaking the representation of a fiduciary or beneficiary of an estate or trust can be difficult. The following issues may arise:

1. What ethical duties a fiduciary's lawyer owes to the beneficiaries of an estate or trust;
2. What expectations the beneficiaries have about the role of the lawyer for "the trust" or for "the estate";
3. What expectations the beneficiaries have about the role of the lawyer for the fiduciary;
4. Whether a lawyer may represent a client in both fiduciary and individual capacities;
5. Whether a lawyer may represent both a fiduciary and a beneficiary in the same matter; and
6. Special ethical considerations in representing a corporate fiduciary.

Identifying and making clear to all interested parties both the identity and the fiduciary capacity of the lawyer's client in a trust or estate administration is especially important because the unsophisticated beneficiary often believes that the lawyer for the fiduciary is representing "the estate" or "the trust," and by extension is also representing the interest of the beneficiaries. In fact, the lawyer represents only the fiduciary and advises on the duties that the fiduciary must fulfill in completing the administration. However, the lawyer may inadvertently undertake responsibilities to beneficiaries by telling or implying to the beneficiaries that the lawyer represents the "estate" or "trust" or is otherwise protecting the interests of the beneficiaries. Misguided expectations may result in the lawyer effectively representing multiple parties with adverse interests, implicating all the ethical duties and limitations surrounding joint representation.

When the lawyer represents the fiduciary, the lawyer should advise the beneficiaries that representation is not extended to them and advise them to seek separate counsel if they have questions about their legal rights. Communication with the beneficiaries is subject to the lawyer's ethical duties to unrepresented persons and other third parties in rules 4.1 and 4.3 of the Rules of Professional Conduct. For a discussion of the ethical duties regarding unrepresented persons and a sample notice of nonrepresentation to beneficiaries, see chapter 7 of this Guide, Communication, sections 7.4 and 7.5.

Concurrent representation of the fiduciary and one or more beneficiaries may be permissible in appropriate circumstances, provided that the lawyer obtains an informed consent from all the proposed clients after a detailed disclosure of the actual and potential conflicts that may arise in the course of the representation. For a further discussion of appropriate client disclosures, see rule 1.0.1(e) of the Rules of Professional Conduct and section 4.10 of this chapter.

In an estate planning context, the lawyer can anticipate future questions about representation, and when possible, should discuss with the estate planning client the functions that a personal representative, trustee, or other fiduciary will perform in the client's estate plan. In anticipation that the lawyer may later owe ethical duties to the beneficiaries as well as to the fiduciary selected by the client, the lawyer should appropriately educate the client as to the role that the lawyer for a fiduciary usually plays in the administration of the trust or estate. These consultations better equip the client to select fiduciaries and to give directions that will prevent or mitigate future conflicts.

While no special ethical considerations generally arise in representing a corporate fiduciary, the duty to avoid conflicts of interest may be implicated when the lawyer represents another client whose interests may be adverse to the corporate fiduciary in an unrelated matter. For a discussion of this controversy, see chapter 5 of this Guide, Conflicts of Interest, section 5.7.

ACTEC Commentaries on Model Rules of Professional Conduct, Model Rule 1.2

> *Communication with Beneficiaries of Fiduciary Estate.* The lawyer engaged by a fiduciary to represent the fiduciary generally in connection with a fiduciary estate may communicate directly with the beneficiaries regarding the nature of the relationship between the lawyer and the beneficiaries. However, the fiduciary is primarily responsible for communicating with the beneficiaries regarding the fiduciary estate. An early meeting between the fiduciary, the lawyer, and the beneficiaries may provide all parties with a better understanding of the proceeding and lead to a more efficient administration. See ACTEC Commentaries on MRPCs 4.1 (Truthfulness in Statements to Others) and 4.3 (Dealing with Unrepresented Person). As a general rule, the lawyer for the fiduciary should consider informing the beneficiaries that the lawyer has been retained by the fiduciary regarding the fiduciary estate and that the fiduciary is the lawyer's client; that while the fiduciary and the lawyer will, from time to time, provide information to the beneficiaries regarding the fiduciary estate, the lawyer does not represent them; and that the beneficiaries may wish to retain independent counsel to represent their interests.

Cases

A law firm could represent an executor and a beneficiary of estate simultaneously. Even when the represented beneficiary was in dispute with another beneficiary of the estate, the Court of Appeal held that the representation did not present a conflict between the executor and the represented beneficiary. The court further found the fact that the law firm had represented the testator in drafting the will did not create a conflict since the representation of the testator in this manner did not create a lawyer-client relationship with the will beneficiaries. *Baker Manock & Jensen v. Super. Ct.* (*Salwasser*) (2009) 175 Cal.App.4th 1414.

The court found that California authorities have uniformly held "that the legal representation of a fiduciary, standing alone, does not impose upon the lawyer a fiduciary obligation to the beneficiary." The holding of *Morales v. Field,* below, was distinguished and limited in this case on the grounds that in *Morales*, the lawyers had made affirmative representations to the beneficiaries that they would keep the beneficiaries informed and that the beneficiaries "should feel reasonably assured that [their] interests will be protected." *Johnson v. Super. Ct.* (*Sheppard Mullin Richter & Hampton*) (1995) 38 Cal.App.4th 463, 472-74.

In holding that no lawyer-client relationship exists between the lawyer for the personal representative of an estate and the estate's beneficiaries, the court stated:

> Contrary to the allegations of the complaint, it is well established that the attorney for the administrator of an estate represents the administrator, and not the estate. [Citations omitted.] A key element of any action for professional malpractice is the establishment of a duty by the professional to the claimant. Absent duty there can be no breach and no negligence. [Citations omitted.] By assuming a duty to the administrator of an estate, an attorney undertakes to perform services which may benefit legatees of the estate, but he has no contractual privity with the beneficiaries of the estate.

Goldberg v. Frye (1990) 217 Cal.App.3d 1258, 1267.

In holding that the beneficiaries of a trust may bring a malpractice action against the lawyer for the trustee, the court stated:

> An attorney who acts as counsel for a trustee provides advice and guidance as to how that trustee may and must act to fulfill his obligations to all beneficiaries. It follows that when an attorney undertakes a relationship as adviser to a trustee, he in reality also assumes a relationship with the beneficiary akin to that between trustee and beneficiary. In contrast to the third party asserting a claim in *Goodman*, appellant here was not someone with whom respondent's client, the trustee Wells Fargo, was to negotiate at arms' length.

Morales v. Field, DeGoff, Huppert & McGowan (1979) 99 Cal.App.3d 307, 316 (citing *Goodman v. Kennedy* (1976) 18 Cal.3d 335).

The Court of Appeal upheld the trial court findings that a lawyer led the nominated executor reasonably to believe the lawyer was representing him, and that it must have been clear to th307e lawyer that the nominated executor was led to so believe. That the nominated executor had not retained the lawyer as a client was irrelevant because the lawyer did not perform the necessary probate work whoever the client was, and the lawyer led the nominated executor to believe that the lawyer was representing him without ever advising him otherwise. A lawyer's duty to communicate includes the duty to communicate with unrepresented persons at least to the extent of advising them that they are not clients. This duty extends only to persons who, to the lawyer's knowledge, may reasonably believe that they are clients. *Butler v. State Bar* (1986) 42 Cal.3d 323, 329.

Article

Kohlmann & Scharre, *Both Attorney and Trustee: Doubling Down or a Bad Bet?* (2019) 25 Cal. Trust and Estates Q., Issue 3.

4.7 Sample Engagement Letter – Fiduciary in Connection with a Trust Administration

The following letter could be adapted for sending to a single trustee who engages the lawyer for advice on fiduciary duties and the completion of an estate or trust administration. In the summary of services section, the engagement letter should include a detailed list of the services that the lawyer or firm will provide to the trustee and specify services that will not be provided to avoid miscommunication.

The sample also provides alternatives if the lawyer is engaged by co-fiduciaries or by a trustee who is also a beneficiary of the trusts under administration. The alternatives are intended to obtain the client's consent to a representation that implicates actual or potential adverse interests. Rules Prof. Conduct, rule 1.7 and chapter 5 of this Guide, Conflicts of Interest, section 5.5. The lawyer should adapt it thoughtfully to the lawyer's customary practice and the needs of a particular client representation.

> Dear [Name of Trustee]:
>
> The purpose of this letter is to confirm our representation of you as Trustee of the trust created by [DECEDENT], and to set forth the terms of our engagement. We appreciate your confidence and trust in engaging this firm as your lawyers. I will be primarily responsible for this representation, but other lawyers or paralegals will assist me.
>
> *Summary of Services to be Performed for You as Trustee.* We will provide those services that are necessary and appropriate to administer the trust under California law. The normal services include the following:
>
> [DESCRIBE SERVICES TO BE RENDERED]
>
> [OPTIONAL:] We will advise you of your powers and responsibilities with respect to trust investment but cannot provide investment advice as such.

If Additional Services are Necessary. If there are other legal services that you wish us to perform for you as Trustee, we should first consult one another and supplement this letter agreement before undertaking those tasks. If a probate of [DECEDENT]'s estate becomes necessary and you would like us to assist you with it, we will provide a separate engagement letter regarding legal services for the probate administration.

Identification of the Client. Please understand that we represent you only in your fiduciary capacity as Trustee. We do not represent individual trust beneficiaries, even though we will from time to time provide them with information about your administration of the trust. In appropriate circumstances, we may advise beneficiaries to obtain independent counsel, as we do not represent them.

[*OPTIONAL PROVISION where the trustee is also a beneficiary*] Because you are a beneficiary of the trust, we cannot advocate for you to maximize your share. If there is a dispute with another beneficiary about your entitlements, we cannot represent you individually in that dispute, and you will have to seek your own independent counsel.

[*OPTIONAL PROVISIONS for use when representing more than one trustee*] It is common for cotrustees to employ the same law firm to assist them in administering a trust, as you have requested us to do. Please understand that, because we will represent you jointly, we must communicate with [BOTH/ALL] of you and receive instructions from [BOTH/ALL] of you. Accordingly, by agreeing to this form of representation, each of you authorizes us to disclose to the [OTHER/OTHERS] information that one of you shares with us or that we acquire from another source that is pertinent to the administration of the trust. We will not take any action or refrain from taking an action that affects the trust without the [OTHER'S/OTHERS'] knowledge and consent. Of course, anything one of you discusses with us is privileged from disclosure to third parties except as limited by the discussion above. If a conflict arises between you during the course of the trust administration or if you have a difference of opinion on any matter concerning the trust, we can point out the pros and cons of your respective positions. However, we cannot advocate one of your positions over the [OTHER/OTHERS]. [Note that in some jurisdictions, it may be necessary to provide examples of potential conflicts.] By signing this letter, you waive any conflict of interest which may arise by virtue of the fact that we represent [BOTH/ALL] of you together.

If an actual conflict of interest arises [BETWEEN/AMONG] you that, in our judgment, makes it impossible for us to live up to our ethical obligations to [BOTH/ALL] of you, we will withdraw as your joint lawyers and advise each of you to seek other legal counsel.

Lawyer-Client Communications. Any relationship between a lawyer and client is subject to Rules of Professional Conduct. In trusts, ethical rules applicable to conflicts of interests and confidentiality are of special concern because of the close relationship of the parties. We cannot overemphasize the need for complete and full disclosure to us at all times of all your acts and doings in order to avoid potential problems that may arise. [CITE EXAMPLES]

The lawyer-client privilege generally applies to communications between us. The privilege encompasses more than confidentiality. It is also an evidence rule in the context of litigation that prevents third parties from gaining access to our communications with you. However, there are exceptions to the lawyer-client privilege. If a beneficiary, accountant, or financial planner is included in a meeting or phone call, or is copied on correspondence or email, then the lawyer-client privilege may be lost as to matters disclosed in that meeting or correspondence. As a result, the beneficiary or other third party may be forced to disclose the information in a court of law or otherwise in the context of litigation, or may use that information to your detriment. Please keep this in mind when asking us to share information with third parties or when you share information with others who are not part of our lawyer-client relationship. That is why, as indicated above, we prefer that communications with beneficiaries originate with you.

Generally, communications made via fax, e-mail, computer transmission or cellular phone are not as secure from inadvertent disclosure to others. Unless you tell us otherwise, you acknowledge that by furnishing us with an e-mail address or cell phone or fax number, you authorize us to communicate with you using these modes of communication notwithstanding the inherent confidentiality risks. By giving us an email address to use to communicate with you, you are indicating to us that your email is secure, that you do not use your employer's server to receive communications from us (as doing so would violate the confidentiality of our communications), and that we have your permission to use the address which you are satisfied is confidential.

Lawyer-Client Privilege. [For a sample provision discussing that the lawyer-client privilege belongs to the office of trustee and not the individual, see chapter 6 of this Guide, Confidentiality of Information, sections 6.13 and 6.14.]

Fees and Billing. [See chapter 8 of this Guide, Compensation]

Our Policies Concerning Client Files. [See chapter 6 of this Guide, Confidentiality of Information, sections 6.15 and 6.16.]

Termination of Engagement. You may terminate this engagement at any time by notice in writing to us. If we receive notice of termination from you, we will promptly cease providing any service to you as Trustee. You will be responsible for paying for our services rendered up to the time we receive such notice and for additional reasonable services that we provide after that in connection with the transfer of responsibility for the trust administration to other counsel.

We may terminate this engagement by giving you written notice. If we send you notice of termination, you will be responsible for paying for our services rendered up to the time we terminate our engagement, and for reasonable services that we provide to transfer responsibility for the matter to your new counsel. However, whether you terminate or we terminate the representation, if we represent you in court proceedings and prior court approval is needed in order for us to cease rendering legal services, we will continue to render legal services to you until such time as the court determines that we may cease rendering services.

Conclusion of Representation. After the trust is terminated (except for the distribution of assets held in reserve or separate trusts created under [DECEDENT]'s trust have been funded), our engagement will be concluded. Of course, we will be happy to provide additional or continuing services. Unless arrangements are made for such services and agreed upon in writing, however, we will have no further responsibility to you or to the trust with any future or ongoing legal issues nor will we have a duty to notify you of changes in the laws.

If you have any questions about anything discussed in this letter, please let us know. In addition, you should feel free to consult with another lawyer about the effect of signing this letter. If you approve this arrangement, please sign the approval copy of this letter and return it in the envelope provided. We welcome and look forward to serving you.

Very truly yours,

[Lawyer]

CONSENT

[I/WE] have reviewed, understand, and agree to the provisions set out in the representation letter referred to above, including those provisions dealing with [CONFLICT DISCLOSURE AND] confidentiality of communications. [I/WE] further agree to the provisions in this letter regarding disclosures to the beneficiaries or their legal representatives under the circumstances described herein. Further, [I/WE] acknowledge receiving and reviewing the informational material provided with this letter, including your fee and billing information. At this time, [I/WE] wish to use your services to go forward with the trust administration.

Dated: ________________ ________________________
[Client 1]

Dated: ________________ ________________________
[Client 2]

Reprinted with permission from The American College of Trust and Estate Counsel.

4.8 Representation of a Trustee on Issues of Personal Liability

Under current California law, the ethical duty of confidentiality and the related lawyer-client privilege are held in the office of the trustee, not the individual trustee. Upon a change of trustee, the right to assert the privilege passes to the successor. See chapter 6 of this Guide, Confidentiality of Information, section 6.13. At the beginning of the representation, the lawyer should advise the proposed client fiduciary that the beneficiaries and other interested parties may assert claims of personal liability against the fiduciary—for example, breach of trust, self-dealing, failure to deal with beneficiaries impartially, and claims on the fiduciary's account. To preserve the right to assert the lawyer-client privilege in defending those claims, the client should obtain separate representation in an individual capacity.

For a sample Disclosure to Fiduciaries Regarding the Lawyer-Client Privilege for possible inclusion in an engagement letter, see chapter 6 of this Guide, Confidentiality of Information, section 6.14.

4.9 Certificate of Independent Review

A lawyer who accepts an engagement to prepare a certificate of independent review pursuant to Probate Code section 21384, subdivision (a), should make it clear from the outset that the only client is the transferor, and that neither the drafting lawyer nor the intended beneficiary is a client. Before accepting the engagement, the lawyer should clearly define the scope of the representation in a letter agreement with the client, limiting the engagement solely to preparing and drafting the certificate.

Probate Code section 21384, subdivision (a) allows a lawyer-prepared certificate of independent review to validate a transfer to a person described in Probate Code section 21380, subdivision (a), to whom donative transfers are otherwise presumed to be the product of fraud or undue influence. That transferee may be the lawyer who drafted the instrument making the transfer, in which case the certificate of independent review may not only validate the transfer, but also save the drafting lawyer transferee from discipline for a violation of rules 1.7 and 1.8.1 of the Rules of Professional Conduct.

The lawyer who accepts an engagement to prepare and execute a certificate of independent review must have no legal, business, financial, professional, or personal relationship with the beneficiary of the donative transfer, and cannot be appointed as a fiduciary or receive any pecuniary benefit as a result of the operation of the instrument containing the transfer. Prob. Code, sec. 21370. Meeting these requirements should be the first concern of the certifying lawyer.

The lawyer engaged to prepare a certificate of independent review should appreciate the risk that the client or the client's beneficiaries someday may assert that the lawyer failed to identify an unrelated flaw in the estate plan. To avoid such a claim, the lawyer should take care to have the client sign a written agreement expressly limiting the lawyer's engagement solely to compliance with the requirements of Probate Code section 21384. If the lawyer has such a written agreement, under Probate Code section 21384, subdivision (b), the lawyer "shall not be considered to otherwise represent the transferor as a client."

Specifically, the engagement letter should (1) state that the lawyer has no legal, business, financial, professional, or personal relationship with the beneficiary of the donative transfer at issue; (2) describe the scope of work necessary to issue the certificate; (3) warn the client that the lawyer is not engaged to determine the legal validity or effect of the instrument or any of its provisions other than the donative transfer at issue; and (4) advise the client that in signing the certificate, counsel does not offer or express a determinative legal opinion, which only can be made by a court.

Although Probate Code section 21384, subdivision (a) does not require the reviewing lawyer to determine that the client has capacity to make the donative transfer, a review with the client as outlined below will help to determine the presence of fraud or undue influence.

1. Does the client understand the nature of the gift, whether testamentary or inter vivos?
    (a) the type of document;
    (b) the dispositive effect of the document; and
    (c) the alternate dispositive effects if the intended beneficiary dies.

2. Does the client fully comprehend the nature and extent of the client's property? Confirm the client's understanding of:
    (a) the extent of the client's estate;
    (b) how title is held (e.g., joint tenancy); and
    (c) the total value of the estate and of individual assets if the particular transfer so warrants.

3. Does the client fully recollect the members of the client's family?
    (a) Note all living and deceased relatives (including surviving descendants of deceased relatives) within the third degree of the client;
    (b) Note all members of a class, degree, or group if gifts are proposed to some but not all members of such class, degree, or group of beneficiaries; and
    (c) Confirm the proposed beneficiary's relationship, if any, to the client's heirs.

4. Does the client appear coherent, alert, and oriented as to place, time, and date? Does the client appreciate the purpose of the consultation?

5. Establish the relationship that the client enjoys with the proposed beneficiary.
    (a) Solicit and document the reasons for the client's gift;
    (b) Determine how long has the client known the beneficiary;
    (c) Ask the client to discuss and note what led the client to make this gift;
    (d) Confirm with the client the effect that the intended gift will have on the client's heirs and on beneficiaries of prior donative instruments;
    (e) Confirm with the client the value of the intended gift to the beneficiary relative to other intended gifts to beneficiaries;

(f) Establish the degree of access that the beneficiary of the intended gift has to the client, and whether the intended beneficiary knows about the intended gift; and
(g) Confirm that the client is not reacting to implied promises made by the intended beneficiary and is not threatened with the loss of emotional or physical assistance that the intended beneficiary currently provides.

Cases

A gift to the drafting lawyer and the family in a trust instrument was invalidated because a certificate of independent review was not prepared by an independent lawyer. Probate Code section 21384 includes an "independent attorney" requirement that applied retroactively. *Schwan v. Permann* (2018) 28 Cal.App.5th 678, 698.

Reversing the trial court's grant of a motion for summary judgment regarding an instrument that was irrevocable before 2011, the Court of Appeal held that triable issues of fact existed regarding the certificate of independent review. The reviewing lawyer failed to counsel the client adequately about the "nature and consequences" of the testamentary gift to a care custodian under former Probate Code section 21351, subdivision (b) because no evidence showed that the lawyer discussed with the client the decision to exclude the client's nieces and nephews from a contemplated will or even that the reviewing lawyer was fully aware of the natural objects of the client's bounty. Nor did the evidence show that the lawyer counseled the client confidentially because other persons were present during the counseling who were not necessary to accomplish the counseling. Finally, the reviewing lawyer was not "independent" within the meaning of Probate Code section 21351 because the instrument at issue designated the reviewing lawyer as executor and because the reviewing lawyer shared an office with the drafter. *Estate of Winans* (2010) 183 Cal.App.4th 102.

When preparing a will or other testamentary instrument giving property to a beneficiary who, under applicable state law, is presumptively disqualified from receiving such a gift, the testator's lawyer owed a duty of care to the nonclient intended beneficiary. In this case, the disqualified beneficiary was the testator's caregiver, and the lawyer should have advised the testator to obtain a certificate of independent review from a disinterested and independent lawyer. Without that certificate, the gift failed. The certificate would have evidenced what the testator-client intended, and that the testator had not been unduly influenced to make the gift, and avoided the legal presumption that the caregiver unduly influenced the testator, which could now only be rebutted by clear and convincing evidence. *Osornio v. Weingarten* (2004) 124 Cal.App.4th 304.

4.10 Defining the Scope of the Representation Through Disclosures and Informed Consent

The clients and the lawyer, working together, may define the scope and objectives of the representation, and the extent to which information will be shared among multiple clients. Through this consultation, the lawyer can comply with the ethical duty of confidentiality and avoid representing clients with adverse interests.

When undertaking to represent multiple clients jointly, rules 1.7 and 1.0.1(e) of the Rules of Professional Conduct require that the lawyer must first obtain an informed written consent of all the joint clients to the representation, notwithstanding direct or potential conflicts. To obtain that consent the lawyer must discuss with each client, and should ultimately reduce to writing, detailed examples of such conflicts. The process of preparing, circulating, discussing, and obtaining signatures on the consent letter will many times bring to light reasons why the multiple representation is not feasible or advisable. When the representation involves an entity and some of its constituents individually, for example a lease or a buy-sell agreement with a controlling owner, the lawyer should have the consent agreement either approved by a majority of disinterested constituents or reviewed by separate counsel for the controlling constituent to insulate the agreement from later attack.

Clients in a joint representation should understand the effect that the ethical duty of confidentiality has on the *practical* ability of the lawyer to keep the confidences of each of them as a client. The lawyer should discuss these practical limitations with the clients in advance, memorialize the discussion, and set forth guidelines in the initial engagement letter.

Before determining that multiple representation is appropriate, the lawyer may, at the outset, meet separately with the prospective clients to give them the opportunity to be more candid, and, perhaps, to reveal conflicts of interest or objectives that would not be apparent in meetings with everyone present. Hidden agendas can be avoided, and the potential client who can foresee not wanting to disclose information to the other client or clients can say so before the lawyer undertakes the representation. The lawyer may conclude from these separate discussions that joint representation is not possible, and that disclosure, waivers, and consents are not likely to resolve conflicts and preserve confidentiality in the course of the representation.

If the lawyer concludes that the informed written consent required by the Rules of Professional Conduct is possible, the lawyer should advise the clients, in writing and in detail, of the potential conflicts of interest. A consent letter should disclose the relevant circumstances and the actual and reasonably foreseeable adverse consequences to the clients of the joint representation. That letter should also disclose, in the case of joint representation, that communications from any of them are not protected by the lawyer's duty of confidentiality, and that the lawyer may have to disclose any such communications to the other client or clients.

Cases

An advance waiver of conflicts of interest in an engagement letter was ineffective when the law firm had a current client with directly adverse interests, and the law firm did not tell either client of its representation of the other. The simultaneous representation of clients with adverse interests in violation of the rules of professional conduct rendered the engagement letter, including its arbitration clause, unenforceable as a matter of public policy. A successful motion for disqualification of a lawyer or firm may require disgorgement of fees. In this case, the court allowed the law firm to recover fees under a theory of quantum meruit. *Sheppard, Mullin, Richter & Hampton v. J-M Manufacturing Co., Inc.* (2018) 6 Cal.5th 59.

Citing *Zador* below, the court found that signed written consents notwithstanding potential conflicts of interest were sufficient when a lawyer disclosed the relevant circumstances and the actual and reasonably foreseeable adverse consequences to the client. *Sharp v. Next Entertainment, Inc.* (2008) 163 Cal.App.4th 410, 429-30.

Citing *Zador* below, the court held "a conflict of interest generally may be waived by the persons who are personally interested in the matter." *McPhearson v. The Michaels Co.* (2002) 96 Cal.App.4th 843, 850.

Advance consent to continued representation of a real property purchaser was effective to allow the law firm to continue representation despite cross-complaint being asserted against a former co-client. That consent stated, "[w]e are now asking that you consent to our continued and future representation of the Companies and agree not to assert any such conflict of interest or to seek to disqualify us from representing the Companies, notwithstanding any adversity that may develop. By signing and returning to us the agreement and consent set forth at the end of this letter, you will consent to such arrangement and waive any conflicts regarding that arrangement. Notwithstanding such waiver and consent, depending on the circumstances, there remains some degree of risk that we would be disqualified from representing any of you in the event of a dispute." *Zador Corp. v. Kwan* (1995) 31 Cal.App.4th 1285, 1290.

A lawyer may limit the scope of the representation, but such limitations must be made very clear to the client. Even when the scope of the representation is properly limited, the lawyer still retains the duty to alert and advise the client of relevant legal issues and the possible need to retain separate counsel. *Nichols v. Keller* (1993) 15 Cal.App.4th 1672.

CHAPTER 5 CONFLICTS OF INTEREST

California Rules of Professional Conduct, Rule 1.7 - Conflicts of Interest: Current Clients

(a) A lawyer shall not, without informed written consent* from each client and compliance with paragraph (d), represent a client if the representation is directly adverse to another client in the same or a separate matter.

(b) A lawyer shall not, without informed written consent* from each affected client and compliance with paragraph (d), represent a client if there is a significant risk the lawyer's representation of the client will be materially limited by the lawyer's responsibilities to or relationships with another client, a former client or a third person,* or by the lawyer's own interests.

(c) Even when a significant risk requiring a lawyer to comply with paragraph (b) is not present, a lawyer shall not represent a client without written* disclosure of the relationship to the client and compliance with paragraph (d) where:

(1) the lawyer has, or knows* that another lawyer in the lawyer's firm* has, a legal, business, financial, professional, or personal relationship with or responsibility to a party or witness in the same matter; or

(2) the lawyer knows* or reasonably should know* that another party's lawyer is a spouse, parent, child, or sibling of the lawyer, lives with the lawyer, is a client of the lawyer or another lawyer in the lawyer's firm,* or has an intimate personal relationship with the lawyer.

(d) Representation is permitted under this rule only if the lawyer complies with paragraphs (a), (b), and (c), and:

(1) the lawyer reasonably believes* that the lawyer will be able to provide competent and diligent representation to each affected client;

(2) the representation is not prohibited by law; and

(3) the representation does not involve the assertion of a claim by one client against another client represented by the lawyer in the same litigation or other proceeding before a tribunal.

(e) For purposes of this rule, "matter" includes any judicial or other proceeding, application, request for a ruling or other determination, contract, transaction, claim, controversy, investigation, charge, accusation, arrest, or other deliberation, decision, or action that is focused on the interests of specific persons,* or a discrete and identifiable class of persons.*

An asterisk (*) identifies a defined term in rule 1.0.1 of the Rules of Professional Conduct. For further discussion of a defined term, see chapter 2 of this Guide, Terminology.

5.1 Introduction

A well-crafted engagement letter identifies the client to whom the lawyer owes ethical duties and sets the terms of the representation within those duties. The trusts and estates lawyer must also be aware of potential conflicts of interest as the representation proceeds and address those conflicts as the need arises. Most commonly, the ethical issue of conflicts of interest arises in the following situations:

1. The lawyer undertakes a joint representation when the parties may have directly adverse interests, for example, both spouses preparing a common estate plan;
2. The lawyer undertakes to represent the child of parents for whom the lawyer prepared an estate plan that purports to transfer assets to the child or disinherits the child;
3. The lawyer undertakes to represent an individual who owns an interest in a business for which the lawyer already provided performed succession planning through a buy-sell agreement;
4. The lawyer undertakes to represent an individual who has competing rights and duties, for example, a trustee who is also a settlor or beneficiary of a trust;
5. The lawyer is involved in a transaction in which the lawyer's personal interests may be adverse to those of the client (e.g., appointment as fiduciary) or those of the beneficiaries of the estate (e.g., the purchase of estate assets by the lawyer); or
6. A new client of the lawyer wants to take an action adverse to a current client.

Each of these circumstances has its own problems and solutions.

Rule 1.7(c) of the Rules of Professional Conduct is a departure from former rule 3-310(C). A literal reading of the informed consent requirements in the former rule did not limit the scope of the required explanations or allow *de minimis* exceptions. The current rule gives the lawyer more latitude to determine, in the lawyer's reasonable belief, that the lawyer can represent each client consistent with the ethical duties of complete loyalty and unimpaired judgment. See chapter 2 of this Guide, Terminology, for further guidance on what constitutes a reasonable belief.

Rule 1.7(b) of the Rules of Professional Conduct allows estate planning lawyers to use their own informed judgment in determining whether a potential conflict of interest poses a significant risk of compromising the lawyer's exercise of independent judgment and loyalty to the client. The lawyer may conclude that the risk from potential conflicts is minimal, and those potential conflicts can be addressed by thoughtful communication. See discussion at chapter 7 of this Guide, Communication, sections 7.2 and 7.4, regarding communication with unrepresented parties. Nevertheless, the lawyer has the ethical duty to analyze the risk from potential conflicts and should resolve any doubtful situation in favor of disclosure and informed written consent.

Rule 1.7(c) of the Rules of Professional Conduct establishes a different standard when a potential conflict arises out of the personal interest of the lawyer or the lawyer's firm. The duty to disclose the lawyer's personal conflicts, in writing, is absolute, and risk analysis is irrelevant. For example, two young associates from different law firms may share an apartment in response to high housing costs. That personal relationship would need to be disclosed if the two law firms take opposing sides in a litigation. In addition, if the personal interest of the lawyer or firm poses a significant risk of compromising the lawyer's exercise of independent judgment and loyalty to the client, the client's informed written consent to the representation is required under rule 1.7(b) of the Rules of Professional Conduct.

Practitioners commonly refer to a waiver of conflicts of interest, but this language is misleading. The term "waiver" does not appear in the Rules of Professional Conduct pertaining to conflicts of interest. Instead, the prospective clients each consent to a lawyer's representation notwithstanding the ongoing direct or potential conflicts of interest. The conflicts do not cease to exist, and the lawyer has a continuing ethical duty to monitor those conflicts throughout the representation and to communicate regularly with the clients how adverse interests may affect that representation. That communication is the basis for the clients' informed consent that complies with rule 1.0.1(e) of the Rules of Professional Conduct.

Comment on California Rules of Professional Conduct, Rule 1.7

> [1] Loyalty and independent judgment are essential elements in the lawyer's relationship to a client. The duty of undivided loyalty to a current client prohibits undertaking representation directly adverse to that client without that client's informed written consent.* Thus, absent consent, a lawyer may not act as an advocate in one matter against a person* the lawyer represents in some other matter, even when the matters are wholly unrelated. (See *Flatt v. Superior Court* (1994) 9 Cal.4th 275 [36 Cal.Rptr.2d 537].) A directly adverse conflict under paragraph (a) can arise in a number of ways, for example, when: (i) a lawyer accepts representation of more than one client in a matter in which the interests of the clients actually conflict; (ii) a lawyer, while representing a client, accepts in another matter the representation of a person* who, in the first matter, is directly adverse to the lawyer's client; or (iii) a lawyer accepts representation of a person* in a matter in which an opposing party is a client of the lawyer or the lawyer's law firm.* Similarly, direct adversity can arise when a lawyer cross-examines a non-party witness who is the lawyer's client in another matter, if the examination is likely to harm or embarrass the witness. On the other hand, simultaneous representation in unrelated matters of clients whose interests are only economically adverse, such as representation of competing economic enterprises in unrelated litigation, does not ordinarily constitute a conflict of interest and thus may not require informed written consent* of the respective clients.
>
> [2] Paragraphs (a) and (b) apply to all types of legal representations, including the concurrent representation of multiple parties in litigation or in a single transaction or in some other common enterprise or legal relationship. Examples of the latter include the formation of a partnership for several partners* or a corporation for several shareholders, the preparation of a pre-nuptial agreement, or joint or reciprocal wills for a husband and wife, or the resolution of an "uncontested" marital dissolution. If a lawyer initially represents multiple clients with the informed written consent* as required under paragraph (b), and circumstances later

develop indicating that direct adversity exists between the clients, the lawyer must obtain further informed written consent* of the clients under paragraph (a).

...

[5] Paragraph (c) requires written* disclosure of any of the specified relationships even if there is not a significant risk the relationship will materially limit the lawyer's representation of the client. However, if the particular circumstances present a significant risk the relationship will materially limit the lawyer's representation of the client, informed written consent* is required under paragraph (b).

Former California Rules of Professional Conduct, Rule 3-310 – Avoiding the Representation of Adverse Interests

(A) For purposes of this rule:

(1) "Disclosure" means informing the client or former client of the relevant circumstances and of the actual and reasonably foreseeable adverse consequences to the client or former client;

(2) "Informed written consent" means the client's or former client's written agreement to the representation following written disclosures;

(3) "Written" means any writing as defined in Evidence Code section 250.

(B) A member shall not accept or continue representation of a client without providing written disclosure to the client where:

(1) The member has a legal, business, financial, professional, or personal relationship with a party or witness in the same matter; or

(2) The member knows or reasonably should know that:

(a) the member previously had a legal, business, financial, professional, or personal relationship with a party or witness in the same matter; and

(b) the previous relationship would substantially affect the member's representation; or

(3) The member has or had a legal, business, financial, professional, or personal relationship with another person or entity the member knows or reasonably should know would be affected substantially by resolution of the matter; or

(4) The member has or had a legal, business, financial, or professional interest in the subject matter of the representation.

(C) A member shall not, without the informed written consent of each client:

(1) Accept representation of more than one client in a matter in which the interests of the clients potentially conflict; or

(2) Accept or continue representation of more than one client in a matter in which the interests of the clients actually conflict; or

(3) Represent a client in a matter and at the same time in a separate matter accept as a client a person or entity whose interest in the first matter is adverse to the client in the first matter.

(D) A member who represents two or more clients shall not enter into an aggregate settlement of the claims of or against the clients, without the informed written consent of each client.

(E) A member shall not, without the informed written consent of the client or former client, accept employment adverse to the client or former client where, by reason of the representation of the client or former client, the member has obtained confidential information material to the employment.

(F) A member shall not accept compensation for representing a client from one other than the client unless:

(1) There is no interference with the member's independence of professional judgment or with the client-lawyer relationship; and

(2) Information relating to representation of a client is protected as required by Business and Professions Code Section 6068, subdivision (e); and

(3) The member obtains the client's informed written consent, provided that no disclosure or consent is required if

(a) such nondisclosure is otherwise authorized by law, or

(b) the member is rendering legal services on behalf of any public agency which provides legal services to other public agencies or the public.

Rule 1.8.1. Business Transactions with a Client and Pecuniary Interests Adverse to a Client, addresses the matters set forth in former rule 3-310(B). See the discussion in section 5.10 of this chapter.

Rule 1.4.1. Communication of Settlement Offers, addresses the matters set forth in former rule 3-310(D). See the discussion in Chapter 7 of this Guide, Communication, section 7.1.

Rule 1.9. Duties to Former Clients, addresses the matters set forth in former rule 3-310(E). See the discussion in section 5.14 of this chapter.

Rule 1.8.6. Compensation from One Other Than Client, addresses the matters set forth in former rule 3-310(F). See the discussion in chapter 8 of this Guide, Compensation, section 8.7.

5.2 Representing More Than One Client

It is often appropriate for a lawyer to represent more than one member of the same family in connection with their estate plans; more than one beneficiary with common interests in an estate or trust administration matter; co-fiduciaries of an estate or trust; or more than one of the owners or investors in a closely held business. Such representation may be more economical and better coordinated, if common interests may outweigh limited inconsistent interests of multiple clients. In such circumstances, the lawyer must discuss with the parties (1) the implications of a joint representation (or separate representations if the lawyer believes that mode of representation is more appropriate); (2) the extent to which material information imparted by any client may be shared with the others; and (3) the possibility that the lawyer may be required to withdraw if a conflict in their interests develops to the degree that the lawyer cannot effectively represent each of them. The clients will best understand the information if it is discussed with them in person, but it must also be provided to them in a written engagement letter. See chapter 4 of this Guide, Identifying the Client and the Scope of the Representation, discussing the necessary informed written consent.

In smaller estate plans, interests of modest value are often spread among many family members. For example, in the case of irrevocable life insurance trusts containing Crummey powers, the lapse of a withdrawal right resulting from the beneficiaries' failing to exercise it timely is often advantageous to everyone in the family. All family members may want the estate planning lawyer, who usually represents the settlors, to assist them with a basic understanding of the plan and their rights.

A lawyer who is asked to represent multiple clients regarding related matters has an ethical duty to consider at the outset whether the representation may involve unavoidable conflicts. Some conflicts are so serious that the informed consent of the parties is insufficient to allow the lawyer to undertake or continue the representation. A lawyer may not represent clients whose interests directly conflict to such a degree that the lawyer cannot adequately represent their individual interests. In sophisticated estate plans, for example, senior family members may create a multitude of entities, trusts, and agreements for children, grandchildren, and charities. There may be many potentially conflicting economic interests among family members sharing in the dispositions under such planning. One family member may serve as trustee or controlling power holder for any number of others.

Comment on California Rules of Professional Conduct, Rule 1.7

> [4] Even where there is no direct adversity, a conflict of interest requiring informed written consent* under paragraph (b) exists if there is a significant risk that a lawyer's ability to consider, recommend or carry out an appropriate course of action for the client will be materially limited as a result of the lawyer's other responsibilities, interests, or relationships, whether legal, business, financial, professional, or personal. For example, a lawyer's obligations to two or more clients in the same matter, such as several individuals seeking to form a joint venture, may materially limit the lawyer's ability to recommend or advocate all possible positions that each might take because of the lawyer's duty of loyalty to the other clients. The

> risk is that the lawyer may not be able to offer alternatives that would otherwise be available to each of the clients. The mere possibility of subsequent harm does not itself require disclosure and informed written consent.* The critical questions are the likelihood that a difference in interests exists or will eventuate and, if it does, whether it will materially interfere with the lawyer's independent professional judgment in considering alternatives or foreclose courses of action that reasonably* should be pursued on behalf of each client. The risk that the lawyer's representation may be materially limited may also arise from present or past relationships between the lawyer, or another member of the lawyer's firm*, with a party, a witness, or another person* who may be affected substantially by the resolution of the matter.

ACTEC Commentaries on ABA Model Rules of Professional Conduct, Model Rule 1.7

> Multiple representation is also generally appropriate because the interests of the clients in cooperation, including obtaining cost effective representation and achieving common objectives, often clearly predominate over their limited inconsistent interests. Recognition should be given to the fact that estate planning is fundamentally nonadversarial in nature and estate administration is usually nonadversarial.

5.3 Joint Representation of Spouses

The presumption in California law appears to be that when a lawyer represents spouses they are joint clients, in the absence of a contrary agreement. Implicit in a joint representation are the assumptions that (1) no actual adversity exists between the spouses; and (2) all information will be shared by the clients with respect to the joint estate plan that is the subject of the representation. If no adversity exists between the spouses, joint representation better serves their interests because it will result in a more coordinated estate plan at a lower cost than if each spouse were represented by a separate lawyer. The lawyer who represents both spouses will have a better understanding of all relevant family and property considerations and will be better able to serve both spouses to achieve their individual and common goals. Rule 1.7(a) and (d) of the Rules of Professional Conduct allow a lawyer to represent spouses with adverse interests if the lawyer obtains their informed written consent and if the lawyer reasonably believes that the lawyer can provide competent and diligent representation to both spouses.

Even if the estate planning goals of the couple are not entirely consistent, the lawyer is not necessarily precluded from representing both spouses. The lawyer may be able to advise spouses who have somewhat different objectives with respect to their estate planning, consistent with their mutual interests and common goals.

Disclosures and Informed Consent to the Representation. When a lawyer represents spouses jointly, such representation must be undertaken only with their informed written consent after full disclosure of relevant implications of the joint representation. The lawyer's view of the mode of representation alters the rights and duties of the spouses with respect to one another and dictates the rights and duties of the lawyer. The terms of the representation must be clearly delineated and the written consent of both clients obtained, in accordance with rule 1.7(a) of the

Rules of Professional Conduct regarding the representation of clients with directly adverse interests.

Under rule 1.0.1(e) of the Rules of Professional Conduct, the lawyer must first discuss with the clients that they have conflicting interests for their consent to be "informed." The lawyer must explain the significant risk that the lawyer's representation of one spouse, and the ability to recommend or advocate a particular position, could be materially limited by the lawyer's responsibilities to the other spouse. For the consent to be "informed," the lawyer must explain the lawyer's responsibilities to each spouse and the potential that the clients may have adverse interests. Such explanation usually appears in the engagement letter by giving examples of circumstances under which those conflicts could surface and discussing "the material risks, including any actual and reasonably foreseeable adverse consequences" of a joint representation. Rules Prof. Conduct, rule 1.0.1(e). The engagement letter can also serve to memorialize the lawyer's discussion of the potential conflicts between the spouses. The clients' consent to the joint representation notwithstanding the potential conflicts must also be "written." Rules Prof. Conduct, rule 1.0.1(e-1). For a discussion of the initial engagement letter, see chapter 4 of this Guide, Identifying the Client and the Scope of the Representation, sections 4.3 and 4.4. For a sample disclosure of conflicts of interest in an engagement letter for spouses seeking a joint estate plan, see section 5.4 of this chapter.

The engagement letter appropriately contains a full discussion of the lawyer's policy concerning joint meetings with the spouses and separate meetings with either of them, how and when copies of correspondence will be disseminated to either or both of the spouses, and the extent of the lawyer's duty to keep each spouse advised of the other's communications and activities with respect to the representation. Explaining the ground rules of the representation ensures that each spouse's interest is protected, and that each of them is fully informed of the status of confidential communications and their waiver of the lawyer's duty of confidentiality between them. The lawyer may also explain that in the event of litigation between the spouses, confidential communications with joint clients are not protected from disclosure. Evid. Code, sec. 962.

Finally, the engagement letter should address the subject of the lawyer's withdrawal from representation in the event of an irreconcilable conflict between the spouses. Generally, the lawyer will withdraw from representing both parties in that case, and the letter should make that possibility clear. In those rare cases in which both spouses agree that the lawyer may withdraw as to only one of them and continue to represent the other, the clients must clearly understand and agree to the continuing representation.

Comment on California Rules of Professional Conduct, Rule 1.7

> [10] A material change in circumstances relevant to application of this rule may trigger a requirement to make new disclosures and, where applicable, obtain new informed written consents.* In the absence of such consents, depending on the circumstances, the lawyer may have the option to withdraw from one or more of the representations in order to avoid the conflict. The lawyer must seek court approval where necessary and take steps to minimize harm to the clients. See rule 1.16. The lawyer must continue to protect the confidences of the clients from whose representation the lawyer has withdrawn. (See rule 1.9(c).)

Cases

One spouse, who was a lawyer, was advised of a potential conflict of interest in relation to entering into a postnuptial agreement. That spouse's signature on the agreement was tantamount to a written consent to having the lawyer prepare that agreement, even though both spouses were represented previously by the same law firm for their joint estate plan. *Marriage of Friedman* (2002) 100 Cal.App.4th 65.

Articles

Hazard, *Conflicts of Interest in Estate Planning for Husband and Wife*, 20 The Probate Law. 1 (Joseph Trachtman Lecture 1994). In Professor Hazard's view:

> There are basic principles of practice that apply when concurrent representation is undertaken in any such situation:
>
> - An assessment must be made whether both clients are genuinely autonomous in their situation, and whether either may have a tendency to fabricate or fantasize, either presently or in the future.
>
> - Separate interviews should be held with each client, more than once if necessary. Separate interviews can reveal divergences in the clients' respective assumptions and purposes that otherwise would be masked by polite conversation.
>
> - The lawyer should feel entirely comfortable in informing each client of the substance of the other client's wishes and purposes.
>
> - There should be a written consent letter, the simpler the better.
>
> - The lawyer should document the progress of the representation with both memos to the file and letters to the clients at important stages.

Moore & Hilker, *Representing Both Spouses: The New Section Recommendations* (July/Aug. 1993) 7 Prob. and Prop. 26, 30. An ABA Special Probate and Trust Division Study Committee on Professional Responsibility published a report in 1993 recognizing that lawyers may represent spouses separately and agree to maintain the confidences of each, but the report recommended that "such a representation be undertaken only by agreement and only by those who believe they can represent independently each spouse despite the knowledge of the other spouse's plan."

5.4 Sample Disclosures for an Engagement Letter - Consent of Spouses to Joint Representation

The following disclosure of conflicts of interests may be adapted into an engagement letter for joint representation of spouses. The disclosures can be modified or expanded as needed to comply with rule 1.0.1(e) of the Rules of Professional Conduct regarding informed client consent. The lawyer should review and adapt it appropriately for the circumstances of the lawyer's practice and a particular representation.

> *Conflicts of Interest.* You have asked me to represent both of you regarding your estate planning. The California Rules of Professional Conduct require that I obtain the informed written consent of parties with directly adverse interests before I represent them jointly. The two of you may not always agree regarding your estate plan.
>
> You may have conflicting interests in the following issues to be addressed in the course of developing your joint estate plan:
>
> 1. Identification of community property versus separate property assets;
> 2. Different life expectancies;
> 3. Unequal bargaining power or skill or experience of one spouse;
> 4. Federal law that may require, in the absence of an agreement to the contrary, that a spouse be designated a beneficiary of part or all of a deceased spouse's retirement plan benefits;
> 5. Different tax consequences of specific assets;
> 6. Different desires for distribution of assets at each spouse's death;
> 7. Reluctance to disclose confidential information to the other spouse; or
> 8. The likelihood that a court may find the estate plan unenforceable in whole or in part because of the absence of an independent lawyer for each spouse.
>
> This list is illustrative and not exhaustive.
>
> Absence of separate lawyers might increase the likelihood of one spouse, or the heirs or beneficiaries of that spouse, challenging the estate plan on the ground that the other spouse forced a joint estate plan that was fraudulent, unconscionable or unfair, or that was signed under a material mistake, duress, or undue influence.
>
> By this letter, I am confirming that I have explained to you that your individual interests may best be advanced if each of you had a separate lawyer. I also explained to you that I will not represent each of you individually; instead, I will respond to your joint instructions. Furthermore, any communication from one of you to me will not be kept confidential by me from the other spouse. You have agreed that I may disclose and exchange all information that I receive from either or both of you in the course of

the joint representation. Such information shall not be considered confidential between you regardless of the manner in which I obtain it, whether in conferences with both of you or in private conferences with only one of you, including any conferences that may have taken place before the date of this letter.

I will not take any action or refrain from taking an action pertaining to the subject matter of this representation that affects either of you without the other's knowledge and consent. Of course, anything either of you discusses with me is protected from disclosure to third parties, unless you authorize me to disclose the information or disclosure is required or permitted by law or my professional obligations as your lawyer.

Minor disagreements between you will ordinarily not affect my ability to represent each of you fully and fairly. If a conflict of interest arises between you during the course of your planning or if the two of you have a difference of opinion on any subject, I can point out the pros and cons of your respective positions. However, I cannot advocate one of your positions over the other. Furthermore, I cannot advocate in favor of either of you if you disagree as to your respective property rights or interests. Serious disputes may render it impossible for me to continue my joint representation in a manner consistent with my professional obligations to both of you. In the event that you cannot reconcile a disagreement between you, I may find it necessary to withdraw my services and advise you each to retain an independent lawyer. Under those circumstances, I will submit my statement for services rendered to the date of such withdrawal, which you agree to pay promptly.

If one of you becomes mentally incapacitated, by your consent to the terms of this agreement you agree to my continued representation of the other spouse as a fiduciary for the incapacitated spouse.

I do not expect that any of these issues will actually arise in representing you jointly. Nevertheless, the ethical rules governing the conduct of lawyers requires that I explain to you the problems that could arise if I represent both of you at the same time and obtain your consent to this joint representation.

By signing this letter, you consent to the joint representation understanding the conflicts of interest that exist in preparing your estate plan jointly, you agree that I cannot recommend an estate planning approach that favors one of you to the disadvantage of the other, and you consent that I may disclose to the other all confidential communications that I may receive from either of you.

Should either of you feel for any reason that you need advice regarding any aspect of the services I am providing under the terms of this agreement, you should feel free to obtain your own lawyer to advise you. I ask that you let me know if you obtain such representation, so that I can clarify my role as your estate planning lawyer.

[*Optional Disclosure of Other Conflicts*] In addition to the conflicts of interest that are inherent in my representing you in preparing your joint estate plan, I have disclosed to you that I also represent other family members. I will address the conflicts inherent in such representation in a separate letter.

5.5 Joint Representation of Family Members

Family groups often desire to use the same lawyer for estate planning due to the clients' confidence in the particular lawyer or firm and the benefits of continuity of representation. The "family" lawyer is already familiar with the family relationships, philosophies, customs, history, assets, existing trusts, or other estate planning devices whenever a new family member becomes involved. Consequently, the family does not have to educate the lawyer about such matters. Furthermore, a comprehensive approach to a family's estate planning can maximize the assets passing to the next generation and facilitate the responsible transfer of management and control.

The nature of family representation may evolve over time. For example, a couple may first consult a lawyer for estate planning. Sometime later, one spouse's parent dies, and the surviving parent needs legal assistance in handling the deceased parent's estate and in preparing a living trust. Then, a sibling of one of the original clients contacts the lawyer for advice regarding a new business venture which may not involve them. Years later, the lawyer revises the estate plan of the original clients, who shortly thereafter send in their now grown child for advice on a prenuptial agreement. In each of these ongoing engagements the lawyer must separately identify the client and the scope of the representation.

In the midst of all these discrete contacts over many years, the lawyer may have received numerous telephone calls from family members with questions of varying importance and complexity. Some calls may relate to services already performed and some may not. In each case, the lawyer must identify current, former, and prospective clients and the proposed scope of the representation to comply with rule 1.7 of the Rules of Professional Conduct, to determine when clients have directly adverse interests and to obtain their informed written consent to a joint, concurrent, or successive representation.

The lawyer also has a duty to evaluate potential conflicts of interest to determine whether those conflicts may affect the lawyer's independent judgment and loyalty to each family member as a separate client. Some potential conflicts are obvious—a parent could seek to disinherit or substantially reduce the share of a child who previously took under the parent's estate plan. Others, however, are not so obvious. Consider whether implementing the following planning for a parent may be directly adverse to the interests of another family member:

1. Nominating one child or someone other than a child to serve as personal representative in the parent's estate plan;
2. Placing the inheritance of a child or other beneficiary in a trust, whether for tax, creditor protection, or other reasons;
3. Creating and funding a generation-skipping trust for the benefit of a grandchild, either the issue of a child or of the child's siblings; or

4. Making a gift of separate property assets to a child who changes title to those assets to community property in connection with the child's own estate planning.

These sample provisions all commonly arise in the context of estate planning for various family members. A family member who is, or reasonably could be, an intestate heir of a client could have a directly adverse interest to the client desiring to alter the rules of intestacy or the statutory order of priority to serve as personal representative. Because a change in statutory rights is implicit in any estate plan, the lawyer should always consider a detailed consent letter before representing multiple family members.

Outside the disposition context, a potential conflict of interest may arise in suggesting to a parent the use of a living trust and durable powers of attorney, effectively eliminating the protections of probate and conservatorship proceedings, while also representing the children in their own estate planning matters or other legal matters. In common practice, lawyers usually find that these potential conflicts do not bear a significant risk of impairing the lawyer's independent judgment; however, in some family relationships, a detailed consent letter may be warranted.

Disclosures and Informed Consent to the Representation. When undertaking to represent multiple family members, the lawyer most clearly complies with the lawyer's ethical duties by obtaining the informed written consent of the clients after full disclosure of relevant implications of the joint representation. Rules Prof. Conduct, rules 1.7 and 1.0.1(e). This written consent must be *informed.* The engagement letter cannot simply say that the clients have potential conflicts of interest. The clients must be "informed" about those conflicts—the letter must explain the nature of the conflicts, usually by giving examples of circumstances under which conflicting interests could surface, and discuss "the material risks, including any actual and reasonably foreseeable adverse consequences" of a joint representation. Rules Prof. Conduct, rule 1.0.1(e). For a discussion of the equally difficult problems that arise in the area of confidentiality among multiple family members, see chapter 6 of this Guide, Confidentiality of Information, section 6.8.

Communication with Nonclients. It is common practice for an estate planning lawyer to lead a "family meeting" regarding the estate plan of a senior family member, in which the legal implications of the estate plan are reviewed. While this practice may foster open communication and can facilitate the efficient transfer of wealth, the lawyer should identify which family members are being represented and communicate that representation to all family members.

A lawyer who does not represent younger generation family members in such a family plan must communicate that fact to them, preferably in writing. In the absence of that communication, those family members may believe that they are clients by virtue of being present when legal issues are being discussed. "The attorney's duty to communicate with a client includes the duty to communicate to persons who reasonably believe they are clients to the attorney's knowledge, at least to the extent of advising them that they are not clients." *Butler v. State Bar* (1986) 42 Cal.3d 323, 329. Communications with unrepresented parties must conform to the ethical duties in rules 4.1 and 4.3 of the Rules of Professional Conduct. For a discussion of the ethical duties regarding unrepresented persons and a sample notice of nonrepresentation to beneficiaries, see chapter 7 of this Guide, Communication, sections 7.4 and 7.5.

This ethical duty to unrepresented parties extends to nonclients for whom the lawyer prepares documents for signature. For example, a lawyer representing a fiduciary commonly prepares documents for signature by beneficiaries or other interested parties (e.g., a waiver of bond or a consent to proposed action). An ethics opinion from the San Diego County Bar Association takes the position that the preparation of such documents may be enough to form a lawyer-client relationship: "When an attorney agrees to draft a document with legal significance for another person, the person who must sign the document for it to have any effect becomes a client, regardless of who asked the attorney to draft the document, who paid for the services, or whether the attorney ever meets with the person who will be signing...." San Diego County Bar Assn., Ethics opn. No. 1990-3.

While this opinion analyzed the issue in the context of one family member procuring a lawyer to draft a will for another, it may also reach documents routinely drafted by a lawyer for a fiduciary in the course of a post-death administration. This opinion is most likely at the outer reaches of what a court would hold; however, any document drafted for the signature of a person who is not a client should be accompanied by a written statement that the lawyer does not represent the person whose signature is sought on the document.

A lawyer representing a family group may consider a form of separate or limited representation. Implicit in most estate plans is that most, if not all, of the documents are completely and unilaterally revocable or amendable so long as the client is alive and competent. Most rational family members do recognize that their relatives can disinherit them, give their property away unequally during lifetime or at death, or give all of their property to charity, a new spouse, or others. Family members may also recognize that their parents, grandparents, and other relatives can allocate the family member's inheritance to restrictive spendthrift trusts designed to protect the intended beneficiary from marital property claims, potential creditors, or the family member's improvidence.

ACTEC Commentaries on ABA Model Rules of Professional Conduct, Model Rule 1.7

> *Joint or Separate Representation.* As indicated in the ACTEC Commentary on Rule 1.6 of the Model Rules of Professional Conduct (Confidentiality of Information), a lawyer usually represents multiple clients jointly. Representing a husband and wife is the most common situation. In that context, attempting to represent a husband and wife separately while simultaneously doing estate planning for each, is generally inconsistent with the lawyer's duty of loyalty to each client. Either the lawyer should represent them jointly or the lawyer should represent only one of them. See generally Price on Contemporary Estate Planning (2014 ed.) section 1.66, p. 1059. In other contexts, however, some experienced estate planners undertake to represent related clients separately with respect to related matters. Such representations should only be undertaken if the lawyer reasonably believes it will be possible to provide impartial, competent, and diligent representation to each client and even then, only with the informed consent of each client, confirmed in writing. See ACTEC Commentaries on MRPC 1.0(e) (Terminology) (defining informed consent) and MRPC Rule 1.0(b) (Terminology) (defining confirmed in writing). The writing may be contained in an engagement letter that covers other subjects as well.

Example 1.7-1. Lawyer (L) was asked to represent Husband (H) and Wife (W) in connection with estate planning matters. L had previously not represented either H or W. At the outset L should discuss with H and W their estate planning goals and the terms upon which L would represent them, including the extent to which confidentiality would be maintained with respect to communications made by each. Assuming that the lawyer reasonably concludes that there is no actual or potential conflict between the spouses, it is permissible to represent a husband and wife as joint clients. Before undertaking such a representation, the lawyer should elicit from the spouses an informed agreement in writing that the lawyer may share any information disclosed by one of them with the other. See ACTEC Commentary on MRPC 1.6 (Confidentiality of Information).

Example 1.7-1a. Lawyer (L) was asked to represent Father (F) and Son (S) in connection with estate planning matters. L had previously not represented either F or S. At the outset L should discuss with F and S their estate planning goals and the terms upon which L would represent them, including the extent to which confidentiality would be maintained with respect to communications made by each. If the prospective clients have common estate planning objectives and coordination is important to them, and there do not appear to be any prohibitive conflicts, the best practice would be for the lawyer to undertake the representation of the two clients jointly with an agreement that information can be shared. Depending on the circumstances, however, a lawyer may be able to represent the father and son as separate clients between whom information communicated by one client will not be shared with the other. Even then, the circumstances may be such that the lawyer knows or should know that their estate plans are interconnected. In that situation, separate representation may be appropriate, provided that there is no obvious conflict of interest between the clients. But even so the lawyer will need to make a conflict determination and may need to obtain the informed consent of each client if there is a "significant risk" that the representation of one might be materially limited by the representation of the other. In such a case, each client must give informed consent confirmed in writing. The same requirements apply to the representation of others as joint or separate multiple clients, such as the representation of other family members, business associates, etc.

5.6 Representation of an Organization and Its Constituents

California Rules of Professional Conduct, Rule 1.13 - Organization as Client

(a) A lawyer employed or retained by an organization shall conform his or her representation to the concept that the client is the organization itself, acting through its duly authorized directors, officers, employees, members, shareholders, or other constituents overseeing the particular engagement.

(b) If a lawyer representing an organization knows* that a constituent is acting, intends to act or refuses to act in a matter related to the representation in a manner that the lawyer knows* or reasonably should know* is (i) a violation of a legal obligation to the organization or a violation of law reasonably* imputable to the organization, and (ii) likely to result in substantial* injury to the organization, the lawyer shall proceed as is reasonably* necessary in the best lawful interest of the organization. Unless the lawyer reasonably believes* that it is not necessary in the best lawful interest of the organization to do so, the lawyer shall refer the matter to higher authority in the organization, including, if warranted by the circumstances, to the highest authority that can act on behalf of the organization as determined by applicable law.

(c) In taking any action pursuant to paragraph (b), the lawyer shall not reveal information protected by Business and Professions Code section 6068, subdivision (e).

(d) If, despite the lawyer's actions in accordance with paragraph (b), the highest authority that can act on behalf of the organization insists upon action, or fails to act, in a manner that is a violation of a legal obligation to the organization or a violation of law reasonably* imputable to the organization, and is likely to result in substantial* injury to the organization, the lawyer shall continue to proceed as is reasonably* necessary in the best lawful interests of the organization. The lawyer's response may include the lawyer's right and, where appropriate, duty to resign or withdraw in accordance with rule 1.16.

(e) A lawyer who reasonably believes* that he or she has been discharged because of the lawyer's actions taken pursuant to paragraph (b), or who resigns or withdraws under circumstances described in paragraph (d), shall proceed as the lawyer reasonably believes* necessary to assure that the organization's highest authority is informed of the lawyer's discharge, resignation, or withdrawal.

(f) In dealing with an organization's constituents, a lawyer representing the organization shall explain the identity of the lawyer's client whenever the lawyer knows* or reasonably should know* that the organization's interests are adverse to those of the constituent(s) with whom the lawyer is dealing.

(g) A lawyer representing an organization may also represent any of its constituents, subject to the provisions of rules 1.7, 1.8.2, 1.8.6, and 1.8.7. If the organization's consent to the dual representation is required by any of these rules, the consent shall be given by an appropriate official, constituent, or body of the organization other than the individual who is to be represented, or by the shareholders.

An asterisk (*) identifies a defined term in rule 1.0.1 of the Rules of Professional Conduct. For further discussion of a defined term, see chapter 2 of this Guide, Terminology.

The comment on rule 1.13 of the Rules of Professional Conduct defines "constituents" to include officers, directors, employees, and shareholders and persons who hold equivalent roles in other organizations.

A lawyer may represent more than one client with related, but not necessarily identical, interests. In connection with the organization of a business, the constituents and the organization may choose to employ a single lawyer for convenience or economic efficiency. The trusts and estates lawyer may also consider this kind of joint representation to address the estate planning aspects of buy-sell agreements, life insurance, and corporate death benefits sponsored by the organization, reorganizations, and other approaches to the transfer of business ownership.

To address the appropriate ethical duties in representing a constituent, multiple constituents and the related organization, or any or all of them, the lawyer must first understand the nature of the relationships and rights among the constituents. The lawyer should identify as soon as possible who will be the client and make that representation clear, both to the clients and to others who might mistakenly believe that the lawyer is representing them. The lawyer should understand and consider the potential liability to persons that the lawyer is not representing but who nonetheless hold an interest in the organization.

Among the possible clients a lawyer may represent in connection with the formation of, operation of, or estate planning with a business organization are:

1. The organization alone;
2. One of the constituents alone;
3. One or more constituents and the organization; or
4. More than one of the constituents, but not the organization.

If the lawyer represents the organization itself, the lawyer's owes ethical duties to the organization and not to its shareholders, directors, officers, managers, members, or partners as individual participants in the organization. A lawyer may also have a duty to the individual constituents in certain circumstances as discussed in the cases cited later in this section.

If the lawyer represents one of the constituents, the lawyer's duties are to that individual and that individual's confidences should be maintained. The lawyer may also have liability to the other constituents and to the organization if the lawyer aids and abets a client's breach of fiduciary duty.

If the lawyer represents the organization and one of its constituents, the lawyer will owe ethical duties to both of them as clients. In that case, the interests of the individual constituent and the organization may be directly adverse.

Representation of the Organization Alone. When a lawyer represents a business organization, the lawyer is presumed to represent only the organization itself, acting through its authorized representatives, and is not presumed also to represent the shareholders, directors, officers, managers, members, partners, or other constituents in the organization. Rules Prof. Conduct, rule 1.13. The lawyer's primary ethical duty is to the organization. Where the interests of the organization and its controlling constituents collide, such as, for example, when a change in control occurs, California case law provides further guidance. *People ex rel. Deukmejian v. Brown* (1981) 29 Cal.3d 150; *Woods v. Super. Ct.* (1983) 149 Cal.App.3d 931; *Goldstein v. Lees* (1975) 46 Cal.App.3d 614.

Notwithstanding that the lawyer's duty is solely to the organization, the lawyer should take steps to ensure that the individual constituents do not operate under the mistaken belief that the organization's lawyer also represents their interests. Those steps can range from simply having a conversation to memorializing the discussion in a writing signed by all the interested parties. Rule 1.13(f) of the Rules of Professional Conduct makes these steps mandatory, when a lawyer should know that the interests of the organization are adverse to those of a constituent. Significantly, rule 1.13(f) of the Rules of Professional Conduct does not further qualify whether such adverse interests may be either direct or material. Notifying unrepresented constituents is required if any potential or actual adverse interest exists. Communications with unrepresented parties must conform to the ethical duties in rules 4.1 and 4.3 of the Rules of Professional Conduct. For a discussion of the ethical duties regarding unrepresented persons and a sample notice of nonrepresentation to beneficiaries that could be adapted for constituents, see chapter 7 of this Guide, Communication, sections 7.4 and 7.5.

Representation of One Constituent Only. A lawyer who represents one constituent as an individual should have no direct ethical duty to the organization, even if the constituent has a fiduciary relationship with the organization. Rule 1.13 of the Rules of Professional Conduct is not implicated when the organization is not being represented. However, to the extent a constituent owes a fiduciary duty to the organization, as a director, officer, manager, member, partner, or otherwise, the lawyer representing the constituent has a professional obligation to the organization and its other constituents not to participate in a breach of that fiduciary duty. The representation of a constituent who owes a fiduciary duty to the organization must specifically address this conflict. The lawyer is well advised to communicate to the constituent, and preferably to the organization, that the lawyer's representation is of the constituent alone.

Representation of More Than One Constituent but Not the Organization. A lawyer may represent more than one of the constituents of an organization while not representing the organization. Rule 1.13 of the Rules of Professional Conduct is not implicated when the organization is not represented. Joint representation of multiple constituents will often best serve the clients if no actual adversity exists, and the lawyer determines that there is no significant risk that the lawyer's loyalty and independent judgment on behalf of each joint client will be impaired. Nonetheless, before undertaking the representation of more than one constituent, the lawyer is ethically required to comply with the informed written consent requirements of rule 1.7 of the Rules of Professional Conduct and to address the confidentiality issues arising from joint or concurrent representation. The lawyer is ethically required to explain the scope of the representation and must notify the clients that, to the extent they are not able to resolve any differences among themselves, the lawyer may have to withdraw from the representation of any or all of them, depending on the circumstances. Rule 1.16 of the Rules of Professional Conduct sets forth the lawyer's ethical duties in withdrawing from a representation.

Joint or concurrent representation of this type should be approached cautiously and never considered when discussions among the constituents are contentious. At the outset the lawyer should reasonably believe that (1) the matter can be resolved on terms compatible with the best interests of each and all the clients; (2) the clients can make reasonably informed decisions regarding the matter; and (3) if the representation is unsuccessful, the clients will not be prejudiced. When the lawyer concludes that risk of an actual conflict is not significant and that the lawyer's independent judgment is not materially limited by the joint representation, the lawyer should memorialize the terms of the representation in an engagement letter and obtain the signature of all parties before commencing work. For a discussion of the ethical duty of confidentiality in connection with joint representation of multiple constituents of an organization, see chapter 6 of this Guide, Confidentiality of Information, section 6.11.

Representation of One or More Constituents and the Organization. An estate planning lawyer who undertakes to represent both an organization and one or more of its constituents may need to address ethical concerns in the following circumstances:

1. The business organization is being formed and two or more of the constituents, one of whom may be a current client, ask the lawyer to represent them regarding its formation;
2. The lawyer is preparing a buy-sell agreement for execution by the business organization and its constituents;
3. One constituent of the organization consults the lawyer for the organization with respect to personal estate planning, which will entail provisions for that constituent's disposition of an interest in the organization; or
4. The lawyer represents a fiduciary that holds a controlling interest in the organization.

Joint representation of the organization and its constituents may, in fact, best serve the clients where their common interests predominate over their separate interests and the circumstances do not suggest a significant risk of ethical dilemmas in the lawyer's loyalty and independent judgment for each client. The Rules of Professional Conduct allow for such a joint or concurrent representation provided that the lawyer obtains the informed written consent of all the potential clients as required by rule 1.7 of the Rules of Professional Conduct or determines that such consent is unnecessary.

If a lawyer for an organization will also represent its individual constituents and their interests are directly adverse, rules 1.7 and 1.13 of the Rules of Professional Conduct require the informed written consent of each potential client. In the case of a transaction between the organization and its controlling constituent such as a lease or a buy-sell agreement, the lawyer may need to have the transaction either approved by a majority of disinterested constituents or reviewed by separate counsel for the controlling constituent to insulate the agreement from later attack.

Before or within a reasonable time after commencing the representation, a lawyer who is consulted by an organization and one or more of its constituents should discuss with them the implications of a joint representation, or a separate representation if the lawyer believes that mode of representation to be more appropriate. The conflicts may be so serious that the informed consent of the parties is insufficient to allow the lawyer to undertake or to continue the representation, if the lawyer cannot fulfill the ethical duty of loyalty and confidentiality to each of them. The prospective clients and the lawyer should discuss the possibility that the lawyer would be required to withdraw if a direct conflict in their interests develops in the course of the joint representation. Rule 1.16 of the Rules of Professional Conduct sets forth the lawyer's ethical duties in withdrawing from a representation. For a further discussion of the ethical duty to withdraw, see section 5.8 of this chapter.

Before accepting a representation involving multiple parties, a lawyer may wish to consider meeting with the prospective clients separately, thereby allowing each of them to be more candid and, perhaps, reveal conflicts of interest that would be hidden in a meeting attended by everyone. The clients may best understand the information if it is discussed with them in person and also provided to them in written form, as in an engagement letter. See the discussion in chapter 4 of this Guide, Identifying the Client and the Scope of Representation, section 4.10.

Disclosures and Informed Consent to the Representation. When undertaking to represent an organization and one or more of its constituents, or multiple constituents when not representing the organization, the lawyer most clearly complies with the lawyer's ethical duties by obtaining the informed written consent of the clients after full disclosure of relevant implications of the joint representation. Rules Prof. Conduct, rules 1.7 and 1.0.1(e). The lawyer should write detailed engagement letters outlining the terms of engagement to the various clients and obtain the written consent to joint representation by all constituents of the organization and closely related family members being represented by the same counsel. This written consent must be informed. The letter cannot simply say that the clients have potential conflicts of interest. To comply with rule 1.0.1(e) of the Rules of Professional Conduct, the clients must be "informed" about those conflicts—the engagement letter must give examples of circumstances under which conflicting interests could surface, and discuss "the material risks, including any actual and reasonably foreseeable adverse consequences" of a joint representation. Rules Prof. Conduct, rule 1.0.1(e). If the organization's consent to the joint or concurrent representation is required under rule 1.7, the consent must be given by an appropriate official, constituent, or body of the organization other than the constituent who is to be represented, or by the shareholders. Rules Prof. Conduct, rule 1.13(g). For a discussion of the ethical duty of confidentiality and the disclosure and engagement letter requirements, see chapter 6 of this Guide, Confidentiality of Information, section 6.11.

Comment on California Rules of Professional Conduct, Rule 1.13

> [1] This rule applies to all forms of private, public and governmental organizations. (See Comment [6].) An organizational client can only act through individuals who are authorized to conduct its affairs. The identity of an organization's constituents will depend on its form, structure, and chosen terminology. For example, in the case of a corporation, constituents include officers, directors, employees and shareholders. In the case of other organizational forms, constituents include the equivalents of officers, directors, employees, and shareholders. For purposes of this rule, any agent or fiduciary authorized to act on behalf of an organization is a constituent of the organization.
>
> [2] A lawyer ordinarily must accept decisions an organization's constituents make on behalf of the organization, even if the lawyer questions their utility or prudence. It is not within the lawyer's province to make decisions on behalf of the organization concerning policy and operations, including ones entailing serious risk. A lawyer, however, has a duty to inform the client of significant developments related to the representation under Business and Professions Code section 6068, subdivision (m) and rule 1.4. Even when a lawyer is not obligated to proceed in accordance with

paragraph (b), the lawyer may refer to higher authority, including the organization's highest authority, matters that the lawyer reasonably believes* are sufficiently important to refer in the best interest of the organization subject to Business and Professions Code section 6068, subdivision (e) and rule 1.6.

[3] Paragraph (b) distinguishes between knowledge of the conduct and knowledge of the consequences of that conduct. When a lawyer knows* of the conduct, the lawyer's obligations under paragraph (b) are triggered when the lawyer knows* or reasonably should know* that the conduct is (i) a violation of a legal obligation to the organization, or a violation of law reasonably* imputable to the organization, and (ii) likely to result in substantial* injury to the organization.

[4] In determining how to proceed under paragraph (b), the lawyer should consider the seriousness of the violation and its potential consequences, the responsibility in the organization and the apparent motivation of the person* involved, the policies of the organization concerning such matters, and any other relevant considerations. Ordinarily, referral to a higher authority would be necessary. In some circumstances, however, the lawyer may ask the constituent to reconsider the matter. For example, if the circumstances involve a constituent's innocent misunderstanding of law and subsequent acceptance of the lawyer's advice, the lawyer may reasonably* conclude that the best interest of the organization does not require that the matter be referred to higher authority. If a constituent persists in conduct contrary to the lawyer's advice, it will be necessary for the lawyer to take steps to have the matter reviewed by a higher authority in the organization. If the matter is of sufficient seriousness and importance or urgency to the organization, referral to higher authority in the organization may be necessary even if the lawyer has not communicated with the constituent. For the responsibility of a subordinate lawyer in representing an organization, see rule 5.2.

[5] In determining how to proceed in the best lawful interests of the organization, a lawyer should consider the extent to which the organization should be informed of the circumstances, the actions taken by the organization with respect to the matter and the direction the lawyer has received from the organizational client.

Case Study

Two brothers owned equal interests in a limited partnership. The brothers and partners were unable to agree on the disposition of certain real estate owned by the partnership. One partner filed a partition action naming the other partner and the partnership as defendants. The defendant partner retained Lawyer to represent the partnership in the partition action, and also retained a second lawyer to represent him individually. The plaintiff partner objected to retaining Lawyer to represent the partnership. Lawyer was paid by the defendant partner, and Lawyer stated his belief that he could act on behalf of the partnership without direction from either of the partners.

What ethical issues arise from this set of facts and how should Lawyer have addressed them?

These facts do not raise an ethical issue of conflicts of interest. Lawyer has only one client: the partnership. Lawyer did not undertake to represent the partnership and either partner jointly. In addition, the court found no allegation that Lawyer formerly represented the plaintiff partner, which could have resulted in the potential adverse use of confidential information. Nevertheless, the facts raised legitimate concerns regarding Lawyer's duty of loyalty, not as between multiple clients, but as to his representation of the partnership. Since the defendant partner selected Lawyer, paid Lawyer, and directed the litigation, Lawyer may appear to advance the defendant partner's interests over the interests of the plaintiff partner. Such representation may not necessarily be in the best interests of the partnership, and Lawyer's disqualification was affirmed. *Jarvis v. Jarvis* (2019) 33 Cal.App.5th 113.

Cases

Former president and chief operating officer of defendant was not disqualified from representing plaintiff in wrongful termination claim against defendant because the lawyer lacked confidential information relevant to the representation. The president and chief operating officer had not investigated or had any discussion with outside counsel regarding the plaintiff's claims. *Wu v. O'Gara Coach Co., LLC* (2019) 38 Cal.App.5th 1069, compare *O'Gara Coach Co., LLC v. Ra* (2019) 30 Cal.App.5th 1115 (former president and chief operating officer of the company and his law firm were disqualified from representing the company's former employees in a suit against the company as a prophylactic measure, even though the lawyer was not a lawyer when serving as president and chief operating officer. Such disqualification was based on a non-lawyer's fiduciary duties when receiving privileged communications and was necessary to protect the integrity of the judicial process).

A management dispute arose between two 50% owners of an LLC. One owner brought an action for malpractice against the lawyers who represented the LLC in connection with the dispute. The court held under former Rules of Professional Conduct, rule 3-600 that the LLC lawyers owed no professional duty to the individual members. The plaintiff owner produced no evidence to support an implied lawyer-client privilege. The Court of Appeal affirmed the trial court dismissal of the case for lack of standing. *Sprengel v. Zyblut* (2019) 40 Cal.App.5th 1028, 1044-1046.

A law firm represented two opposing parties concurrently for approximately 10 years, without a written consent. Given this extensive time period, disqualification was inappropriate because the moving party had implicitly consented to the concurrent representation and was estopped to raise it. *Antelope Valley Groundwater Cases* (2018) 30 Cal.App.5th 602.

A limited liability company was owned by Beachcomber Management (Beachcomber) and five other members, the plaintiffs. Although the plaintiffs invested in the limited liability company, Beachcomber had the exclusive right of management. Beachcomber in turn was owned by the individual defendant who had exclusive management rights. A lawyer represented Beachcomber and the individual defendant. The lawyer had represented the limited liability company in the past, but did not represent it in this case. Plaintiffs filed a derivative suit, and sought the lawyer's disqualification, which the trial court granted. Issuing a writ, the Court of Appeal directed the trial court to consider the closely held entity exception. Since the source of all closely held entity's confidential information was from the insiders, counsel could represent the insiders, not the entity, and disqualification was not appropriate. *Beachcomber Management Crystal Cove, LLC v. Super. Ct. (Salisbury)* (2017) 13 Cal.App.5th 1105.

Counsel for the majority shareholder and the corporation were properly disqualified as to the corporation, but not the majority shareholder, in minority shareholder's derivative lawsuit over the corporation and its assets. Counsel had a conflict because the claims created adversity between the corporation and the majority shareholder, and the majority shareholder could not waive the conflict on behalf of the corporation. *Ontiveros v. Constable* (2016) 245 Cal.App.4th 686.

A lawyer who had represented the company filed a cross-complaint on behalf of one of the shareholders against the company. Reversing the trial court, the Court of Appeal held that the lawyer was automatically disqualified because of the lawyer's concurrent representation of both the shareholder and the company. *M'Guinness v. Johnson* (2015) 243 Cal.App.4th 602.

A lawyer and a lawyer's wife sued a former firm and partner, asserting several claims arising from the lawyer's retirement. Holding that the lawyer lacked standing to seek disqualification of the defendants' counsel because the claims were not derivative, the Court of Appeal also held that counsel representing the partner and the corporation did not have a conflict of interest. *Coldren v. Hart, King & Coldren, Inc.* (2015) 239 Cal.App.4th 237.

A law firm was not disqualified from representing an LLC, managing member, and another member in a dispute with two minority members involving an option agreement because no actual conflict or reasonable likelihood that a conflict might arise existed, and the defendant minority members did not allege mismanagement or misuse of the LLC property. *Havasu Lakeshore Investments, LLC v. Fleming* (2013) 217 Cal.App.4th 770, accord *Centex Homes v. St. Paul Fire and Marine Ins. Co.* (2018) 19 Cal.App.5th 789 (in an insurance coverage dispute, the court determined that independent counsel—paid by the insurer but taking direction from the insured—was unnecessary under former rule 3-310(c) of the Rules of Professional Conduct because the rule requiring independent counsel is only triggered "when there is a reasonable likelihood an actual conflict will arise.").

Citing *Knight v. Ferguson,* below, the court held that a rational link between the subject matter of the two cases will suffice to disqualify a lawyer, without an in-depth analysis of the facts of each matter. *j2 Global Communications, Inc. v. Easylink Services Internat. Corp.* (C.D. Cal.) 2012 U.S. Dist. LEXIS 179673.

In a derivative action, a lawyer was disqualified for simultaneously representing a limited liability company and a member with conflicting interests and without written consent. *Blue Water Sunset, LLC v. Markowitz* (2011) 192 Cal.App.4th 477, accord *Ontiveros v. Constable*, 245 Cal.App.4th 686. Compare *Shen v. Miller* (2012) 212 Cal.App.4th 48, where the court held that filing a derivative action on behalf of a shareholder did not create a lawyer-client relationship with the corporation, and the representing lawyer obtained information only through an inspection of the corporate records.

A majority shareholder and the corporation had adverse interests because the minority shareholder alleged harm to the corporation through the majority shareholder's misuse of corporate funds, and corporate counsel could not satisfy an undivided duty of loyalty to the corporation and the majority shareholder. *Gong v. RFG Oil, Inc.* (2008) 166 Cal.App.4th 209.

A lawyer represented a manager in negotiating a partnership arrangement and later undertook to represent unrelated investors who sought to remove the manager. The court found that a lawyer who successively represents two clients with adverse interests must be disqualified from representing the second client where there is a substantial relationship between the two matters. *Knight v. Ferguson* (2007) 149 Cal.App.4th 1207.

No conflict of interest arose from a lawyer's drafting of limited partnership agreement for current clients where the clients sought to accomplish a common end, had already formed their organization, and engaged the lawyer's services only to implement their joint plan by memorializing their agreement. *Buehler v. Sbardellati* (1995) 34 Cal.App.4th 1527.

By representing a partnership generally, partnership counsel assumed a duty of care and loyalty to the partnership and all the partners. *Johnson v. Super. Ct.* (*Sheppard Mullin Richter & Hampton*) (1995) 38 Cal.App.4th 463.

A lawyer representing a partnership did not necessarily have a lawyer-client relationship with an individual partner for purposes of applying the conflict of interest rules. The court held that the determination whether the lawyer was deemed to represent the individual partner depended upon the totality of the circumstances, citing former rule 3-600 of the Rules of Professional Conduct as applied to partnerships. *Responsible Citizens v. Super. Ct.* (1993) 16 Cal.App.4th 1717.

The paramount duty of the lawyer for a corporation was to the corporation. A lawyer for the corporation does not become a representative of its shareholders merely because the lawyer's actions on behalf of the corporation concurrently benefit the shareholders. Although shareholders might receive indirect or tangential benefits from legal advice rendered for the corporation, the primary duty of corporate counsel was owed to the corporate entity. *Skarbrevick v. Cohen, England & Whitfield* (1991) 231 Cal.App.3d 692.

Ethics Opinion

A lawyer may jointly represent a corporation and shareholder A in a suit brought by the only other shareholder, B; shareholder A may also consent to the joint representation on behalf of the corporation. State Bar of Cal. Com. on Prof. Resp. and Conduct, formal opn. No. 1999-153.

5.7 Fiduciaries and Beneficiaries

Concurrent representation of a fiduciary and a beneficiary can arise in the following contexts:

1. The lawyer represents a fiduciary in both fiduciary and individual capacities; or
2. The lawyer represents both a fiduciary and a beneficiary in the same matter.

Representation of a Fiduciary Who Is Also A Beneficiary. A person who is a beneficiary of a trust or estate is commonly named to act as the fiduciary. A lawyer may represent such person in both capacities, however, the lawyer should be alert to the potential conflicts that the client may have as a result of those dual roles. If a lawyer will represent a fiduciary to administer a trust or estate who is also a beneficiary and the fiduciary's beneficial interest may be in dispute, the lawyer should advise the fiduciary to seek separate counsel for representation as a beneficiary.

A lawyer who can diligently represent a client as both a fiduciary and beneficiary should advise the client of the fiduciary duty in Probate Code section 16003. Under that section a trustee has a duty to act impartially and not in a manner that gives preference to the client's own interests over the interests of the other beneficiaries. For example, if a client who is both the fiduciary and a residuary beneficiary proposes a non-pro-rata distribution of real property to the residuary beneficiaries, the client's self-interest may conflict with the fiduciary duty of impartiality. The lawyer should point out the potential conflict to the client and help the client resolve this conflict by obtaining the consent of the other beneficiaries, by obtaining court approval or, if necessary, by resigning as fiduciary. Because the fiduciary-beneficiary is the same person, rule 1.7 of the Rules of Professional Conduct, which deals with representing multiple clients with directly adverse interests, does not apply. Further, while the lawyer's fees to advise the client as a fiduciary may be paid by with trust or estate assets, any fees incurred to further the client's interest as a beneficiary must be paid directly by the client.

Even if the fiduciary is not a beneficiary, the lawyer for the fiduciary may be called upon to represent the individual both as a fiduciary and individually. A lawyer should be careful to distinguish between services to a client as fiduciary and to the client individually, should charge for them separately, and should advise the client that the services to the client in an individual capacity must be paid for personally and not from the trust or estate. For a discussion of the ethical issues surrounding confidentiality of the records of the fiduciary and the fiduciary's lawyer, see chapter 6 of this Guide, Confidentiality of Information, section 6.12.

Unless the fiduciary waives compensation or intends to request only the fee prescribed by statute or the trust or will, the fiduciary may submit a request for compensation without violating the fiduciary duty to avoid conflicts of interest. A court may ultimately determine that the fiduciary acted individually in defending a challenge to an accounting or a claim of breach of fiduciary duties. Nevertheless, pending such determination, a fiduciary may seek a fee for services rendered to the trust or estate. If the fiduciary is not successful, however, in defending their accounting, not awarded all or any extraordinary fees, or determined to be in breach of fiduciary duties, the fiduciary may be compelled to reimburse all or a part of the fees. The lawyer should advise the fiduciary client to keep separate records concerning services and fees related to the defense of an accounting or other claims. For a discussion of advising a fiduciary client on a disclosure and retention policy for trust administration records stored digitally, see chapter 10 of this Guide, Ethics and Technology, section 10.4.

A fiduciary who is also a creditor of the trust or estate must bring a claim to determine if a valid debt exists. If the fiduciary presents such a claim, the fiduciary is in an adverse relationship with the trust or estate, and the fiduciary may not represent the trust or estate with regard that claim. The fiduciary duty to avoid conflicts of interest in Probate Code section 16004 may compel the fiduciary to resign to pursue the claim. If the fiduciary intends to pursue a claim as an individual creditor, the lawyer for the fiduciary must advise the fiduciary client to seek separate counsel for that individual claim. Such advice complies with the lawyer's ethical duty to avoid representing two current clients with directly adverse interests. Rules Prof. Conduct, rule 1.7.

Conflicting interests may be a matter of degree. For example, a creditor claim for reimbursement for burial or funeral expenses or a creditor claim by a lawyer for legal fees incurred in drawing the decedent's will likely be non-controversial. In probate estates, a petition must be made for reimbursement or payment because only the court may approve or reject a claim made by a personal representative or the personal representative's lawyer. Prob. Code, secs. 9252, 9830 et seq. If the claim is more than simply reimbursement or a non-controversial payment, however, the ethical duty to avoid representation of clients with directly adverse interests requires the lawyer's withdrawal from representation or referral to separate counsel to adjudicate or settle the claim.

A lawyer and client may by agreement limit the scope of the lawyer's representation. See discussion in chapter 4 of this Guide, Identifying the Client and the Scope of Representation, section 4.10. They may agree that the lawyer will advise the client only with regard to the administration of the estate and not with respect to matters such as compensation, when the fiduciary's individual interest may be directly adverse to the beneficiaries. Although no ethical duty prohibits a lawyer from representing a client in dual capacities, the lawyer and client may wish to limit the scope of the representation for practical reasons. The lawyer or client may anticipate that administration of the trust or estate will be difficult because of divergent interests between the fiduciary and interested parties, either because of their relationship (for example, a stepparent and stepchild) or because of particular assets (such as a family home that both the fiduciary and another beneficiary wish to receive as part of their share). In such case, the lawyer and client may agree that the lawyer will represent the client only as the fiduciary to avoid concern that the lawyer's duty of loyalty to the client individually will interfere with the lawyer's representation of the client as fiduciary; to preserve the lawyer's credibility; and to preserve the lawyer's ability to communicate with all beneficiaries in connection with administration matters. In such a representation, the lawyer and client may appropriately agree that the lawyer may disclose all information to the beneficiaries, including otherwise confidential communications between the lawyer and client and information discovered by the lawyer that may be detrimental to the client personally. See further discussion at chapter 6 of this Guide, Confidentiality of Information, section 6.12.

For similar reasons, the fiduciary's lawyer may wish to suggest that the fiduciary obtain separate counsel to represent the fiduciary's individual interests. For example, a fiduciary joining in estate litigation as a beneficiary may choose to have separate counsel in the litigation to eliminate any question that the confidential communications with the litigation lawyer are privileged. Likewise, having separate counsel in each capacity could discourage claims by other beneficiaries that the fees of the fiduciary's lawyer are partly personal, and, therefore, should not be paid from the trust or probate estate.

Representation of a Fiduciary and a Beneficiary Who Are Not the Same Person. Under rule 1.7 of the Rules of Professional Conduct, a lawyer may represent a fiduciary and a beneficiary whose interests are directly adverse, but only with the informed written consent of both clients. Conflicts of interest are inherent in such a joint representation, including issues of fiduciary fees, settlement of the fiduciary's accounting, alleged breaches of fiduciary duties, and the fiduciary's treatment of other beneficiaries. To be certain that the clients' consents are informed, the lawyer should describe these potential conflicts in the initial engagement letter and obtain written consent from both clients before representation begins. The lawyer's engagement letter should also discuss whether the lawyer may disclose to one client confidential information obtained from the other; and whether the lawyer may continue to represent one client if an irreconcilable conflict arises that materially limits the lawyer's ethical representation of each client.

The lawyer representing the fiduciary and fewer than all the beneficiaries will have at least the appearance of being biased in favor of the client fiduciary and beneficiaries. This apparent bias may implicate the fiduciary duty of impartiality under Probate Code section 16003. To protect the fiduciary from accusations of favoritism, the lawyer should advise the fiduciary to obtain the informed written consent of all beneficiaries, or court approval, for any action by the fiduciary that would affect the individual beneficiaries differently. If the fiduciary takes actions and incurs additional fees solely because of the lawyer's representation of fewer than all the beneficiaries, it may be appropriate to charge such fees to the lawyer's clients and not the trust or estate. The lawyer's potential conflict of interest may also need to be disclosed to the other beneficiaries or to the court, as the case may be, to avoid accusations of extrinsic fraud, and, therefore, questions about the finality of any settled matter. *Potter v. Moran* (1966) 239 Cal.App.2d 873.The lawyer may avoid ethical conflicts of interest arising from joint representation of multiple beneficiaries by only representing the fiduciary.

Representation Imposed by Circumstances. Although the general rule is that the lawyer for the fiduciary represents only the fiduciary and does not represent the "estate" or the "trust" or the beneficiaries, there are circumstances under which a duty may be imposed on the lawyer and the ethical duties governing the lawyer-client relationship may apply.

The general rule in California is that a lawyer owes ethical duties to a client, but not to third parties who are not the lawyer's own clients. Although the lawyer performs services that may benefit estate or trust beneficiaries, the lawyer has no contractual privity with the beneficiaries, and the beneficiaries are only incidental beneficiaries to whom no duty is owed. An action for malpractice by the estate beneficiaries against the lawyer for the administrator will not lie because the administrator did not retain the lawyer "for the principal purpose of providing benefit to the legatees," and the fact that such beneficiaries may be benefited or damaged by the lawyer's performance "does not give rise to a duty by the attorney to such third parties." *Goldberg v. Frye* (1990) 217 Cal.App.3d 1258, 1268.

Despite a lack of contractual or privity relationship with a third party, the lawyer may be found to owe a duty in specific cases upon the balancing of various factors, including the extent to which the transaction was intended to benefit the third party and the closeness of the connection between the lawyer's conduct and the alleged injury suffered. The cases that have considered and found such a duty have arisen not in the ethics area, but in the civil liability area. Nonetheless, the facts and conduct which gave rise to civil liability are instructive on the ethical duties to avoid conflicts of interest. If a duty is found for civil liability and a lawyer-client relationship is the foundation for that duty, the lawyer may also be found to have breached an ethical duty.

Among the circumstances under which civil liability to the beneficiaries may be imposed are:

1. The lawyer may be held liable to the beneficiaries if the lawyer actively participates in a breach of trust by the trustee;
2. The lawyer has a responsibility to disclose to the beneficiaries any potential conflict of interest that the lawyer may have that affects the beneficiaries' interests; or
3. The lawyer may assume responsibilities to the beneficiaries that the lawyer would otherwise not have by telling, or implying to, the beneficiaries that the lawyer represents the "estate" or "trust" or is otherwise protecting the interests of the beneficiaries. In some instances, those beneficiaries may actually become "clients" of the lawyer.

In *Morales v. Field, DeGoff, Huppert & MacGowan* (1979) 99 Cal.App.3d 307, the lawyers for the executor sent letters to the estate beneficiaries assuring them that they would "keep [them] advised if anything unusual arises" and that, since the estate proceeding was subject to court supervision, the beneficiaries "should feel reasonably assured that [their] interests will be protected." The lawyer representing a fiduciary should avoid such communications because they may create a duty of care that the lawyer owes to someone other than the fiduciary-client. If a dispute arises, the lawyer may have duties to multiple parties with directly adverse interests in violation of rule 1.7 of the Rules of Professional Conduct.

To avoid inadvertent representation imposed by circumstances, most lawyers for fiduciaries notify all the beneficiaries in writing that they represent only the fiduciary and that the beneficiaries may retain their own lawyers. Such an approach is required if the beneficiaries have reason to believe that the fiduciary's lawyer is representing them, because a lawyer has a duty to communicate to persons who reasonably believe they are clients, at least to the extent of advising them that they are not clients. *Butler v. State Bar* (1986) 42 Cal.3d 323, 329. For a discussion of the ethical duties regarding unrepresented persons and a sample notice of nonrepresentation to beneficiaries, see chapter 7 of this Guide, Communication, sections 7.4 and 7.5.

Representation of Corporate Fiduciaries. Rule 1.7 of the Rules of Professional Conduct prohibits a lawyer from representing two different clients, even in unrelated matters, if the interest of one client is directly adverse to the interest of the other in either matter. While representing a corporate fiduciary of a trust or probate estate, the lawyer is clearly prohibited from representing a person who has an interest adverse to that fiduciary, even if the representation is in connection with an entirely different matter. Less clear is the application of rule 1.9 of the Rules of Professional Conduct relating to the lawyer's accepting employment adverse to the corporate fiduciary as a former client, when the earlier matter has concluded. Rule 1.9 of the Rules of Professional Conduct is not an absolute prohibition against the lawyer's ever representing a client against the fiduciary; it prohibits such representation in a substantially related matter when the interests of the current and former client are materially adverse, or if the lawyer has acquired confidential information that is material to the related matter.

Some California corporate fiduciaries take the position that a lawyer who has represented them may never represent another client in a matter adverse to the corporate fiduciary. They assert that the lawyer always has "confidential information material to the employment," and they insist that consent must first be obtained. When such consent is requested, they often refuse to give it. A client seeking representation will unlikely be willing to undergo the litigation needed to resolve the issue in favor of the lawyer. Consequently, a lawyer who is asked to represent a corporate fiduciary of a trust or probate estate should consider discussing with the fiduciary at the outset the extent to which the representation might preclude the lawyer from representing a client in an unrelated future matter.

One approach for a lawyer engaged by a corporate fiduciary is to specify in the engagement letter the scope of the engagement and the fiduciary's consent to ongoing representation notwithstanding conflicts of interest that may arise between the fiduciary and the lawyer's other clients in unrelated matters. Otherwise, the lawyer may find the fiduciary unwilling to consent to the lawyer's representation of a beneficiary of a different estate seeking to contest the corporate fiduciary's accounting or fee request.

ACTEC Commentaries on Model Rules of Professional Conduct, Rule 1.7

> A lawyer who is asked to represent a corporate fiduciary in connection with a fiduciary estate should consider discussing with the fiduciary the extent to which the representation might preclude the lawyer from representing an adverse party in an unrelated matter. In the absence of a contrary agreement, a lawyer who represents a corporate fiduciary in connection with the administration of a fiduciary estate should not be treated as representing the fiduciary generally for purposes of applying MRPC 1.7 (Conflict of Interest: Current Clients) with regard to a wholly unrelated matter. In particular, the representation of a corporate fiduciary in a representative capacity should not preclude the lawyer from representing a party adverse to the corporate fiduciary in connection with a wholly unrelated matter, such as a real estate transaction, labor negotiation, or another estate or trust administration. Nonetheless, the corporate fiduciary might be of a different view; and it would be useful to clarify this in advance. Where the lawyer is trying to keep open the possibility of such a future adverse representation on an unrelated matter, the lawyer should ask the corporate fiduciary for a prospective consent to such representations, as explored in the next section. Where a lawyer is already representing another party adverse to the corporate fiduciary on an unrelated matter, it will be necessary for the lawyer to comply with MRPC 1.7(b) as to both clients before undertaking to represent the corporate fiduciary.

Statutes

California Probate Code section 16003

> If a trust has two or more beneficiaries, the trustee has a duty to deal impartially with them and shall act impartially in investing and managing the trust property, taking into account any differing interests of the beneficiaries.

California Probate Code section 16004

> (a) The trustee has a duty not to use or deal with trust property for the trustee's own profit or for any other purpose unconnected with the trust, nor to take part in any transaction in which the trustee has an interest adverse to the beneficiary.
>
> (b) The trustee may not enforce any claim against the trust property that the trustee purchased after or in contemplation of appointment as trustee, but the court may allow the trustee to be reimbursed from trust property the amount that the trustee paid in good faith for the claim.
>
> (c) A transaction between the trustee and a beneficiary which occurs during the existence of the trust or while the trustee's influence with the beneficiary remains and by which the trustee obtains an advantage from the beneficiary is presumed to be a violation of the trustee's fiduciary duties. This presumption is a presumption affecting the burden of proof. This subdivision does not apply to the provisions of an agreement between a trustee and a beneficiary relating to the hiring or compensation of the trustee.

California Probate Code section 16005

> The trustee of one trust has a duty not to knowingly become a trustee of another trust adverse in its nature to the interest of the beneficiary of the first trust, and a duty to eliminate the conflict or resign as trustee when the conflict is discovered.

Cases

When a lawyer represents a fiduciary, the lawyer owes duties to the client trustee or administrator alone. This single representation rings especially true when the lawyer's client and a third party are adverse, as the lawyer's duty of loyalty to a client cannot be divided or diluted by a duty owed to a third party. The court held that plaintiff's claim that the defendant lawyer participated in breach of trust amounted to an allegation of conspiracy with the trustee, even though it was not labeled as such. Therefore, the prefiling requirements of Code of Civil Procedure section 1714.10 applied. The Court of Appeal overruled the trial court and ordered it to sustain the defendant lawyer's demurrer to the complaint. *Cortese v. Sherwood* (2018) 26 Cal.App.5th 445.

Disappointed heirs brought a malpractice claim against the estate planning lawyers claiming that the testator lacked testamentary capacity at the time the estate plan amendments were executed, that the lawyers should have known that the testator's testamentary capacity was questionable, and that the lawyers acted negligently in failing to assure, confirm, and document the testator's capacity to execute the governing will and trust amendments. The Court of Appeal upheld the trial court's grant of a demurrer dismissing the claim without leave to amend. The court found that the lawyer's duty of loyalty to the client may be compromised by imposing a duty to nonclient beneficiaries on issues of determining incapacity. The court cited favorably rule 1.14(a) of the Model Rules of Professional Conduct: "When a client's ability to make adequately considered decisions in connection with the representation is impaired, whether because of minority, mental disability or for some other reason, the lawyer shall, as far as reasonably possible, maintain a normal client-lawyer relationship with the client." None of the authorities imposing a duty upon the lawyer to assess the capacity of the testator indicate that such duty would run to beneficiaries rather than solely to the testator. *Moore v. Anderson Zigler Disharoon Gallagher and Grey, P.C.* (2003) 109 Cal.App.4th 1287, 1294.

"The attorney for the trustee of a trust is not, by virtue of this relationship, also the attorney for the beneficiaries of the trust. The attorney represents only the trustee. [citations]." *Wells Fargo Bank v. Super. Ct. (Boltwood)* (2000) 22 Cal.4th 201, 212. For a further discussion of the competing fiduciary and ethical duties in this case, see chapter 9 of this Guide, Ethics and Litigation, section 9.4.

Where the plaintiff alleged that the defendant performed legal services intended to prevent the plaintiff from discovering the dissipation of the trust assets and the trustee's inappropriate investments, advised the plaintiff to waive rights to ongoing accountings, and made misrepresentations of material fact, these allegations were sufficient to state a cause of action under exception to the general rule that trust beneficiaries are not represented by the trustee's lawyer. *Wolf v. Mitchell* (1999) 76 Cal.App.4th 1030, 1040.

Trust beneficiaries may sue brokers who participated with a trustee in alleged breaches of trust as long as the third parties' participation was both active and for the purpose of advancing their own interests or financial advantage. *City of Atascadero, et al., v. Merrill Lynch Pierce Fenner and Smith, Inc., et al.* (1998) 68 Cal.App.4th 445.

A lawyer must be careful not to lead the beneficiaries to believe that the lawyer is protecting the interests of the beneficiaries; such communications could create an obligation of care by the lawyers, apart from the representation of a direct client, the fiduciary. *Johnson v. Super. Ct.* (*Sheppard Mullin Richter & Hampton*) (1995) 38 Cal.App.4th 463, 474.

Estate beneficiaries could not sue the administrator's lawyer for malfeasance because the lawyer's representation of the administrator was "not entered into for the principal purpose of providing benefit to the legatee," and the fact that such beneficiaries may be benefited or damaged by the lawyer's performance "does not give rise to a duty by the attorney to such third parties." *Goldberg v. Frye* (1990) 217 Cal.App.3d 1258, 1268.

The Court of Appeal upheld the trial court findings that a lawyer led the nominated executor reasonably to believe the lawyer was representing him, and that it must have been clear to the lawyer that the nominated executor was led to so believe. That the nominated executor had not retained the lawyer as a client was irrelevant because the lawyer did not perform the necessary probate work whoever the client was, and the lawyer led the nominated executor to believe that the lawyer was representing him without ever advising him otherwise. A lawyer's duty to communicate includes the duty to communicate with unrepresented persons at least to the extent of advising them that they are not clients. This duty extends only to persons who, to the lawyer's knowledge, may reasonably believe that they are clients. *Butler v. State Bar* (1986) 42 Cal.3d 323, 329.

A lawyer has a duty to disclose to the trust beneficiaries the lawyer's concurrent representation of the executor and a third party who had entered into a transaction with the executor. A lawyer may be held liable to beneficiaries if the lawyer actively participates in a breach of trust by the trustee. *Morales v. Field, DeGoff, Huppert & MacGowan* (1979) 99 Cal.App.3d 307.

The trustee's lawyers had a duty to inform the court that they also represented the guardian for the minor beneficiaries; no valid order approving the trustee's accounts could be made while the lawyers represented the conflicting interests. *Potter v. Moran* (1966) 239 Cal.App.2d 873, 876-879.

5.8 Duty to Withdraw

If joint clients have directly adverse interests, the lawyer has a duty to obtain their written consent to the continuing joint representation and may have to withdraw from representing both of them. Withdrawal must comply with the ethical duties set forth in rule 1.16 of the Rules of Professional Conduct. The lawyer may not continue to represent either client separately without the informed written consent of the other. For a discussion of the requirements of informed consent, see rule 1.0.1(e) of the Rules of Professional Conduct and chapter 2 of this Guide, Terminology.

Certain direct conflicts would preclude the lawyer from representing both spouses in a joint representation, notwithstanding their informed written consent. For example, a lawyer should not represent both parties to a prenuptial or postnuptial agreement. A direct conflict may also exist if the spouses assert different rights to the same assets or one spouse undertakes to conceal assets belonging to the other. In such examples, the two spouses have directly adverse interests and one lawyer cannot maintain loyalty and independent judgment to them both.

If jointly represented spouses later decide to divorce, their interests will directly conflict such that continuing representation of both of them during divorce proceedings is generally inappropriate. Even with the written consent of both spouses, representation of either spouse in estate planning matters may be inappropriate until the dissolution of their marriage is concluded and the marital property has been divided between them. Some estate planners will only represent one or both of the former clients after the divorce proceeding is concluded, and with the consent of the other former spouse. For a discussion of representing a client whose interest is materially adverse to a former client, see section 5.14 of this chapter.

In a joint representation, one spouse may communicate matters to the lawyer not to be disclosed to the other spouse, but that the lawyer feels are material to the representation and the knowledge of which will influence the representation. In that case, the lawyer may have to examine whether continued representation of the couple is possible or whether withdrawal is required. For additional discussion of the rules governing confidential information and the representation of couples in their estate planning, see chapter 6 of this Guide, Confidentiality of Information, section 6.8.

Ethics Opinion

Former rule 3-700(A)(2) of the Rules of Professional Conduct provided that a member may not withdraw from the representation of a client until the member has taken reasonable steps to avoid reasonably foreseeable prejudice to the rights of the client. The requirements of rule 3-700(A)(2) applied when a lawyer's withdrawal was prompted by the dissolution of the lawyer's law firm. In the event of dissolution, all lawyers who are employed by or partners of a firm were required to comply with rule 3-700(A)(2) as to all clients of the firm, regardless of their connection to any specific client or the specific nature of their affiliation with the firm. What "reasonable steps" a lawyer must take to protect a particular client's rights may vary considerably, however, depending on the circumstances, including the lawyer's relationship to the client and its matter and the lawyer's position within the firm. State Bar of Cal. Com. on Prof. Resp. and Conduct, formal opn. No. 2014-190. The same analysis would apply under Rules of Professional Conduct, rule 1.16, For a further discussion of the ethical duties arising out of departure from a law firm, see section 5.14 of this chapter and State Bar of Cal. Com. on Prof. Resp. and Conduct, formal opn. No. 2020-201.

5.9 Advance Consent to Representation with Conflicts of Interest

The comment on rule 1.7 of the Rules of Professional Conduct expressly states that it does not supersede existing California case law regarding advance consent to future conflicts of interest. "An advance waiver of potential future conflicts … is permitted under California law, even if the waiver does not specifically state the exact nature of the future conflict." *Visa U.S.A., Inc. v. First Data Corp.* (N.D. Cal. 2003) 241 F.Supp.2d 1100, 1105. "The only inquiry that need be made is whether the waiver was fully informed." *Id.* The requirements for informed written consent are set forth in rule 1.0.1(e) of the Rules of Professional Conduct and applicable case law.

The following factors may be considered in determining whether an advance consent is fully informed: the breadth of the consent, the temporal scope of the consent, the quality of the conflicts discussion between the lawyer and the client, the specificity of the consent, the nature of the actual conflict, the sophistication of the client, and the interest of justice. *Visa U.S.A., Inc. v. First Data Corp., supra,* 241 F.Supp.2d at p. 1106; see also *Concat LP v. Unilever, PLC* (N.D. Cal. 2004) 350 F.Supp.2d 796, 820. The determination of the enforceability of an advance consent is fact intensive and based on the facts available at the time the consent is signed. The disclosure should be as detailed as possible in its description of potential conflicts that may arise, and the lawyer should confirm that the client understands the potential future conflicts at the time the advance consent is signed.

The requirement of a detailed disclosure of current facts most likely precludes a blanket consent to all future conflicts. The circumstances of a representation may change, and unforeseen conflicts may arise through client disclosures, additional parties or claims, or new lawyers joining a firm. The lawyer must address such changed circumstances by additional disclosures and a contemporaneous consent from the client or clients to the continued representation.

Furthermore, any informed consent should also confirm the client's understanding that the consent may be later withdrawn and the method for doing so.

Comment on California Rules of Professional Conduct, Rule 1.7

> [9] This rule does not preclude an informed written consent* to a future conflict in compliance with applicable case law. The effectiveness of an advance consent is generally determined by the extent to which the client reasonably* understands the material risks that the consent entails. The more comprehensive the explanation of the types of future representations that might arise and the actual and reasonably* foreseeable adverse consequences to the client of those representations, the greater the likelihood that the client will have the requisite understanding. The experience and sophistication of the client giving consent, as well as whether the client is independently represented in connection with giving consent, are also relevant in determining whether the client reasonably* understands the risks involved in giving consent. An advance consent cannot be effective if the circumstances that materialize in the future make the conflict nonconsentable under paragraph (d). A lawyer who obtains from a client an advance consent that complies with this rule will have all the duties of a lawyer to that client except as expressly limited by the consent. A lawyer cannot obtain an advance consent to incompetent representation. (See rule 1.8.8.)

Case Study

Lawyer represents two clients who are defendants in the same litigation regarding a boundary dispute. One client owns land that borders plaintiff's property to the east; the other client owns property that borders both plaintiff's and the other client's property to the north. The engagement agreement between Lawyer and both clients has a general consent to concurrent representation but does not specifically address potential conflicts during settlement discussions.

During the course of the litigation, the plaintiff's counsel proposes a settlement that would benefit one of Lawyer's clients to the detriment of the other. The client who would benefit from the proposed settlement asks Lawyer not to disclose the terms of the proposed settlement to Lawyer's other client. In response to the conflict, Lawyer does not disclose the settlement offer. Instead, Lawyer declines to represent both clients with respect to further settlement negotiations but will continue to represent them in the litigation with respect to defending plaintiff's claims.

What ethical issues arise from this set of facts and how should Lawyer have addressed them?

Lawyer cannot keep the settlement offer secret; Lawyer has an ethical duty to keep both clients reasonably informed of significant developments in the representation. A general consent to concurrent representation in an engagement agreement does not allow a lawyer to continue that representation after an actual and irreconcilable conflict of interest arises. Lawyer must obtain the further informed written consent of the clients before providing advice that would be detrimental to one client's interests. Otherwise, Lawyer must withdraw from both representations. San Diego

County Bar Assn., formal opn. No. 2013-1. See also Rules of Professional Conduct, rule 1.4.1 and chapter 7 of this Guide, Communication, section 7.1.

Cases

An advance waiver of conflicts of interest in an engagement letter was ineffective when the law firm had a current client with directly adverse interests, and the law firm did not tell either client of its representation of the other. The simultaneous representation of clients with adverse interests in violation of the rules of professional conduct rendered the engagement letter, including its arbitration clause, unenforceable as a matter of public policy. A successful motion for disqualification of a lawyer or firm may require disgorgement of fees. In this case, the court allowed the law firm to recover fees under a theory of quantum meruit. *Sheppard, Mullin, Richter & Hampton, LLP v. J-M Manufacturing Co., Inc.* (2018) 6 Cal.5th 59.

A consent to joint representation was held unenforceable because it was not specific enough about the potential conflicts and did not cover a conflict that arose when the law firm later represented a subsidiary. Consents to such a representation may need to be revisited and revised based on subsequent events. *Lennar Mare Island, LLC v. Steadfast Insurance Co.* (E.D. Cal. 2015) 105 F.Supp.3d 1100.

Advance consent to continued representation of a real property purchaser was effective to allow the law firm to continue representation despite cross-complaint being asserted against a former co-client. That consent stated, "[w]e are now asking that you consent to our continued and future representation of the Companies and agree not to assert any such conflict of interest or to seek to disqualify us from representing the Companies, notwithstanding any adversity that may develop. By signing and returning to us the agreement and consent set forth at the end of this letter, you will consent to such arrangement and waive any conflicts regarding that arrangement. Notwithstanding such waiver and consent, depending on the circumstances, there remains some degree of risk that we would be disqualified from representing any of you in the event of a dispute." *Zador Corp. v. Kwan* (1995) 31 Cal.App.4th 1285, 1290.

5.10 Transactions with Clients Implicating Lawyer's Personal Interests

California Rules of Professional Conduct, Rule 1.8.1 - Business Transactions with a Client and Pecuniary Interests Adverse to a Client

> A lawyer shall not enter into a business transaction with a client, or knowingly* acquire an ownership, possessory, security or other pecuniary interest adverse to a client, unless each of the following requirements has been satisfied:
>
> (a) the transaction or acquisition and its terms are fair and reasonable* to the client and the terms and the lawyer's role in the transaction or acquisition are fully

disclosed and transmitted in writing* to the client in a manner that should reasonably* have been understood by the client;

(b) the client either is represented in the transaction or acquisition by an independent lawyer of the client's choice or the client is advised in writing* to seek the advice of an independent lawyer of the client's choice and is given a reasonable* opportunity to seek that advice; and

(c) the client thereafter provides informed written consent* to the terms of the transaction or acquisition, and to the lawyer's role in it.

An asterisk (*) identifies a defined term in rule 1.0.1 of the Rules of Professional Conduct. For further discussion of a defined term, see chapter 2 of this Guide, Terminology.

Rule 1.8.1 of the Rules of Professional Conduct departs from former rule 3-300 by specifically requiring that the lawyer disclose not only the terms of the transaction implicating the lawyer's personal interest but also the lawyer's role in that transaction. Both the transaction and the lawyer's role in the transaction are subject to the informed written consent of the client, as prescribed in rule 1.0.1(e) of the Rules of Professional Conduct.

Rule 1.8.1 of the Rules of Professional Conduct is not intended to apply to a fee agreement between a lawyer and a client unless the agreement confers on the lawyer a property interest adverse to the client. Fee agreements are governed generally by rule 1.5 of the Rules of Professional Conduct, discussed in chapter 8 of this Guide, Compensation. When a lawyer seeks to obtain an interest in a client's property to secure payment of past due or future fees, rule 1.8.1 may apply. For example, a lawyer may receive a security in a client's expected probate inheritance to secure payment of the lawyer's fees and court costs.

Sale of Insurance Products. Although there is no absolute prohibition against the trusts and estates lawyer entering into a business transaction with a client, some transactions should be approached with particular caution, if not avoided altogether. In particular, the lawyer who also sells life insurance, long-term care insurance, annuities, and other financial products to estate planning clients runs a serious risk of a claim of undue influence to unravel the transaction, and discipline for ethical violations in not obtaining the necessary informed consent from the client and in failing to act competently by not advising the client of reasonable alternatives.

In the course of estate planning, lawyers are told their clients' most private family problems and complete financial details, details which would often not be disclosed to insurance or investment sellers. The implicit understanding when this information is given is that it will be used by the lawyer for the client's benefit, not the lawyer's profit. Rule 1.8.2 of the Rules of Professional Conduct prohibits a lawyer from using confidential information to the detriment of the client. When the lawyer later converts the meeting into a sales pitch for investment products, many clients may be unable to make a critical, independent evaluation of the products. That vulnerability of the estate planning client makes it unlikely that the client can enter into an arm's length transaction with the lawyer regardless of any efforts of the lawyer to meet the technical requirements of rule 1.8.1 of the Rules of Professional Conduct.

Although these specific circumstances have not arisen in case law, the courts can be expected to view such transactions with the same, if not greater, skepticism than they view the naming of the drafting lawyer as a fiduciary for the client. See the discussion at section 5.11 of this chapter. That skepticism recognizes that the personal and confidential relationship of the trusts and estates lawyer with a client can make it impossible for the client to stand at the necessary "arm's length" and evaluate the financial product being purveyed by the lawyer. If the lawyer and client are not at arm's length, the client cannot give the informed written consent required under rule 1.8.1 of the Rules of Professional Conduct.

The ethical duty of competence in rule 1.1 of the Rules of Professional Conduct may also pose a bar to the sale of insurance and other financial products by the lawyer to the client. While the insurance or other investment broker has no duty to advise the buyer how to evaluate the product or what alternatives may be available, the lawyer clearly has an ethical duty to do so. In the insurance context, the duty would include, at the least, either a referral to an expert independent insurance analyst, or, alternatively, an explanation of the company rating systems, the commission structure, alternative products from other companies, and the costs of early termination of the product. If, for example, the lawyer suggests an annuity in the context of Medi-Cal planning, the lawyer must explain all reasonable non-insurance alternatives, such as seeking an enlarged community spouse resource allowance by administrative or judicial procedure. For a discussion of the ethical duties of competence and diligence, see chapter 3 of this Guide, Competence and Diligence, and section 3.10 regarding the ethical issues raised by participating in the marketing of form-based trust documents.

Business and Professions Code section 6175.3 prescribes the required disclosures if a lawyer, while acting as a fiduciary, sells financial products to a client who is an elder or dependent adult. Those disclosures are required to any such person with whom the lawyer has or has had, within the preceding three years, a lawyer-client relationship. The statutory disclosures must be presented to the client at or prior to the time the lawyer recommends a financial product.

Purchasing Property at a Foreclosure Sale. Rule 1.8.9 of the Rules of Professional Conduct prohibits a lawyer from directly or indirectly purchasing property at a foreclosure or judicial sale in an action in which the lawyer, or any lawyer affiliated by reason of personal, business, or professional relationship with that lawyer or with that lawyer's law firm, is acting as a lawyer for a party or as a fiduciary. This ethical prohibition does not apply to sales pursuant to Probate Code sections 9880 to 9885 requiring judicial authorization for the sale of estate property to the personal representative or the lawyer for the personal representative, with the written consent of all beneficiaries and a showing that the transaction is to the advantage of the estate. In the case of *Sodikoff v. State Bar* (1975) 14 Cal.3d 422, the court held that a lawyer was subject to discipline for encouraging a client to sell estate real property below its appraised value. The lawyer failed to disclose to the client that the purchaser corporation was the lawyer's alter ego.

Former California Rules of Professional Conduct, Rule 3-300 - Avoiding Interests Adverse to a Client

> A member shall not enter into a business transaction with a client; or knowingly acquire an ownership, possessory, security, or other pecuniary interest adverse to a client, unless each of the following requirements has been satisfied:

(A) The transaction or acquisition and its terms are fair and reasonable to the client and are fully disclosed and transmitted in writing to the client in a manner which should reasonably have been understood by the client; and

(B) The client is advised in writing that the client may seek the advice of an independent lawyer of the client's choice and is given a reasonable opportunity to seek that advice; and

(C) The client thereafter consents in writing to the terms of the transaction or the terms of the acquisition.

Cases

The Rule of Professional Conduct subjecting a lawyer to discipline for entering into a business transaction with a client without first satisfying certain substantive and procedural prerequisites does not itself provide a basis for civil liability. Former Rules Prof. Conduct, rule 3–300. The statutory presumption that transactions between a lawyer and client by which the lawyer obtains an advantage are a breach of the lawyer's fiduciary duty and are the product of undue influence is rebuttable, and the lawyer's inability to do so renders the transaction voidable at the client's option. *Ferguson v. Yaspan* (2014) 233 Cal.App.4th 676. See also Prob. Code, sec. 16004, subd. (c);

A lawyer was denied recovery of fees in quantum meruit after business agreements with a client were voided for failure to comply with former rule 3-300 of the Rules of Professional Conduct. The fiduciary duty in Probate Code section 16004 is the statutory complement to rule 3-300, entitling the client to recover damages under a fiduciary standard, irrespective of whether the business transactions were successful. *Fair v. Bakhtiari* (2011) 195 Cal.App.4th 1135. The court distinguished the *Shopoff* and *Fergus* cases, discussed below.

A lawyer's offer to discount fees as an incentive for the client to settle did not violate former rule 3-300 of the Rules of Professional Conduct because the lawyer did not thereby obtain an interest in the client's claims or in any settlement proceeds. *Chan v. Lund* (2010) 188 Cal.App.4th 1159. See also *Modtech Holdings, Inc. v. Monteleone & McCrory LLP* (C.D. Cal. 2011) 2011 U.S. Dist. LEXIS 42367 (compliance with requirements of former rule 3-300 of the Rules of Professional Conduct is sufficient without further advising the client of the reasons why the lawyer has an adverse interest).

The inclusion of a charging lien in a contingency fee agreement does not create an interest adverse to a client under former rule 3-300 of the Rules of Professional Conduct. *Plummer v. Day/Eisenberg LLP* (2010) 184 Cal.App.4th 38 (citing State Bar of Cal. Com. on Prof. Resp. and Conduct, formal opn. No. 2006-170), compare *Fletcher v. Davis* (2004) 33 Cal.4th 61 (requiring compliance with former rule 3-300 of the Rules of Professional Conduct to secure payment of an agreement for hourly fees).

Under the doctrine of severability of contracts, charging liens in a fee agreement that did not comply with former rule 3-300 of the Rules of Professional Conduct did not invalidate the underlying contract and the obligation to pay lawyer fees. *Shopoff & Cavallo LLP v. Hyon* (2008)

167 Cal.App.4th 1489. This decision was distinguished in *Fair v. Bakhtiari, supra,* 195 Cal.App.4th at pp. 1165-66.

A contingency fee agreement to collect a judgment was transformed into a partnership agreement to renovate a hotel purchased at a sheriff's sale. Both agreements were voidable by the client. *Fergus v. Songer* (2007) 150 Cal.App.4th 552. This case was distinguished in *Fair v. Bakhtiari, supra,* 195 Cal.App.4th at pp. 1166-67.

Inter vivos gifts to and a will making gifts to the testator's lawyer and family were invalidated following proof of undue influence exercised by the lawyer over the client. *In re Estate of Auen* (1994) 30 Cal.App.4th 300. See section 5.13 of this chapter, Donative Transfers Presumed to be the Product of Fraud or Undue Influence.

A lawyer has enhanced liability in business transactions with a client, even if the potential risk faced by the client would come about primarily through lawyer's inadvertence or circumstances beyond the lawyer's control rather than deliberate misdeeds by the lawyer. The case also demonstrates need to create a clear written record of client instructions in business transactions with a client. *McKnight v. State Bar* (1991) 53 Cal.3d 1025.

A lawyer was subject to disciplinary action when the lawyer borrowed money from client on an unsecured note and then filed for bankruptcy. The client had not been advised of the terms of the note and or of the right to seek advice of an independent lawyer. *Sugarman v. State Bar* (1990) 51 Cal.3d 609.

A lawyer was reproved for entering into a financing arrangement with a client without advising the client to obtain separate counsel and giving a reasonable time to do so. *Connor v. State Bar* (1990) 50 Cal.3d 1047.

A lawyer was suspended for five years for encouraging the conservator, whom the lawyer represented, to loan funds to a third party whom the lawyer did not disclose was a client and former business partner of the lawyer. *Rodgers v. State Bar* (1989) 48 Cal.3d 300.

A lawyer encouraged a litigation client to invest settlement proceeds in a franchise business without disclosing the "finder's fee" to be received for bringing in an investor; the lawyer also failed to discuss and emphasize substantial risks of the investment. The court stated that a lawyer should encourage independent counsel for a client with whom the lawyer is engaging in a business transaction, not just mention the availability of such counsel. *Rose v. State Bar* (1989) 49 Cal.3d 646, 663.

The court emphasized that the strict scrutiny of loans from clients and former clients continues even after the representation has ended. The rules are drawn to protect clients from their lawyer's use of confidential financial information disclosed during the lawyer-client relationship. *Hunniecutt v. State Bar* (1988) 44 Cal.3d 362.

A lawyer took unauthorized loans from a trust while serving as trustee. *Schneider v. State Bar of Cal.* (1987) 43 Cal.3d 784.

A new lawyer was placed on probation for making an unsecured loan to himself from probate estate funds without appropriate disclosure, without the beneficiary's written consent, and without prior court order. *Lewis v. State Bar* (1981) 28 Cal.3d 683.

A lawyer representing a client in probate proceedings was disciplined for failing to disclose to the client or the probate court that the lawyer owed money to the estate. *Mayo v. State Bar* (1978) 23 Cal.3d 72.

In a disciplinary action, the court imposed a six-month suspension on a lawyer who represented the administrator of an estate. The lawyer violated the position of trust and confidence that the lawyer voluntarily assumed with an elderly beneficiary who lived in England. The lawyer falsely advised the beneficiary that "one of our clients by the name of Acquistate, a California corporation" had made an offer to buy the property for $20,000. The lawyer failed to disclose to the beneficiary that Acquistate was not a client of the law firm but was the lawyer's alter ego. The lawyer also failed to disclose that the property had been appraised at $46,500. *Sodikoff v. State Bar* (1975) 14 Cal.3d 422.

"An attorney's duty of fidelity to his client involves far more than refraining from exercising undue influence.... For this reason all business dealings between attorney and client whereby attorney benefits are strictly scrutinized for any unfairness on the attorney's part [citations]." *Magee v. State Bar of Cal.* (1962) 58 Cal.2d 423, 430.

Business transactions between a lawyer and a client "are always scrutinized by the courts with zealous care" because they are fraught with ethical peril. *Felton v. LeBreton* (1891) 92 Cal. 457.

Ethics Opinions

A lawyer and the lawyer's firm prepared all the documents for a public offering and the related SEC filings. It was in the law firm's interest, as well as that of the client company and its officers and directors, that the litigation result in a finding of no failure to disclose material information in those documents. The opinion concludes that the lawyer and firm had vested financial and professional interests in the outcome of the subject matter of this representation and must make full disclosure of the potential conflict to the client company, and each officer and director, under former rule 3-310(B) of the Rules of Professional Conduct. When the lawyer later found notes of a meeting with directors and officers at which they discussed related-party transactions, the firm was to fully disclose that fact and its ramifications to each client, including the new, inherent conflicts of interest between the firm and its clients. San Diego County Bar Assn., Ethics opn. No. 2017-1.

Although fee agreements are statutorily exempt from this rule, when a client waives the right to recovery of fees in a civil rights suit, compliance with former rule 3-300 of the Rules of Professional Conduct should be considered. State Bar of Cal. Com. On Prof. Resp. and Conduct, formal opn. No. 1994-136.

For a lawyer to receive compensation both as personal representative of the probate estate and a commission as a real estate broker, compliance with former rule 3-300 of the Rules of Professional Conduct was required. San Diego County Bar Assn., Ethics opn. No. 1992-1.

5.11 Designation of Drafting Lawyer as Fiduciary

No California Rule of Professional Conduct deals explicitly with the propriety of a lawyer preparing for a client a will or other document that designates the lawyer as executor or trustee or nominates the lawyer as conservator. The drafting lawyer may include such a provision without contravening the lawyer's ethical duties so long as the client is properly informed, the designation does not violate the conflict of interest rules, and the designation or nomination is not the product of undue influence or improper solicitation by the lawyer. In such a case, the client must be properly informed regarding the role and duties of the fiduciary, the ability of someone other than a lawyer to serve as fiduciary with legal and other professional assistance, and the comparative costs of designating the lawyer or another person or institution as fiduciary.

Nevertheless, Probate Code section 21380 establishes a legal presumption of fraud and undue influence if the lawyer who drafts the instrument receives a donative transfer under its terms. Section 21380 includes important exceptions to the presumption, notably no disqualification if the transferor is related by blood or marriage to, or cohabits with, the drafting lawyer. In the absence of an applicable exception, the presumption of fraud and undue influence is conclusive with respect to the drafting lawyer or a person related to or affiliated with the drafting lawyer. In addition, California Business and Professions Code section 6103.6 provides that a violation of section 21380 is grounds for discipline, if the lawyer knew or should have known of the facts leading to the violation.

In light of this legislation and developing case law, and in consideration of other ethical duties in the Rules of Professional Conduct, the drafting lawyer who is named as fiduciary must consider the following potential issues:

1. Whether by self-nominating in the document the lawyer violates rule 1.8.1 of the Rules of Professional Conduct governing when and how the lawyer may enter into a business transaction with the client;
2. Whether the lawyer, if named as sole trustee, is likely to face a petition by the beneficiaries to remove the trustee under Probate Code section 15642, subdivision (b)(6);
3. Whether the lawyer, if assuming the fiduciary role during the lifetime of the client, can perform the duties of a fiduciary and at the same time fulfill the lawyer's ethical duties of loyalty and confidentiality to the client;
4. Whether the lawyer, if assuming or continuing the fiduciary role after the death of the client, will have potential future conflicts of interest that impair the lawyer's independent judgment in a dispute arising between the lawyer, as fiduciary, and beneficiaries whom the lawyer represented in the past;
5. Whether the lawyer, if assuming or continuing the fiduciary role after the death of the client, can preserve client confidentiality because the lawyer obtained confidential information from one or more beneficiaries in a prior representation; and
6. Whether the lawyer be adequately compensated as fiduciary given the restrictions on dual compensation in the Probate Code.

Despite the absence of an outright prohibition, most commentators take the position that a lawyer should avoid the practice of routinely naming himself or herself as fiduciary because this practice creates an appearance of impropriety and unprofessionalism. Nevertheless, in certain cases the lawyer may be the logical and appropriate choice.

Drawing a document that directs a fiduciary to retain the drafting lawyer as counsel involves essentially the same ethical issues as the appointment of the drafting lawyer as fiduciary. Before drawing such a document, the drafting lawyer should advise the client that it is neither necessary nor customary to include such a direction in a will or trust. A client who wishes to include such a direction in a document should be advised that under California law such a direction is not enforceable. The fiduciary is free to select and retain counsel of the fiduciary's own choice without regard to such a direction.

ACTEC Commentaries on Model Rules of Professional Conduct, Rule 1.7

> *Selection of Fiduciaries*. The lawyer advising a client regarding the selection and appointment of a fiduciary should make full disclosure to the client of any benefits that the lawyer may receive as a result of the appointment. In particular, the lawyer should inform the client of any policies or practices known to the lawyer that the fiduciaries under consideration may follow with respect to the employment of the scrivener of an estate planning document as counsel for the fiduciary. The lawyer may also point out that a fiduciary has the right to choose any counsel it wishes. If there is a significant risk that the lawyer's independent professional judgment in the selection of a fiduciary would be materially limited by the lawyer's self-interest or any other factor, the lawyer must obtain the client's informed consent, confirmed in writing. If the client is selecting a fiduciary that is affiliated with the lawyer, such as a trust company owned by the lawyer's firm, the lawyer must obtain the client's informed consent, confirmed in writing.

Cases

The court invalidated a $5 million donative transfer to a lawyer and removed the lawyer as trustee of a revocable trust. The lawyer drafted and transcribed the will and trust for personal enrichment. *Butler v. Lebouef* (2016) 248 Cal.App.4th 198.

A provision in a will directing employment of a particular lawyer by the fiduciary was not enforceable. *Estate of Ogier* (1894) 101 Cal. 381.

5.12 Lawyer Acting as Fiduciary

At times, a client may ask to name the drafting lawyer as successor trustee, executor, or agent under a power of attorney because the client has no one else to name. The drafting lawyer should consider declining such a nomination, due to the inherent conflicts of interest. Even if the selection of the drafting lawyer as fiduciary represents the client's free and informed decision, conflicts of interest may prove troublesome and render the appointment inadvisable. Depending upon the lawyer's prior relationship with the client, the client's family, or the beneficiaries of the trust or estate, appointment as a fiduciary may place the lawyer in a potential conflict with a former or current client. The lawyer must evaluate these issues not only at the time that the nomination is made, but also prior to acceptance of the appointment.

Two cases in which actual or potential conflicts are most troublesome are when the lawyer serves as trustee of the client's revocable trust; and when the lawyer serves as conservator for the client.

Lawyer Serving as Trustee of the Client's Revocable Trust. The lawyer who serves as trustee of a revocable trust may have interests adverse to the client during the client's lifetime. In that case, the lawyer must resign because rule 1.9 of the Rules of Professional Conduct prohibits the lawyer from accepting employment adverse to a client or former client when the lawyer obtained confidential information material to the employment by virtue of the prior lawyer-client relationship. In another example, the trustee-lawyer may have interests adverse to the surviving spouse, who was also a client of the lawyer, in the management of a trust created by the now deceased spouse. Again, the lawyer probably must resign because of the prohibition of rule 1.9 of the Rules of Professional Conduct since confidential information obtained while the lawyer was representing the couple is likely to be material to the lawyer's later employment as trustee.

Probate Code section 15642, subdivision (b)(6) provides that a person described in subdivision (a) of section 21380 who is acting as sole trustee may be removed by the court, upon petition by the beneficiaries or upon its own motion. That section applies to a drafting lawyer regardless of whether the lawyer receives a donative gift. The drafting lawyer who acts as sole trustee is subject to removal unless the court finds that the appointment is consistent with the settlor's intent and was not the product of fraud, menace, duress, or undue influence. Consequently, faced with the prospect of a battle to remove the lawyer as sole trustee and the difficulties of proving the settlor's intent, many lawyers have a policy of refusing to serve as sole trustee except in limited narrow circumstances.

The client may not waive the provisions of Probate Code section 15642, subdivision (b)(6) in a trust instrument or will. No disclosures or consent by the client will negate the power of the trust beneficiaries to remove the trustee under that statute. Similarly, any attempt by the testator to confer on the testator's lawyer the right to receive compensation as both trustee and lawyer may be subject to court review and not approved.

Removal under section 15642, subdivision (b)(6) may be avoided if the instrument is reviewed by an independent lawyer who certifies that the conditions under that section are satisfied. These provisions authorizing the use of a certificate of independent review are modeled on the provisions of Probate Code section 21384 regarding donative transfers to the drafting lawyer. A lawyer who is engaged to provide a certificate of independent review is not deemed to otherwise represent the client. Prob. Code, sec. 21385. For a discussion of the ethical duties related to the preparation of a certificate of independent review, see chapter 4 of this Guide, Identifying the Client and the Scope of the Representation, section 4.9.

Lawyer Serving as Conservator. The lawyer serving as conservator faces ethical dilemmas at two stages: at the time of the appointment and then during the ongoing administration of the conservatorship. If the proposed conservatee does not object to the lawyer's appointment, no ethical duties prohibit the lawyer assuming that role. If, however, the proposed conservatee client expresses any opposition to the appointment of the lawyer as conservator, the lawyer may not serve because the lawyer may not accept employment adverse to a current or former client. Even if the appointment is made without objection by the client conservatee, the lawyer must watch for conflicts that arise in the future. In the event there is a dispute, the lawyer must consider the propriety of remaining as conservator, and may not do so if the conservator's duties require actions adverse to the client.

Dual Compensation. In California, without prior court approval, the lawyer-fiduciary is not entitled to compensation for legal services in addition to fiduciary fees. In the case of a trust, timely notice to the beneficiaries can be substituted for court approval. The testator or settlor cannot waive this prohibition in the trust or will that names or appoints the fiduciary.

A lawyer serving as conservator or executor is also precluded from dual compensation. The court may not approve such dual compensation unless it finds that it is to the advantage, benefit, and best interest of the conservatee under Probate Code section 2645, subdivision (c) or to the advantage, benefit, and best interest of the decedent's estate under Probate Code section 10804. Unless the lawyer presents adequate evidence that the client was properly informed of the costs of the arrangement and the available alternatives, such a provision creates the appearance of impropriety and the court is not likely to approve dual compensation. For these reasons alone, it may be more practical for the lawyer-conservator or lawyer-executor to hire other legal counsel.

While it is inadvisable for a lawyer to accept appointment as a fiduciary on a routine basis, the lawyer may be the most appropriate choice in certain circumstances. In these instances, the lawyer who drafts the instrument should be allowed to accept appointment as a fiduciary provided the client is adequately informed, the appointment is not the result of any undue influence exerted by the lawyer, and the appointment does not violate the conflict of interest rules. In those cases, the lawyer must be aware of the serious restrictions on dual compensation and be prepared either to accept those restrictions or take the action necessary to obtain court or beneficiary approval of a greater amount.

Statute

California Probate Code section 15642, subdivision (b)(6)

> (b) The grounds for removal of a trustee by the court include the following:
>
> . . .
>
> (6) Where the sole trustee is a person described in subdivision (a) of Section 21350 or subdivision (a) of Section 21380, whether or not the person is the transferee of a donative transfer by the transferor, unless, based upon any evidence of the intent of the settlor and all other facts and circumstances, which shall be made known to the court, the court finds that it is consistent with the settlor's intent that the trustee continue to serve and that this intent was not the product of fraud or undue influence. Any waiver by the settlor of this provision is against public policy and shall be void. This paragraph shall not apply to

instruments that became irrevocable on or before January 1, 1994. This paragraph shall not apply if any of the following conditions are met:

(A) The settlor is related by blood or marriage to, or is a cohabitant with, any one or more of the trustees, the person who drafted or transcribed the instrument, or the person who caused the instrument to be transcribed.

(B) The instrument is reviewed by an independent attorney who (1) counsels the settlor about the nature of his or her intended trustee designation and (2) signs and delivers to the settlor and the designated trustee a certificate in substantially the following form:

"CERTIFICATE OF INDEPENDENT REVIEW

I, ____, have reviewed

(attorney's name)

_______________________________________, and have counseled my client,

(name of instrument)

_____________________________________, fully and privately on the nature

(name of client)

and legal effect of the designation as trustee of ______________________________

(name of trustee)

contained in that instrument. I am so disassociated from the interest of the person named as trustee as to be in a position to advise my client impartially and confidentially as to the consequences of the designation. On the basis of this counsel, I conclude that the designation of a person who would otherwise be subject to removal under paragraph (6) of subdivision (b) of Section 15642 of the Probate Code is clearly the settlor's intent and that intent is not the product of fraud * * * or undue influence.

_________________________________ _______________________

(name of attorney) (date)"

This independent review and certification may occur either before or after the instrument has been executed, and if it occurs after the date of execution, the named trustee shall not be subject to removal under this paragraph. Any attorney whose written engagement signed by the client is expressly limited to the preparation of a certificate under this subdivision, including the prior counseling, shall not be considered to otherwise represent the client.

(C) After full disclosure of the relationships of the persons involved, the instrument is approved pursuant to an order under Article 10 (commencing with Section 2580) of Chapter 6 of Part 4 of Division 4.

California Probate Code section 15687

(a) Notwithstanding any provision of a trust to the contrary, a trustee who is an attorney may receive only (1) the trustee's compensation provided in the trust or otherwise provided in this article or (2) compensation for legal services performed for the trustee, unless the trustee obtains approval for the right to dual compensation as provided in subdivision (d).

(b) No parent, child, sibling, or spouse of a person who is a trustee, and no law partnership or corporation whose partner, shareholder, or employee is serving as a trustee shall receive any compensation for legal services performed for the trustee unless the trustee waives trustee compensation or unless the trustee obtains approval for the right to dual compensation as provided in subdivision (d).

(c) This section shall not apply if the trustee is related by blood or marriage to, or is a cohabitant with, the settlor.

(d) After full disclosure of the nature of the compensation and relationship of the trustee to all persons receiving compensation under this section, the trustee may obtain approval for dual compensation by either of the following:

(1) An order pursuant to paragraph (21) of subdivision(b) of Section 17200.

(2) Giving 30 days' advance written notice to the persons entitled to notice under Section 17203. Within that 30-day period, any person entitled to notice may object to the proposed action by written notice to the trustee or by filing a petition pursuant to paragraph (21) of subdivision (b) of Section 17200. If the trustee receives this objection during that 30-day period and if the trustee wishes dual compensation, the trustee shall file a petition for approval pursuant to paragraph (21) of subdivision (b) of Section 17200.

(e) Any waiver of the requirements of this section is against public policy and shall be void.

(f) This section applies to services rendered on or after January 1, 1994.

California Business and Professions Code section 6103.6. Violation of Certain Probate Code Provisions as Grounds for Discipline

Violation of Section 15687 of the California Probate Code, or of Part 3.5 (commencing with Section 21350) or of Part 3.7 (commencing with Section 21360) of Division 11 of the Probate Code, shall be grounds for discipline, if the attorney knew or should have known of the facts leading to the violation. This section shall only apply to violations that occur on or after January 1, 1994.

Cases

The Court of Appeal upheld the trial court's application of a presumption of undue influence based on the existence of a lawyer-client relationship. *In Re Estate of Auen* (1994) 30 Cal.App.4th 300. See section 5.13 of this chapter, Donative Transfers Presumed to the Product of Fraud or Undue Influence.

The lawyer violated former rule 5-101 of the Rules of Professional Conduct (now rule 1.8.1 of the Rules of Professional Conduct) in drafting documents that named the lawyer as successor trustee with the power to make self-dealing loans. The lawyer did not adequately disclose the import of the self-dealing provision to the clients, did not advise them in writing of their right to independent counsel, and did not secure their consent in writing. *Schneider v. State Bar* (1987) 43 Cal.3d 784.

Ethics Opinion

Under the Model Rules of Professional Conduct, a lawyer may accept appointment as a personal representative or trustee named in a will or trust the lawyer is preparing for a client, subject to complying with model rule 1.4(b) and, in some circumstances, with model rule 1.7(b). ABA Com. on Ethics and Prof. Resp., formal opn. No. 2002-426, Lawyer Serving as Fiduciary for an Estate or Trust.

Articles

Kohlmann & Scharre, *Both Attorney & Trustee: Doubling Down or a Bad Bet?* (2019) 25 Cal. Trusts and Estates Q., Issue 3.

Johnstone & House, *California Conservatorships and Guardianships*, sec. 1.76 (Cont.Ed.Bar., rev. 2003). The authors discuss the conflicts of interest inherent in the lawyer serving as conservator for a former client.

Avery, *The Role of the Attorney in Estate Planning*, 1 Estate Planning Prac., sec. 1.19(c) (Cont.Ed.Bar. 1995).

5.13 Donative Transfers Presumed to be the Product of Fraud or Undue Influence

California Rules of Professional Conduct, Rule 1.8.3 - Gifts from Client

(a) A lawyer shall not:

(1) solicit a client to make a substantial* gift, including a testamentary gift, to the lawyer or a person* related to the lawyer, unless the lawyer or other recipient of the gift is related to the client, or

(2) prepare on behalf of a client an instrument giving the lawyer or a person* related to the lawyer any substantial* gift, unless (i) the lawyer or other recipient of the gift is related to the client, or (ii) the client has been advised by an independent lawyer who has provided a certificate of independent review that complies with the requirements of Probate Code section 21384.

(b) For purposes of this rule, related persons* include a person* who is "related by blood or affinity" as that term is defined in California Probate Code section 21374, subdivision (a).

An asterisk (*) identifies a defined term in rule 1.0.1 of the Rules of Professional Conduct. For further discussion of a defined term, see chapter 2 of this Guide, Terminology.

It is a breach of rule 1.8.3 of the Rules of Professional Conduct for a lawyer to induce a client to make a substantial gift to the lawyer unless the lawyer and client are related by blood or marriage. Furthermore, under Probate Code section 21380, a donative transfer to a lawyer who drafts an instrument, transcribes an instrument, or causes an instrument to be transcribed is presumed to be the product of fraud or undue influence if the instrument makes a donative transfer to (1) the lawyer; (2) a person related by blood or affinity within the third degree to the lawyer; (3) a cohabitant or employee of the lawyer; or (4) a partner, shareholder, or employee of a law firm in which the lawyer has an ownership interest.

The presumption does not apply, under Probate Code section 21382, however, to any of the following instruments or transfers: (1) the lawyer is related by blood or affinity, within the fourth degree, to the transferor or is the transferor's cohabitant; (2) the instrument is drafted or transcribed by a person who is related by blood or affinity, within the fourth degree, to the transferor or is the transferor's cohabitant; (3) the court approves the instrument on a petition for substituted judgment under Probate Code section 2580 after full disclosure of the relationships of the persons involved; (4) the value of the transferred property is $5,000 or less, if the total value of the transferor's estate equals or exceeds the amount stated in Probate Code section 13100; or (5) the instrument was executed outside California by a transferor who was not a California resident when the instrument was executed. If the provisions of Probate Code section 21380 invalidate the gift to the lawyer or those related to the lawyer as described above, the lawyer may be subject to discipline if the lawyer knew or should have known of the facts leading to the violation. Bus. & Prof. Code, sec. 6103.6.

Preparing a Certificate of Independent Review. The preparation of a certificate of independent review should not give rise to the ethical duty to avoid conflicting interests because the reviewing lawyer has a single client. The drafting lawyer may prepare a certificate if the gift is to a care custodian as defined in Probate Code section 21380, subdivision (a)(3). In all other circumstances, however, only a second lawyer may prepare the certificate. Prob. Code, sec. 21384, subd. (c). The lawyer who performs the review and signs the certificate will likely be called to testify if a beneficiary, heir, or other third party later challenges the drafted instrument after the client dies.

Whether the certificate is prepared by the drafting lawyer in the case of a gift to a care custodian or a reviewing lawyer in the case of all other presumptively invalid gifts, the reviewing lawyer must be independent, defined by reference to the beneficiary of the gift. The reviewing lawyer must have no legal, business, financial, professional, or personal relationship with the beneficiary of a donative transfer at issue. In addition, the reviewing lawyer is not independent if the instrument names the reviewing lawyer as a fiduciary or if the reviewing lawyer receives any pecuniary benefit other than payment for services rendered in connection with preparing the certificate. Prob. Code, sec. 21370.

The reviewing lawyer must counsel the client, out of the presence of any heir or proposed beneficiary, about the nature and consequences of the intended transfer, including the effect of the intended transfer on the client's heirs and on any beneficiary of a prior donative instrument. Prob. Code, sec. 21384, subd. (a). If the reviewing lawyer is unable to certify that the intended transfer is not the product of fraud or undue influence, the reviewing lawyer should consider recommending to the client other ways in which the client may be able to achieve the client's objective. Among the alternatives are establishing a conservatorship proceeding for purposes of obtaining an order of substituted judgment under Probate Code section 2580, an order authorizing a particular transaction under Probate Code section 3100, giving a trusted family member a power to appoint property to a care custodian, or giving a trusted family member an asset coupled with a precatory request that the family member gift the asset to the care custodian.

Former California Rules of Professional Conduct, Rule 4-400 - Gifts from Client

> A member shall not induce a client to make a substantial gift, including a testamentary gift, to the member or to the member's parent, child, sibling, or spouse, except where the client is related to the member.

Cases

Gift to a drafting lawyer and family in a trust instrument was invalidated because a certificate of independent review was not prepared by an independent lawyer. Probate Code section 21384 includes an "independent attorney" requirement that applied retroactively. *Schwan v. Permann* (2018) 28 Cal.App.5th 678, 698.

Reversing the trial court's grant of a motion for summary judgment regarding an instrument that was irrevocable before 2011, the Court of Appeal held that triable issues of fact existed regarding the certificate of independent review. The reviewing lawyer failed to adequately counsel the client about the nature and consequences of the testamentary gift to a care custodian under Probate Code section 21351, subdivision (b) because no evidence showed that the lawyer discussed with the client the decision to exclude the client's nieces and nephews from a contemplated will or even that the reviewing lawyer was fully aware of the natural objects of the client's bounty. Nor did the evidence show that the lawyer counseled the client confidentially because other persons were present during the counseling who were not necessary to accomplish the counseling. Finally, the reviewing lawyer was not independent within the meaning of Probate Code section 21351 because the instrument at issue designated the reviewing lawyer as executor and because the reviewing lawyer shared an office with the drafter. *Estate of Winans* (2010) 183 Cal.App.4th 102.

A handyman who helped an elderly widow with bills, bookkeeping, and taxes and had a fiduciary relationship with her was not a disqualified person under Probate Code section 21350 because he neither transcribed nor caused to be transcribed the will and the instruments making inter vivos gifts to him and his wife. *Rice v. Clark* (2002) 28 Cal.4th 89.

Ethics Opinion

The signatory of a will is the drafting lawyer's client, regardless of who initially retains the lawyer and pays the lawyer's fees. When a child, who is the proposed beneficiary of the parent's will, asks the lawyer to prepare the will, the lawyer must be assured that the proposed document is made with the true consent of the person who will sign the document; that the client is competent; that the client is not acting under undue influence; and the lawyer must clarify who is the client and disclose potential conflicts in writing and obtain written consents from the mutual clients (parent and child) before proceeding further. The lawyer should have an extended interview with the client outside the presence of interested parties and should keep a detailed and complete record of the interview. San Diego County Bar Assn., Ethics opn. No. 1990-3.

5.14 Conflicts of Interest: Former Clients

California Rules of Professional Conduct, Rule 1.9 - Duties to Former Clients

(a) A lawyer who has formerly represented a client in a matter shall not thereafter represent another person* in the same or a substantially related matter in which that person's* interests are materially adverse to the interests of the former client unless the former client gives informed written consent.*

(b) A lawyer shall not knowingly* represent a person* in the same or a substantially related matter in which a firm* with which the lawyer formerly was associated had previously represented a client

(1) whose interests are materially adverse to that person;* and

(2) about whom the lawyer had acquired information protected by Business and Professions Code section 6068, subdivision (e) and rules 1.6 and 1.9(c) that is material to the matter; unless the former client gives informed written consent.*

(c) A lawyer who has formerly represented a client in a matter or whose present or former firm* has formerly represented a client in a matter shall not thereafter:

(1) use information protected by Business and Professions Code section 6068, subdivision (e) and rule 1.6 acquired by virtue of the representation of the former client to the disadvantage of the former client except as these rules or the State Bar Act would permit with respect to a current client, or when the information has become generally known;* or

(2) reveal information protected by Business and Professions Code section 6068, subdivision (e) and rule 1.6 acquired by virtue of the representation of the former

client except as these rules or the State Bar Act permit with respect to a current client.

An asterisk (*) identifies a defined term in rule 1.0.1 of the Rules of Professional Conduct. For further discussion of a defined term, see chapter 2 of this Guide, Terminology.

Rule 1.9 of the Rules of Professional Conduct prescribes the ongoing duties that a lawyer owes to a client after the current representation terminates. The interests of a former client protected by rule 1.9 differ from the interests of current clients protected by rule 1.7. Rule 1.7 requires the informed written consent of current clients whose interests are *directly* adverse. Rule 1.9 requires the informed written consent of a former client whose interests are *materially* adverse to those of a successive or prospective client. The requirement of materiality in rule 1.9 of the Rules of Professional Conduct is consistent with California case law that the ethical duties owed to a former client are only implicated in substantially related matters. *City Nat. Bank v. Adams* (2002) 96 Cal.App.4th 315, 324.

Rule 1.9 of the Rules of Professional Conduct also protects the confidentiality of information received during the representation of a former client, and materiality is again the governing standard. A lawyer is prohibited from taking a representation in the same or a substantially related matter if confidential information received from a former client is *material* to that matter. Even if the two matters are not so closely related, the lawyer may not reveal any confidential information obtained in the former representation or use that information to the detriment of the former client. Rules Prof. Conduct, rule 1.8.2. For a further discussion of the ethical duty of confidentiality to former clients, see chapter 6 of this Guide, Confidentiality of Information, section 6.4.

Determining when an engagement for estate planning or a trust administration terminates is not always clear. When the representation is for a specific and limited matter, such as an estate or trust administration or litigation of a disputed accounting, the completion of the matter normally results in the termination of the lawyer-client relationship. However, the preparation of estate plan documents may not be so limited. Either the lawyer or the client may believe that the relationship continues, and thus the estate planning client continues to be a client of the lawyer even if their contact is sporadic or even dormant. In some cases, the lawyer or the client may specifically terminate the representation after completion of the estate plan by giving notice to the other. The lawyer's duties are then governed by rule 1.9 of the Rules of Professional Conduct regarding former clients. For a further discussion of ethical duties after a representation terminates, see chapter 7 of this Guide, Communication, section 7.7.

For example, if a lawyer assists a client in establishing a trust, the lawyer cannot later represent a creditor in challenging the validity of the trust or attempting to reach its assets. Similarly, if a lawyer represents both spouses on estate planning matters, and they later divorce, the original lawyer cannot continue to represent one of the spouses in changing the estate plan unless the other spouse consents. The interests of the spouses are materially adverse because the estate plan is being changed, and the lawyer will have obtained confidential information from both spouses concerning their assets and other matters relating to the estate plan.

Some experienced estate planners who represent both spouses on estate planning matters will decline to represent either spouse while a divorce is pending, even if both are separately represented in the divorce proceeding, and will only represent one of the former spouses in changing their estate plan after the dissolution is completed if they both consent.

Departure from a Firm. A lawyer's departure from a law firm implicates specific ethical duties on both the departing lawyer and the firm regarding conflicts of interest. Cal. State Bar Com. on Prof. Responsibility and Conduct, formal opn. No. 2020-201. A detailed conflicts check must be conducted with respect to the departing lawyer's client relationships and those of a new firm that the departing lawyer will join. Such a comprehensive inquiry should bring to light whether any of the departing lawyer's clients have conflicts of interest with the new firm, and whether the current, and sometimes former, client relationships of the departing lawyer may be adverse to the interests or affect the representation of clients at the new firm. The new firm also should consider whether any screening protocols should be implemented once the departing lawyer joins and whether there are potential conflicts with respect to prospective clients, as set forth in rule 1.18 of the Rules of Professional Conduct. For a further discussion of appropriate ethical screening, see rule 1.0.1(k) of the Rules of Professional Conduct and chapter 2 of this Guide, Terminology.

During all phases of any transition or departure, the departing lawyer should be mindful of the ethical duty to protect client confidences. That duty is often implicated when a departing lawyer checks for conflicts of interest with a potential new law firm; it can also arise when a departing lawyer communicates with a new firm before, during, and after the departure. The tension between the duty of confidentiality and other ethical duties should be managed by every lawyer involved in the transition to protect and preserve confidential client information.

Comment on California Rules of Professional Conduct, Rule 1.9

> [1] After termination of a lawyer-client relationship, the lawyer owes two duties to a former client. The lawyer may not (i) do anything that will injuriously affect the former client in any matter in which the lawyer represented the former client, or (ii) at any time use against the former client knowledge or information acquired by virtue of the previous relationship. (See *Oasis West Realty, LLC v. Goldman* (2011) 51 Cal.4th 811 [124 Cal.Rptr.3d 256]; *Wutchumna Water Co. v. Bailey* (1932) 216 Cal. 564 [15 P.2d 505].) For example, (i) a lawyer could not properly seek to rescind on behalf of new client a contract drafted on behalf of the former client and (ii) a lawyer who has prosecuted an accused person* could not represent the accused in a subsequent civil action against the government concerning the same matter. (See also Bus. and Prof. Code, sec. 6131; 18 U.S.C. sec. 207(a).) These duties exist to preserve a client's trust in the lawyer and to encourage the client's candor in communications with the lawyer.
>
> [2] For what constitutes a "matter" for purposes of this rule, see rule 1.7(e).
>
> [3] Two matters are "the same or substantially related" for purposes of this rule if they involve a substantial* risk of violation of one of the two duties to a former client described above in Comment [1]. For example, this will occur: (i) if the

matters involve the same transaction or legal dispute or other work performed by the lawyer for the former client; or (ii) if the lawyer normally would have obtained information in the prior representation that is protected by Business and Professions Code section 6068, subdivision (e) and rule 1.6, and the lawyer would be expected to use or disclose that information in the subsequent representation because it is material to the subsequent representation.

[4] Paragraph (b) addresses a lawyer's duties to a client who has become a former client because the lawyer no longer is associated with the law firm* that represents or represented the client. In that situation, the lawyer has a conflict of interest only when the lawyer involved has actual knowledge of information protected by Business and Professions Code section 6068, subdivision (e) and rules 1.6 and 1.9(c). Thus, if a lawyer while with one firm* acquired no knowledge or information relating to a particular client of the firm,* and that lawyer later joined another firm,* neither the lawyer individually nor lawyers in the second firm* would violate this rule by representing another client in the same or a related matter even though the interests of the two clients conflict. See rule 1.10(b) for the restrictions on lawyers in a firm* once a lawyer has terminated association with the firm.*

Former California Rules of Professional Conduct, Rule 3-310(E) – Avoiding the Representation of Adverse Interests

(E) A member shall not, without the informed written consent of the client or former client, accept employment adverse to the client or former client where, by reason of the representation of the client or former client, the member has obtained confidential information material to the employment.

Cases

The lawyers who formulated the spouses' estate plan were disqualified from representing the marital trust in a tax dispute. The dispute arose after the death of the surviving spouse and concerned the apportionment of estate tax to the marital trust under the terms of the governing instrument. The trustees did not dispute that the lawyers' prior representation of the spouse was direct in nature and substantially related to the current tax dispute. In such a directly related matter, the sharing of confidential information was presumed without further inquiry as to whether it was in fact received. The court ordered the entry of motion allowing disqualification of the lawyers for the trustees. *Fiduciary Trust Internat. of Cal. v. Super. Ct.* (2013) 218 Cal.App.4th 465, 481 (citing *Brand v. 20th Century Ins. Co./21st Century Ins. Co.* (2004) 124 Cal.App.4th 594, 607.)

The court cited with approval the American Law Institute definition of substantially related matters: Matters are substantially related if "(1) the current matter involves work a lawyer performed for the former client; or (2) there is a substantial risk that representation of the present client will involve the use of information acquired in the course of representing the former client…." An exception to the substantial relationship rule may apply in unusual cases, upon a showing that there was no opportunity for confidential information to be divulged. But this exception was not available when the clients were on opposite sides of the same matter. *City Nat. Bank v. Adams* (2002) 96 Cal.App.4th 315, 324, fn. 2.

The Supreme Court distinguished simultaneous representation from successive representation of two clients with adverse interests. The court held that there was no malpractice when the conflict of interest related to a *simultaneous* representation of clients with adverse interests. In such cases, the chief fiduciary value in jeopardy is that of client loyalty. That duty requires that the lawyer withdraw from the new representation as soon as the conflict is discovered; the lawyer has no duty and in fact is prohibited from advising the new client. In contrast, the ethical conflict arises in *successive* representations only if there is a substantial relationship between the subject matters in the two cases. The lawyer's primary duty to a former client is of confidentiality. If the former and new matter are substantially related then access to confidential information in the course of the first representation is "presumed," and disqualification of the lawyer's representation of the second client is mandatory. *Flatt v. Super. Ct.* (1994) 9 Cal.4th 275, 289.

In a successive representation is successive, a lawyer cannot accept or continue representing one client without consent of the former client if the lawyer received confidential information from the former client that is material to the current engagement. If a substantial relationship exists between the former representation and the current representation, then it will be presumed that the lawyer obtained confidential information related to the current matter and the lawyer must withdraw. Under the facts of this case, knowledge of each lawyer was imputed to all other members of the firm. The imputation of confidential information also extended to all lawyers who were of counsel to the firm because clients would expect that client information would be shared between the firm lawyers and the of counsel lawyer. *People ex rel. Dept of Corporations v. SpeeDee Oil Change Systems* (1999) 20 Cal.4th 1135, 1154-1156. Imputation of conflicts of interest among members of a law firm is now prescribed under Rules of Professional Conduct, rule 1.10.

Ethics Opinion

The client's right to counsel of the client's choice and the protection of the client's best interests are the ethical principles that should guide any lawyer departure from a law firm. The departing lawyer and law firm each have ethical obligations related to the departure and must prioritize their ethical obligations to clients over their own competing interests. These ethical obligations include properly notifying relevant clients of the departure, protecting client confidences, addressing conflicts of interests with clients, ensuring that clients continue to have competent representation, and avoiding reasonably foreseeable prejudice to the rights of clients during any changes in the representation. Both the departing lawyer and firm have a duty to cooperate in the transition of any client matter. State Bar of Cal. Com. on Prof. Resp. and Conduct, formal opn. No. 2020-201.

5.15 Sample Client Letter – Termination of Representation

The following explanation could be adapted for inclusion in a letter to a client-fiduciary terminating the representation when the trust administration is substantially complete. That letter would also advise the client of any closing matters that remain for the client's attention. The lawyer should adapt it thoughtfully to the lawyer's customary practice and the needs of a particular client representation.

Dear [Client],

You retained me to represent you as trustee of the [Name of Trust] and to advise you on the administration of the trust in accordance with your fiduciary duties. The written consent of all the beneficiaries to your final account concludes this engagement and our lawyer-client relationship. You should retain a sufficient reserve for the costs of making distribution to the beneficiaries, closing the trust financial accounts, and filing federal and California fiduciary income tax returns. As trustee, you have responsibility for filing final income tax returns for the trust. After you file those returns, you must send the beneficiaries a summary of the expenses paid from the reserve and distribute the balance.

If you need my services in the future, please feel free to contact me and renew our relationship. In the meantime, I will not take any further action with reference to your affairs unless and until I hear otherwise from you.

Sincerely,
[Lawyer]

5.16 Imputation of Conflicts of Interest: Client Representation

California Rules of Professional Conduct, Rule 1.10 - Imputation of Conflicts of Interest: General Rule

(a) While lawyers are associated in a firm,* none of them shall knowingly* represent a client when any one of them practicing alone would be prohibited from doing so by rules 1.7 or 1.9, unless:

(1) the prohibition is based on a personal interest of the prohibited lawyer and does not present a significant risk of materially limiting the representation of the client by the remaining lawyers in the firm;* or

(2) the prohibition is based upon rule 1.9(a) or (b) and arises out of the prohibited lawyer's association with a prior firm,* and

(i) the prohibited lawyer did not substantially participate in the same or a substantially related matter;

(ii) the prohibited lawyer is timely screened* from any participation in the matter and is apportioned no part of the fee therefrom; and

(iii) written* notice is promptly given to any affected former client to enable the former client to ascertain compliance with the provisions of this rule, which shall include a description of the screening* procedures employed;

and an agreement by the firm* to respond promptly to any written* inquiries or objections by the former client about the screening* procedures.

(b) When a lawyer has terminated an association with a firm,* the firm* is not prohibited from thereafter representing a person* with interests materially adverse to those of a client represented by the formerly associated lawyer and not currently represented by the firm,* unless:

(1) the matter is the same or substantially related to that in which the formerly associated lawyer represented the client; and

(2) any lawyer remaining in the firm* has information protected by Business and Professions Code section 6068, subdivision (e) and rules 1.6 and 1.9(c) that is material to the matter.

(c) A prohibition under this rule may be waived by each affected client under the conditions stated in rule 1.7.

(d) The imputation of a conflict of interest to lawyers associated in a firm* with former or current government lawyers is governed by rule 1.11.

An asterisk (*) identifies a defined term in rule 1.0.1 of the Rules of Professional Conduct. For further discussion of a defined term, see chapter 2 of this Guide, Terminology.

Rule 1.10 of the Rules of Professional Conduct specifies the imputation of conflicts of interest among the lawyers associated in a firm. Imputation tracks the same ethical issues of the materiality of adverse interests and substantial relationship of the former and current client matters that are the subject of the representations.

Lawyers within a firm may have current or former clients with conflicts of interest, or conflicts may arise when a lawyer moves from one firm to another. The confidential information acquired by the lawyer in the course of a representation is imputed to the law firm as a whole, creating a conflict of interest even though different lawyers represent the various clients. Rule 1.10(b)(2) of the Rules of Professional Conduct limits imputation after a lawyer leaves a firm to substantially related matters in which the departing lawyer formerly represented the client. In addition, imputation is required if the remaining lawyers have received confidential information material to the new matter. Conflicts checks after termination require evaluation from the perspective of both the lawyer who departs the firm and the lawyers who remain.

Screening and Ethical Walls. When a lawyer joins a new firm, the presence of the new lawyer should not create a conflict for the existing lawyers if the new lawyer can be properly screened from the representation. In some cases, however, such an ethical screen may not be possible, either because of the nature of the proceeding involved, or because of the nature of the relationship of the lawyer to the firm as a whole. In *City and County of San Francisco v. Cobra Solutions, Inc.* (2006) 38 Cal.4th 839, the court found that when a lawyer previously engaged in private practice representing a client was later hired as the head of a government office, the entire office was conflicted out of a representation that was adverse to that former client because the new lawyer was in a policy-making position for the entire office.

As with other conflicts, an informed written consent can be effective to permit the firm to accept or continue the representation and may be appropriate in some cases. For a further discussion of appropriate ethical screening, see rule 1.0.1(k) of the Rules of Professional Conduct and chapter 2 of this Guide.

Comment on California Rules of Professional Conduct, Rule 1.10

> [1] In determining whether a prohibited lawyer's previous participation was substantial,* a number of factors should be considered, such as the lawyer's level of responsibility in the prior matter, the duration of the lawyer's participation, the extent to which the lawyer advised or had personal contact with the former client, and the extent to which the lawyer was exposed to confidential information of the former client likely to be material in the current matter.
>
> [2] Paragraph (a) does not prohibit representation by others in the law firm* where the person* prohibited from involvement in a matter is a nonlawyer, such as a paralegal or legal secretary. Nor does paragraph (a) prohibit representation if the lawyer is prohibited from acting because of events before the person* became a lawyer, for example, work that the person* did as a law student. Such persons,* however, ordinarily must be screened* from any personal participation in the matter. (See rules 1.0.1(k) and 5.3.)
>
> [3] Paragraph (a)(2)(ii) does not prohibit the screened* lawyer from receiving a salary or partnership share established by prior independent agreement, but that lawyer may not receive compensation directly related to the matter in which the lawyer is prohibited.
>
> [4] Where a lawyer is prohibited from engaging in certain transactions under rules 1.8.1 through 1.8.9, rule 1.8.11, and not this rule, determines whether that prohibition also applies to other lawyers associated in a firm* with the personally prohibited lawyer.
>
> [5] The responsibilities of managerial and supervisory lawyers prescribed by rules 5.1 and 5.3 apply to screening* arrangements implemented under this rule.
>
> [6] Standards for disqualification, and whether in a particular matter (1) a lawyer's conflict will be imputed to other lawyers in the same firm,* or (2) the use of a timely screen* is effective to avoid that imputation, are also the subject of statutes and case law. (See, e.g., Code Civ. Proc., sec. 128, subd. (a)(5); Pen. Code, sec. 1424; *In re Charlisse C.* (2008) 45 Cal.4th 145 [84 Cal.Rptr.3d 597]; *Rhaburn v. Superior Court* (2006) 140 Cal.App.4th 1566 [45 Cal.Rptr.3d 464]; *Kirk v. First American Title Ins. Co.* (2010) 183 Cal.App.4th 776 [108 Cal.Rptr.3d 620].)

Cases

The trial court, on remand, was required to engage in factual analysis before exercising its discretion to disqualify a law firm. "Automatically finding that [lawyer's] very short tenure at [law firm] is sufficient to impute knowledge to the entire firm, including attorneys working on the matter in a different office, places form over substance." *Cal. Self-Insurers' Security Fund v. Super. Ct.* (2018) 19 Cal.App.5th 1065.

A lawyer's receipt of confidential information as settlement officer would bar the lawyer's firm from representing the employer. *Castaneda v. Super. Ct.* (2015) 237 Cal.App.4th 1434.

Vicarious disqualification of an entire law firm based on the confidential information possessed by a lateral lawyer in a previous matter was not automatic but should be determined based on the facts of each case. An ethical wall around the "tainted" lawyer might be effective to rebut the presumption that client confidences are shared among lawyers in the same firm and so avoid disqualification of the entire law firm. This case has an extensive discussion of the development of the vicarious disqualification rule in California, and of policy considerations for allowing the presumption to be overcome. *Kirk v. First American Title Insurance Co.* (2010) 183 Cal.App.4th 776.

In a case involving a public law office, disqualification of the entire office was not automatically required when one unit previously represented the mother when a minor, and a different unit now represented the mother's minor child in a dependency proceeding, even though the two matters were substantially related. The trial court instead needed to determine whether the current lawyer obtained or would acquire confidential information concerning the prior representation. Special considerations limited vicarious disqualification in the context of a public law office. *In re Charlisse C.* (2008) 45 Cal.4th 145.

Ethics Opinion

A client's blanket waiver of the right to disqualify the lawyer in any other matter based on alleged breach of the lawyer's duty of confidentiality or duty to avoid conflicts of interest is not of itself ethically improper, but such a waiver may not be enforceable depending upon the circumstances existing when the waiver was signed and when an actual conflict of interest develops. In any event, such a waiver may not be asserted as a defense to a disciplinary proceeding charging incompetent performance nor may such a waiver be used to limit a lawyer's civil liability for malpractice. State Bar of Cal. Com. on Prof. Resp. and Conduct, formal opn. No. 1989-115.

5.17 Imputation of Conflicts of Interest: Personal Interests

California Rules of Professional Conduct, Rule 1.8.11 - Imputation of Prohibitions Under Rules 1.8.1 to 1.8.9

> While lawyers are associated in a law firm,* a prohibition in rules 1.8.1 through 1.8.9 that applies to any one of them shall apply to all of them.

An asterisk (*) identifies a defined term in rule 1.0.1 of the Rules of Professional Conduct. For further discussion of a defined term, see chapter 2 of this Guide, Terminology.

The Rules of Professional Conduct specify when conflicts of interest are imputed between a lawyer and the lawyer's firm. Rule 1.10 of the Rules of Professional Conduct imputes conflicts to all members of a lawyer's firm in representing current or former clients. Rule 1.8.11 imputes those conflicts that arise from a lawyer's personal interests or transactions with a client.

The pairing of these two rules requires that lawyers in a firm broaden the traditional conflicts check when undertaking a new representation, typically a review of all client matters that the firm has handled. Ethical and competent practice requires that lawyers in a firm disclose all transactions with a client described in rules 1.8.1 through 1.8.9 of the Rules of Professional Conduct so that those transactions can be incorporated into a future conflicts check.

Comment on California Rules of Professional Conduct, Rule 1.8.11

> A prohibition on conduct by an individual lawyer in rules 1.8.1 through 1.8.9 also applies to all lawyers associated in a law firm* with the personally prohibited lawyer. For example, one lawyer in a law firm* may not enter into a business transaction with a client of another lawyer associated in the law firm* without complying with rule 1.8.1, even if the first lawyer is not personally involved in the representation of the client. This rule does not apply to rule 1.8.10 since the prohibition in that rule is personal and is not applied to associated lawyers.

Note: Rule 1.8.10 of the Rules of Professional Conduct prohibits sexual relations with a client unless the client is the lawyer's spouse or registered domestic partner or a consensual sexual relationship existed before the lawyer-client relationship.

Ethics Opinions

Lawyers at times may seek legal advice concerning their ethical and other obligations to clients. This advice may be provided by, among others, outside counsel or a lawyer within the law firm serving as in-house counsel. The act of seeking legal advice concerning ethical obligations owed to a client by itself does not create a conflict with the client. Once a lawyer becomes aware of an error that could prejudice the client, the lawyer ethically may seek legal advice concerning obligations to the client and options available, but must comply with the rules governing disclosure to the client and the ethical rules governing conflicts of interest. State Bar of Cal. Com. on Prof. Resp. and Conduct, formal opn. No. 2019-197.

A lawyer and the lawyer's firm prepared all the documents for a public offering and the related SEC filings. It was in the law firm's interest, as well as that of the client company and its officers and directors, that the litigation result in a finding of no failure to disclose material information in those documents. The opinion concludes that the lawyer and firm had vested financial and professional interests in the outcome of the subject matter of this representation and must make full disclosure of the potential conflict to the client company, and each officer and director, under former rule 3-310(B) of the Rules of Professional Conduct. When the lawyer later found notes of a meeting with directors and officers at which they discussed related-party transactions, the firm was to fully disclose that fact and its ramifications to each client, including the new, inherent conflicts of interest between the firm and its clients. San Diego County Bar Assn., Ethics opn. No. 2017-1.

CHAPTER 6 CONFIDENTIALITY OF INFORMATION

California Rules of Professional Conduct, Rule 1.6 - Confidential Information of a Client

(a) A lawyer shall not reveal information protected from disclosure by Business and Professions Code section 6068, subdivision (e)(1) unless the client gives informed consent,* or the disclosure is permitted by paragraph (b) of this rule.

(b) A lawyer may, but is not required to, reveal information protected by Business and Professions Code section 6068, subdivision (e)(1) to the extent that the lawyer reasonably believes* the disclosure is necessary to prevent a criminal act that the lawyer reasonably believes* is likely to result in death of, or substantial* bodily harm to, an individual, as provided in paragraph (c).

(c) Before revealing information protected by Business and Professions Code section 6068, subdivision (e)(1) to prevent a criminal act as provided in paragraph (b), a lawyer shall, if reasonable* under the circumstances:

(1) make a good faith effort to persuade the client: (i) not to commit or to continue the criminal act; or (ii) to pursue a course of conduct that will prevent the threatened death or substantial* bodily harm; or do both (i) and (ii); and

(2) inform the client, at an appropriate time, of the lawyer's ability or decision to reveal information protected by Business and Professions Code section 6068, subdivision (e)(1) as provided in paragraph (b).

(d) In revealing information protected by Business and Professions Code section 6068, subdivision (e)(1) as provided in paragraph (b), the lawyer's disclosure must be no more than is necessary to prevent the criminal act, given the information known* to the lawyer at the time of the disclosure.

(e) A lawyer who does not reveal information permitted by paragraph (b) does not violate this rule.

An asterisk (*) identifies a defined term in rule 1.0.1 of the Rules of Professional Conduct. For further discussion of a defined term, see chapter 2 of this Guide, Terminology.

Business and Professions Code section 6068, subdivision (e)

It is the duty of an attorney to do all of the following:

...

(e)(1) To maintain inviolate the confidence, and at every peril to himself or herself to preserve the secrets, of his or her client.

(2) Notwithstanding paragraph (1), an attorney may, but is not required to, reveal confidential information relating to the representation of a client to the extent that the attorney reasonably believes the disclosure is necessary to prevent a criminal act that the attorney reasonably believes is likely to result in death of, or substantial bodily harm to, an individual.

6.1 Introduction

What a lawyer learns about a client by observation or communication is a client "confidence" or "secret," and is therefore protected from disclosure to third parties under the strict confidentiality rule of Business and Professions Code section 6068, subdivision (e)(1). Moreover, the duty to safeguard a client's confidences extends from the time that the lawyer learns of the confidence beyond the end of the representation. As discussed below, with certain exceptions, the duty even extends beyond the death of the client.

A lawyer's duty to preserve client secrets "at every peril" to the lawyer, has been described as absolute. *Gordon v. Super. Ct.* (1997) 55 Cal.App.4th 1546, 1557. Business and Professions Code section 6068, subdivision (e)(2) permits a lawyer to disclose confidential information to prevent a criminal act that the lawyer reasonably believes is likely to result in death or substantial bodily harm. Rule 1.6 of the Rules of Professional Conduct restates this same exception to the duty of confidentiality. Although trust and estate disputes are often heated and may involve long-standing grudges and family feuds, they do not, as a rule, involve the potential for such harm. However, if such a circumstance arises, a lawyer could permissibly violate the duty of client confidentiality.

Neither the statute nor the rule imposes an affirmative obligation on the lawyer to reveal the information, leaving it up to the lawyer to decide when to reveal confidential information. A lawyer who chooses not to reveal the information does not violate the statute or rule 1.6 of the Rules of Professional Conduct.

Before disclosing confidential information, the lawyer must, if reasonable under the circumstances, make a good faith effort to dissuade the client from the client's possible criminal conduct or to take other action that will prevent the threatened harm, or both. The reasonableness of the circumstances includes the risk of harm to the lawyer or the lawyer's family or associates. Rule 1.6 of the Rules of Professional Conduct further directs the lawyer to inform the client "at an appropriate time" of the lawyer's ability or decision to reveal confidential communications, if the lawyer can reasonably do so. In determining whether to disclose confidential communications, the lawyer is to consider a series of factors: whether the client has ever acted on threats in the past, whether the lawyer believes the efforts to dissuade the client from possible criminal conduct have been successful, the imminence of the harm, and the client's rights under the U.S. and California Constitutions.

Rule of Professional Conduct 4.1, Truthfulness in Statements to Others, provides further guidance:

In the course of representing a client a lawyer shall not knowingly:

(a) make a false statement of material fact or law to a third person; or

(b) fail to disclose a material fact to a third person* when disclosure is necessary to avoid assisting a criminal or fraudulent* act by a client, unless disclosure is prohibited by Business and Professions Code section 6068, subdivision (e)(1) or rule 1.6.

Rule 1.6 of the Rules of Professional Conduct conforms to the absolute prohibition in the statute, subject only to the limited exception in Business and Professions Code section 6068, subdivision (e)(2). The ABA Model Rules of Professional Conduct, rule 1.6 is more permissive than California law in allowing the disclosure of confidential client information. That model rule allows revelation of otherwise confidential client information to prevent the client's commission of a crime or fraud "reasonably certain to result in substantial injury to the financial interests or property of another and in furtherance of which the client has used or is using the lawyer's services"; or to prevent, mitigate, or rectify substantial injury related to such crime or fraud in furtherance of which the client used the lawyer's services.

The ethical duty of confidentiality in California is statutory. In the most recent revision of the Rules of Professional Conduct, the Supreme Court declined to broaden the exception to the duty of confidentiality, if needed to protect a physically or mentally incapacitated client from financial or physical abuse. For a further discussion of the ethical duty of confidentiality owed to a client with diminished capacity, see section 6.7 of this chapter.

Former California Rules of Professional Conduct, Rule 3-100 - Confidential Information of a Client

(A) A member shall not reveal information protected from disclosure by Business and Professions Code section 6068, subdivision (e)(1) without the informed consent of the client, or as provided in paragraph (B) of this rule.

(B) A member may, but is not required to, reveal confidential information relating to the representation of a client to the extent that the member reasonably believes the disclosure is necessary to prevent a criminal act that the member reasonably believes is likely to result in death of, or substantial* bodily harm to, an individual.

(C) Before revealing confidential information to prevent a criminal act as provided in paragraph (B), a member shall, if reasonable* under the circumstances:

(1) make a good faith effort to persuade the client: (i) not to commit or to continue the criminal act; or (ii) to pursue a course of conduct that will prevent the threatened death or substantial bodily harm; or do both (i) and (ii); and

(2) inform the client, at an appropriate time, of the member's ability or decision to reveal information as provided in paragraph (B).

(D) In revealing confidential information as provided in paragraph (B), the member's disclosure must be no more than is necessary to prevent the criminal act, given the information known to the member at the time of the disclosure.

(E) A member who does not reveal information permitted by paragraph (B) does not violate this rule.

Ethics Opinions

Every lawyer must act competently to protect confidential client information against inadvertent or other unauthorized disclosure. While lawyers always should be cautious about disclosing any information related to a client, online communications present particular risks. One example of such a risk arises when someone attempts to elicit information from a lawyer through social media pretexting. A lawyer's unguarded disclosure of client information might result in violations of the duties of competence and confidentiality and might cause the loss of the lawyer-client privilege and work product protection. L.A. County Bar Assn., Ethics opn. No. 529 (Aug. 23, 2017).

Whether a lawyer violates the ethical duties of confidentiality and competence when using technology to transmit or store confidential client information will depend on the particular technology being used and the circumstances surrounding such use. Before using a particular technology in the course of representing a client, a lawyer must take appropriate steps to evaluate: (1) the level of security attendant to the use of that technology, including whether reasonable precautions may be taken when using the technology to increase the level of security; (2) the legal ramifications to a third party who intercepts, accesses, or exceeds authorized use of the electronic information; (3) the degree of sensitivity of the information; (4) the possible impact on the client of an inadvertent disclosure of privileged or confidential information or work product; (5) the urgency of the situation; and (6) the client's instructions and circumstances, such as access by others to the client's devices and communications. State Bar of Cal. Com. on Prof. Resp. and Conduct, formal opn. No. 2010-179.

Construing model rule 1.6, a lawyer for the fiduciary of an estate has no duty to disclose the client's intent to commit a nonviolent crime to a nonclient beneficiary. ABA Com. on Ethics and Prof. Resp., formal opn. No. 1994-380.

6.2 Use of Confidential Information

California Rules of Professional Conduct, Rule 1.8.2 - Use of Current Client's Information

> A lawyer shall not use a client's information protected by Business and Professions Code section 6068, subdivision (e)(1) to the disadvantage of the client unless the client gives informed consent,* except as permitted by these rules or the State Bar Act.

An asterisk (*) identifies a defined term in rule 1.0.1 of the Rules of Professional Conduct. For further discussion of a defined term, see chapter 2 of this Guide, Terminology.

The ethical duty of confidentiality prohibits not only the disclosure of client communications, but also the use of confidential information to the client's disadvantage. Such use may include acquiring a property or financial interest adverse to a client, as prohibited by rule 1.8.1 of the Rules of Professional Conduct. See chapter 5 of this Guide, Conflicts of Interest, sections 5.10 and 5.17. The ethical prohibition also includes a broader range of disclosures that may be either embarrassing or detrimental to the client. As with other client confidences, the ethical duty extends beyond the termination of the representation and protects former clients from the disclosure of detrimental information.

Case Study

Hedge Fund Manager retained Lawyer for representation in defending a fraud claim brought by several investors. In the course of that lawsuit, Lawyer interviewed Former Investor who told Lawyer that several years earlier Hedge Fund Manager paid her $100,000 to resolve a disputed fraud claim before a lawsuit was filed. Former Investor also posted this information on a public blog.

Several months after the settlement of the current lawsuit and the conclusion of Lawyer's representation, Lawyer read an interview with Former Investor in the Wall Street Journal that recited the details of that prior dispute with Hedge Fund Manager. In response, Lawyer wrote a letter to the editor of the Journal, commenting on the interview with Former Investor and discussing the lawsuit that Lawyer handled for Hedge Fund Manager concerning similar allegations, including the settlement of that matter.

Several years later, Hedge Fund Manager was arrested for driving under the influence of alcohol. Lawyer commented on the arrest on a Facebook page, stating, "[d]rinking and driving is irresponsible."

What ethical issues arise from this set of facts and how should Lawyer have addressed them?

Lawyer violated the duty of confidentiality by commenting on the interview with the Wall Street Journal. Even though the Former Investor made information publicly available by that interview and a personal blog post, Lawyer had a duty to protect that information as a client secret, and not disseminate or further publicize it. A lawyer may not disclose a client's secrets, which include not only confidential information communicated between the client and the lawyer but also publicly available information that the lawyer obtained during the professional relationship that the client has requested be kept secret, or the disclosure of which is likely to be embarrassing or detrimental to the client. Even after termination of the lawyer-client relationship, the lawyer may not disclose potentially embarrassing or detrimental information about the former client if that information was acquired by virtue of the lawyer's prior representation.

The arrest for drunk driving was not information obtained in the course of the prior representation and does not constitute a client secret. State Bar of Cal. Com. On Prof. Resp. and Conduct, formal opn. No. 2016-195 (discussing former rule 3-100 of the Rules of Professional Conduct).

6.3 Duty of Confidentiality and the Lawyer-Client Privilege

Both Business and Professions Code section 6068, subdivision (e) and Evidence Code sections 950 et. seq. deal with the confidentiality of information obtained in the course of representing a client. The Evidence Code sections relate to the production or disclosure of evidence in a court proceeding. The ethical duty to protect client confidences in the Business and Professions Code appears to be absolute, with one limited exception. In the Evidence Code, the lawyer-client privilege against disclosure has several more express exceptions, for example in a fee dispute with the client. The statutory exceptions in the Evidence Code limit the ability of a client to assert the lawyer's ethical duty to prevent disclosures of the client's own confidential information.

In *Fox Searchlight Pictures, Inc. v. Paladino* (2001) 89 Cal.App.4th 297, the Court of Appeal reviewed a claim whether a lawyer suing a former employer for wrongful termination had violated the prohibition on disclosing confidential information by sharing that information with counsel in the employment litigation. The court held that the plaintiff, even though a lawyer, "may disclose to her attorney all facts relevant to the termination, including employer confidences and privileged communications." *Id.* at p. 308. The court emphasized that it was determining only that "narrow issue," commenting, "[w]e are not faced with, and do not decide, whether the former in-house counsel or her attorney can be held liable to the employer for the public disclosure of those confidences and communications." *Id.*

In analyzing the prohibition of section 6068, subdivision (e) as it existed at the time the case was decided, the court stated that "[a]lthough the statute on its face brooks no exceptions, it must be read in conjunction with other statutes and ethical rules which specifically permit the attorney to depart from the usual rules of client confidentiality." *Fox Searchlight Pictures, Inc. v. Paladino, supra,* 89 Cal.App.4th at p. 313. The Court of Appeal cited with approval cases from the State Bar Court that had held that "the duty of confidentiality expressed in Business and Professions Code Section 6068, subdivision (e) is modified by the exceptions to the attorney-client privilege contained in the Evidence Code." *Id.* at p. 314 (footnotes omitted).

The *Fox Searchlight* case clarified what had been an uncertain area. However, considerable caution is still required as indicated in the case itself, in rule 1.6 of the Rules of Professional Conduct, and in the case of *Solin v. O'Melveny & Myers* (2001) 89 Cal.App.4th 451. In the *Solin* case, a lawyer sought advice from a specialist in criminal law with the defendant firm regarding the obligations arising from potential criminal conduct of the lawyer's clients. Rather than limiting the inquiry to hypothetical facts the lawyer disclosed confidential client information to the specialist. When the lawyer sued the specialist for malpractice, the lawyer's client intervened to maintain the confidentiality of information that had been disclosed, and the trial court dismissed the case. The Court of Appeal affirmed, holding that "unless a statutory provision removes the protection afforded by the attorney-client privilege to confidential communications between attorney and client, an attorney plaintiff may not prosecute a lawsuit if in doing so client confidences would be disclosed." *Id.* at 458. See also *Dietz v. Meisenheimer & Herron* (2009) 177 Cal.App.4th 771 in which the Court of Appeal ruled that a lawyer could not assert the lawyer-client privilege to avoid liability to pay a referral fee, when the client waived the lawyer-client privilege sufficiently to allow the lawyer to defend the claim.

Comment on California Rules of Professional Conduct, Rule 1.6

> [2] The principle of lawyer-client confidentiality applies to information a lawyer acquires by virtue of the representation, whatever its source, and encompasses matters communicated in confidence by the client, and therefore protected by the lawyer-client privilege, matters protected by the work product doctrine, and matters protected under ethical standards of confidentiality, all as established in law, rule and policy. (See *In the Matter of Johnson* (Review Dept. 2000) 4 Cal. State Bar Ct. Rptr. 179; *Goldstein v. Lees* (1975) 46 Cal.App.3d 614, 621 [120 Cal. Rptr. 253].) The lawyer-client privilege and work-product doctrine apply in judicial and other proceedings in which a lawyer may be called as a witness or be otherwise compelled to produce evidence concerning a client. A lawyer's ethical duty of confidentiality is not so limited in its scope of protection for the lawyer-client relationship of trust and prevents a lawyer from revealing the client's information even when not subjected to such compulsion. Thus, a lawyer may not reveal such information except with the informed consent* of the client or as authorized or required by the State Bar Act, these rules, or other law.
>
> ...
>
> [13] This rule is not intended to augment, diminish, or preclude any other exceptions to the duty to preserve information protected by Business and Professions Code section 6068, subdivision (e)(1) recognized under California law.

6.4 Duties to Former Clients

California Rules of Professional Conduct, Rule 1.9 - Duties to Former Clients

> (a) A lawyer who has formerly represented a client in a matter shall not thereafter represent another person* in the same or a substantially related matter in which that person's* interests are materially adverse to the interests of the former client unless the former client gives informed written consent.
>
> (b) A lawyer shall not knowingly* represent a person* in the same or a substantially related matter in which a firm* with which the lawyer formerly was associated had previously represented a client

(1) whose interests are materially adverse to that person;* and

(2) about whom the lawyer had acquired information protected by Business and Professions Code section 6068, subdivision (e) and rules 1.6 and 1.9(c) that is material to the matter; unless the former client gives informed written consent.*

(c) A lawyer who has formerly represented a client in a matter or whose present or former firm* has formerly represented a client in a matter shall not thereafter:

(1) use information protected by Business and Professions Code section 6068, subdivision (e) and rule 1.6 acquired by virtue of the representation of the former client to the disadvantage of the former client except as these rules or the State Bar Act would permit with respect to a current client, or when the information has become generally known;* or

(2) reveal information protected by Business and Professions Code section 6068, subdivision (e) and rule 1.6 acquired by virtue of the representation of the former client except as these rules or the State Bar Act permit with respect to a current client.

An asterisk (*) identifies a defined term in rule 1.0.1 of the Rules of Professional Conduct. For further discussion of a defined term, see chapter 2 of this Guide, Terminology.

The duty of a lawyer not to represent a current client and a former client whose interests are materially adverse is closely tied to the lawyer's duty to protect a client's confidences. Rule 1.9 of the Rules of Professional Conduct expressly links the ethical duty to avoid conflicts to the duty of confidentiality owed to former clients. Under that rule, a lawyer who obtained confidential information from former Client A that is material to a current controversy between Client A and Client B may not represent Client B in that controversy, without the informed written consent of Client A.

The interrelated ethical duties in rule 1.9 of the Rules of Professional Conduct may arise in a trusts and estates practice when the lawyer has represented a corporate fiduciary in one matter and is later engaged to represent an individual with interests adverse to corporate fiduciary in an unrelated matter. For example, a lawyer may represent a corporate fiduciary in the administration of a trust or probate estate and may later undertake to represent the beneficiary of an unrelated trust in an action for surcharge and removal of the corporate fiduciary. For a discussion of the ethical duties to a corporate fiduciary client, see chapter 5 this Guide, Conflicts of Interest, section 5.7.

Comment on California Rules of Professional Conduct, Rule 1.9

[1] After termination of a lawyer-client relationship, the lawyer owes two duties to a former client. The lawyer may not (i) do anything that will injuriously affect the former client in any matter in which the lawyer represented the former client, or (ii)

at any time use against the former client knowledge or information acquired by virtue of the previous relationship. (See *Oasis West Realty, LLC v. Goldman* (2011) 51 Cal.4th 811 [124 Cal.Rptr.3d 256]; *Wutchumna Water Co. v. Bailey* (1932) 216 Cal. 564 [15 P.2d 505].) For example, (i) a lawyer could not properly seek to rescind on behalf of a new client a contract drafted on behalf of the former client and (ii) a lawyer who has prosecuted an accused person* could not represent the accused in a subsequent civil action against the government concerning the same matter. (See also Bus. and Prof. Code sec. 6131; 18 U.S.C. sec. 207(a).) These duties exist to preserve a client's trust in the lawyer and to encourage the client's candor in communications with the lawyer.

6.5 Disclosure of Confidential Information

When a lawyer proposes to represent multiple clients in a single matter, such joint representation requires the informed written consent of each client. The clients' consent would appropriately include the consent for the lawyer to share information between or among the clients, and to disclose what would otherwise be confidential information. For a further discussion of such consent, see section 6.9 of this chapter, Disclosures Between Joint Clients.

In a few limited circumstances, a lawyer may disclose confidential information without the client's consent:

1. Evidence Code section 947 provides that, "[t]here is no privilege under this article as to a communication relevant to an issue between parties all of whom claim through a deceased client, regardless of whether the claims are by testate or intestate succession, nonprobate transfer, or inter vivos transaction."
2. Evidence Code section 956 provides that there is no lawyer-client privilege if the lawyer's services are sought to enable or aid the client to commit or plan to commit a crime or a fraud.
3. Evidence Code section 956.5 provides that there is no privilege if the lawyer "reasonably believes that disclosure ... is necessary to prevent a criminal act that the lawyer reasonably believes is likely to result in the death of, or substantial bodily harm to, an individual."
4. Evidence Code section 958 provides that, "[t]here is no privilege under this article relevant to an issue of breach, by the lawyer or by the client, of a duty arising out of the lawyer-client relationship."

These Evidence Code statutes are exceptions to the assertion of the lawyer-client privilege in a litigated proceeding, and not limitations on the absolute ethical duty of confidentiality.

The advent of new technologies requires that the lawyer consider the extent to which the use of a new technology may risk disclosure of client confidences. For a discussion of related ethical issues, see chapter 10 of this Guide, Ethics and Technology, section 10.4.

Ethics Opinions

A lawyer may disclose to the court only as much as is reasonably necessary to demonstrate the need to withdraw. Ordinarily it will be sufficient to say that ethical considerations require withdrawal or that there has been an irreconcilable breakdown in the lawyer-client relationship. To the extent the court orders a lawyer to disclose confidential information, the lawyer may pursue reasonable avenues of appeal or other further review of such an order. The lawyer must evaluate the relevant legal authorities and the particular circumstances, including the potential prejudice to the client, to reach a conclusion on how to proceed. Whatever choice the lawyer makes must include reasonable steps to minimize the impact of that choice on the client. State Bar of Cal. Com. on Prof. Resp. and Conduct, formal opn. No. 2015-192.

As it pertains to the use of technology, the Business and Professions Code and the Rules of Professional Conduct do not impose greater or different duties upon a virtual law office (VLO) practitioner operating in the cloud than they do upon a lawyer practicing in a traditional law office. While a lawyer may maintain a VLO in the cloud where communications with the client, and storage of and access to all information about the client's matter, are conducted solely through the internet using a third-party's secure servers, the lawyer may be required to take additional steps to confirm compliance with a lawyer's ethical obligations due to distinct issues raised by the hypothetical VLO and its operation. Failure of the lawyer to comply with all ethical obligations relevant to these issues will preclude the operation of a VLO in the cloud. State Bar of Cal. Com. on Prof. Resp. and Conduct, formal opn. No. 2012-184.

The opinion addresses at length the question of whether a lawyer may reasonably use email to communicate confidentially with a client. It describes in detail how different email systems may operate and then concludes that email generally may be regarded as adequately secure even without encryption, likening email security to the same level of security that a lawyer and client might expect from a landline telephone call. The opinion also discusses, without reaching a conclusion, the extent to which the lawyer may rely on other types of technology, such as cordless telephones and cellular telephones. ABA Com. on Ethics and Prof. Resp., formal opn. No. 1999-413.

6.6 Implied Authorization to Disclose

The lawyer-client relationship impliedly confers upon the lawyer the ability to disclose confidential information regarding the client and the client's affairs to members of the lawyer's staff, including other lawyers, legal assistants, and secretaries. This general rule is, of course, subject to express contrary directions from the client. The managerial or supervising lawyer must take reasonable steps to ensure that all members of the lawyer's office understand the duty of confidentiality imposed on the law firm by the Business and Professions Code. Rules Prof. Conduct, rule 5.1. For a further discussion of the duties of managing and supervising lawyers, see chapter 3 of this Guide, Competence and Diligence, section 3.9.

A lawyer should normally confer with other professionals, lawyer or non-lawyer, only with the client's express consent. However, a client's pre-existing relationships with, for example, an insurance adviser or an accountant, may reflect the client's implied authorization to disclose otherwise confidential lawyer-client communications. A lawyer may also properly, at the lawyer's own expense, consult with another professional to assist the lawyer in representing the client. For example, the lawyer may seek tax expertise that the lawyer does not have. In seeking such professional assistance, the lawyer should disclose no information that would identify the client or reveal confidential client communications. If the lawyer harbors any concern that a professional consultation will not protect the client's identity and confidential information, then the client's consent should be obtained. For a further discussion of seeking expert advice to comply with the ethical duty of competence, see chapter 3 of this Guide, Competence and Diligence, section 3.4.

ACTEC Commentaries on Model Rules of Professional Conduct, Model Rule 1.6

> *Legal Assistants, Secretaries and Office Staff.* In the absence of express contrary instructions by a client, the lawyer may share confidential information with members of the lawyer's office staff to the extent reasonably necessary to the representation. As indicated in MRPC 5.3 (Responsibilities Regarding Nonlawyer Assistants), the lawyer is required to assure that staff members respect the confidentiality of clients' affairs. The lawyer should "give such assistants appropriate instructions concerning the ethical aspects of their employment, particularly regarding the obligation not to disclose information relating to the representation of the client, and should be responsible for their work product." Comment to MRPC 5.3 (Responsibilities Regarding Nonlawyer Assistants).
>
> *Consultants and Associated Counsel.* The lawyer should obtain the client's consent to the disclosure of confidential information to other professionals. However, the lawyer may be impliedly authorized to disclose confidential information to other professionals and business consultants to the extent appropriate to the representation. Thus, the client may reasonably anticipate that a lawyer who is preparing an irrevocable life insurance trust for the client will discuss the client's affairs with the client's insurance advisor. Additionally, in order to satisfy the lawyer's duty of competence, the lawyer may, without the express consent of the client, consult with another professional regarding draft documents or the tax consequences of particular actions, provided that the client's identity and other confidential information is not disclosed. In such a case the lawyer is responsible for payment of the consultant's fee. As indicated in the ACTEC Commentary on MRPC 1.1 (Competence), with the client's consent, the lawyer may associate other professionals to assist in the representation.
>
> *Implied Authorization to Disclose.* The lawyer is also impliedly authorized to disclose otherwise confidential information to the courts, administrative agencies, and other individuals and organizations as the lawyer believes is reasonably required by the representation. A lawyer is impliedly authorized to make arrangements, in case of the lawyer's death or disability, for another lawyer to review the files of the clients. As stated in ABA Formal Opinion 92-369 (1992), "[r]easonable clients would likely not object to, but rather approve of, efforts to ensure that their interests are safeguarded." A lawyer has no implied authority to disclose client confidences in the context of electronic bulletin boards, social media, continuing legal education seminars or similar public forums where persons from outside the lawyer's firm may be participating. The prohibition on disclosure includes information that could reasonably lead to the discovery of confidential information. Thus, a lawyer may use a hypothetical to discuss issues relating to a

representation only so long as there is no reasonable likelihood that the listener will be able to ascertain the identity of the client or the situation involved.

Client may reasonably expect lawyer who is preparing an irrevocable life insurance trust to discuss client's affairs with client's insurance advisor; to satisfy lawyer's duty of competence, lawyer may, without express consent of the client, consult with another professional regarding draft documents or the tax consequences of particular actions, provided that client's identity and other confidential information is not disclosed and that lawyer is responsible for payment of the consultant's fee.

Case

Communications among a businessman, lawyer, and public relations consultant were not protected by lawyer-client privilege because there was no common interest "in securing legal advice related to the same shared matter." *Behunin v. Super. Ct. (Schwab)* (2017) 9 Cal.App.5th 833.

Ethics Opinions

If a lawyer chooses to outsource legal and nonlegal services, the lawyer should "minimize the risk that any outside service provider may inadvertently—or perhaps even advertently—reveal client confidential information to adverse parties or to others who are not entitled to access." The lawyer may minimize the risk by procuring written confidentiality agreements with the outside provider and by confirming that the outside service provider does not work for the client's adversaries on the same or a substantially related matter. ABA Com. on Ethics and Prof. Resp., formal opn. No. 2008-451.

The lawyer should be aware that legal and ethical standards applicable to foreign lawyers and legal assistants may differ from California standards, so the lawyer must act competently to ensure that an outside service provider maintains the client's confidences. San Diego County Bar Assn., Ethics opn. No. 2007-1.

To fulfill the obligation to protect client files and property, a lawyer should prepare a future plan providing for the maintenance and protection of those client interests in the event of the lawyer's death. Such a plan should, at a minimum, include the designation of another lawyer who would have the authority to review client files and make determinations as to which files need immediate attention, and who would notify the clients of their lawyer's death. ABA Com. on Ethics and Prof. Resp., formal opn. No. 1992-369.

6.7 Client with Diminished Capacity

The State Bar of California Committee on Professional Responsibility and Conduct addressed the ethical duties of a lawyer who represents a mentally impaired client in Formal Opinion Number 1989-112. The Committee opined that a lawyer for a possibly incapacitated client may not institute conservatorship proceedings for the client without the client's consent, even when the lawyer concludes that the client is incompetent to act in the client's own best interest. The opinion rests on Business and Professions Code section 6068, subdivision (e) requiring a lawyer to "maintain inviolate the confidence, and at every peril to himself or herself to preserve the secrets, of his or her client," and former rule 3-310 of the Rules of Professional Conduct barring a lawyer from representing adverse or conflicting interests.

In 2003, the California Legislature balanced the absolute duty of confidentiality and loyalty against the understandable desire to allow lawyers to protect potential victims of crime. Business and Professions Code section 6068, subdivision (e)(2) was added to allow limited disclosures if the lawyer reasonably believes the disclosure is necessary to prevent a criminal act likely to result in death of, or substantial bodily harm, to an individual. Rule 1.6(b) of the Rules of Professional Conduct adopts this limited exception to the statutory duty of confidentiality.

Formal Opinion Number 1989-112 stands in marked contrast with ABA Model Rules of Professional Conduct, rule 1.14. Model rule 1.14 allows a lawyer to make limited disclosures and take other actions if needed to protect a client whose mental impairments substantially affect their judgment and make them vulnerable to financial or physical abuse.

The Trusts and Estates Section of the California Lawyers Association, formerly of the State Bar of California, sponsored legislation to balance the duties of confidentiality and loyalty with the desire to allow lawyers to take reasonable steps to protect their clients whose mental impairments substantially affect their judgment and make them particularly vulnerable. That legislation proposed a change to the California Rules of Professional Conduct that closely followed ABA Model Rules of Professional Conduct, rule 1.14. The Legislature referred this proposed change to the Commission for the Revision of the Rules of Professional Conduct. The Commission included a proposed version of model rule 1.14 as one of the 70 proposed new and amended Rules of Professional Conduct submitted as their final recommendations to the State Bar Board of Trustees. The Supreme Court declined to adopt the proposed change, without comment, in the revision of the Rules of Professional Conduct effective November 1, 2018.

In connection with the proposed revision of the statutory duty of confidentiality, the Trusts and Estates Section also considered an advance consent to disclosure of confidential information that a client may make while competent. Under current California law, an advance consent without actual disclosure does not appear to waive the duty of confidentiality or the lawyer-client privilege going forward. Evidence Code section 912 provides that "the right of any person to claim" the lawyer-client privilege "is waived with respect to a communication protected by the privilege if any holder of the privilege, without coercion, has disclosed a significant part of the communication or has consented to the disclosure." However, "a mere intention to waive the privilege, evidenced only by a promise … does not waive the privilege." *Tennenbaum v. Deloitte & Touche* (9th Cir. 1996) 77 F.3d 337, 341. "[W]aiver occurs only when the holder of the privilege has, in fact, voluntarily disclosed or consented to a disclosure made, in fact, by someone else. Put another way, the intent to disclose does not operate as a waiver, waiver comes into play after a disclosure has been made." *Lohman v. Super. Ct.* (1978) 81 Cal.App.3d 90, 95. If a client consents to disclosure of confidential or privileged information but the disclosure does not occur, upon the client's subsequently losing capacity, the decision of whether to permit future disclosure of privileged information falls to the "guardian or conservator of the client, if the client has a guardian or conservator." Evid. Code, sec. 953, subd. (b).

ACTEC Commentaries on Model Rules of Professional Conduct, Model Rule 1.14

[The Supreme Court declined to adopt the provisions of ABA Model Rules of Professional Conduct, rule 1.14 in the revisions to the California Rules of Professional Conduct effective November 1, 2018.]

Preventive Measures for Competent Clients. As a matter of routine, the lawyer who represents a competent adult in estate planning matters should provide the client with information regarding the devices the client could employ to protect his or her interests in the event of diminished capacity, including ways the client could avoid the necessity of a guardianship or similar proceeding. Thus, as a service to a client, the lawyer should inform the client regarding the costs, advantages and disadvantages of durable powers of attorney, directives to physicians or living wills, health care proxies, and revocable trusts. A lawyer may properly suggest that a competent client consider executing a letter or other document that would authorize the lawyer to communicate to designated parties (e.g., family members, health care providers, a court) concerns that the lawyer might have regarding the client's capacity. In addition, a lawyer may properly suggest that a durable power of attorney authorize the attorney-in-fact, on behalf of the principal, to give written authorization to one or more of the client's health care providers and to disclose information for such purposes upon such terms as provided in such authorization, including health information regarding the principal, that might otherwise be protected against disclosure by the Health Insurance Portability and Accountability Act of 1996 (HIPAA). If the client wishes the durable power of attorney to become effective at a date when the client is unable to act for him- or herself, the lawyer should consider how to draft that power in light of the restrictions found in HIPAA.

Implied Authority to Disclose and Act. Based on the interaction of subsections (b) and (c) of MRPC 1.14, a lawyer has implied authority to make disclosures of otherwise confidential information and take protective actions when there is a risk of substantial harm to the client and the lawyer reasonably believes that the client is unable because of diminished capacity, either temporary or permanent, to protect him or herself. Under those circumstances, the lawyer may consult with individuals or entities that may be able to assist the client, including family members, trusted friends and other advisors. However, in deciding whether others should be consulted, the lawyer should also consider the client's wishes, the impact of the lawyer's actions on potential challenges to the client's estate plan, and the impact on the lawyer's ability to maintain the client's confidential information. In determining whether to act and in determining what action to take on behalf of a client, the lawyer should consider the impact a particular course of action could have on the client, including the client's right to privacy and the client's physical, mental and emotional well-being. In appropriate cases, the lawyer may seek the appointment of a guardian ad litem, conservator or guardian or take other protective action.

Risk and Substantiality of Harm. For the purposes of this rule, the risk of harm to a client and the amount of harm that a client might suffer should both be determined according to a different scale than if the client were fully capable. In particular, the client's diminished capacity increases the risk of harm and the possibility that any particular harm would be substantial. If the risk and substantiality of potential harm to a client are uncertain, a lawyer may make reasonably appropriate disclosures of otherwise confidential information and take reasonably appropriate protective actions. In determining the risk and substantiality of harm and deciding what action to take, a lawyer should consider any wishes or directions that were clearly expressed by the client during his or her competency. Normally, a lawyer should be permitted to take actions on behalf of a client with apparently diminished capacity that the lawyer reasonably believes are in the best interests of the client.

Case

Disappointed heirs brought a malpractice claim against the estate planning lawyers claiming that the testator lacked testamentary capacity at the time the estate plan amendments were executed, that the lawyers should have known that the testator's testamentary capacity was questionable, and that the lawyers acted negligently in failing to assure, confirm, and document the testator's capacity to execute the governing will and trust amendments. The Court of Appeal upheld the trial court's grant of a demurrer dismissing the claim without leave to amend. The court found that the lawyer's duty of loyalty to the client may be compromised by imposing a duty to nonclient beneficiaries on issues of determining incapacity. The court cited favorably rule 1.14(a) of the Model Rules of Professional Conduct: "When a client's ability to make adequately considered decisions in connection with the representation is impaired, whether because of minority, mental disability or for some other reason, the lawyer shall, as far as reasonably possible, maintain a normal client-lawyer relationship with the client." None of the authorities imposing a duty upon the lawyer to assess the capacity of the testator indicate that such duty would run to beneficiaries rather than solely to the testator. *Moore v. Anderson Zeigler Disharoon Gallagher & Gray, P.C.* (2003) 109 Cal.App.4th 1287.

Ethics Opinions

A lawyer may properly petition the court for appointment of a new guardian ad litem when the lawyer believes that the current guardian ad litem is not properly representing a client but may not disclose confidential information that the current guardian ad litem requests remain confidential. San Diego County Bar Assn., Ethics opn. No. 2017-2.

A lawyer who initiates conservatorship proceedings for a client without the client's consent discloses the client's "secrets" in violation of Business and Professions Code section 6068, subdivision (e), and possibly discloses communications protected by Evidence Code section 952. In addition, a lawyer who seeks to initiate conservatorship proceedings for the client acts in conflict to the client's stated interests under former rule 3-310 of the Rules of Professional

Conduct Rule and in violation of the duty of loyalty to the client. State Bar of Cal. Com. on Prof. Resp. and Conduct, formal opn. No. 1989-112; Orange County Bar Assn., Ethics opn. No. 1995-2; San Diego County Bar Assn., Ethics opn. No. 1978-1.

6.8 Joint Representation

The ethical duty of confidentiality applies when a lawyer represents more than one client with identical or related interests. The lawyer may owe the same duty to each one of multiple parties whose interests diverge. That duty arises, for example, in the context of representing spouses, domestic partners, parents and children, and unmarried couples in joint estate planning, more than one member of the same family in multiple matters, more than one beneficiary in a will contest, more than one party to a business transaction, a fiduciary and beneficiaries, or more than one fiduciary in a trust or estate administration.

When the lawyer represents two or more clients with common or related interests, it is almost impossible to separate the lawyer's duty of keeping the client's confidences inviolate from the lawyer's duty of loyalty to the client. When one joint client asks that certain information not be disclosed to the other, usually their common interests have diverged, and disclosure of that information may prejudice the client seeking to prevent disclosure. At that point, the lawyer is faced with an insoluble dilemma because disclosure of the information will prejudice one client and withholding it will prejudice the other. The interests of the joint clients have become directly adverse, and rule 1.7 of the Rules of Professional Conduct prohibits the lawyer from continuing the representation without the informed written consent of both clients. Informed written consent may require precisely the disclosure that one client is seeking to prevent. The ethical duty of loyalty to one client may preclude the lawyer's joint or concurrent representation of the other client, and the lawyer may need to terminate the representation of both parties as provided in rule 1.16 of the Rules of Professional Conduct.

Spouses. The presumption in California law appears to be that when a lawyer represents spouses they are joint clients, in the absence of a contrary agreement. When representing both spouses jointly, the lawyer advisedly sets forth explicit disclosure rules in a written engagement letter and both spouses waive the duty of confidentiality in Business and Professions Code section 6068, subdivision (e) with respect to each other. The spouses would appropriately consent to full disclosure of all information to each other, and address what happens if their interests become directly adverse. Failure to set specific disclosure rules can leave the lawyer in an insoluble dilemma, if one spouse communicates material information to the lawyer that is not to be disclosed to the other spouse.

In the course of a joint representation of spouses, the lawyer may need to decide whether confidential information imparted by one spouse to the lawyer must be disclosed to the other. If one spouse directs the lawyer not to disclose certain information to the other, those instructions may be evidence of a direct conflict. In that case, rule 1.7 of the Rules of Professional Conduct allows the lawyer to proceed only after making full disclosure of the conflict to both spouses and obtaining the written consent of both of them. Without full disclosure and informed written consent, the lawyer must withdraw from the representation of both parties.

Family Members. Equally difficult is the problem of complying with the ethical duty of confidentiality in representing multiple family members. While a detailed engagement letter can greatly reduce the possibility of conflicting duties by making it clear from the outset that the lawyer cannot and is not expected to keep information confidential among the joint clients, the prohibition of rule 1.7 of the Rules of Professional Conduct in representing clients with directly adverse interests may be hard to reconcile with open communication.

Maintaining confidentiality among multiple clients from one family may not be either realistic or feasible. The usual flow of information from family members to the lawyer generally makes it impossible for the lawyer to remember who said what to whom and when and in what context. It may not be realistic, for example, for the older generation to expect the lawyer not to disclose at least the general outline of the older generation's estate plan to the younger generation who are also clients. If non-disclosure is expected, the lawyer cannot realistically put knowledge of that plan out of mind in advising the younger generation.

While the specifics of disclosure are a matter of degree and may vary, the fundamental dilemma is the same and the ethical duties in California law and the Rules of Professional Conduct are unyielding. As a result, a lawyer representing multiple family members is best advised to obtain the written consent of all clients to complete, open communication by the lawyer. The clients will not have an unrealistic expectation that the lawyer is holding things in confidence, the lawyer will not inadvertently violate the duty of confidentiality in Business and Professions Code section 6068, subdivision (e) by disclosing information that one family member does not want disclosed, and the free exchange of information will enable the lawyer to maximize the benefits of multi-generational estate planning. The lawyer who proposes such open communication and meets resistance from one or more family members should recognize this resistance as evidence of directly adverse interests. The lawyer may then consider declining the joint family representation and representing only one member of the family from the outset.

Case

The Supreme Court distinguished simultaneous representation from successive representation of two clients with adverse interests. The court held that there was no malpractice when the conflict of interest related to a *simultaneous* representation of clients with adverse interests. In such cases, the chief fiduciary value in jeopardy is that of client loyalty. That duty requires that the lawyer withdraw from the new representation as soon as the conflict is discovered; the lawyer has no duty and in fact is prohibited from advising the new client. In contrast, the ethical conflict arises in *successive* representations only if there is a substantial relationship between the subject matters in the two cases. The lawyer's primary duty to a former client is of confidentiality. If the former and new matter are substantially related then access to confidential information in the course of the first representation is "presumed," and disqualification of the lawyer's representation of the second client is mandatory. *Flatt v. Super. Ct.* (1994) 9 Cal.4th 275, 289.

Ethics Opinions

Whether an actual or potential conflict of interest exists in a multiple client engagement depends on whether one or more of six conflict situations exist or may potentially arise during the representation: (1) conflicting instructions from the clients in which the lawyer cannot follow one client's instruction without violating another client's instruction; (2) conflicting objectives of the clients in which the lawyer cannot effectively advance one client's objective without detrimentally affecting another client's objective; (3) advocacy of antagonistic positions of the clients in which the lawyer is called on to advocate both sides of a negotiation or a legal position at the same time; (4) inconsistent expectations of confidentiality in which one client expects the lawyer not to disclose information the lawyer would be required to impart to the other client; (5) a preexisting relationship with one client that would adversely affect the lawyer's independent judgment on behalf of the other client; and (6) conflicting demands by the clients for the original file once the representation has ended. To the extent that one or more of the foregoing conflict situations are reasonably possible, a potential conflict of interest exists that requires both clients' informed written consent under former rule 3-310(C)(1) of the Rules of Professional Conduct. To the extent that any of the conflict situations arise during the representation, an actual conflict of interest exists that, if not resolved before the lawyer must proceed, requires both clients' additional informed written consent under former rule 3-310(C)(2) of the Rules of Professional Conduct. State Bar of Cal. Com. on Prof. Resp. and Conduct, formal opn. No. 1999-153.

If a lawyer's relationship with one client affects the lawyer's loyalty and independent judgment on behalf of another client, an actual conflict of interest exists. This can occur when the lawyer receives conflicting instructions from the clients or is called upon to advance inconsistent objectives of the clients. Such circumstances trigger a duty to obtain further consent under former rule 3-310(C)(2) of the Rules of Professional Conduct. State Bar of Cal. Com. on Prof. Resp. and Conduct, formal opn. No. 1997-148.

A lawyer's obligation of confidentiality precludes disclosure of a client's commission of fraud, but a lawyer may not participate in or further the client's misconduct. State Bar of Cal. Com. on Prof. Resp. and Conduct, formal opn. No. 1996-146.

A lawyer who represented a mother in an individual capacity and as guardian of her child in a personal injury action settled the case with the child's settlement funds to be administered by the mother. Even though the lawyer learns from a reliable source that the mother previously misappropriated her child's trust funds and has reason to believe that the mother would misappropriate the settlement funds, the lawyer may not disclose this information. State Bar of Cal. Com. on Prof. Resp. and Conduct, formal opn. No. 1988-96.

A lawyer should explicitly define confidentiality obligations to office staff. A lawyer must investigate facts surrounding unauthorized disclosure of confidential information, inform the client of the disclosure, and offer to withdraw from representation. State Bar of Cal. Com. on Prof. Resp. and Conduct, formal opn. No. 1979-50. See also rule 5.1 of the Rules of Professional Conduct, Duties of Managerial and Supervisory Lawyers and chapter 3 of this Guide, Competence and Diligence, section 3.9.

A lawyer representing an executor in the probate of an estate discovered that the executor had taken estate funds for personal use and intended to conceal the misappropriation in an accounting to be filed with the court. Communications between the lawyer and the executor were completely confidential. The lawyer must first call on the client to rectify any mismanagement and to forego any advantage the client might have wrongfully gained. If the client refuses to correct the accounting, the lawyer should prepare an alternate accounting and send it to the client for signature. If the client refuses to sign the corrected version, the lawyer may not file any accounting. If cited into court for failure to file an accounting, the lawyer may state in a declaration that an alternate accounting was submitted to the client. Withdrawal may be advisable for the lawyer if it can be done without causing prejudice to the client. The lawyer may not disclose the client's misappropriation to a new lawyer. San Diego County Bar Assn., Ethics opn. No. 1990-2.

Article

Bennett, *Don't Tell My Husband, But ...: Ethics in Spousal Representation* (May 1996) 135 Trusts and Estates 40.

6.9 Disclosures Between Joint Clients

When the lawyer receives information from one joint client that the communicating client does not wish to share, the lawyer must consider the relevance and the significance of the information and decide whether to disclose the communication to the other client. The ACTEC Commentaries on the Model Rules of Professional Conduct, rule 1.6 suggest the following possible courses of action:

1. Taking no action with respect to the communication because it is regarded as trivial or irrelevant to the estate planning or business matter at hand;
2. Encouraging the communicating client to disclose the information to the other client or to allow the lawyer to do so; or
3. Withdrawing from representation of the clients if the communication discloses serious adversity between the clients.

If the lawyer obtains a written waiver of confidentiality from the clients at the outset of the representation and if such waiver clearly specifies that the lawyer is free to disclose to either of them confidential information imparted by the other, this conflict of ethical duties may be easier to address. Such a waiver may impose on the lawyer an obligation to disclose even trivial matters to the other client. Nonetheless, the fact that one client seeks to hide information from another may be evidence of directly adverse interests and may preclude the lawyer from continuing to represent them jointly or either of them separately. By establishing the lawyer's role in writing, some of the conflicting duties that may arise from a joint representation may be avoided. The clients may be educated in advance as to the issues relating to confidential communications and may refrain from disclosing information to the lawyer that would put the lawyer in an ethical dilemma.

The lawyer who jointly represents spouses in an estate planning matter may, for example, conclude that information disclosed by one spouse regarding a past act of marital infidelity is not relevant to the current estate planning engagement and should not necessarily be communicated to the other spouse. In reaching that conclusion, the lawyer must assume that the other client would not change his or her estate plan having that information. Consequently, the lawyer will more likely be concerned that the confidential communication imparted by one spouse is so material that it threatens the other client or impairs the lawyer's ability to represent the interests of the other spouse effectively. If instead one spouse informs the lawyer of an intention to divorce the other, or if one spouse discloses having named a third party as the beneficiary of life insurance or employee benefits, the information is indisputably material and must be disclosed. Additionally, the lawyer should not assist one spouse in taking an action, such as drafting a new codicil or new will, which might damage the economic interests of the other spouse or prevent the lawyer from maintaining the ethical duty of loyalty to both clients. Analogous situations arise among multiple family members or business partners.

If the communicating client continues to oppose disclosing the confidence to the other client, the lawyer should consider the ethical duty of loyalty owed to both clients. That consideration of ethical duties may be informed by an express or implied agreement among the lawyer and the joint clients; the reasonable expectations of the clients; the nature of the confidence; and the harm that may result from disclosure. In some instances, the lawyer must also consider whether the interests of the joint clients are or may become directly adverse, preventing the lawyer from effectively representing either or both of them. The lawyer should also consider whether a letter of withdrawal may arouse the other client's suspicions to the point that the communicating client or the lawyer may ultimately be required to disclose the information.

For a discussion of disclosures and informed consent to representation notwithstanding conflicts of interest, see chapter 4 of this Guide, Identifying the Client and the Scope of Representation, section 4.10 and chapter 5 of this Guide, Conflicts of Interest, section 5.2.

ACTEC Commentaries on Model Rules of Professional Conduct, Model Rule 1.6

> *Confidences Imparted by One Joint Client.* As noted earlier, except in special circumstances, joint clients should be advised at the outset of the representation that information from either client may be required to be shared with the other if the lawyer considers such sharing of information necessary or beneficial to the representation. This advice should be confirmed in writing, and the lawyer should consider asking the clients to acknowledge that understanding in writing. Absent an advance agreement that adequately addresses the handling of confidential information shared by only one joint client, a lawyer who receives information from one joint client (the "communicating client") that the client does not wish to be shared with the other joint client (the "other client") is confronted with a situation that may threaten the lawyer's ability to continue to represent one or both of the clients. As soon as practicable after such a communication, the lawyer should consider the relevance and significance of the information and decide upon the appropriate manner in which to proceed. The potential courses of action include, inter alia, (1) taking no action with respect to communications regarding irrelevant (or trivial) matters; (2) encouraging the communicating client to provide the information to the other client or to allow the lawyer to do so; and, (3) withdrawing from the representation if the communication reflects serious adversity between the parties. For example, a lawyer who represents spouses in estate planning matters might conclude that information imparted by one of the spouses regarding a past act of marital infidelity need not be communicated to the other spouse. On the other hand, the lawyer might conclude that action is required with respect to a confidential communication that threatens the interests of the other client or that

could impair the lawyer's ability to represent the other client effectively (e.g., "After she signs the trust agreement, I intend to leave her..." or "All of the insurance policies on my life that name her as beneficiary have lapsed"). Without the informed consent of the other client, the lawyer should not take any action on behalf of the communicating client, such as drafting a codicil or a new will, that might damage the other client's economic interests or otherwise violate the lawyer's duty of loyalty to the other client.

6.10 Sample Disclosure Letter – Prior Representation of a Family Member

The following letter would be sent to a former client who later refers another family member to the lawyer for estate planning services. The letter assumes that both the former and prospective clients will waive the ethical duty of confidentiality between them. The lawyer should adapt it thoughtfully to the lawyer's customary practice and the needs of a particular client representation.

Dear [Client]:

We were pleased to represent you in connection with your estate planning. This letter discusses our ongoing professional obligations to you in light of our proposed representation of [Family Member].

Our professional obligations to you, as our client, require that we keep confidential any communications that we sent or received from you. We may not disclose any communications or information we received from you or any details of your estate plan without your consent. That ethical duty continues after you signed your estate planning documents and the representation concluded.

If [Family Member] retains this firm for representation regarding estate planning, [Family Member] would also be our client. We would owe the ethical duty of confidentiality to [Family Member] as a client, and we may not disclose any communications or information we receive in that representation unless [Family Member] consents.

You and [Family Member] each agree that we will disclose to the other information regarding your separate estate planning that one of you shares or has shared with us, or that we acquire from another source. We will not withhold information from either of you that is relevant or material to your respective estate planning. Of course, any information we receive from you or [Family Member] continues to be protected from disclosure to third parties, unless both of you authorize us to disclose it.

By signing this letter, you consent to the disclosure to [Family Member] of the material terms of your estate plan. We have sent an engagement letter to [Family Member] that includes a consent to disclose to you the material terms of the proposed planning for [Family Member]. When we receive written consent from both of you, our representation of [Family Member] and related estate planning services will begin. If you have any questions about this letter or the proposed terms of disclosure to [Family Member], I encourage you to consult another lawyer about this letter before signing it.

Sincerely,

[Lawyer]

CONSENT

I have reviewed the foregoing letter and agree to the proposed representation of [Family Member] by Lawyer. I also understand and agree that all communications and information the Lawyer previously received from me regarding my estate planning may be shared with [Family Member].

Dated: ________________ ______________________________
[Client 1]

6.11 Organization as Client

California Rules of Professional Conduct, Rule 1.13 - Organization as Client

(a) A lawyer employed or retained by an organization shall conform his or her representation to the concept that the client is the organization itself, acting through its duly authorized directors, officers, employees, members, shareholders, or other constituents overseeing the particular engagement.

(b) If a lawyer representing an organization knows* that a constituent is acting, intends to act or refuses to act in a matter related to the representation in a manner that the lawyer knows* or reasonably should know* is (i) a violation of a legal obligation to the organization or a violation of law reasonably* imputable to the organization, and (ii) likely to result in substantial* injury to the organization, the lawyer shall proceed as is reasonably* necessary in the best lawful interest of the organization. Unless the lawyer reasonably believes* that it is not necessary in the best lawful interest of the organization to do so, the lawyer shall refer the matter to higher authority in the organization, including, if warranted by the circumstances, to the highest authority that can act on behalf of the organization as determined by applicable law.

(c) In taking any action pursuant to paragraph (b), the lawyer shall not reveal information protected by Business and Professions Code section 6068, subdivision (e).

(d) If, despite the lawyer's actions in accordance with paragraph (b), the highest authority that can act on behalf of the organization insists upon action, or fails to act, in a manner that is a violation of a legal obligation to the organization or a violation of law reasonably* imputable to the organization, and is likely to result in substantial* injury to the organization, the lawyer shall continue to proceed as is reasonably* necessary in the best lawful interests of the organization. The lawyer's response may include the lawyer's right and, where appropriate, duty to resign or withdraw in accordance with rule 1.16.

(e) A lawyer who reasonably believes* that he or she has been discharged because of the lawyer's actions taken pursuant to paragraph (b), or who resigns or withdraws under circumstances described in paragraph (d), shall proceed as the lawyer reasonably believes* necessary to assure that the organization's highest authority is informed of the lawyer's discharge, resignation, or withdrawal.

(f) In dealing with an organization's constituents, a lawyer representing the organization shall explain the identity of the lawyer's client whenever the lawyer knows* or reasonably should know* that the organization's interests are adverse to those of the constituent(s) with whom the lawyer is dealing.

(g) A lawyer representing an organization may also represent any of its constituents, subject to the provisions of rules 1.7, 1.8.2, 1.8.6, and 1.8.7. If the organization's consent to the dual representation is required by any of these rules, the consent shall be given by an appropriate official, constituent, or body of the organization other than the individual who is to be represented, or by the shareholders.

An asterisk (*) identifies a defined term in rule 1.0.1 of the Rules of Professional Conduct. For further discussion of a defined term, see chapter 2 of this Guide, Terminology.

The commentary on rule 1.13 of the Rules of Professional Conduct defines "constituents" to include officers, directors, employees, and shareholders and persons who hold equivalent roles in other organizations.

In the course of an estate planning practice, a lawyer may develop client relationships with business organizations and constituents of those organizations in a variety of ways. The following situations are common but not exhaustive of the possibilities:

1. The lawyer is initially engaged solely by an individual for estate planning or other purposes, and the initial formation of the organization occurs either as a part of the recommended planning or as an additional service;
2. The lawyer is initially engaged solely by an individual for estate or business planning, and the client is an existing officer, director, or major shareholder or controlling owner of an already-formed organization;
3. After an initial representation, the client seeks to retain the lawyer to represent the organization, either in connection with business transfer planning or for other matters related to the ordinary business of the organization or for litigation by the organization against unrelated third parties; or

4. In the course of representing of an organization, the lawyer develops relationships with one or more individual directors, officers, or shareholders, and the lawyer is thereafter approached by an individual to perform personal estate planning services or other personal services for that individual.

Maintaining the confidences of multiple clients when they are intimately involved in the same business organization, or when the client is the organization itself, may not be possible. Accordingly, the most conservative course of action is to decline joint, concurrent, or successive representation of an organization and one or more of its constituents, and to continue the lawyer-client relationship solely with the initial client. Possible conflicts of interest may be either too significant to allow joint representation, or so objectionable to one or both clients that the lawyer cannot obtain the required informed consent to the representation and waiver of confidentiality. Rules Prof. Conduct, rule 1.7. For a discussion of disclosures and informed consent to representation notwithstanding conflicts of interest, see chapter 5 of this Guide, Conflicts of Interest, section 5.6.

If the representation of an organization or its constituents raises possible competing ethical duties, the lawyer must clearly and unequivocally establish the identity of the client. The client and other related persons must not be allowed to be mistaken about whose confidences are to be kept and whose are not, or to whom the lawyer owes a duty of loyalty and to whom the lawyer does not owe that duty.

If the client is the organization, the individual constituents should be told in writing, repeatedly, that the lawyer (1) does not represent any of them or their individual interests, (2) is loyal only to the organization and not to any individual constituent, and (3) cannot hold in confidence any documents or information that any individual constituent provides to the lawyer. Rule 1.13(f) of the Rules of Professional Conduct reflects and responds to existing case law. See *Meehan v. Hopps* (1956) 144 Cal.App.2d 284, holding that a lawyer representing a corporation deals with the organization's constituents in their representative capacities and not individually. To comply with rule 1.13 of the Rules of Professional Conduct, the lawyer must explain to those individual constituents that the organization is the client, and must also clearly explain to them the nature of the lawyer's obligations to the organization, including that confidential information provided by the individual constituents may be used adversely to any of them.

In the case of a partnership, special rules, discussed below, apply with respect to litigation exceptions to the lawyer-client privilege. Those special rules require additional disclosures. The lawyer should educate the representatives of a corporate client as to how to protect the corporation's privilege. Such protection would include defining the rights of officers, directors, and shareholders to inspect documents or obtain communications that may be subject to the lawyer-client or work-product privileges.

If the initial and sole ongoing client is an individual constituent of an organization, the lawyer should advise other officers, directors, and shareholders, in writing and with reasonable regularity, that the lawyer is loyal to the interests of that individual and not to them or to the organization itself. The lawyer should advise the other officers, directors, and shareholders that the lawyer intends to negotiate actions only in accordance with the ethical duty of loyalty owed to that individual client, that the lawyer intends to hold confidential any information obtained from that client, and if circumstances require, that the lawyer will represent that client adversely to the organization or the other constituents.

The lawyer may represent individual constituents on personal matters unrelated to the formation or business of the organization. Frequently, the individual client's need for representation does not touch upon the business of the organization. Such matters may include real estate transactions with third parties, personal income tax advice, the formation of unrelated noncompetitive entities, or family law matters. Other matters may be indirectly related to the lawyer's representation of the organization, such as personal estate planning for disposition of the individual's ownership interests. In that case the lawyer should be familiar with any restrictions on transfers in the organizational documents or by contract. Directly adverse interests are usually rare. On the other hand, when estate planning involves the organization as a party to a contract, such as in the negotiation of a buy-sell agreement, the lawyer must address the ethical issues related to joint, concurrent, or successive representation.

In the interests of practical efficiency, the constituents, individually or as authorized representatives of the organization, may consent to joint or successive representation after the lawyer's disclosure of possible conflicts among them. Joint representation of the organization and participating constituents may, in fact, best serve the clients, where the clients' common interests predominate over their separate interests and the lawyer does not determine that there is a significant risk to the lawyer's loyal and effective representation of all parties. Rules 1.13 and 1.7 of the Rules of Professional Conduct allow joint representation provided that the lawyer discloses the confidentiality issues to the clients and obtains their informed written consent.

Rule 1.13(g) of the Rules of Professional Conduct provides that the lawyer may engage in joint, concurrent, or successive representation of an organization and an individual constituent, provided that the consent of the organization be obtained from an "appropriate" official, constituent, or body of the organization other than the individual constituent, or by the shareholders of the organization. "Appropriate" is not defined, but common sense would dictate that the person or group should not only have authority to give such consent but should also be free of any conflict of interest which would cause such consent to be given for reasons adverse to the organization's best interests.

Adverse Conduct of a Constituent. Rule 1.13(b) of the Rules of Professional Conduct gives specific guidance on the ethical duties of a lawyer representing an organization, when a constituent acts, threatens to act, or refuses to act, contrary to the interest of the organization. The lawyer's duty of loyalty to the organization remains unchanged, as does the duty to preserve confidential information that the lawyer receives in the course of the representation or that may be detrimental to the organization. Within the bounds of those ethical duties, the lawyer may refer the adverse conduct to a higher authority within the organization. If a higher authority fails to address that conduct and the lawyer believes that substantial harm to the organization may result, the lawyer may need to seek to withdraw from the representation in accordance with the procedures set forth in rule 1.16 of the Rules of Professional Conduct.

Litigation. Under present case law, representation of a partnership is a hybrid of sole and joint representation. When the client is a partnership, all the general partners are treated by case law as *de facto* clients for purposes of application of the litigation-related "joint client" exception to the lawyer-client privilege. Evid. Code, sec. 962. Therefore, representation of a partnership in a litigated matter requires adapting the principles applicable to joint representation. Unfortunately, existing case law is not clear whether each general partner is automatically a joint client for all issues involving application of lawyer-client privilege, or only for application of Evidence Code section 962.

As in other instances of joint representation, the lawyer should advise the partners that the lawyer-client privilege may not protect communications between the lawyer and one partner from disclosure to another and should specifically discuss the issue in the context of potential future litigation between the partners. Further, the lawyer should take every opportunity to define in writing the scope of the representation as being restricted to partnership matters only, to guard against the inaccurate impression that the lawyer was engaged to represent any partner individually or on matters unrelated to partnership business.

A partnership as an organization may be a client for purposes of rule 1.13 of the Rules of Professional Conduct. Any partner may become a client subject to the lawyer's attendant duty of loyalty, on facts supporting the creation of a lawyer-client relationship. Thus, the lawyer must be vigilant in advising the partners that only the organization is the client, if the lawyer wishes to avoid being held to represent an individual partner unintentionally. *Wortham & Van Liew v. Super. Ct.* (*Clubb*) (1987) 188 Cal.App.3d 927.

Rule 1.13 of the Rules of Professional Conduct closely tracks model rule 1.13 but differs in one significant respect. Under the model rule, when a constituent acts or threatens to act in a way that is harmful to the organization and refuses the lawyer's entreaties to desist, the lawyer may in certain circumstances reveal confidential communications "but only if and to the extent the lawyer reasonably believes necessary to prevent substantial injury to the organization." Rule 1.13 of the Rules of Professional Conduct, by contrast, requires or allows the lawyer to withdraw or resign, but without violating the ethical duty of confidentiality. Rules Prof. Conduct, rule 1.13(c)-(d).

Former California Rules of Professional Conduct, Rule 3-600 – Organization as Client

> (A) In representing an organization, a member shall conform his or her representation to the concept that the client is the organization itself, acting through its highest authorized officer, employee, body, or constituent overseeing the particular engagement.
>
> (B) If a member acting on behalf of an organization knows that an actual or apparent agent of the organization acts or intends or refuses to act in a manner that is or may be a violation of law reasonably imputable to the organization, or in a manner which is likely to result in substantial injury to the organization, the member shall not violate his or her duty of protecting all confidential information as provided in Business and Professions Code section 6068, subdivision (e). Subject to Business

and Professions Code section 6068, subdivision (e), the member may take such actions as appear to the member to be in the best lawful interest of the organization. Such actions may include among others:

(1) Urging reconsideration of the matter while explaining its likely consequences to the organization; or

(2) Referring the matter to the next higher authority in the organization, including, if warranted by the seriousness of the matter, referral to the highest internal authority that can act on behalf of the organization.

(C) If, despite the member's actions in accordance with paragraph (B), the highest authority that can act on behalf of the organization insists upon action or a refusal to act that is a violation of law and is likely to result in substantial injury to the organization, the member's response is limited to the member's right, and, where appropriate, duty to resign in accordance with rule 3-700.

(D) In dealing with an organization's directors, officers, employees, members, shareholders, or other constituents, a member shall explain the identity of the client for whom the member acts, whenever it is or becomes apparent that the organization's interests are or may become adverse to those of the constituent(s) with whom the member is dealing. The member shall not mislead such a constituent into believing that the constituent may communicate confidential information to the member in a way that will not be used in the organization's interest if that is or becomes adverse to the constituent.

(E) A member representing an organization may also represent any of its directors, officers, employees, members, shareholders, or other constituents, subject to the provisions of rule 3-310. If the organization's consent to the dual representation is required by rule 3-310, the consent shall be given by an appropriate constituent of the organization other than the individual or constituent who is to be represented, or by the shareholder(s) or organization members.

Rule 1.13 of the Rules of Professional Conduct is a reformulation of the substance of former rule 3-600, with the following modifications:

1. Previously, the lawyer had the option of reporting to a higher authority in the organization certain harmful actions of constituents. The new rule mandates such reporting. Rules Prof. Conduct, rule 3-600(b);
2. Rule 3-600(b) now provides a two-part test to determine if a constituent's action should be reported to a person with higher authority in the organization. The obligation to report is triggered only if both parts of the test are satisfied; and
3. If the lawyer is discharged or withdraws as a result of these "reporting up" requirements, the lawyer is explicitly required, to the extent the lawyer "reasonably believes necessary," to report to the organization's highest authority the lawyer's discharge, withdrawal, or other termination. Rules Prof. Conduct, rule 3-600(e).

Statute

California Corporations Code section 15901.04, subdivision (a)

> A limited partnership is an entity distinct from its partners.

Cases

A trial court's decision to deny a disqualification motion was reversed by the Court of Appeal, and a lawyer was accordingly disqualified from representing employees of the lawyer's former employer in litigation against that employer. The lawyer had obtained privileged communications relating to the pending litigation in the course of the lawyer's prior employment as president and chief operating officer of the employer. The reasoning of the Court of Appeal was based in pertinent part on the principle that "[a]lthough the 'classic disqualification case involves the attorney switching sides … [i]n other cases, counsel may be disqualified where counsel has obtained the secrets of an adverse party in some other manner.'; '[d]isqualification is warranted in these cases not because the attorney has a duty to protect the adverse party's confidences, but because the situation implicates the attorney's ethical duty to maintain the integrity of the judicial process.'" *O'Gara Coach Co., LLC v. Ra* (2019) 30 Cal.App.5th 1115, 1128 (quoting *Rousch v. Seagate Technology, LLC* (2007) 150 Cal.App.4th 210, 219). Compare *Wu v. O'Gara Coach Co., LLC* (2019) 38 Cal.App.5th 1069 (A lawyer who was also former president and chief operating officer of the defendant was not disqualified from representing the plaintiff in wrongful termination claim against the defendant because the lawyer lacked confidential information relevant to the representation. The president and chief operating officer had not investigated or had any discussions with outside counsel regarding the plaintiff's claims).

A management dispute arose between two 50% owners of an LLC. One owner brought an action for malpractice against the lawyers who represented the LLC in connection with the dispute. The court held under former Rules of Professional Conduct, rule 3-600 that the LLC lawyers owed no professional duty to the individual members. The plaintiff owner produced no evidence to support an implied lawyer-client privilege. The Court of Appeal affirmed the trial court dismissal of the case for lack of standing. *Sprengel v. Zyblut* (2019) 40 Cal.App.5th 1028, 1044-1046.

An in-house lawyer was fired for reporting to the lawyer's superiors the actions of another corporate employee and sued for retaliatory discharge in violation of public policy. The in-house lawyer argued that the firing was in retaliation for disclosing confidential communications, and the lawyer argued that former rule 3-600 of the Rules of Professional Conduct required that disclosure. The court held that a plain reading of rule 3-600 showed that the lawyer's ethical duty to report was merely *permissive,* and therefore the lawyer could not claim that termination resulted from the performance of a mandatory ethical duty. As such, the termination of the lawyer's employment violated no public policy. Performance of a permissive ethical duty also did not support the claim of wrongful termination. The court held that any actions the lawyer chose to take under former rule 3-600(B) were subject to the ethical duty to protect confidential client information. A claim must fail if it can only be proven by the disclosure of such confidential information. *Tam v. Qualcomm* (S.D. Cal. 2018) 300 F.Supp.3d 1130, 1144. The result in this case might have been different under rule 1.13(b) of the Rules of Professional Conduct, where the reporting requirement under certain circumstances is mandatory.

"Substantial evidence supported the trial court's findings that disqualification of defense attorney was necessary to prevent doubts about the integrity of the judicial process and to prevent future prejudice or harm to client from defense attorney's exploitation of contents of e-mail, which contained privileged attorney-client information and was inadvertently disclosed to third parties, and thus trial court did not abuse its discretion in disqualifying attorney in client's underlying legal malpractice action against one of those third parties. The evidence showed that attorney thought it was permissible to use e-mail to oppose client's claims and that attorney's previous access to the e-mail would undermine public trust in the integrity of the adjudicatory process. Evid. Code 954." *McDermott, Will & Emery LLP v. Super. Ct.* (*Hausman*) (2017) 10 Cal.App.5th 1083.

Because the existence of the corporate lawyer-client privilege would deny the defendant lawyer the ability to mount a meaningful defense, a shareholder may not bring a derivative suit for malpractice against the corporate lawyer notwithstanding that the corporation refuses a proper demand to commence the action. The shareholders do not stand in the shoes of the corporation for purposes of waiver of the privilege or obtain the right to waive the privilege by virtue of filing the action. *McDermott, Will & Emery v. Super. Ct.* (*James*) (2000) 83 Cal.App.4th 378.

In the absence of the applicability of a specific Evidence Code exception, or the existence of an independent confidential relationship between the shareholder and corporate counsel, a shareholder of a corporation does not have a right, merely by virtue of status as a shareholder, to inspect corporate documents that are protected by the lawyer-client privilege. Also, a director of a corporation is not a "partner" for purposes of the rule of *Wortham & Van Liew v. Super. Ct.* (*Clubb*) (1987) 188 Cal.App.3d 927, and *McCain v. Phoenix Resources* (1986) 185 Cal.App.3d 578, that a partner is entitled to confidential documents. The rule in those cases does not apply to corporations. A director cannot delegate any director's rights of inspection to a shareholder or use status as a director to pass confidential information to a shareholder to be used adversely to the corporation, as such acts would be a breach of the director's fiduciary duties to the corporation. *Nat. Football League Properties v. Super. Ct.* (*Oakland Raiders*) (1998) 65 Cal.App.4th 100.

A limited partner's right to obtain records of the partnership extends to records in the possession of the partnership's lawyers. Purely private or personal records of one of the partners may be distinguished from partnership records such that the lawyer-client privilege may prevent disclosure of them. However, the lawyers represented the partnership as an entity, not just the general partner in particular. *McCain v. Phoenix Resources* (1986) 185 Cal.App.3d 578.

Over many years, corporate counsel to a closely held family corporation, in which all of the shareholders were the children of the original sole shareholder and their spouses, also acted as an individual lawyer to many members of the family, including each of the shareholders. In a family scuffle over control, meetings were held between corporate counsel and members of two families, which sometimes included other nonfamily corporate officers, but did not include the presence of one "troublemaking" brother. In the ensuing action to dissolve the corporation, the plaintiff sought discovery of the communications at these meetings. In this context (1) a closely held corporation enjoys a lawyer-client privilege and there is no exception for disclosure of protected communications to a shareholder on the basis of shareholder status alone; (2) the presence of spouses or other family members at meetings did not cause the communications to be unprotected, as the court viewed disclosures to those persons as being reasonably necessary to furtherance of the interests of the corporation, within the meaning of Evidence Code section 952; and (3) plaintiff had not sued in the capacity of a director and could not assert a right to obtain disclosure of confidential communications in that capacity. The court noted in dicta that a director may only obtain confidential information for proper purposes consistent with a director's fiduciary obligations and not for a hostile purpose. The court stated in a footnote that the existence of a conflict of interest in a lawyer's representation of both a corporation and of the principals of the corporation does not in and of itself impair the corporation's lawyer-client privilege, but did not analyze the relationship between this assertion and the rules relating to joint representation. *Hoiles v. Super. Ct.* (*Freedom Newspapers, Inc.*) (1984) 157 Cal.App.3d 1192.

A lawyer may not represent a client if the nature of the representation inherently required the lawyer either to serve the new client loyally by revealing and utilizing previously obtained confidences in a manner adverse to the interests of a former client, or else to protect the confidences of the former client and thereby impair the ethical duty of undivided loyalty to the new client. The lawyer initially represented the corporation and subsequently undertook representation of a minority shareholder and director adverse to the corporation. The public policy in favor of encouraging confidential communication between the lawyer and the first client was found to be of such importance that the agreement for the second representation was declared void, and the lawyer was not permitted to collect fees with respect to that representation. While it may have been theoretically possible under the Rules of Professional Conduct to obtain "the informed and written consent of the client or former client," such consent had not been obtained. *Goldstein v. Lees* (1975) 46 Cal.App.3d 614.

An avoidable expenditure of significant resources was devoted to the factual determination of whether a corporate officer was personally a client of the lawyer at the same time that the corporation was a client. Once it was determined that the lawyer represented only the corporation, the court followed and clearly articulated the rule that information provided by an officer to corporate counsel could properly be disclosed and used in a manner adverse to the interests of the individual officer. *Meehan v. Hopps* (1956) 144 Cal.App.2d 284.

Articles

Wertlieb, *The Importance of Knowing Who Is, and Who Is Not, My Client* (Sept. 3, 2019) Cal. Lawyers Assn.

Garner, *A Representational Trinity: The Parent, the Sub, and Holy Lawyer* (Mar. 2013) State Bar of Cal. MCLE.

Mermelstein & Amer, *When Transactional Attorneys Face Criminal Liability* (Dec. 2009) 32 L.A. Law. 17.

Stewart, *In-House Counsel as Whistleblower: A Rat Without a Remedy?* (2008) 240 N.Y. Law J. 24, col. 3.

Rothstein, *"Anything You Say May Be Used Against You": A Proposed Seminar on the Lawyer's Duty to Warn of Confidentiality's Limits in Today's Post-Enron World* (2007) 76 Fordham Law Rev. 1745.

Serwin & Pandika, *Who is the Client? Confidentiality When Representing Organizations* (Jul./Aug. 2007) 24 GPSolo 22 (publication of the ABA Solo, Small Firm, and General Practice Division (GPSolo)).

6.12 Fiduciaries and Beneficiaries

A lawyer who represents a beneficiary or beneficiaries must maintain each beneficiary's confidences when dealing with the fiduciary and the fiduciary's lawyer.

If a lawyer represents the fiduciary or fiduciaries, there is much greater potential for confusion and controversy regarding the scope of the lawyer's representation. At least insofar as private express trusts are concerned, the client under California law is the fiduciary or fiduciaries and not the estate or trust as a whole, and not the fiduciary and beneficiaries as joint clients. This rule is materially different than the law in many states and federal law under ERISA.

If the lawyer represents both the fiduciary and another person as the beneficiary of the fiduciary relationship, the lawyer likely has an ethical duty to protect the confidences of each from the other. As always with joint clients, disclosure authority and expectations of confidentiality should be memorialized in writing, most appropriately in the engagement letter. See chapter 4 of this Guide, Identifying the Client and the Scope of Representation, section 4.10. In addition, the fiduciary and beneficiary clients have likely "retained or consulted" the lawyer on "a matter of common interest" for purposes of Evidence Code section 962. Neither of them may claim the lawyer-client privilege if litigation arises between the two of them about that matter.

More complicated is the case when the lawyer believes that the only client is the fiduciary, but a beneficiary or the settlor or testator incorrectly believes that the lawyer represents that interested party as well. Applicable case law has found a *de facto* lawyer-client relationship as a result of failing to clarify the representation to nonclients. The lawyer is well advised to tell the beneficiaries or other interested parties, in writing and at the outset of an engagement for the fiduciary, that the lawyer represents only the fiduciary. Subsequent communications with an unrepresented beneficiary should advise the beneficiary to engage a separate lawyer to avoid the impression of a lawyer-client relationship with that beneficiary.

If the lawyer represents a fiduciary who is separately represented in a beneficiary capacity, the lawyer must be wary of disclosing the client's confidences to the other lawyer without the explicit consent of the client. In representing a fiduciary, the lawyer must be sensitive to the client's duty of impartiality in dealing with beneficiaries. Other beneficiaries and, perhaps, unrepresented beneficiaries may object if the lawyer discloses information to the fiduciary's personal lawyer but does not make similar disclosures to them.

The fiduciary client is generally owed the same duty of confidentiality as any other client, and the lawyer must exercise the same care to avoid unauthorized disclosure. Communication with the beneficiaries may be required or permitted under the notice provisions of the Probate Code, and the fiduciary client and the lawyer may believe that disclosure to beneficiaries or their lawyer sometimes is an appropriate way to keep the beneficiaries informed about the administration of the trust. In undertaking such communication, the lawyer is well-advised to consult with the fiduciary client regularly about expectations of confidentiality and disclosure.

6.13 The Lawyer-Client Privilege in Fiduciary Litigation

Fiduciary matters warrant particular care, because disclosure to a beneficiary may constitute a waiver of the lawyer-client privilege for the subject matter. Such a waiver may work to the detriment of both the fiduciary and the beneficiary in dealing with other interested parties. For example, a discussion between the fiduciary and a beneficiary about the advice the fiduciary's lawyer has rendered concerning a commercial lease dispute may waive the privilege and make the content of an otherwise confidential communication discoverable by the other party to the lease. Similar waiver questions may arise as a result of discussions with a beneficiary or a beneficiary's lawyer about a federal tax controversy or potential controversy, making the content of an otherwise confidential communication between the fiduciary and the fiduciary's lawyer discoverable by an agent of the Internal Revenue Service. A discussion between the fiduciary's lawyer and the lawyer for a beneficiary may give rise to litigation over the applicability of the so-called "common-interest" exception to the general waiver rules, even if it does not constitute a waiver.

The holder of the lawyer-client privilege has the authority to waive that privilege and authorize disclosure. The lawyer should advise a fiduciary client that the privilege belongs to the fiduciary office, not the individual, and that confidential lawyer-client communications on trust administration matters may be discovered by successor fiduciaries. If the identity of the fiduciary changes, a successor fiduciary holds the privilege with respect to "confidential communications that occurred when the predecessor, *in its fiduciary capacity*, sought the lawyer's advice *for guidance in administering the trust*. If a predecessor trustee seeks legal advice in its personal capacity out of a genuine concern for possible future charges of breach of fiduciary duty, the predecessor may be able to avoid disclosing the advice to a successor trustee by hiring a separate lawyer and paying for the advice out if its personal funds." *Moeller v. Super. Ct.* (1997) 16 Cal.4th 1124, 1134 (italics in original). Separate representation for issues of personal liability may preclude the successor from waiving the privilege, as would be allowed for general trust administration issues. By analogy, this rationale regarding the lawyer-client privilege in litigation could apply to the ethical duty of confidentiality in the Business and Professions Code as well.

The transfer of the privilege upon a change of trustee has been analogized to a corporate change of control, when new management generally holds the privilege as to communications between prior management and corporate counsel. If a communication was "personal" to a prior manager or board of directors, however, the individual client remains the holder of the privilege.

Exceptions to the Assertion of the Privilege. Evidence Code sections 956 to 962 identify the exceptions to the lawyer-client privilege in California. Those sections likely to be of most concern to trust and probate lawyers are the crime-fraud exception and the exceptions related to determining the competency and intent of a deceased client.

Exceptions in other jurisdictions may be broader. The so-called "fiduciary" exception to the lawyer-client privilege derives from common law and is recognized in federal tax controversies. Many states and the federal courts generally hold that a fiduciary has no privilege with respect to the trust beneficiaries regarding any communication related to the administration of a trust, as opposed to a communication concerning the "personal" defense against breach-of-trust claims against the fiduciary. The California Supreme Court employed a similar analysis in *Moeller v. Superior Court* in determining that the holder of the privilege changes with the identity of the trustee.

Conservators and Guardians. Evidence Code section 953, subdivision (b), as amended effective January 1, 2019, makes a statutory exception to a guardian or conservator holding and exercising the lawyer-client privilege. The conservator or guardian may not assert or waive the lawyer-client privilege if the conservator or guardian has an *actual or apparent* conflict of interest with the client. This exception protects a client's rights in the event of a dispute between the client and the client's conservator or guardian. Nevertheless, the new statutory exception is broad. It applies to both actual and apparent conflicts and is not limited to conflicts that may relate directly to the exercise of the privilege. The lawyer should resolve any doubts as to possible conflicts in favor of the conserved client.

Statute

California Evidence Code section 953

> As used in this article, "holder of the privilege" means:
>
> (a) The client, if the client has no guardian or conservator.
>
> (b) (1) A guardian or conservator of the client, if the client has a guardian or conservator, except as provided in paragraph (2).
>
> (2) If the guardian or conservator has an actual or apparent conflict of interest with the client, then the guardian or conservator does not hold the privilege.
>
> (c) The personal representative of the client if the client is dead, including a personal representative appointed pursuant to Section 12252 of the Probate Code.
>
> (d) A successor, assign, trustee in dissolution, or any similar representative of a firm, association, organization, partnership, business trust, corporation, or public entity that is no longer in existence.

Cases

Under the holding in *Moeller v. Super. Ct.* (1997) 16 Cal.4th 1124, the lawyer-client privilege vests in the office of the trustee, and the right to assert the privilege passes to the successor trustee. A former trustee sought legal advice from a lawyer. No contention was made in this case that the former trustee retained separate counsel for advice regarding the trustee's separate interests. The court held no communications between the former trustee and counsel may be withheld from a successor trustee. Any trust provision seeking to do so would violate public policy and be unenforceable. *Morgan v. Super. Ct.* (2018) 23 Cal.App.5th 1026, 1037.

Predecessor trustees must show they communicated with trust lawyers in their personal capacity to rely on lawyer-client privilege to deny documents to the successor trustee. More than 40 communications were identified in the supplemental privilege log as protected because they were 'defensive'. Labeling a document as `defensive' does not by itself fulfill the criteria described in *Moeller*. "Further, the burden falls on the predecessor trustee claiming the privilege 'to distinguish, scrupulously and painstakingly, his or her own interests from those of the beneficiaries.'" *Fiduciary Trust Internat. of Cal. v. Klein* (2017) 9 Cal.App.5th 1184, 1201 citing *Moeller v. Super. Ct.* (1997) 16 Cal.4th 1124, 1134.

A court may not review the contents of a communication to determine whether the lawyer-client privilege protects that communication. The lawyer-client privilege was absolute and prevented disclosure, no matter how necessary or relevant to the lawsuit. It was neither necessary nor appropriate to review a communication to determine whether the lawyer-client privilege protected it. *DP Pham, LLC v. Cheadle* (2016) 246 Cal.App.4th 653.

A successor conservator could pursue a malpractice cause of action against the lawyers for the prior conservator. Citing *Moeller v. Super. Ct.* (1997) 16 Cal.4th 1124, 1127, the court held that a successor fiduciary "assumes all the powers of [the predecessor], including the power to assert the attorney-client privilege as to confidential communications on the subject of trust administration." The malfeasance of the prior conservator did not bar the malpractice claim. *Stine v. Dell'Osso* (2014) 230 Cal.App.4th 834, 841-842.

The lawyer-client privilege did not protect third party information unless the third party was an agent of the client. *Zimmerman v. Super. Ct.* (2013) 220 Cal.App.4th 389.

The Court of Appeal found that nonclient plaintiffs adequately pled a claim of civil conspiracy between defendants and the lawyers representing defendants. The lawyers had an independent legal duty to refrain from defrauding nonclients and to disburse funds from a client trust account in a fair manner. The court further held that an independent legal duty also arises when a lawyer engages in conduct that goes beyond the role of a legal representative. The litigation privilege did not apply because the communications and affirmative misconduct of the lawyers interfered with the court-approved plan of remediation and did not further the objects of the litigation. The court concluded that the lawyer-client privilege did not bar the claim that could be proved by circumstantial evidence, and that assertion of the privilege could make civil conspiracy claims not viable. *Rickley v. Goodfriend* (2013) 212 Cal.App.4th 1136.

Normal civil discovery rules apply in breach-of-trust litigation. Beneficiaries are not entitled to discover the contents of confidential communications with the trustee's lawyers. They are not entitled to discover any work product memorializing the lawyers' impressions, conclusions, opinions, or legal research or theories unless there was a waiver of the privilege, nor are they entitled to discover any other work product absent a finding that denial of discovery will unfairly prejudice them in preparing their claim or defense or will result in injustice. *Wells Fargo Bank, N.A., v. Super. Ct. (Boltwood)* (2000) 22 Cal.4th 201.

The successor trustee holds the lawyer-client privilege for most communications between a prior trustee and the trustee's lawyer about the trust administration, except for defensive communications sought for the trustee's own protection. *Moeller v. Super. Ct.* (1997) 16 Cal.4th 1124.

Trust beneficiaries are not joint clients of the trustee's lawyer and are not entitled to discover otherwise privileged lawyer work product of trustee's lawyer that has not been communicated to the trustee. *Lasky, Haas, Cohler & Munter v. Super. Ct.* (*Getty*) (1985) 172 Cal.App.3d 264.

6.14 Sample Disclosure to Fiduciaries Regarding the Lawyer - Client Privilege

The following sample paragraph may be adapted for inclusion in an engagement letter for the representation of a trustee. Even if litigation is not foreseen at the outset of the representation, the lawyer should inform the proposed trustee-client of the necessary steps to preserve the evidentiary privilege if the trust administration turns acrimonious. The lawyer should adapt it thoughtfully to the lawyer's customary practice and the needs of a particular client representation.

> *Lawyer-Client Privilege.* Upon acceptance of this representation, confidential communications between Lawyer and Client will be protected by the lawyer-client privilege. The term "confidential communication" means information transmitted between the Client and Lawyer in the course of that relationship and in confidence. A communication is confidential if, so far as Client is aware, it discloses information to no one other than those present to further Client's interest or those to whom disclosure is reasonably necessary for the accomplishment of the matter for which Lawyer is consulted.
>
> Client must take reasonable steps to ensure that emails between Lawyer and Client are not disclosed to third persons. For example, emails sent and received from Client's work computer or work email address may be subject to review by Client's employer and, therefore, not protected by the lawyer-client privilege. Use of an employer email account may compromise the communication and open the door for discovery by opposing counsel or parties if the matter becomes contested in the future. Client agrees to provide a preferred email account to be used by Lawyer in this matter. Also, emails forwarded or copied to third persons may constitute a waiver of the lawyer-client privilege.
>
> Under California law, a trustee may assert the lawyer-client privilege to prevent disclosure of confidential communications between the trustee and a lawyer consulted on behalf of the trust. However, the authority to assert the lawyer-client privilege passes from the predecessor trustee to a successor trustee when the successor assumes the office of trustee. Any confidential communications between Client and Lawyer concerning the trust administration may not be privileged with respect to a successor trustee.
>
> Issues may arise in the trust administration for which Client may be at risk of personal liability for actions taken as trustee. For example, the beneficiaries may bring a claim against Client for breach of fiduciary duty or dispute Client's account

as trustee. The scope of this representation is limited to the trust administration and Client's fiduciary duties as trustee. If Client has concerns regarding personal liability for actions taken as trustee, Client would appropriately obtain advice from an independent lawyer. Communications with an independent lawyer regarding any such liability would be protected from disclosure by a separate lawyer-client privilege.

6.15 Retention of Client's Original Documents

A lawyer who has drawn a will or other estate planning documents for a client may offer to retain the executed originals of the documents subject to the client's order. Historically, retention of original wills by the drafting lawyer was common practice. Those who advocate for the practice assert that retention by the lawyer makes it less likely the document will be lost, destroyed, altered, or overlooked at the death of the testator or settlor. The contrary assertion is that retention of the documents is done primarily for the benefit of the lawyer, hoping to be retained by the named executor or trustee in the post-death administration. By keeping the documents, the lawyer assumes an enormous responsibility to store the documents indefinitely. The current trend seems to be against retaining original documents, partly because the accumulation of original documents belonging to clients who can no longer be located presents a storage problem, and partly in recognition that clients are now less likely to die in the same community where they signed their documents. Nonetheless, no ethical duty prohibits the practice, provided that the lawyer complies with as the provisions of Probate Code sections 700 to 735.

A lawyer who retains a client's documents for safekeeping should provide the client with a written notice acknowledging that the documents are held subject to the client's order. That written notice may be in the form of a letter. The receipt may, but need not, also indicate that the fiduciary designated in the documents is not required to retain as counsel the lawyer with whom the documents were left for safekeeping. In particular, the documents should be properly identified and appropriately safeguarded from loss or destruction. Subject to otherwise applicable laws, the lawyer should comply with the client's written directions regarding disposition of the documents. Probate Code sections 700 to 735 set forth the duties of a lawyer who holds original client documents. Before assuming responsibility for storing original client documents, the lawyer should review the provisions of Probate Code sections 732 to 734 governing deposit of the documents on the death, incapacity, or retirement of the lawyer and Probate Code section 8200 governing deposit of the documents upon the death of the client. Pursuant to Probate Code section 8200, a custodian of a will has the statutory obligation to lodge the original of that will with the court and to pay to the court a fee for that lodging ($50.00 under Government Code section 70626 as of the date of publication of this edition of the Guide).

The retention of the client's original estate planning documents does not itself make the client an active client or impose any obligation on the lawyer to take steps to keep informed regarding the client's management of property and family status. Similarly, sending a client periodic letters encouraging the client to review the sufficiency of the client's estate plan or calling the client's attention to subsequent legal developments do not increase the lawyer's obligation to the client. For a discussion of the ethical duties owed to a client after a representation terminates, see chapter 7 of this Guide, Communication, section 7.7.

Ethics Opinions

A lawyer may not ethically deposit a client's will with a private will depository absent the client's express consent, since the Probate Code provides the exclusive legal means for disposing of wills and other estate planning documents held on deposit by a lawyer. A lawyer may ethically register a will with a will registry without the client's express consent, only if the lawyer concludes that disclosure would further the client's interest and not be embarrassing or detrimental to the client. If the lawyer cannot locate the client, the lawyer may only terminate the deposit pursuant to Probate Code sections 700 et seq. A lawyer may register certain identifying information about a client's will or other estate planning documents with a private will registry if the lawyer can determine that registration will not violate the lawyer's fiduciary duties of confidentiality and competence. State Bar of Cal. Com. on Prof. Resp. and Conduct, formal opn. No. 2007-173.

Before a law firm may destroy its office files of a deceased client, the firm must attempt to give notice to the legal representatives or successors in interest, except where (1) there is no pending matter or any reasonably foreseeable possibility that the files may be needed to protect the legal interests of the deceased client; and (2) the firm lawyers reasonably believe that the documents have no significant pecuniary or intrinsic value. In responding to a request from the legal representative or successors in interest to inspect or obtain return of documents, the law firm has an ethical duty to maintain the deceased client's confidences and secrets. L.A. County Bar Assn., Ethics opn. No. 491 (Oct. 20, 1997).

6.16 Sample Provisions on Retention of Client Documents

The following optional provisions may be included in an engagement letter to clarify and obtain the client's advance consent to the documents retention policy of the lawyer or the firm. The lawyer should adapt it thoughtfully to the lawyer's customary practice and the needs of a particular client representation.

> Dear [Client],
>
> We do not hold original estate planning documents for clients. Therefore, you will have to make arrangements to safeguard your own original documents. We generally do not recommend that you place your original documents in safe deposit box unless another person has access.
>
> You agree that we have the right to destroy the client file we create for you [NUMBER] years after we cease to actively represent you (i.e., after we last perform legal services for you). Your "client file" consists of all paper and electronic copies of the trust administration file, documents sent to us by you or third parties (such as deeds, beneficiary designations and statements from financial institutions), correspondence and other written communications between us and others that pertain to the trust. You agree that all other pertinent materials (such as

our notes and internal memoranda) are proprietary to us and not part of your client file.

Before destroying your client file, we will attempt to contact you to make arrangements to deliver the file contents to you. If we are unable to contact you at the most recent address contained in our file, then, subject to applicable law, we may destroy your file without further notice. It will be your responsibility to notify us of any change in your address and other contact information.

Sincerely,

[Lawyer]

Reprinted with permission from The American College of Trust and Estate Counsel.

6.17 Duty to Preserve Confidences After Death of Client

After a client's death, the lawyer has a continuing ethical duty to maintain inviolate the confidences and to preserve the secrets of the now deceased client. The privilege may be waived by the client's successor in interest, typically, though not always, the client's personal representative.

However, the Evidence Code provides specific exceptions to the lawyer-client communications privilege in the following cases:

1. When the otherwise privileged communication is relevant to an issue between parties, all whom claim through a deceased client, regardless of whether the claims are by testate or intestate succession, nonprobate transfer, or by inter vivos transaction. Evid. Code, sec. 957;
2. When the communication is relevant to an issue concerning the intention or competence of a client executing an attested document of which the lawyer is an attesting witness, or concerning the execution or attestation of such a document. Evid. Code, sec. 959;
3. When the communication is relevant to an issue concerning the intention of a client, now deceased, with respect to a deed of conveyance, will, or other writing executed by the client, purporting to affect an interest in property. Evid. Code, sec. 960;
4. When the communication is relevant to an issue concerning the validity of a deed of conveyance, will, or other writing, executed by a client, now deceased, purporting to affect an interest in property. Evid. Code, sec. 961; and
5. When no holder of the privilege exists for a deceased client. Evid. Code, sec. 954, subd. (c).

Nevertheless, the estate planning lawyer for a now deceased client may be authorized to make limited disclosures of communications with that client.

In general, the lawyer's duty of confidentiality continues after the death of a client. Accordingly, a lawyer ordinarily should not disclose confidential information

> following a client's death. However, if consent is given by the client's personal representative, or if the decedent had expressly or impliedly authorized disclosure, the lawyer who represented the deceased client may provide an interested party, including a potential litigant, with information regarding a deceased client's dispositive instruments and intent, including prior instruments and communications relevant thereto. The personal representative or client may also authorize disclosure of other confidential information learned during the representation if there is a need for that information A lawyer may be impliedly authorized to make appropriate disclosure of client confidential information that would promote the client's estate plan, forestall litigation, preserve assets, and further family understanding of the decedent's intention. Disclosures should ordinarily be limited to information that the lawyer would be required to reveal as a witness.

ACTEC Commentaries on the Model Rules of Prof. Conduct, rule 1.6. As a witness, the lawyer would be required to testify as to confidential information relevant to the decedent's estate planning and specifically excepted from the lawyer-client privilege under the provisions of the Evidence Code.

Case

The lawyer-client privilege terminates when there is no person [or personal representative] to claim it. *HLC Properties, Ltd. v. Super. Ct.* (2005) 35 Cal.4th 54, 65-66.

Ethics Opinion

A lawyer's duty of confidentiality survives client's death except as to the testator-client's conversations with the lawyer regarding drafting of a will. L.A. County Bar Assn, Ethics opn. No. 491 (Oct. 20, 1997). The opinion discusses the disposition of office files of a deceased client. In that context, it concludes that the lawyer-client privilege devolves on the death of the client to the client's personal representative until discharge, and disclosure of confidential information or secrets to the personal representative would not violate the ethical duty of confidentiality or the lawyer-client privilege.

Article

Frankel, *The Attorney-Client Privilege After the Death of the Client* (1992) 6 Georgetown J. of Legal Ethics 45.

6.18 Prospective Clients

California Rules of Professional Conduct, Rule 1.18 - Duties to Prospective Client

> (a) A person* who, directly or through an authorized representative, consults a lawyer for the purpose of retaining the lawyer or securing legal service or advice from the lawyer in the lawyer's professional capacity, is a prospective client.

(b) Even when no lawyer-client relationship ensues, a lawyer who has communicated with a prospective client shall not use or reveal information protected by Business and Professions Code section 6068, subdivision (e) and rule 1.6 that the lawyer learned as a result of the consultation, except as rule 1.9 would permit with respect to information of a former client.

(c) A lawyer subject to paragraph (b) shall not represent a client with interests materially adverse to those of a prospective client in the same or a substantially related matter if the lawyer received from the prospective client information protected by Business and Professions Code section 6068, subdivision (e) and rule 1.6 that is material to the matter, except as provided in paragraph (d). If a lawyer is prohibited from representation under this paragraph, no lawyer in a firm* with which that lawyer is associated may knowingly* undertake or continue representation in such a matter, except as provided in paragraph (d).

(d) When the lawyer has received information that prohibits representation as provided in paragraph (c), representation of the affected client is permissible if:

(1) both the affected client and the prospective client have given informed written consent,* or

(2) the lawyer who received the information took reasonable* measures to avoid exposure to more information than was reasonably* necessary to determine whether to represent the prospective client; and (i) the prohibited lawyer is timely screened* from any participation in the matter and is apportioned no part of the fee therefrom; and (ii) written* notice is promptly given to the prospective client to enable the prospective client to ascertain compliance with the provisions of this rule.

An asterisk (*) identifies a defined term in rule 1.0.1 of the Rules of Professional Conduct. For further discussion of a defined term, see chapter 2 of this Guide, Terminology.

Rule 1.18 of the Rules of Professional Conduct prescribes the ethical duties that a lawyer owes to a prospective client. The lawyer's duty of confidentiality extends to a prospective client who provides confidential information with a view to retaining the lawyer. The ethical duty applies even if the prospective client does not retain the lawyer following consultation. Rule 1.18 extends that ethical duty to an authorized representative of a prospective client who proffers that confidential information to the lawyer.

The ethical duty under rule 1.18 of the Rules of Professional Conduct is primarily preservation of confidential information. In taking an initial consultation, a lawyer should receive only such information as needed to determine if the lawyer can undertake the representation without conflicts of interest. Prudence suggests a prompt and thorough conflicts of interest search of the lawyer's files before the lawyer receives information beyond the names and relationships of the prospective client and adverse or potentially adverse parties.

Terminating the consultation once the client and scope of representation are identified may avoid potential conflicts of interest, but the duty of confidentiality continues. The lawyer's receipt of confidential information from a prospective client may disqualify the lawyer from later representing a party in a substantially related matter whose interests are materially adverse to the prospective client. Rules Prof. Conduct, rule 1.9. For a further discussion of the ethical duty of confidentiality owed to a former client, see section 6.4 of this chapter.

Rule 1.18 of the Rules of Professional Conduct allows a law firm to create an ethical wall between the interviewing lawyer and that lawyer's colleagues and authorize the law firm to represent a different client in the same matter so long as the disqualified lawyer is "timely screened," does not participate in the legal fees, and written notice of these arrangements is given to the prospective client. California case law has recognized that a tainted lawyer in receipt of confidential information from a former client may be timely and effectively screened. *Kirk v. First American Title Ins. Co.* (2010) 183 Cal.App.4th 776. For a further discussion of ethical screening, see chapter 2 of this Guide, Terminology.

Comment on California Rules of Professional Conduct, Rule 1.18

> [1] As used in this rule, a prospective client includes a person's* authorized representative. A lawyer's discussions with a prospective client can be limited in time and depth and leave both the prospective client and the lawyer free, and sometimes required, to proceed no further. Although a prospective client's information is protected by Business and Professions Code section 6068, subdivision (e) and rule 1.6 the same as that of a client, in limited circumstances provided under paragraph (d), a law firm* is permitted to accept or continue representation of a client with interests adverse to the prospective client. This rule is not intended to limit the application of Evidence Code section 951 (defining "client" within the meaning of the Evidence Code).
>
> [2] Not all persons* who communicate information to a lawyer are entitled to protection under this rule. A person* who by any means communicates information unilaterally to a lawyer, without reasonable* expectation that the lawyer is willing to discuss the possibility of forming a lawyer-client relationship or provide legal advice is not a "prospective client" within the meaning of paragraph (a). In addition, a person* who discloses information to a lawyer after the lawyer has stated his or her unwillingness or inability to consult with the person* (*People v. Gionis* (1995) 9 Cal.4th 1196 [40 Cal.Rptr.2d 456]), or who communicates information to a lawyer without a good faith intention to seek legal advice or representation, is not a prospective client within the meaning of paragraph (a).
>
> [3] In order to avoid acquiring information from a prospective client that would prohibit representation as provided in paragraph (c), a lawyer considering whether or not to undertake a new matter must limit the initial interview to only such information as reasonably* appears necessary for that purpose.
>
> [4] Under paragraph (c), the prohibition in this rule is imputed to other lawyers in a law firm* as provided in rule 1.10. However, under paragraph (d)(1), the

consequences of imputation may be avoided if the informed written consent* of both the prospective and affected clients is obtained. (See rule 1.0.1(e-1) [informed written consent].) In the alternative, imputation may be avoided if the conditions of paragraph (d)(2) are met and all prohibited lawyers are timely screened* and written* notice is promptly given to the prospective client. Paragraph (d)(2)(i) does not prohibit the screened* lawyer from receiving a salary or partnership share established by prior independent agreement, but that lawyer may not receive compensation directly related to the matter in which the lawyer is prohibited.

[5] Notice under paragraph (d)(2)(ii) must include a general description of the subject matter about which the lawyer was consulted, and the screening* procedures employed.

Cases

A lawyer-client relationship may exist when a lawyer provides a legal service without providing advice. The court found that the defendant had a lawyer-client relationship with outside counsel hired as an investigator. Even though the investigator's role was limited to fact-finding and did not extend to providing advice, outside counsel had expertise in employment law that was used to further that investigation. *City of Petaluma v. Super. Ct.* (2016) 248 Cal.App.4th 1023.

Whether a lawyer was consulted in a professional capacity as a lawyer, rather than for nonlegal services or for advice in the lawyer's capacity as a friend, is a question of fact, and evidence supported the conclusion that the lawyer was consulted in a professional capacity and a lawyer-client relationship was formed. *Kerner v. Super. Ct.* (2012) 206 Cal.App.4th 84.

When a lawyer obtained confidential information from a client, that lawyer was prohibited from accepting representation adverse to the client in a matter to which the confidential information would be material. Nevertheless, automatic vicarious disqualification of the lawyer's entire law firm was not required. Instead, there was a rebuttable presumption that the lawyer's knowledge of client confidences was imputed to the firm, which could be refuted by evidence that the firm adequately screened the lawyer from the others at the firm representing the adverse party. *Kirk v. First American Title Ins. Co.* (2010) 183 Cal.App.4th 776.

When a lawyer unequivocally refused to represent a prospective client, no lawyer-client relationship existed and the lawyer-client communications privilege did not extend to communications made after the lawyer's refusal to represent the client. Nor was a communication privileged that was unrelated to any professional relationship established between the lawyer and the prospective client. *People v. Gionis* (1995) 9 Cal.4th 1196.

Ethics Opinion

Lawyer websites that invite inquiries from a website visitor may, inadvertently to the lawyer, create a prospective client-lawyer relationship with expectation of confidentiality, even if the website visitor does not retain the lawyer following submission of the information. ABA Com. on Ethics and Prof. Resp., Formal opn. No. 2010-457. For a further discussion of ethical communication of a lawyer's services and advertising, see chapter 10 of this Guide, Ethics and Technology, sections 10.9 and 10.10

CHAPTER 7 COMMUNICATION

California Rules of Professional Conduct, Rule 1.4 - Communication with Clients

(a) A lawyer shall:

(1) promptly inform the client of any decision or circumstance with respect to which disclosure or the client's informed consent* is required by these rules or the State Bar Act;

(2) reasonably* consult with the client about the means by which to accomplish the client's objectives in the representation;

(3) keep the client reasonably* informed about significant developments relating to the representation, including promptly complying with reasonable* requests for information and copies of significant documents when necessary to keep the client so informed; and

(4) advise the client about any relevant limitation on the lawyer's conduct when the lawyer knows* that the client expects assistance not permitted by the Rules of Professional Conduct or other law.

(b) A lawyer shall explain a matter to the extent reasonably* necessary to permit the client to make informed decisions regarding the representation.

(c) A lawyer may delay transmission of information to a client if the lawyer reasonably believes* that the client would be likely to react in a way that may cause imminent harm to the client or others.

(d) A lawyer's obligation under this rule to provide information and documents is subject to any applicable protective order, non-disclosure agreement, or limitation under statutory or decisional law.

An asterisk (*) identifies a defined term in rule 1.0.1 of the Rules of Professional Conduct. For further discussion of a defined term, see chapter 2 of this Guide, Terminology.

California Business and Professions Code section 6068, subdivision (m)

It is the duty of an attorney:

. . .

(m) [t]o respond promptly to reasonable status inquiries of clients and to keep clients reasonably informed of significant developments in matters with regard to which the attorney has agreed to provide legal services.

7.1 Introduction

A lawyer has an ethical duty to foster communication with the client. The generally confidential nature of those communications should encourage candor and full disclosure, attributes of the communicative process that in turn promotes the quality of the legal services that the lawyer provides to the client.

The nature and extent of the contents of communications between lawyer and client are affected by numerous factors, including the age, competence, and experience of the client, the complexity of the matter, cost control, and other relevant considerations. The governing statute and rule 1.4 of the Rules of Professional Conduct do not require a lawyer to communicate insignificant or irrelevant information to the client. Nevertheless, a lawyer is ethically obligated to respond promptly to reasonable requests from the client for information and for documents related to the matter of the representation.

The client defines both the scope of representation and the means by which the goals of the representation are pursued. See chapter 4 of this Guide, Identifying the Client and the Scope of Representation, section 4.1. The lawyer must reasonably consult with the client about the means by which the client's objectives are to be accomplished. The ethical duty of communication in rule 1.4 of the Rules of Professional Conduct includes not only notifying the client of significant developments in the course of the representation but framing the goals of the representation and the means of achieving the goals that the client sets.

Rule 1.4 of the Rules of Professional Conduct provides further guidance on the requirements for informed consent. The ethical duty of communication includes explaining a matter to the extent reasonably necessary to permit the client to make informed decisions regarding the representation. Written communication may allow the client additional time to reflect on the legal issues and alternative approaches to accomplishing the client's goals. That written communication can also memorialize the communication with the client for future reference.

Rule 1.4(c) of the Rules of Professional Conduct allows a lawyer to delay communication if a client reaction may cause imminent harm to the client or others. For example, a lawyer may delay communicating an adverse administration issue to a trustee, to allow additional time to determine the best approach to addressing that issue. Another example might be a claim by a tenant who occupies trust real property, requiring time for the trustee to investigate the claim and determine the most appropriate response.

A lawyer's departure from a law firm implicates specific ethical duties of communication on both the departing lawyer and the firm. The departure of a lawyer is a "significant development" under rule 1.4(a)(3) of the Rules of Professional Conduct if the lawyer provides meaningful legal services to the client. Cal. State Bar Com. on Prof. Resp. and Conduct, formal opn. No. 2020-201. The departing lawyer and the firm must notify clients about a lawyer's departure as soon as reasonably practical to allow clients to make an informed choice about further representation, to provide for a smooth transition, and to avoid prejudice to the clients' interests. The opinion cautions against firm policies or contractual provisions that limit a departing lawyer's contact with a client after the firm gives notice of a lawyer's departure.

A separate ethical duty to communicate settlement offers to the client is set forth in rule 1.4.1 of the Rules of Professional Conduct. Although not specifically addressed in rule 1.4.1, an offer to mediate a claim would most likely be included within the duty to communicate settlement proposals to the client, and within the concurrent duty in rule 1.4 of the Rules of Professional Conduct to keep the client informed of significant developments. For a discussion of the lawyer's professional obligations regarding the conduct of mediation, see chapter 9 of this Guide, Ethics and Litigation, section 9.8.

For a discussion of the lawyer's professional obligations regarding communications with the court, see chapter 9 of this Guide, Ethics and Litigation, section 9.6.

Comment on California Rules of Professional Conduct, Rule 1.4

> [1] A lawyer will not be subject to discipline under paragraph (a)(3) of this rule for failing to communicate insignificant or irrelevant information. (See Bus. and Prof. Code, sec. 6068, subd. (m).) Whether a particular development is significant will generally depend on the surrounding facts and circumstances.
>
> [2] A lawyer may comply with paragraph (a)(3) by providing to the client copies of significant documents by electronic or other means. This rule does not prohibit a lawyer from seeking recovery of the lawyer's expense in any subsequent legal proceeding.
>
> [3] Paragraph (c) applies during a representation and does not alter the obligations applicable at termination of a representation. (See rule 1.16(e)(1).)
>
> [4] This rule is not intended to create, augment, diminish, or eliminate any application of the work product rule. The obligation of the lawyer to provide work product to the client shall be governed by relevant statutory and decisional law.

Former California Rules of Professional Conduct, Rule 3-500 – Communication

> A member shall keep a client reasonably informed about significant developments relating to the employment or representation, including promptly complying with reasonable requests for information and copies of significant documents when necessary to keep the client so informed.

Case

A retainer agreement that gave the lawyer "unqualified authority to settle" client cases breached the lawyer's fiduciary obligations. *In the Matter of Guzman* (Review Dept. 2014) 5 Cal. State Bar Ct. Rptr. 308.

Ethics Opinion

The client's right to counsel of the client's choice and the protection of the client's best interests are the ethical principles that should guide any lawyer departure. The departing lawyer and law firm each have ethical obligations related to the departure and must prioritize their ethical obligations to clients over their own competing interests. These ethical obligations include properly notifying relevant clients of the departure, protecting client confidences, addressing conflicts of interests with clients, ensuring that clients continue to have competent representation, and avoiding reasonably foreseeable prejudice to the rights of clients during any changes in the representation. Both the departing lawyer and firm have a duty to cooperate in the transition of any client matter. State Bar of Cal. Com. on Prof. Resp. and Conduct, formal opn. No. 2020-201.

7.2 Accuracy of Communications

California Rules of Professional Conduct, Rule 4.1 - Truthfulness in Statements to Others

> In the course of representing a client a lawyer shall not knowingly:* (a) make a false statement of material fact or law to a third person;* or (b) fail to disclose a material fact to a third person* when disclosure is necessary to avoid assisting a criminal or fraudulent* act by a client, unless disclosure is prohibited by Business and Professions Code section 6068, subdivision (e)(1) or rule 1.6.

An asterisk (*) identifies a defined term in rule 1.0.1 of the Rules of Professional Conduct. For further discussion of a defined term, see chapter 2 of this Guide, Terminology.

Rule 4.1 of the Rules of Professional Conduct broadens the lawyer's ethical duty of communication to include third parties with whom the lawyer may communicate in the course of a representation. Those third parties may include other lawyers in a litigation context and represented and unrepresented parties. The trusts and estates lawyer properly communicates with third parties—to comply with statutory notice requirements, to facilitate a probate or trust administration, and to fulfill the duty to advise third parties that the lawyer does not represent their interest. When the lawyer represents a trustee and communicates with the trust beneficiaries as part of that representation, when the lawyer represents an organization or one of its constituents and communicates with the other constituents, or when a client requests that the lawyer inform other family members of the details and purpose of a tax-motivated estate plan, the ethical duty in rule 4.1 of the Rules of Professional Conduct is implicated.

Rule 1.6 of the Rules of Professional Conduct permits a breach of client confidentiality if necessary to prevent a criminal act that the lawyer reasonably believes is likely to result in death or substantial bodily harm. See chapter 6 of this Guide, Confidentiality of Information, section 6.1. Such disclosure is permissive, not mandatory. In contrast, rule 4.1 of the Rules of Professional Conduct imposes an affirmative duty on the lawyer to disclose material facts, if necessary, to avoid either a criminal or a fraudulent act by a client. Such disclosure is nonetheless subject to the lawyer's ethical duty not to disclose confidential client communications.

Comment on California Rules of Professional Conduct, Rule 4.1

[1] A lawyer is required to be truthful when dealing with others on a client's behalf, but generally has no affirmative duty to inform an opposing party of relevant facts. A misrepresentation can occur if the lawyer incorporates or affirms the truth of a statement of another person* that the lawyer knows* is false. However, in drafting an agreement or other document on behalf of a client, a lawyer does not necessarily affirm or vouch for the truthfulness of representations made by the client in the agreement or document. A nondisclosure can be the equivalent of a false statement of material fact or law under paragraph (a) where a lawyer makes a partially true but misleading material statement or material omission. In addition to this rule, lawyers remain bound by Business and Professions Code section 6106 and rule 8.4.

[2] This rule refers to statements of fact. Whether a particular statement should be regarded as one of fact can depend on the circumstances. For example, in negotiation, certain types of statements ordinarily are not taken as statements of material fact. Estimates of price or value placed on the subject of a transaction and a party's intentions as to an acceptable settlement of a claim are ordinarily in this category, and so is the existence of an undisclosed principal except where nondisclosure of the principal would constitute fraud.*

[3] Under rule 1.2.1, a lawyer is prohibited from counseling or assisting a client in conduct that the lawyer knows* is criminal or fraudulent.* See rule 1.4(a)(4) regarding a lawyer's obligation to consult with the client about limitations on the lawyer's conduct. In some circumstances, a lawyer can avoid assisting a client's crime or fraud* by withdrawing from the representation in compliance with rule 1.16.

Case Study

The trial court entered judgment for Plaintiffs in a claim for illegal dumping of contaminated debris on Plaintiffs' property. The judgment required Defendants to remove the debris pursuant to a court-approved remediation plan, and the remediation funds were placed in the trust account of Defendants' lawyers. Defendants failed to remove the contaminated debris, and Defendants' lawyers disbursed the funds in a manner contrary to Plaintiffs' interest in the court-approved plan. Plaintiffs filed a second suit claiming a civil conspiracy between Defendants and Defendants' lawyers to defraud Plaintiffs.

Defendants' lawyers asserted that Code of Civil Procedure section 1714.10 prohibits civil conspiracy claims between a lawyer and a client regarding the settlement of disputes. In addition, Defendants' lawyers asserted that proof of a civil conspiracy claim would require the disclosure of work product protected by the litigation privilege and client communications protected by the lawyer-client privilege, and those prohibitions on disclosure barred prosecution of the claim.

What ethical issues arise from this set of facts and what duties do Defendants' lawyers owe to nonclient Plaintiffs?

Code of Civil Procedure section 1714.10 prohibits civil conspiracy claims arising from any attempt to contest or compromise a claim or dispute, based upon a lawyer's representation of a client. Nevertheless, that prohibition does not apply to a conspiracy claim if "(1) the attorney has an independent legal duty to the plaintiff, or (2) the attorney's acts go beyond the performance of a professional duty to serve the client and involve a conspiracy to violate a legal duty in furtherance of the attorney's financial gain." The Court of Appeal held that Defendants' lawyers owed independent legal duties to nonclient Plaintiffs not to interfere with the remediation plan and not to disburse the remediation funds unfairly, and the Plaintiffs adequately pleaded a civil conspiracy. *Rickley v. Goodfriend* (2013) 212 Cal.App.4th 1136, 1158.

The court further found that the litigation privilege offered no protection for the collaborative efforts of the Defendants and Defendants' lawyers to interfere with a court-approved remediation plan. The goals of the litigation privilege would not be advanced by conferring immunity on the Defendants and Defendants' lawyers given that, together, they allegedly conspired to interfere with the abatement of a nuisance. The court declined to apply the litigation privilege where to do so would, in essence, abolish a cause of action for civil conspiracy. *Rickley v. Goodfriend, supra*, 212 Cal.App.4th at p. 1164.

The court also dismissed the claim of Defendants' lawyers that permitting a conspiracy claim would require the disclosure of communications protected by the lawyer-client privilege. The court found that conspiracies could be proved by circumstantial evidence. A ruling that the lawyer-client privilege bars the Plaintiffs' claim could well lead to the conclusion that no lawyer-client conspiracy claims are viable. *Rickley v. Goodfriend, supra*, 212 Cal.App.4th. at p.1166.

Case

An arbitrator stated that a law firm acknowledged the falsity of a lawyer's statement that the firm had never represented the three affiliated entities involved in the transaction that was the subject to the client's legal malpractice claim. That statement did not establish that the arbitration award was "procured by corruption, fraud or other undue means," as would require vacatur under Code of Civil Procedure section 1286.2, subdivision (a)(1). The arbitrator did not rely at any point on the portion of the lawyer's declaration that was allegedly false. *ECC Capital Corp. et al. v. Manatt, Phelps & Phillips, LLP* (2017) 9 Cal.App.5th 885.

Ethics Opinion

Statements made by counsel during negotiations are subject to the ethical rules prohibiting a lawyer from engaging in dishonesty, deceit, or collusion. Thus, it is improper for a lawyer to make false statements of fact or implicit misrepresentations of material fact during negotiations. However, puffery and posturing, such as statements about a party's negotiating goals or willingness to compromise, are generally permissible because they are not considered statements of fact. State Bar of Cal. Com. on Prof. Resp. and Conduct, formal opn. No. 2015-194.

7.3 Communication with Persons Represented by Counsel

California Rules of Professional Conduct, Rule 4.2 - Communication with a Represented Person

> (a) In representing a client, a lawyer shall not communicate directly or indirectly about the subject of the representation with a person* the lawyer knows* to be represented by another lawyer in the matter, unless the lawyer has the consent of the other lawyer.
>
> (b) In the case of a represented corporation, partnership, association, or other private or governmental organization, this rule prohibits communications with:
>
> > (1) A current officer, director, partner,*or managing agent of the organization; or
> >
> > (2) A current employee, member, agent, or other constituent of the organization, if the subject of the communication is any act or omission of such a person* in connection with the matter which may be binding upon or imputed to the organization for purposes of civil or criminal liability.
>
> (c) This rule shall not prohibit:
>
> > (1) communications with a public official, board, committee, or body; or
> >
> > (2) communications otherwise authorized by law or a court order.
>
> (d) For purposes of this rule:
>
> > (1) "Managing agent" means an employee, member, agent, or other constituent of an organization with substantial* discretionary authority over decisions that determine organizational policy.
> >
> > (2) "Public official" means a public officer of the United States government, or of a state, county, city, town, political subdivision, or other governmental organization, with the comparable decision-making authority and responsibilities as the organizational constituents described in paragraph (b)(1).

An asterisk (*) identifies a defined term in rule 1.0.1 of the Rules of Professional Conduct. For further discussion of a defined term, see chapter 2 of this Guide, Terminology.

Rule 4.2 of the Rules of Professional Conduct is intended to prevent a lawyer from taking advantage of a person who is represented by another lawyer in a matter. Significantly, the rule is not limited to litigation, and it applies even if the communication is well-intentioned. *Graham vs. U.S.* (9th Cir. 1996) 96 F.3d 446, 449; *Abeles vs. State Bar* (1973) 9 Cal.3d 603. Knowledge that a person is represented is imputed if a lawyer of reasonable prudence and competence would ascertain that fact. Rules Prof. Conduct, rule 1.0.1(f) and (j). This imputed knowledge of representation may even override the person's statement to the contrary. Cal. State Bar Com. on Prof. Resp. and Conduct, formal opn. No. 1996-145.

Rule 4.2 of the Rules of Professional Conduct governs all communications between a lawyer and a person whom the lawyer knows to be represented by counsel "in the matter." Any form of communication with a represented person is prohibited, whether in person, by telephone, letter, fax, text message, or email. Represented persons include directors, officers, and partners of business entities, and may include employees. For a detailed discussion of connection requests on social media in a litigation context, see chapter 9 of this Guide, Ethics and Litigation, section 9.7.

For the trusts and estates lawyer, the problem most likely to be encountered in applying rule 4.2 will be defining the scope of "the matter." For example, a lawyer may represent a trustee in connection with a disputed accounting relating to the continued operation of a business owned in trust. Assume that a beneficiary engages another lawyer to represent the beneficiary in this dispute. If the trustee proposes selling an unrelated trust asset and the lawyer must communicate with the beneficiary about the sale, the question arises whether the lawyer for the trustee may contact the beneficiary directly. Arguably, the sale is not the same "matter" as the accounting dispute. In this example, however, the lawyer for the trustee would prudently construe the scope of the matter most broadly, and refrain from direct communication with a beneficiary until advised otherwise by the beneficiary's lawyer.

Direct party-to-party communications are not prohibited. A lawyer who is a party to an action, even if self-representing, may communicate with another party to the action directly, even if that other party is represented. Encouraging a client to speak directly to another party who is represented by counsel may be advantageous to help narrow or resolve issues between the parties. Nevertheless, a lawyer may not use a client as a substitute to argue or negotiate with a represented party. State Bar of California Committee on Professional Responsibility and Conduct, Formal Opinion Number 1993-131 distinguishes between permitted party-to-party communications and prohibited indirect communications, based on the origin of the content of the communication. If the content originates with the lawyer, the contact is indirect and prohibited; if it originates with the client, it is a permissible party-to-party communication.

Rule 4.2 of the Rules of Professional Conduct does not prohibit communications by the lawyer with a person who acts *in propria persona*, even if that person retains counsel to assist in the matter. The lawyer must recognize the self-representing party as the lawyer of record and communicate with that party accordingly. The self-representing party who is assisted by a lawyer cannot invoke the protections of rule 4.2 of the Rules of Professional Conduct to prohibit direct contact by an opposing lawyer.

Consent under rule 4.2 of the Rules of Professional Conduct need not be express; rather, it may be implied by the facts and circumstances surrounding the communication with the represented party. State Bar of California Committee on Professional Responsibility and Conduct, Formal Opinion Number 2011-181 sets forth several facts and circumstances that might establish implied consent including "whether the communication is in the presence of the other attorney; prior course of conduct; the nature of the matter; how the communication is initiated and by whom; the formality of the communication; the extent to which the communication might interfere with the attorney-client relationship; whether there exists a common interest or joint defense privilege between the parties; whether the other attorney will have a reasonable opportunity to counsel the represented party with regard to the communication contemporaneously or immediately following such communication; and the instructions of the represented party's attorney."

Rule 4.4 of the Rules of Professional Conduct prescribes the lawyer's duties concerning inadvertently transmitted emails and other writings. In compliance with that rule, a lawyer must refrain from examining the writing any more than is necessary to determine whether it is privileged or confidential, and promptly notify the sender. The ethical duty does not appear to extend to deleting or destroying the writing. *McDermott Will & Emery LLP v. Super. Ct. (Hausman)* (2017) 10 Cal.App.5th 1083; *Ardon v. City of L.A.* (2016) 62 Cal.4th 1176. For a further discussion of this ethical issue, see chapter 9 of this Guide, Ethics and Litigation, section 9.7.

Comment on California Rules of Professional Conduct, Rule 4.2

> [1] This rule applies even though the represented person* initiates or consents to the communication. A lawyer must immediately terminate communication with a person* if, after commencing communication, the lawyer learns that the person* is one with whom communication is not permitted by this rule.
>
> [2] "Subject of the representation," "matter," and "person" are not limited to a litigation context. This rule applies to communications with any person,* whether or not a party to a formal adjudicative proceeding, contract, or negotiation, who is represented by counsel concerning the matter to which the communication relates.
>
> [3] The prohibition against communicating "indirectly" with a person* represented by counsel in paragraph (a) is intended to address situations where a lawyer seeks to communicate with a represented person* through an intermediary such as an agent, investigator or the lawyer's client. This rule, however, does not prevent represented persons* from communicating directly with one another with respect to the subject of the representation, nor does it prohibit a lawyer from advising a client concerning such a communication. A lawyer may also advise a client not to accept or engage in such communications. The rule also does not prohibit a lawyer who is a party to a legal matter from communicating on his or her own behalf with a represented person* in that matter.
>
> [4] This rule does not prohibit communications with a represented person* concerning matters outside the representation. Similarly, a lawyer who knows* that a person* is being provided with limited scope representation is not prohibited from communicating with that person* with respect to matters that are outside the scope of the limited representation. (See, e.g., Cal. Rules of Court, rules 3.35- 3.37, 5.425 [Limited Scope Representation].)

[5] This rule does not prohibit communications initiated by a represented person* seeking advice or representation from an independent lawyer of the person's* choice.

[6] If a current constituent of the organization is represented in the matter by his or her own counsel, the consent by that counsel to a communication is sufficient for purposes of this rule.

Former California Rules of Professional Conduct, Rule 2-100 - Communication with a Represented Party

(A) While representing a client, a member shall not communicate directly or indirectly about the subject of the representation with a party the member knows to be represented by another lawyer in the matter, unless the member has the consent of the other lawyer.

(B) For the purposes of this rule, a "party" includes:

(1) An officer, director, or managing agent of a corporation or association, and a partner or managing agent of a partnership; or

(2) An association member or an employee of an association, corporation, or partnership, if the subject of the communication is any act or omission of such person in connection with the matter which may be binding upon or imputed to the organization for purposes of criminal liability or whose statement may constitute an admission on the part of the organization.

(C) This rule shall not prohibit:

(1) Communications with a public officer, board, committee, or body; or

(2) Communications initiated by a party seeking advice or representation from an independent lawyer of the party's choice; or

(3) Communications otherwise authorized by law.

Cases

The public officer exception in former rule 2-100(c)(1) of the Rules of Professional Conduct did not apply to communications with all government employees; rather it applied only to communications with a represented party when the communication was constitutionally protected by the First Amendment right to petition the government to seek redress of a grievance or to address a particular issue before the official being contacted. The court discussed the relevance of model rule 4.2. "Although ABA Rule 4.2 is not necessarily controlling here, that rule was violated as well. Unconsented questioning of an opposing party's employees on matters that counsel has reason to believe are at issue in the pending litigation is barred under ABA Rule 4.2 unless the sole purpose of the communication is to exercise a constitutional right of access to officials having the authority to act upon or decide the policy matter being presented. In addition, advance notice to the government's counsel is required." *U. S. v. Sierra Pacific Industries* (E.D. Cal. 2010) 759 F.Supp.2d 1206, 1214.

The Rules of Professional Conduct are not equivalent to court orders or local rules for the purpose of awarding sanctions under Code of Civil Procedure sections 177.5 or 575.2. In this case, the trial court ordered sanctions based on its belief that the lawyer had knowingly violated the Rules of Professional Conduct, including communication with the conservatee without obtaining permission from the conservatee's lawyer. The Court of Appeal vacated that order and directed the entry of a new order denying sanctions. The court held that ethical rules, although binding upon a lawyer, are not normally regarded as court orders or local rules for the purpose of awarding sanctions. Responsibility for enforcing the Rules of Professional Conduct is lodged in the Supreme Court, which has delegated it to the State Bar Court. *Conservatorship of Becerra* (2009) 175 Cal.App.4th 1474.

While a party proceeding *in propria persona* has every right to be assisted by a lawyer not of record, neither the party nor the assisting lawyer can unilaterally limit opposing counsel's ability to confer with the lawyer of record. *McMillan v. Shadow Ridge at Oak Park Homeowners* (2008) 165 Cal.App.4th 960.

The ethical duties regarding communication with represented parties are intended to permit a lawyer to function adequately in the lawyer's proper role and to prevent opposing counsel from impeding the lawyer's performance. *Mitton v. State Bar* (1969) 71 Cal.2d 525, 534.

Ethics Opinion

A lawyer's duty not to deceive prohibits sending social media "friend" requests to unrepresented witnesses without disclosing the purpose of the request. The opinion notes that the privacy of an unrepresented non-party could be surreptitiously circumvented by being misled into accepting a friend request. San Diego County Bar Assn., Ethics opn. No. 2011-2. See also chapter 9 of this Guide, Ethics and Litigation, section 9.7.

7.4 Communications with Unrepresented Persons

California Rules of Professional Conduct Rule 4.3 - Communicating with an Unrepresented Person

> (a) In communicating on behalf of a client with a person who is not represented by counsel, a lawyer shall not state or imply that the lawyer is disinterested. When the lawyer knows or reasonably should know that the unrepresented person incorrectly believes* the lawyer is disinterested in the matter, the lawyer shall make reasonable efforts to correct the misunderstanding. If the lawyer knows or reasonably should know that the interests of the unrepresented person are in conflict with the interests of the client, the lawyer shall not give legal advice to that person,* except that the lawyer may, but is not required to, advise the person* to secure counsel.
>
> (b) In communicating on behalf of a client with a person* who is not represented by counsel, a lawyer shall not seek to obtain privileged or other confidential

information the lawyer knows* or reasonably should know* the person* may not reveal without violating a duty to another or which the lawyer is not otherwise entitled to receive.

An asterisk (*) identifies a defined term in rule 1.0.1 of the Rules of Professional Conduct. For further discussion of a defined term, see chapter 2 of this Guide, Terminology.

This rule guides a trusts and estates lawyer in dealing with parties to a matter who are not likely to be represented by counsel. In an uncontested probate proceeding when the lawyer represents the executor or administrator and the beneficiaries are not represented by counsel, the first step in communicating with unrepresented beneficiaries should be to explain who the lawyer does and does not represent, the possibility of conflict between the interests of the lawyer's client and a beneficiary, and the suggestion that the beneficiary consult independent counsel. Such notification, if given effect at the beginning of the matter and pursued diligently throughout the representation, can prevent serious misunderstandings that often arise in what starts out to be an uncontested matter.

A lawyer's ethical duty to unrepresented persons includes not requesting or accepting privileged or confidential information from such persons. For a discussion of rule 1.18 of the Rules of Professional Conduct and a lawyer's duties to prospective clients, see chapter 6 of this Guide, Confidentiality of Information, section 6.18.

Rule 4.3(a) of the Rules of Professional Conduct specifies ethical duties when a lawyer reasonably should know that the interests of the lawyer's client conflict with the unrepresented party's interests. In that case, the rule prohibits giving any advice to the unrepresented party apart from the advice to obtain counsel.

The sophistication of the unrepresented person and the setting in which the communication takes place will further distinguish permissible from impermissible contact. The lawyer must first explain that the lawyer represents a party that is, or may be, adverse to the unrepresented person and does not represent the unrepresented person. With that said and understood, the lawyer may negotiate a transaction or settle a dispute with the unrepresented person.

Comment on California Rules of Professional Conduct, Rule 4.3

[1] This rule is intended to protect unrepresented persons,* whatever their interests, from being misled when communicating with a lawyer who is acting for a client.

[2] Paragraph (a) distinguishes between situations in which a lawyer knows* or reasonably should know* that the interests of an unrepresented person* are in conflict with the interests of the lawyer's client and situations in which the lawyer does not. In the former situation, the possibility that the lawyer will compromise the unrepresented person's* interests is so great that the rule prohibits the giving of any legal advice, apart from the advice to obtain counsel. A lawyer does not give legal advice merely by stating a legal position on behalf of the lawyer's client. This rule does not prohibit a lawyer from negotiating the terms of a transaction or settling

a dispute with an unrepresented person.* So long as the lawyer discloses that the lawyer represents an adverse party and not the person,* the lawyer may inform the person* of the terms on which the lawyer's client will enter into the agreement or settle the matter, prepare documents that require the person's* signature, and explain the lawyer's own view of the meaning of the document and the underlying legal obligations.

ACTEC Commentaries on Model Rules of Professional Conduct, Rule 4.3

The lawyer for a fiduciary is required to comply with MRPC 4.3 in communicating with the beneficiaries of the fiduciary estate, or with the protected person in the case of guardianships and conservatorships, when such persons are not represented by counsel. In dealing with unrepresented beneficiaries or the protected person, the lawyer for the fiduciary may not suggest that he or she is disinterested. As indicated in the ACTEC Commentary on MRPC 1.2 (Scope of Representation and Allocation of Authority Between Client and Lawyer), the lawyer should inform the beneficiaries of the fiduciary estate regarding various matters, including the fact that the lawyer does not represent them and that they may wish to obtain independent counsel. If the lawyer knows, or reasonably should know, that an unrepresented beneficiary, or another unrepresented person, misunderstands the lawyer's role in the matter, the lawyer should make reasonable efforts to correct the misunderstanding. The lawyer should not permit the beneficiaries to believe that the lawyer is the lawyer for the parties interested in the matter if the lawyer is representing only the fiduciary.

Cases

The Court of Appeal upheld the trial court findings that a lawyer led the nominated executor reasonably to believe the lawyer was representing him, and that it must have been clear to the lawyer that the nominated executor was led to so believe. That the nominated executor had not retained the lawyer as a client was irrelevant because the lawyer did not perform the necessary probate work whoever the client was, and the lawyer led the nominated executor to believe that the lawyer was representing him without ever advising him otherwise. A lawyer's duty to communicate includes the duty to communicate with unrepresented persons at least to the extent of advising them that they are not clients. This duty extends only to persons who, to the lawyer's knowledge, may reasonably believe that they are clients. *Butler v. State Bar* (1986) 42 Cal.3d 323, 329.

A lawyer's direct communication with a represented third party violated the ethical rule prohibiting such communications because the lawyer knew the party still had a lawyer of record. *Abeles v. State Bar* (1973) 9 Cal.3d 603, 609.

Ethics Opinion

A lawyer who has actual knowledge that an opposing party is represented by counsel may not contact the party about the subject of the representation without the consent of that party's counsel. Knowledge of such representation can be inferred from the surrounding circumstances and is determined by an objective standard rather than the subjective knowledge of the lawyer. If the lawyer has no reason to know whether a party is represented, the lawyer is not required to inquire if a party is represented. Nevertheless, a lawyer would prudently inquire when it is not clear whether a party is represented. When the lawyer has reason to know that a party is represented, the party's statement to the contrary will not relieve the lawyer of the duty to obtain consent. The ethical obligations of the lawyer apply regardless of the means of communication. The means of communication, however, is one factor that may lead to the inference of knowledge or the need for the lawyer to inquire further. State Bar of Cal. Com. on Prof. Resp. and Conduct, formal opn. No. 1996-145.

7.5 Notice to Beneficiaries of Nonrepresentation

The following paragraph may be adapted and included in a longer letter to unrepresented parties, to comply with the lawyer's professional obligation to communicate to such parties that the lawyer does not represent them. That letter might include, for example, a statutory notification of the terms of the trust, financial information or an accounting by the trustee, a detailed notice of a proposed action by the trustee, or a response to a beneficiary request for a report. The following paragraph would be included in that letter to clarify that the communication of such information does not create a lawyer-client relationship with the beneficiary.

> Dear [Beneficiary],
>
> You are receiving this letter in compliance with California law requiring notice to the trust (estate) beneficiaries of significant events regarding the trust (estate) administration. The trustee (executor) and I will endeavor to answer any questions or concerns you have related to this letter. However, please note that I represent ______________ (name), as (trustee / executor / petitioner) and not any of the heirs or beneficiaries individually. If you have any questions regarding your interest in the trust (estate) and your rights as a beneficiary, I encourage you to retain a lawyer of your choice to advise you. The retention of an independent lawyer would be at your own expense.
>
> Sincerely,
>
> [Lawyer]

7.6 Client with Diminished Capacity

Rule 1.4 of the Rules of Professional Conduct allows no exception regarding a lawyer's duty to communicate with a client if that client becomes incapacitated during the representation. The duty of client communication applies even if the client has difficulty understanding or retaining the lawyer's communications or articulating the client's wishes regarding the goals of the representation or the steps required to accomplish those goals. The California Supreme Court declined to amend the Rules of Professional Conduct to allow a limited breach of the duty of confidentiality to protect a client from financial or physical abuse, as provided in ABA Model Rules of Professional Conduct, rule 1.14. The ethical duties to the client are absolute, and the lawyer may not substitute the lawyer's judgment for the wishes of the client, however well-intentioned. If difficulties in communication prevent effective representation of the client, the lawyer should consider withdrawing from the representation consistent with the procedures set forth in rule 1.16 of the Rules of Professional Conduct.

Rule 1.16 of the Rules of Professional Conduct allows a lawyer to withdraw from representing a client due to the lawyer's impaired physical or mental condition; it does not allow withdrawal for a client's incapacity. Nevertheless, paragraph (b) of that rule allows withdrawal from representation if the conduct of a client renders it unreasonably difficult for the lawyer to carry out the representation effectively, or a continued representation is likely to result in a violation of the Rules of Professional Conduct. Those ethical rules include following the client's decisions regarding the goals of the representation and consulting with the client on the means by which those goals are pursued, obtaining the client's informed written consent if required under the Rules of Professional Conduct, and communicating to the client all significant developments related to the representation. The client's inability to read, understand, or reflect on communications from the lawyer may impair the lawyer's compliance with these professional obligations and be grounds for permissive withdrawal.

A client's diminished capacity may limit the lawyer's ability to terminate a representation. Rule 1.16(d) of the Rules of Professional Conduct requires, as a precondition to withdrawal, that a lawyer take reasonable steps to prevent prejudice to the client's rights, including giving the client sufficient notice to allow the client to retain another lawyer. Communicating such notice may itself be impaired by the client's incapacity.

Article

Rudolph & Hughes, *A Lawyer is a Lawyer is a Lawyer* (2019) 25 Cal. Trust and Estates Q., Issue 1.

7.7 Client Communications After a Representation Terminates

The execution of estate planning documents and the completion of related matters, as the engagement letter defines the subject matter of the representation, normally ends the active representation of an estate planning client. The scope of work set out in the engagement letter has the importance of defining when the agreed-upon services have been completed. Unless the lawyer or client can show that the services have been completed and that the representation is terminated, the representation may become dormant subject to activation by the client. A lawyer could have unintended and ongoing ethical duties to the client if the representation becomes dormant rather than clearly terminated.

A client becomes a former client if either the client or the lawyer terminates the representation. Rules Prof. Conduct, rules 1.9 and 1.16. A lawyer may terminate the representation by a letter advising the client that the current representation is concluded, and that any subsequent representation will be the matter of a new engagement. The client may terminate the representation by retaining another lawyer to represent the client in estate and trust matters. The preparation of estate planning documents is a discrete representation that lends itself most appropriately to a termination letter when the documents are executed. For a sample provision that could be included in an engagement letter and revisited in a termination letter after the client has executed the estate planning documents, see chapter 4 of this Guide, Identifying the Client and the Scope of Representation, section 4.2. A termination letter would also be appropriate for a representation regarding an estate or trust administration. See chapter 5 of this Guide, Conflicts of Interest, section 5.15 for a sample letter.

Although the lawyer owes ethical duties to a former client, including the duties of confidentiality and avoidance of conflicts of interest, the lawyer's responsibilities are diminished when the subject matter of the representation, as defined in the engagement letter, is completed. After the conclusion of the initial representation, the lawyer may communicate periodically with the client regarding the desirability of reviewing the executed estate planning documents. Similarly, the lawyer may send the client an individual letter or a form letter, pamphlet, or brochure regarding changes in the law that may affect the client. In the absence of an agreement to the contrary, the lawyer is not obligated to remind a former client to update estate planning documents periodically or to advise a former client of the effect that changes in the law or the client's circumstances might have on the client's legal affairs.

A lawyer may desire to offer continuing services to a client after the initial estate planning representation terminates, as a means of continuing the client contact. For example, a lawyer may offer a periodic review of the client's estate planning documents for developments in applicable law, growth of or additions to assets, or other changes in the clients' family circumstances. Such continuing services should be clearly outlined as the scope of representation in a separate engagement letter, and the related fees disclosed to the client in that letter. If the continuing services involve a review of the client's estate planning documents in light of changes in applicable law, then that engagement letter would appropriately include detailed disclosures to the client as to the lawyer's undertaking to inform the client of those changes or to communicate with the client periodically to see if changes to the initial estate plan may be warranted.

At the client's request, the lawyer may retain the original documents executed by the client. For a further discussion on retention of documents and a sample disclosure to clients of a documents retention policy, see chapter 6 of this Guide, Confidentiality of Information, sections 6.15 and 6.16.

ACTEC Commentaries on Model Rules of Professional Conduct, Rule 1.4

> *Termination of Representation.* A client whose representation by the lawyer is dormant becomes a former client if the lawyer or the client terminates the representation. See MRPC 1.16 (Declining or Terminating Representation) and MRPC 1.9 (Duties to Former Clients) and the ACTEC Commentaries thereon. The lawyer may terminate the relationship in most circumstances, although the disability of a client may limit the lawyer's ability to do so. Thus, the lawyer may terminate the representation of a competent client by a letter, sometimes called an "exit" letter, that informs the client that the relationship is terminated. The representation is also terminated if the client informs the lawyer that another lawyer has undertaken to represent the client in trusts and estates matters. Finally, the representation may be terminated by the passage of an extended period of time during which the lawyer is not consulted. In general, a lawyer may communicate

with a former client regarding the subject of the former representation and matters of potential interest to the former client. See MRPCs 7.3 (Direct Contact with Prospective Clients) and 7.4 (Communication of Fields of Practice).

> Example 1.4-1. Lawyer (L) prepared and completed an estate plan for Client (C). At C's request, L retained the original documents executed by C. L performed no other legal work for C in the following two years but has no reason to believe that C has engaged other estate planning counsel. L's representation of C is dormant. L may, but is not obligated to, communicate with C regarding changes in the law. If L communicates with C about changes in the law but is not asked by C to perform any legal services, L's representation remains dormant. C is properly characterized as a client and not a former client for purposes of MRPCs 1.7 (Conflict of Interest: Current Client) and 1.9 (Duties to Former Clients).

> Example 1.4-2. Assume the same facts as in Example 1.4-1 except that L's partner (P) in the two years following the preparation of the estate plan renders legal services to C in matters completely unrelated to estate planning, such as a criminal representation. L's representation of C with respect to estate planning matters remains dormant, subject to activation by C.

Case Study

Lawyer prepared a will and trust for a client, naming a bank as trustee. The client discussed with a trust officer at the bank the possibility of transferring a valuable parcel of commercial real property to the trustee and amending the trust instrument to add other children as beneficiaries. The trust officer communicated this possibility to Lawyer, who declined to act until hearing from the client. The client died without having amended the trust. The client's children brought suit against the bank and Lawyer for failure to accomplish the client's desire to amend the trust instrument.

What ethical issues arise from this set of facts and how should Lawyer have addressed them?

The court affirmed a summary judgment in favor of Lawyer, observing, "[Lawyer] fully discharged whatever duty his prior representation imposed by his request through the intermediary that the client communicate with him personally. [Lawyer]'s conduct satisfied rather than violated his duty as a lawyer. It was designed to assure that the personal nature of the attorney-client relationship was protected." *Brandlin v. Belcher* (1977) 67 Cal.App.3d 997, 1001.

Cases

Written termination of the initial representation may also clarify the applicability of the statute of limitations on actions for legal malpractice. Code of Civil Procedure section 340.6 provides that the limitations period on malpractice claims is tolled during the time that "[t]he attorney continues to represent the plaintiff regarding the specific subject matter in which the alleged wrongful act or omission occurred." In this case the defendant lawyer asserted that representation of the plaintiff client ceased, as a matter of law, more than one year before the plaintiff's action was filed, when the plaintiff consulted with another lawyer. The plaintiff claimed that the defendant lawyer continued to represent her until eleven months before suit was filed. The trial court's grant of summary judgment was reversed because the evidence disclosed a triable issue of material fact regarding the date on which the defendant's representation of the plaintiff ended. "Continuity of representation ultimately depends, not on the client's subjective beliefs, but rather on evidence of an ongoing mutual relationship and of activities in furtherance of the relationship." *Worthington v. Rusconi* (1994) 29 Cal.App.4th 1488.

The Court of Appeal upheld the trial court findings that a lawyer led the nominated executor reasonably to believe the lawyer was representing him, and that it must have been clear to the lawyer that the nominated executor was led to so believe. That the nominated executor had not retained the lawyer as a client was irrelevant because the lawyer did not perform the necessary probate work whoever the client was, and the lawyer led the nominated executor to believe that the lawyer was representing him without ever advising him otherwise. A lawyer's duty to communicate includes the duty to communicate with unrepresented persons at least to the extent of advising them that they are not clients. This duty extends only to persons who, to the lawyer's knowledge, may reasonably believe that they are clients. *Butler v. State Bar* (1986) 42 Cal.3d 323, 329.

CHAPTER 8 COMPENSATION

California Rules of Professional Conduct, Rule 1.5 - Fees for Legal Services

(a) A lawyer shall not make an agreement for, charge, or collect an unconscionable or illegal fee.

(b) Unconscionability of a fee shall be determined on the basis of all the facts and circumstances existing at the time the agreement is entered into except where the parties contemplate that the fee will be affected by later events. The factors to be considered in determining the unconscionability of a fee include without limitation the following:

(1) whether the lawyer engaged in fraud* or overreaching in negotiating or setting the fee;

(2) whether the lawyer has failed to disclose material facts;

(3) the amount of the fee in proportion to the value of the services performed;

(4) the relative sophistication of the lawyer and the client;

(5) the novelty and difficulty of the questions involved, and the skill requisite to perform the legal service properly;

(6) the likelihood, if apparent to the client, that the acceptance of the particular employment will preclude other employment by the lawyer;

(7) the amount involved and the results obtained;

(8) the time limitations imposed by the client or by the circumstances;

(9) the nature and length of the professional relationship with the client;

(10) the experience, reputation, and ability of the lawyer or lawyers performing the services;

(11) whether the fee is fixed or contingent;

(12) the time and labor required; and

(13) whether the client gave informed consent* to the fee.

(c) A lawyer shall not make an agreement for, charge, or collect:

(1) any fee in a family law matter, the payment or amount of which is contingent upon the securing of a dissolution or declaration of nullity of a marriage or upon the amount of spousal or child support, or property settlement in lieu thereof; or

(2) a contingent fee for representing a defendant in a criminal case.

(d) A lawyer may make an agreement for, charge, or collect a fee that is denominated as "earned on receipt" or "non-refundable," or in similar terms, only if the fee is a true retainer and the client agrees in writing* after disclosure that the client will not be entitled to a refund of all or part of the fee charged. A true retainer is a fee that a client pays to a lawyer to ensure the lawyer's availability to the client during a specified period or on a specified matter, but not to any extent as compensation for legal services performed or to be performed.

(e) A lawyer may make an agreement for, charge, or collect a flat fee for specified legal services. A flat fee is a fixed amount that constitutes complete payment for the performance of described services regardless of the amount of work ultimately involved, and which may be paid in whole or in part in advance of the lawyer providing those services.

An asterisk (*) identifies a defined term in rule 1.0.1 of the Rules of Professional Conduct. For further discussion of a defined term, see chapter 2 of this Guide, Terminology.

8.1 Introduction

Fees negotiated for estate planning, probate administration, trust administration, guardianship administration, conservatorship administration, elder law, and probate litigation work are subject to the requirements of rule 1.5 of the Rules of Professional Conduct. Those requirements apply even if the lawyer undertakes new work for a current client. Renegotiation of an existing fee agreement with a client is also subject to the provisions of rule 1.8.1 of the Rules of Professional Conduct regarding business transactions with a client. *Matter of Silverton* (Review Dept. 2001) 4 Cal. St. Bar Ct. Rptr. 252.

If the negotiated agreement provides for a security interest for the lawyer's fee, a transfer of ownership from the client to the lawyer, or an assignment of a present interest such as a statutory executor's fee by the client to the lawyer, the fee agreement must comply with rule 1.8.1. *Matter of Yagman* (Review Dept. 1997) 3 Cal. St. Bar Ct. Rptr. 788, referring to former rule 3-300 of the Rules of Professional Conduct. An interest in the client's recovery in a represented matter or a contingency fee agreement is not within the purview of rule 1.5 of the Rules of Professional Conduct.

In addition to the requirements imposed by the Rules of Professional Conduct, fee agreements must meet the general requirements regarding financial arrangements between lawyers and clients. Fee agreements may only be between the lawyer and a client. A paralegal may not establish a fee agreement directly with a client. Bus. & Prof. Code, sec. 6450, subd. (b)(8).

If a lawyer charges an hourly or flat fee and expects that fee to exceed $1,000, the contract for services must be in writing. Bus. & Prof. Code, sec. 6148, subd. (a). The contract must provide the basis for the compensation, the general nature of the legal services to be provided, and the respective responsibilities of the lawyer and the client as to the performance of the contract. The lawyer must provide a duplicate, fully signed copy of the contract to the client. Bus. & Prof. Code, sec. 6148, subd. (b). Failure to comply with these statutory requirements allows the client to void the agreement. Bus. & Prof. Code, sec 6148, subd. (c). If the client voids the agreement, the lawyer can nevertheless collect “a reasonable fee.” Bus. & Prof. Code, sec 6148, subd. (c).

If the lawyer intends to charge a contingency fee, the contract for services must be in writing. Bus. & Prof. Code, sec. 6147, subd. (a). The contract must also provide statements of the contingency fee rate, how disbursements and costs will affect the contingency fee and recovery of the client, how additional compensation could arise for other matters not covered by the contingency fee agreement, and that the fee is not set by law and is negotiable. The lawyer must provide a duplicate, fully signed copy of the contract to the client. Bus. & Prof. Code, sec. 6147, subd. (a). Failure to comply with these statutory requirements allows the client to void the agreement. Bus. & Prof. Code, sec. 6147, subd. (b). If the client voids the agreement, the lawyer can nevertheless collect “a reasonable fee.” Bus. & Prof. Code, sec. 6147, subd. (b).

A lawyer may accept payment of earned fees by credit card. Cal. State Bar Com. on Prof. Resp. and Conduct, formal opn. No. 2007-172. The part of that opinion regarding a deposit by credit card for fees not yet earned has been superseded by rule 1.15 of the Rules of Professional Conduct. Rule 1.15 now mandates that unearned fees must be deposited into the client trust account. Also, a lawyer may not accept a deposit for advances applicable to costs and expenses by credit card, since ethically those funds must be held in a client trust account and could be subject to invasion under the terms of the credit card companies’ merchant account rules.

ACTEC Commentaries on Model Rules of Professional Conduct, Model Rule 1.5

> *Basis of Fees for Trusts and Estates Services.* Fees for legal services in trusts and estates matters may be established in a variety of ways provided that the fee ultimately charged is a reasonable one taking into account the factors described in MRPC 1.5(a) (Fees). Fees in such matters frequently are primarily based on the hourly rates charged by the lawyers and legal assistants rendering the legal services or upon a mutually agreed-upon fee determined in advance. There is nothing improper, in principle, with charging a flat fee for estate planning or estate administration if the fee is reasonable after considering all the factors enumerated in Rule 1.5(a). If a statute or other authority in the lawyer’s state authorizes certain flat fees or declares them reasonable, then a flat fee consistent with that state authority is reasonable under Rule 1.5. See, e.g., Fla. Stat. 733.6171. Unless the lawyer has regularly represented the client on the same basis or rate, the lawyer must advise the client of the basis upon which the legal fees will be charged and obtain the client’s consent to the fee arrangement. The rule also requires a lawyer to inform the client, preferably in writing, before or within a reasonable time after commencing the representation, of the extent to which the client will be charged for other items, including duplicating expenses and the time of secretarial or clerical personnel.
>
> Any changes in the basis or rate of the fee or expenses shall be communicated to the client. Basing a fee for legal services solely on any single factor set forth in MRPC 1.5 (Fees) is generally inappropriate unless required or allowed by the law of the applicable jurisdiction. See Cal. Prob. Code section 10810 and Fla. Stat. Ann. section 733.6171 described in the Annotations to this Commentary. In recent years

courts in several states have, in effect, prohibited or seriously limited the use of fees based upon a percentage of the value of the estate.

Most states allow a lawyer who serves as a fiduciary and as the lawyer for the fiduciary to be compensated for work done in both capacities. However, it is inappropriate for the lawyer to receive double compensation for the same work.

Statutes

California Business and Professions Code section 6147

(a) An attorney who contracts to represent a client on a contingency fee basis shall, at the time the contract is entered into, provide a duplicate copy of the contract, signed by both the attorney and the client, or the client's guardian or representative, to the plaintiff, or to the client's guardian or representative. The contract shall be in writing and shall include, but is not limited to, all of the following:

(1) A statement of the contingency fee rate that the client and attorney have agreed upon.

(2) A statement as to how disbursements and costs incurred in connection with the prosecution or settlement of the claim will affect the contingency fee and the client's recovery.

(3) A statement as to what extent, if any, the client could be required to pay any compensation to the attorney for related matters that arise out of their relationship not covered by their contingency fee contract. This may include any amounts collected for the plaintiff by the attorney.

(4) Unless the claim is subject to the provisions of Section 6146 , a statement that the fee is not set by law but is negotiable between attorney and client.

(5) If the claim is subject to the provisions of Section 6146 , a statement that the rates set forth in that section are the maximum limits for the contingency fee agreement, and that the attorney and client may negotiate a lower rate.

(b) Failure to comply with any provision of this section renders the agreement voidable at the option of the plaintiff, and the attorney shall thereupon be entitled to collect a reasonable fee.

(c) This section shall not apply to contingency fee contracts for the recovery of workers' compensation benefits.

(d) This section shall become operative on January 1, 2000.

California Business and Professions Code section 6148

(a) In any case not coming within Section 6147 in which it is reasonably foreseeable that total expense to a client, including attorney fees, will exceed one thousand dollars ($1,000), the contract for services in the case shall be in writing. At the time the contract is entered into, the attorney shall provide a duplicate copy of the contract signed by both the attorney and the client, or the client's guardian or representative, to the client or to the client's guardian or representative. The written contract shall contain all of the following:

(1) Any basis of compensation including, but not limited to, hourly rates, statutory fees or flat fees, and other standard rates, fees, and charges applicable to the case.

(2) The general nature of the legal services to be provided to the client.

(3) The respective responsibilities of the attorney and the client as to the performance of the contract.

(b) All bills rendered by an attorney to a client shall clearly state the basis thereof. Bills for the fee portion of the bill shall include the amount, rate, basis for calculation, or other method of determination of the attorney's fees and costs. Bills for the cost and expense portion of the bill shall clearly identify the costs and expenses incurred and the amount of the costs and expenses. Upon request by the client, the attorney shall provide a bill to the client no later than 10 days following the request unless the attorney has provided a bill to the client within 31 days prior to the request, in which case the attorney may provide a bill to the client no later than 31 days following the date the most recent bill was provided. The client is entitled to make similar requests at intervals of no less than 30 days following the initial request. In providing responses to client requests for billing information, the attorney may use billing data that is currently effective on the date of the request, or, if any fees or costs to that date cannot be accurately determined, they shall be described and estimated.

(c) Failure to comply with any provision of this section renders the agreement voidable at the option of the client, and the attorney shall, upon the agreement being voided, be entitled to collect a reasonable fee.

(d) This section shall not apply to any of the following:

(1) Services rendered in an emergency to avoid foreseeable prejudice to the rights or interests of the client or where a writing is otherwise impractical.

(2) An arrangement as to the fee implied by the fact that the attorney's services are of the same general kind as previously rendered to and paid for by the client.

(3) If the client knowingly states in writing, after full disclosure of this section, that a writing concerning fees is not required.

(4) If the client is a corporation.

(e) This section applies prospectively only to fee agreements following its operative date.

(f) This section shall become operative on January 1, 2000.

Former California Rules of Professional Conduct, Rule 4-200 - Fees for Legal Services

(A) A member shall not enter into an agreement for, charge, or collect an illegal or unconscionable fee.

(B) Unconscionability of a fee shall be determined on the basis of all the facts and circumstances existing at the time the agreement is entered into except where the parties contemplate that the fee will be affected by later events. Among the factors to be considered, where appropriate, in determining the conscionability of a fee are the following:

(1) The amount of the fee in proportion to the value of the services performed.

(2) The relative sophistication of the member and the client.

(3) The novelty and difficulty of the questions involved and the skill requisite to perform the legal services properly.

(4) The likelihood, if apparent to the client, that the acceptance of the particular employment will preclude other employment by the member.

(5) The amount involved and the results obtained.

(6) The time limitations imposed by the client or by the circumstances.

(7) The nature and length of the professional relationship with the client.

(8) The experience, reputation, and ability of the member or members performing the services.

(9) Whether the fee is fixed or contingent.

(10) The time and labor required.

(11) The informed consent of the client to the fee.

Cases

A client did not consent to pay the lawyer's invoice for services rendered under an unsigned fee agreement between the lawyer and the client's late husband that did not comply with statutory disclosure requirements, and the client was not liable on the lawyer's cause of action for account stated. Even though the client filed an objection to the lawyer's request to withdraw from limited scope representation, the client sent the lawyer an email requesting more information and stating that the client would make future payments only "provided I understand and approve what it is I am paying for." *Leighton v. Forster* (2017) 8 Cal.App.5th 467.

Binding private arbitration clause in a lawyer-client fee agreement may be enforced under the California Arbitration Act when the arbitration process is completed, without filing a superior court action to compel arbitration. *Rosenson v. Greenberg Glusker Fields Claman and Machtinger LLP* (2012) 203 Cal.App.4th 688.

In the absence of a written contract between counsel and a client, the agreement was voidable. Further, counsel was still required to comply with ethical obligations regarding client trust accounts. *Gutierrez v. Girardi* (2011) 194 Cal. App.4th 925.

Failure of contingency fee agreement to contain a statement that the fee is not set by law but is negotiable renders the agreement voidable. *Arnall v. Super. Ct.* (2010) 190 Cal.App.4th 360.

"When a law firm quotes specific hourly rates for the services of named attorneys to a prospective client who then agrees in writing to pay the firm's 'regular hourly rates,' the law firm cannot raise the rates charged by the named attorneys without first notifying the client." *Severson & Werson v. Bolinger* (1991) 235 Cal.App.3d 1569, 1570. The Northern District of California relied on the ruling in this case to hold "an attorney cannot seek a rate increase after the fee for engagement has already been established, unless he reserves the right to do so." *Thelen Reid Brown Raysman & Steiner LLP v. Marland* (N.D. Cal., Aug. 1, 2007, No. C 06-2071 VRW) 2007 WL 9812750, at *12.

The Court of Appeal declined to enforce a prior approved fee agreement where insufficient notice had been provided to creditors. The trial court improperly approved the agreement by way of an ex parte petition, dispensed with notice of the hearing, and ordered the petition sealed until the administrator concluded all litigation related to the estate. The opinion reviews extensively the legislative history of the enactment of Probate Code section 10811, subdivision (c) allowing a lawyer to charge a contingent fee for extraordinary services rendered in probate matters. *Estate of Stevenson* (2006) 141 Cal.App.4th 1074.

A lawyer is required to comply with requirements of former rule 3-300 of the Rules of Professional Conduct when requesting an additional fee agreement after the original fee agreement was signed. *Matter of Silverton* (Review Dept. 2001) 4 Cal. State Bar Ct. Rptr. 252.

Ethics Opinions

A lawyer may enter into a binding and enforceable contingency fee agreement that provides to the lawyer some or all of the first proceeds of suit so as to impose on the client greater risk that the defendant's financial condition will limit the amount recovered from a settlement agreement or judgment. Any such risk-shifting agreement requires the client's informed consent based on the lawyer's full and fair disclosure of pertinent information known to the lawyer. L.A. County Bar Assn., Ethics opn. No. 526 (Feb. 9, 2015).

A lawyer may ethically accept payment for earned fees by credit card, but not a deposit applicable to advances for costs and expenses. State Bar of Cal. Com. on Prof. Resp. and Conduct, formal opn. No. 2007-172.

8.2 Sample Agreement for Compensation at Hourly Rate

The following provisions can be adapted for inclusion in an engagement letter that sets forth the terms of the representation when the proposed lawyer's compensation is an hourly fee. The lawyer should adapt them thoughtfully to the lawyer's customary practice and the needs of a particular client representation. The provisions may also be modified to explain procedures for arbitration of fee disputes that are required or permitted under rules of the local bar association.

> Dear [Client],
>
> Our fee in connection with the [subject matter of the engagement] will be the product of the time spent by our lawyers and other professionals multiplied times their respective hourly rates. The time for which we are to be paid includes not only normal office conferences, research, analysis, and advice associated with the [subject matter of the engagement], but also the time involved in telephone calls, faxes, e-mail, and other forms of communication. We will bill you for our services on a monthly basis.
>
> We adjust our hourly rates periodically. We consider the ability, experience, and reputation of our lawyers and paralegals when we set hourly rates. Changes are usually made each January 1, but sometimes they are made at other times. Any increase in rates will apply to all time beginning with the month when the rates are changed. Work done before that month will be billed at the hourly rate that was previously in effect.
>
> Different lawyers and paralegals in our firm may be involved in your work if that will result in lower fees, provide a specialized legal talent, or help us do your work more efficiently. We will try to assign lawyers and paralegals having the lowest hourly rates consistent with the skills, time demands, and other factors required for your work. We might not assign a lawyer or paralegal with the lowest hourly rate if, in our judgment, it may be in your best interests to assign a lawyer or paralegal with a higher hourly rate because of that lawyer's or paralegal's skill and experience or because of the time constraints of the work.
>
> We record and bill our time in one-tenth hour (six-minute) units. If a lawyer's or paralegal's total time on your work is less than three-tenths of an hour for the entire day, three-tenths of an hour will be billed for that day. If the lawyer's or paralegal's total time on your work is more than three-tenths of an hour for that day (whether done at one time or not), only the time actually spent will be billed.
>
> In addition to our legal fees, as described above, we will be entitled to be reimbursed by you for out-of-pocket expenses that we pay on your behalf and for our internal costs. Out-of-pocket expenses include items such as filing fees charged by government agencies and travel expenses. Our internal costs include things like photocopying, long-distance telephone calls, fax transmissions, document scanning and electronic transmission, storage, and retrieval, courier services, computer research charges, and complex document production. Rather than tracking precise

costs for every single internal charge (which would ultimately result in higher hourly rates for our clients), we charge fixed costs for these types of expenses. Our charges for these internal costs may exceed the actual direct costs that we pay to outsiders such as the telephone company or photocopying contractors.

Sometimes it is necessary to hire other persons to provide services for you, such as accounting or appraisal firms. Their work may have more confidentiality if we (rather than you) request their services, and so we may hire them. However, you will be responsible for paying their fees and expenses, whether paid directly to them or to us in reimbursement.

Our bills are due when rendered. If a bill is not paid within 30 days after it is mailed to you, interest will accrue on the unpaid balance of that bill beginning on the thirty-first (31st) day and accruing thereafter at the rate of one percent (1%) per month. Interest charges will apply to specific monthly bills. Payments made on past-due accounts will be applied first to the oldest outstanding bill. If our bills are not paid reasonably soon after they are rendered, we reserve the right to stop work until your account is brought current and appropriate measures are taken to ensure prompt payment in the future. If we have to bring collection efforts for payment, you agree that you will pay the costs of collection procedures, including reasonable attorneys' fees incurred by us (whether paid to our firm or another firm retained by us).

We may require a retainer or advance fee deposit for your work. Unless you and we agree otherwise, the retainer or advance fee deposit will be applied to our final statement, and any unused portion will be returned to you. We may also request an advance cost deposit (in addition to the retainer or advance fee deposit) when we expect that we will incur substantial costs on your behalf.

[*Alternative for Joint Representation*] Each of you agrees that you will all be jointly and severally responsible for the payment of all amounts owed to us and that we can seek payment in full from any one of you at our election. Any agreement between any of you to limit your responsibility for payment of amounts owed to us will not be binding upon us unless we agree in writing to those limits. Your joint and several responsibility for the payment of our fees and expenses includes the situation in which our representation is terminated for any reason prior to the completion of the [subject matter of the engagement].

Sincerely,

[Lawyer]

Reprinted with permission from The American College of Trust and Estate Counsel.

8.3 Retainers and Flat Fees

Rule 1.5 of the Rules of Professional Conduct permits and distinguishes a retainer from a flat fee, both as forms of the lawyer's compensation. Each of those forms of compensation is subject to client consent after specified disclosures.

A retainer subject to the provisions of rule 1.5(d) is a "true retainer" rather than a payment on account to be applied as fees are earned. A lawyer may charge such a retainer that is not refundable and not applied as services are performed. The client must consent in writing to such a nonrefundable fee. In all other cases, rule 1.16(e) of the Rules of Professional Conduct requires that any unearned portion of a lawyer's fee must be returned to the client when the representation terminates. A true retainer is excepted from that ethical duty.

A lawyer may also charge a flat fee for services rendered. Defining the scope of the representation and the specific services covered by the flat fee will avoid later fee disputes. For a further discussion of engagement letters to specify the terms of a representation, see chapter 4 of this Guide, Identifying the Client and the Scope of Representation. A lawyer may draw on any part or all of a flat fee at any time during the course of the representation.

Because a flat fee is full payment subject to draw at any time, the lawyer may deposit that fee into the lawyer's operating account. Rule 1.15(b) of the Rules of Professional Conduct prescribes written disclosures to the client for such a flat fee:

> (b) Notwithstanding paragraph (a), a flat fee paid in advance for legal services may be deposited in a lawyer's or law firm's operating account, provided:
>
> > (1) the lawyer or law firm* discloses to the client in writing*(i) that the client has a right under paragraph (a) to require that the flat fee be deposited in an identified trust account until the fee is earned, and (ii) that the client is entitled to a refund of any amount of the fee that has not been earned in the event the representation is terminated or the services for which the fee has been paid are not completed; and
> >
> > (2) if the flat fee exceeds $1,000.00, the client's agreement to deposit the flat fee in the lawyer's operating account and the disclosures required by paragraph (b)(1) are set forth in a writing* signed by the client.

These written disclosures are most appropriately included in the initial engagement letter and fee agreement with the client. If the client does not consent, the flat fee must be deposited in the lawyer's client trust account.

Charging a flat fee may raise a calculation issue if the representation is terminated before the agreed upon work is completed. In that case, the lawyer must refund the unearned portion of the fee in accordance with rule 1.16(e) of the Rules of Professional Conduct. The San Diego Bar Association discusses the calculation of the refund amount in its Ethics Opinion Number 2019-3. A lawyer and client may agree on a method of calculating the unearned portion of the fee, provided that the methodology results in a fee commensurate with the reasonable value of the lawyer's services and is not unconscionable, as determined under the factors in rule 1.5 of the Rules of Professional Conduct. The opinion analyzes two such methodologies: tracking the hours spent on the flat fee matter to termination of employment and identifying milestones in the progress of the representation. The first approach has the benefit of simplicity but can raise the ethical issue of an unconscionable fee. The opinion cites authorities that providing for agreed representation benchmarks or milestones for the earning of a portion of a flat fee is permissible.

Article

Wertlieb, *Advance Fee Deposits and Your Client Trust Account* (Dec. 2019) Cal. Lawyers Assn. eNews.

8.4 Sample Flat Fee Agreement

The following provisions can be included in an engagement letter that sets forth the terms of the representation when the proposed lawyer's compensation is a flat fee. The lawyer should adapt them thoughtfully to the lawyer's customary practice and the needs of a particular client representation.

> Dear [Client],
>
> Our fee in connection with the [subject matter of the engagement] will be a flat fee of $____. This fee includes the normal office and telephone conferences, research, analysis, and advice associated with the [subject matter of the engagement]. Significant changes in the scope of the services required or significant revisions to any documents that we have prepared will be charged separately, but any additional charges will be explained to you before any revisions are begun. One-half of this fee is payable once this engagement letter is signed and you authorize us to proceed. The balance of the fee will be payable at the time when the [subject matter of the engagement] is complete.
>
> Sincerely,
>
> [Lawyer]

Reprinted with permission from The American College of Trust and Estate Counsel.

The following provision could also be added to the engagement letter to comply with the disclosure requirements in rule 1.15 of the Rules of Professional Conduct.

> Upon payment, the fee will be deposited into our business operating account. You may require instead that the fee be deposited in a client trust account until the fee is earned. In either case you are entitled to a refund of any part of the fee that has not been earned in the event the representation is terminated or the services set forth in this engagement letter are not completed. We would be pleased to answer any questions you may have regarding these disclosures. Your signature on the enclosed copy of this engagement letter acknowledges receipt of the disclosures and your agreement that we may deposit the fee into our business operating account.

8.5 Compensation in Estate, Conservatorship, or Guardianship Proceedings

Lawyers must also comply with statutory and court rules applicable to probate, guardianship, and conservatorship cases. In a probate proceeding, compensation for the statutory services of the personal representative and lawyer may not exceed the statutory rate provided in Probate Code sections 10800 and 10810, respectively. The lawyer and the client cannot agree to pay the lawyer's fee from other sources, if the statutory formula applied to a low value probate estate results in an unreasonably low fee. Agreements between probate counsel and the estate representative for compensation exceeding that allowed by statute are void as against public policy. *Estate of Gilkison* (1998) 65 Cal.App.4th 1443, 1446, fn. 2. An agreement between the personal representative and the lawyer for higher lawyer's compensation than provided by Probate Code section 10813 is void.

Charging a contingency fee for ordinary services in a probate proceeding is also impermissible. *Denton v. Smith* (1951) 101 Cal.App.2d 841. However, Probate Code section 10811, subdivision (c) requires that an agreement for a contingency fee related to extraordinary services be in writing and comply with all the requirements of section 6147 of the Business and Professions Code. Such an agreement must be approved by the court at a noticed hearing, upon a court determination that the compensation is just and reasonable and the agreement is to the advantage of the estate and in the best interests of the persons interested in the estate.

Fees charged for extraordinary services that the personal representative and lawyer provide on behalf of the probate estate must be just and reasonable. Prob. Code, secs. 10801, 10811. Reasonableness of a fee in probate matters has been determined using the following factors: the gross income of the estate; the success or failure of the administration of the fiduciary; any unusual skill or experience that the fiduciary in question may have brought to the fiduciary's work; the fidelity or disloyalty displayed by the fiduciary; the amount of risk and responsibility assumed; the time spent in carrying out the fiduciary's duties; the custom in the community as to allowances by settlors or courts, and as to charges of corporate fiduciaries; the character of the work performed, i.e., whether routine or involving skill or judgment; and the fiduciary's own estimate of the value of the fiduciary's services. *Estate of Nazro* (1971) 15 Cal.App.3d 218, 221.

In determining whether the fees for extraordinary services are just and reasonable, the court may determine that the statutory fee payment adequately compensates the personal representative or lawyer and disallow the extraordinary compensation. There is no absolute right to compensation for extraordinary services. *Estate of Hilton* (1996) 44 Cal.App.4th 890; Cal. Rules of Court, rule 7.703(a). A court finding that a fee is unreasonable does not mean that it is unconscionable. To be unconscionable, a fee must be so exorbitant and wholly disproportionate to the services performed as to shock the conscience. *Tarver v. State Bar* (1984) 37 Cal.3d 122. The trial court may review whether lawyer fees awarded for both ordinary and extraordinary services are adequate, given the value of the estate and the nature of its assets, to compensate the lawyer fully, and denial of a petition for extraordinary fees in light of such review is not an abuse of discretion. *Estate of Trynin* (1989) 49 Cal.3d 868, 880.

Extraordinary services performed by the lawyer may be compensated under the terms of a contingency fee contract if the contract meets the requirements set forth above and is approved by the court at a noticed hearing. Prob. Code, sec. 10811, subd. (c); Cal. Rules of Court, rule 7.703(d). A contingency fee contract with beneficiaries or heirs to protect a claim or share is not illegal and does not need to be approved by the court. *Estate of Kerr* (1966) 63 Cal.2d 875.

The will of the decedent may prescribe the executor's compensation or the lawyer's compensation. If the will specifies such compensation, the personal representative and lawyer are limited to the compensation provided unless the court grants relief from that provision. Prob. Code, secs. 10802 and 10812. California Rules of Court, rule 7.700(a) prohibits a personal representative and the personal representative's lawyer from paying or receiving statutory fees or fees for extraordinary services prior to a court order. Paragraph (b) of that rule of court permits sanctions including surcharge for the amount of the fees paid without court order, with interest. Consistent with rule 7.700, the lawyer must request court relief in advance before taking a fee in an amount greater than the will provides.

If there is more than one personal representative or lawyer, the fees are apportioned based upon the services provided by each or the agreement reached by them. Prob. Code, secs. 10804, 10814; Cal. Rules of Court, rule 7.704.

All fees payable to the personal representative and the lawyer are subject to court allowance. Prob. Code, secs. 10830 et seq.; Cal. Rules of Court, rule 7.700. Charging a fee in a probate proceeding that has not been approved by the court is impermissible and will subject the lawyer to discipline. *Matter of Phillips* (Review Dept. 2001) 4 Cal. St. Bar Ct. Rptr. 315. A petition for payment of fees for extraordinary services must set forth a statement of facts regarding the services performed. Cal. Rules of Court, rule 7.702. Any petition for allowance of extraordinary services performed by a paralegal must state the paralegal's qualifications, hours spent by the paralegal, the paralegal's hourly rate, describe the services provided by the paralegal, state why it was appropriate to use the paralegal, and demonstrate that the total requested does not exceed the amount that would have been appropriate if the lawyer had performed the services without the assistance of a paralegal. Cal. Rules of Court, rule 7.703(e).

In conservatorship and guardianship proceedings, all fees of the conservator or guardian of the person, conservator or guardian of the estate, and of the lawyer are payable from the conservatorship or guardianship estate and subject to court allowance. Prob. Code, secs. 2640 et seq. Petitions for payment of such fees from the conservatorship or guardianship estate must generally comply with the requirements of rule 7.702 concerning extraordinary compensation in decedents' estates and may include a request for compensation for services rendered before appointment of the guardian or conservator. Cal. Rules of Court, rule 7.751. Fees that are paid from other sources are not limited by these sections. Prob. Code, sec. 2646. Fees may be paid under a contingency fee contract if the contract meets the requirements set forth above and is approved by the court upon a noticed hearing. Prob. Code, sec. 2644. A person who sought appointment but was not appointed and the lawyer for that unsuccessful petitioner may file a petition for an order fixing and allowing compensation. Such a petition may be filed any time after the filing of the inventory and appraisal, but not before the expiration of 90 days from the issuance of letters. Prob. Code, sec. 2640.1.

For the limitations on compensation payable to a lawyer serving in both a fiduciary capacity and as a lawyer, see Probate Code sections 2645 and 10806, and chapter 5 of this Guide, Conflicts of Interest, section 5.12.

California Rules of Court

Rule 7.701. Allowance on account of statutory compensation

The court may authorize an allowance of statutory fees or commissions on account before approval of the final account and the decree of final distribution. Any allowance made before settlement of the final account must be low enough to avoid the possibility of overpayment. The allowance:

(1) Must be based on the estimated amount of statutory compensation payable on the estate determined as of the date of the petition for allowance;

(2) Must be in proportion to the work actually performed; and

(3) Must be based upon a detailed description of the ordinary services performed and remaining to be performed.

Rule 7.702. Petition for extraordinary compensation

A petition for extraordinary compensation must include, or be accompanied by, a statement of the facts upon which the petition is based. The statement of facts must:

(1) Show the nature and difficulty of the tasks performed;

(2) Show the results achieved;

(3) Show the benefit of the services to the estate;

(4) Specify the amount requested for each category of service performed;

(5) State the hourly rate of each person who performed services and the hours spent by each of them;

(6) Describe the services rendered in sufficient detail to demonstrate the productivity of the time spent; and

(7) State the estimated amount of statutory compensation to be paid by the estate, if the petition is not part of a final account or report.

Rule 7.703. Extraordinary compensation

(a) Discretion of the court

An award of extraordinary compensation to the personal representative or to the attorney for the personal representative is within the discretion of the court. The court may consider the amount of statutory compensation when determining compensation for extraordinary services.

(b) Examples of extraordinary services by personal representative

The following is a nonexclusive list of activities for which extraordinary compensation may be awarded to the personal representative:

(1) Selling, leasing, exchanging, financing, or foreclosing real or personal property;

(2) Carrying on decedent's business if necessary to preserve the estate or under court order;

(3) Preparing tax returns; and

(4) Handling audits or litigation connected with tax liabilities of the decedent or of the estate.

(c) Examples of extraordinary services by attorney

The following is a nonexclusive list of activities for which extraordinary compensation may be awarded to the attorney for the personal representative:

(1) Legal services in connection with the sale of property held in the estate;

(2) Services to secure a loan to pay estate debts;

(3) Litigation undertaken to benefit the estate or to protect its interests;

(4) Defense of the personal representative's account;

(5) Defense of a will contested after its admission to probate;

(6) Successful defense of a will contested before its admission to probate;

(7) Successful defense of a personal representative in a removal proceeding;

(8) Extraordinary efforts to locate estate assets;

(9) Litigation in support of attorney's request for extraordinary compensation, where prior compensation awards are not adequate compensation under all the circumstances;

(10) Coordination of ancillary administration; and

(11) Accounting for a deceased, incapacitated, or absconded personal representative under Probate Code section 10953.

(d) Contingency fee agreement for extraordinary legal services

An attorney may agree to perform extraordinary services for a personal representative on a contingent-fee basis on the following conditions:

(1) The agreement must be in writing and must comply with section 6147 of the Business and Professions Code;

(2) The court must approve the agreement in the manner provided in Probate Code section 10811(c), based on findings that the compensation under the

agreement is just and reasonable, that the agreement is to the advantage of the estate, and that the agreement is in the best interest of the persons interested in the estate; and

(3) In the absence of an emergency or other unusual circumstances, the personal representative must obtain the court's approval of the contingency fee agreement before services are performed under it.

(e) Use of paralegals in the performance of extraordinary services

Extraordinary legal services may include the services of a paralegal as defined in Business and Professions Code section 6450(a) only if the request for extraordinary legal fees for the paralegal's services:

(1) Describes the qualifications of the paralegal (including education, certification, continuing education, and experience). The description must state that the paralegal:

(A) Acted under the direction and supervision of an attorney;

(B) Satisfies one or more of the minimum qualifications specified in Business and Professions Code section 6450(c); and

(C) Has completed mandatory continuing education required by Business and Professions Code section 6450(d) for the last two-year certification period ending before the year during which any part of the paralegal's services were performed.

(2) States the hours spent by the paralegal and the hourly rate requested for the paralegal's services;

(3) Describes the services performed by the paralegal;

(4) States why it was appropriate to use the paralegal's services in the particular case; and

(5) Demonstrates that the total amount requested for the extraordinary services of the attorney and the paralegal does not exceed the amount appropriate if the attorney had performed the services without the paralegal's assistance.

Rule 7.751. Petitions for orders allowing compensation for guardians or conservators and their attorneys

(a) Petition for allowance of compensation for services performed before appointment of guardian or conservator.

A petition for allowance of compensation to a guardian or conservator or to the attorney for a guardian or conservator may include a request for compensation for services rendered before an order appointing a guardian or conservator. The petition must show facts demonstrating the necessity for preappointment services.

(b) Required showing in petition for allowance of compensation.

All petitions for orders fixing and allowing compensation must comply with the requirements of rule 7.702 concerning petitions for extraordinary compensation in decedents' estates, to the extent applicable to guardianships and conservatorships, except that the best interest of the ward or conservatee is to be considered instead of the interest of beneficiaries of the estate.

Cases

Lawyer compensation paid out of probate estate does not require a written fee agreement. *In re Estate of Wong* (2012) 207 Cal.App.4th 366.

A lawyer may not receive any fee in a probate proceeding prior to court approval as such fee is illegal. *Matter of Phillips* (Review Dept. 2001) 4 Cal. State Bar Ct. Rptr. 315.

A probate lawyer was not entitled to additional compensation when reasonable value of services did not exceed statutory compensation. *Estate of Hilton* (1996) 44 Cal.App.4th 890.

The court outlined factors that the court may and should consider in determining reasonableness of a lawyer's fees in connection with a legal proceeding. *Stokus v. Marsh* (1990) 217 Cal.App.3d 647.

A probate lawyer was disbarred for misappropriation of client funds for demanding and accepting fees before probate proceedings had been commenced or court approval obtained. *Alberton v. State Bar* (1987) 43 Cal.3d 638.

A probate lawyer was disciplined for unilaterally determining a fee without court approval and withdrawing that fee from the estate trust account. Such a payment is misappropriation of client funds and may subject a lawyer to disbarment. *Murray v. State Bar* (1985) 40 Cal.3d 575.

A probate lawyer improperly obtained a $1,500 retainer. *Tarver v. State Bar* (1984) 37 Cal.3d 122.

A lawyer charged an illegal fee for ordinary services based upon recovery from the estate. *Denton v. Smith* (1951) 101 Cal.App.2d 841.

8.6 Sample Compensation Disclosure in Probate Representation

The following provisions can be adapted for inclusion in an engagement letter for the representation of an executor or administrator in a probate matter. The lawyer should adapt them thoughtfully to the lawyer's customary practice and the needs of a particular client representation.

Dear [Client],

Expenses of Administration and Compensation of Personal Representative and Attorneys. The expenses of administering estates vary depending on many factors, one of which is the size of the estate. The expenses of administration may include court fees, certification fees, surety bond premiums, the California probate referee's fees, agency fees, insurance premiums, expenses of selling assets, and the personal representative's, accountants', and lawyers' compensation. Upon your appointment as personal representative, the decedent's will and California law allow you to pay expenses incurred in the collection, care, and administration of the estate. You will include those expenses on your account filed with the court, and you should pay expenses only if you are sure that the estate has sufficient funds to pay all expenses related to the estate administration.

The largest costs are usually the compensation of the personal representative and the lawyer. You must obtain a court order before paying or receiving any fee for your services or for the services of this firm.

As personal representative, you are allowed compensation for your services. Unless the will makes special provision for your compensation, the amount of compensation for your "ordinary" services is fixed by California statute and is based on the value of the estate accounted for. This value generally includes the inventory value of the probate estate and income received during the period of administration. *Compensation can be paid only after the court orders payment.* The compensation for ordinary services for the Personal Representative and the Personal Representative's lawyer is calculated based on the amount of the estate accounted for as follows:

4% on the first $100,000 or fraction thereof;
3% on the next $100,000 or fraction thereof;
2% on the next $800,000 or fraction thereof;
1% on the next $9,000,000;
½% on the next $15,000,000; and
A reasonable fee determined by the court on the excess over $25,000,000.

For purposes of applying this formula the estate accounted for is the inventory value of the probate estate, without reduction for mortgages or loans secured by real property, as increased by income receipts and adjusted for gains or losses on the sale of assets.

Compensation for Extraordinary Services. In addition to the statutory compensation discussed above, the probate court may, in proper instances, authorize payment of additional compensation to the personal representative or lawyer for "extraordinary services" rendered in the administration of the estate. There is no prescribed schedule of compensation of such services. The amount in each instance is fixed by the court on the basis of a declaration by the personal representative or the lawyer as to the nature and extent of the extraordinary services rendered to the estate. The court may consider the amount of statutory compensation when determining compensation for extraordinary services so that the total fee payable is reasonable in amount.

For example, if your duties as personal representative require you to carry on the decedent's business under court order or participate in litigation involving the estate, such services would be regarded as in addition to the ordinary services you are expected to render in administering the estate. You would be entitled to apply for and receive additional compensation for such services.

Similarly, we as lawyers and our paralegal assistants may be called upon to perform legal services in connection with the administration of an estate that are regarded as extraordinary in nature and are not covered by the statutory compensation provided for by the Probate Code. Such services include the following common situations: handling sales or mortgages of real or personal property; contesting or defending litigated claims against the estate; handling litigation relating to property of the estate; arranging for the conduct of ancillary administration in other states where the decedent owned property; and preparing petitions for instructions, to determine heirship, and for preliminary distribution.

Compensation for extraordinary services performed by this firm is based primarily upon our hourly rates from time-to-time prevailing, considering the size and complexity of the matter at issue, the results achieved, and the benefit conferred upon the estate. We will periodically consult with you regarding the probable compensation you will incur as matters calling for extraordinary services arise. All compensation for extraordinary services performed by this firm must be approved by the court.

Waiver of Personal Representative's Compensation. Compensation paid to a personal representative is taxable income to be reported on an income tax return. A personal representative who is also a beneficiary may benefit by waiving the right to receive statutory or extraordinary compensation. I recommend that you discuss the tax consequences of your proposed compensation with your accountant before requesting an order from the court.

Sincerely,

[Lawyer]

8.7 Compensation Paid by Person Other Than Client

California Rules of Professional Conduct, Rule 1.8.6 - Compensation from One Other Than Client

A lawyer shall not enter into an agreement for, charge, or accept compensation for representing a client from one other than the client unless:

(a) there is no interference with the lawyer's independent professional judgment or with the lawyer-client relationship;

(b) information is protected as required by Business and Professions Code section 6068, subdivision (e)(1) and rule 1.6; and

(c) the lawyer obtains the client's informed written consent* at or before the time the lawyer has entered into the agreement for, charged, or accepted the compensation, or as soon thereafter as reasonably* practicable, provided that no disclosure or consent is required if:

(1) nondisclosure or the compensation is otherwise authorized by law or a court order; or

(2) the lawyer is rendering legal services on behalf of any public agency or nonprofit organization that provides legal services to other public agencies or the public.

An asterisk (*) identifies a defined term in rule 1.0.1 of the Rules of Professional Conduct. For further discussion of a defined term, see chapter 2 of this Guide, Terminology.

When the lawyer renders estate planning, administration, elder law, or litigation services to a client with the expectation of payment from a third person, the lawyer must obtain the client's informed written consent. That written consent must be made only after full disclosure that another person will pay the legal fees. Informed consent is a defined term set forth in rule 1.0.1(e) of the Rules of Professional Conduct. The client's consent is "informed" only after the lawyer explains and communicates to the client the relevant circumstances and material risks, including actual and reasonably foreseeable adverse consequences, of the proposed third-party payment of the lawyer's fee.

Rule 1.8.6 of the Rules of Professional Conduct further requires that the lawyer preserve "independence of professional judgment" and maintain all the confidences of the client, notwithstanding the fee arrangement. Bus. & Prof. Code, sec. 6068, subd. (e)(1).

ACTEC Commentaries on Model Rules of Professional Conduct, Model Rule 1.8(f).

Payment of Compensation by Person Other than Client. It is relatively common for a person other than the client to pay for the client's estate planning services. Examples include payment by a parent or other relative or by an employer. A lawyer asked to provide legal services on such terms may do so provided the requirements of MRPCs 1.5 (Fees), 1.7 (Conflict of Interest: Current Clients), and 1.8(f) are satisfied.

Example 1.8-1. Father (F), a client of Lawyer (L), has asked L to prepare an irrevocable trust for F's daughter (D), who will soon attain her majority. D will be the settlor, since F wants D to transfer property to the trust that D will be entitled to receive from a custodianship that was established for D under the Uniform Transfers to Minors Act. F has indicated that he would pay the cost of

L's representation of D in connection with the preparation of the trust. Before undertaking to represent D, L should inform F regarding the requirements of MRPC 1.8—particularly that L must be free to exercise independent judgment in advising D in the matter. L must also obtain D's informed consent to L being compensated by F. Since F is a client, L must be satisfied that representing both F and D is permissible. If there is significant risk that the L's representation of D will be materially limited by the lawyer's own interests in the fee arrangement or by L's responsibilities to F, then L must be able to reasonably conclude that it will be possible to competently and diligently represent both clients and the consent of each must be confirmed in writing. See ACTEC Commentary to MRPC 1.7 (Conflict of Interest: Current Clients). If L cannot represent both F and D consistent with the provisions of MRPC 1.7 (Conflict of Interest: Current Clients), L should decline to represent D. L should not prepare the trust at F's request without meeting with D personally—just as L should not draw D's will without meeting with her personally.

Example 1.8-2. After a review of various forms of fringe benefit programs, Employer (E) is introduced to Lawyer (L) for the purpose of having L provide estate planning services for those of E's employees who desire such services. E agrees to pay L for providing the contemplated professional services "that will benefit E's employees." Provided each employee gives an informed consent to L's representation of the employee under the circumstances and provided L exercises independent judgment on behalf of each employee-client, L may render the services requested by each employee.

Example 1.8-3. L represents Charity. Charity contacts L and tells her that a donor wishes to leave his estate entirely to Charity as long as Charity will cover the costs of drafting the Will. Charity asks L to meet with the client and draft his Will, with the understanding that the Charity will pay L's fees. L should inform Charity regarding the requirements of MRPC 1.8—particularly that L must be free to exercise independent judgment in advising donor in the matter, and that confidentiality of information regarding L's representation of donor will be maintained, even if donor's intentions regarding disposition of his estate vary from what Charity currently understands. L must also obtain donor's informed consent to L being compensated by Charity. Since Charity is a client, L must be satisfied that representing both Charity and donor is permissible. If there is significant risk that the L's representation of donor will be materially limited by the lawyer's own interests in the fee arrangement or by L's responsibilities to Charity, then L must be able to reasonably conclude that it will be possible to competently and diligently represent both clients and the consent must be confirmed in writing.

8.8 Financial Arrangements with Other Lawyers

California Rules of Professional Conduct, Rule 1.5.1 - Fee Divisions Among Lawyers

(a) Lawyers who are not in the same law firm* shall not divide a fee for legal services unless:

(1) the lawyers enter into a written* agreement to divide the fee;

(2) the client has consented in writing,* either at the time the lawyers enter into the agreement to divide the fee or as soon thereafter as reasonably* practicable, after a full written* disclosure to the client of:

(i) the fact that a division of fees will be made;

(ii) the identity of the lawyers or law firms* that are parties to the division; and

(iii) the terms of the division; and

(3) the total fee charged by all lawyers is not increased solely by reason of the agreement to divide fees.

(b) This rule does not apply to a division of fees pursuant to court order.

An asterisk (*) identifies a defined term in rule 1.0.1 of the Rules of Professional Conduct. For further discussion of a defined term, see chapter 2 of this Guide, Terminology.

A lawyer who renders estate planning, administration, elder law, or litigation services to a client may ethically associate additional counsel to assist in representing the client, such as a certified specialist. Such association may fulfill the lawyer's ethical duty to handle the subject matter of the representation competently. See chapter 3 of this Guide, Competence and Diligence, section 3.4. If association with counsel outside the lawyer's firm involves splitting the client fee, the engagement letter with the client must comply with the requirements of rule 1.5.1 of the Rules of Professional Conduct. The disclosures in rule 1.5.1 are specific and should be discussed in detail in the engagement letter. To comply with the ethical rule, the engagement letter must identify the lawyers who share the fee and the terms of the division between them. In addition, the total fee charged for services of both lawyers must be reasonable.

If fees are divided due to a change of lawyer during a probate proceeding, see the comment in section 8.5 above, Probate Code sections 10804 and 10814, and rule 7.704 of the California Rules of Court.

ACTEC Commentaries on Model Rules of Professional Conduct, Model Rule 1.5(e).

Rebates, Discounts, Commissions, Referral Fees and Fee Splitting. Under MRPC 7.2(b), a lawyer may not "give anything of value to a person for recommending the lawyer's services," except that a lawyer may (1) pay for permissible advertisements (MRPC 7.1-7.3), (2) pay the usual charges of a legal service plan or referral service, (3) pay for a law practice as permitted by MRPC 1.17, and (4) "refer clients to another lawyer or a nonlawyer professional pursuant to an agreement not otherwise prohibited under these Rules that provides for the other person to refer clients or customers to the lawyer, if (i) the reciprocal referral agreement is not exclusive, and (ii) the client is informed of the existence and nature of the agreement." Conversely, a lawyer should not accept any rebate, discount, commission or referral fee from a nonlawyer or a lawyer not acting in a legal capacity in connection with the representation of a client except as permitted by MRPC 7.2(b). Even with full disclosure to and consent by the client, such an arrangement involves a risk of overreaching by the lawyer and the potential for actual or apparent abuse. The client is generally entitled to the benefit of any economies that are achieved by the lawyer in connection with the representation. The acceptance by the lawyer of a referral fee from a nonlawyer may involve an improper conflict of interest. See MRPC 1.7 (Conflict of Interest: Current Clients) and MRPC 1.8 (Conflict of Interest: Current Clients: Specific Rules). In those jurisdictions that permit referral fees between lawyers, the lawyer should comply with the requirements of local law governing such matters, including full disclosure to the client. A lawyer is generally prohibited from sharing legal fees with nonlawyers. See MRPC 5.4 (Professional Independence).

While a lawyer is not entitled to accept a referral fee (except as permitted by MRPC 7.2(b)), lawyers are permitted to split fees under the terms of MRPC 1.5(e). Ordinarily this will be done "in proportion to the services performed by each lawyer" as stated in that subsection. Even then, the client must agree to the arrangement, including the share of each lawyer; the agreement must be in writing; and the total fee must be reasonable. But MRPC 1.5(e) also permits fee splitting between law firms not proportional to services performed provided that "each lawyer assumes joint responsibility for the representation." Comment [7] to MRPC 1.5 elaborates that "[j]oint responsibility for the representation entails financial and ethical responsibility for the representation as if the lawyers were associated in a partnership. A lawyer should only refer a matter to a lawyer whom the referring lawyer reasonably believes is competent to handle the matter. See Rule 1.1." It is contemplated by the rule that a referring lawyer who provides no further services for the referred client may receive a share of the fee ultimately paid by the client, provided the technical requirements of the rule are met. To this extent, the Rule allows referral fees "[i]n practical effect." 1 G.C. Hazard, Jr., W.W. Hodes and P.R. Jarvis, *The Law of Lawyering*, section 8.16 at 8-43 (3d ed. 2013).

Former California Rules of Professional Conduct, Rule 2-200 - Financial Arrangements Among Lawyers

(A) A member shall not divide a fee for legal services with a lawyer who is not a partner of, associate of, or shareholder with the member unless:

(1) The client has consented in writing thereto after a full disclosure has been made in writing that a division of fees will be made and the terms of such division; and

(2) The total fee charged by all lawyers is not increased solely by reason of the provision for division of fees and is not unconscionable as that term is defined in rule 4-200.

(B) Except as permitted in paragraph (A) of this rule or rule 2-300, a member shall not compensate, give, or promise anything of value to any lawyer for the purpose of recommending or securing employment of the member or the member's law firm by a client, or as a reward for having made a recommendation resulting in employment of the member or the member's law firm by a client. A member's offering of or giving a gift or gratuity to any lawyer who has made a recommendation resulting in the employment of the member or the member's law firm shall not of itself violate this rule, provided that the gift or gratuity was not offered in consideration of any promise, agreement, or understanding that such a gift or gratuity would be forthcoming or that referrals would be made or encouraged in the future.

Cases

A client's written acknowledgement of receiving and understanding a letter that explained that the lawyer's referral fee would not come from client's percentage of a settlement, did not constitute written consent to the referral fee agreement. The referral fee agreement was unenforceable as against public policy and the lawyer cannot recover for breach of contract. *Reeve v. Meleyco* (2020) 46 Cal.App.5th 1092 (discussing former rule 2-200 of the Rules of Professional Conduct).

Fee division agreement was unenforceable under former rule 3-410 of the Rules of Professional Conduct because the lawyer failed to disclose lack of professional liability insurance. Quantum meruit recovery was not limited to hours reflected in the referring lawyer's time records, but could include the reasonable value of the referral. *Hance v. Super Store Industries* (2020) 44 Cal.App.5th 676.

As with all rules of the Rules of Professional Conduct, violation of the rule permitting a lawyer to share legal fees with another lawyer only with the client's informed, written consent can subject a lawyer to disciplinary action by the State Bar. Lack of informed consent did not foreclose fee-splitting by equitable estoppel. The lawyer was estopped from claiming the agreement was unenforceable due to non-compliance with the ethical rules. *Barnes, Crosby, Fitzgerald and Zeman, LLP v. Ringler* (2012) 212 Cal.App.4th 172.

Ethics Opinion

There is nothing inherently unethical with a client or lawyer hiring another lawyer—often a contract lawyer—to ghostwrite a document to be submitted to court, without identifying the contract lawyer or disclosing the hiring arrangement. Only when the client or lawyer seeks to recover fees must the contract lawyer's role be disclosed to the court. Both lawyers must comply with their ethical obligations, including their duties of competence. In addition, to the extent the contract lawyer is not admitted to practice in California, both lawyers must guard against the potential unauthorized practice of law. Orange County Bar Assn., Ethics opn. No. 2014-1.

Article

Hodel, *The Ethics of Referrals* (2015) Orange County Bar Assn. News (discussing the limitations on referral fees under former rule 1-320 of the Rules of Professional Conduct, Financial Arrangements with Non-Lawyers, and former rule 2-200, Financial Arrangements Among Lawyers). The author also discusses potential malpractice liability for a negligent referral.

8.9 Financial Arrangements with Non-Lawyers

California Rules of Professional Conduct, Rule 5.4 - Financial and Similar Arrangements with Nonlawyers

(a) A lawyer or law firm* shall not share legal fees directly or indirectly with a nonlawyer or with an organization that is not authorized to practice law, except that:

(1) an agreement by a lawyer with the lawyer's firm,* partner,* or associate may provide for the payment of money or other consideration over a reasonable* period of time after the lawyer's death, to the lawyer's estate or to one or more specified persons;*

(2) a lawyer purchasing the practice of a deceased, disabled or disappeared lawyer may pay the agreed-upon purchase price, pursuant to rule 1.17, to the lawyer's estate or other representative;

(3) a lawyer or law firm* may include nonlawyer employees in a compensation or retirement plan, even though the plan is based in whole or in part on a profit-sharing arrangement, provided the plan does not otherwise violate these rules or the State Bar Act;

(4) a lawyer or law firm* may pay a prescribed registration, referral, or other fee to a lawyer referral service established, sponsored and operated in accordance with the State Bar of California's Minimum Standards for Lawyer Referral Services; or

(5) a lawyer or law firm* may share with or pay a court-awarded legal fee to a nonprofit organization that employed, retained or recommended employment of the lawyer or law firm* in the matter.

(b) A lawyer shall not form a partnership or other organization with a nonlawyer if any of the activities of the partnership or other organization consist of the practice of law.

(c) A lawyer shall not permit a person* who recommends, employs, or pays the lawyer to render legal services for another to direct or regulate the lawyer's independent professional judgment or interfere with the lawyer-client relationship in rendering legal services.

(d) A lawyer shall not practice with or in the form of a professional corporation or other organization authorized to practice law for a profit if:

(1) a nonlawyer owns any interest in it, except that a fiduciary representative of a lawyer's estate may hold the lawyer's stock or other interest for a reasonable* time during administration;

(2) a nonlawyer is a director or officer of the corporation or occupies a position of similar responsibility in any other form of organization; or

(3) a nonlawyer has the right or authority to direct or control the lawyer's independent professional judgment.

(e) The Board of Trustees of the State Bar shall formulate and adopt Minimum Standards for Lawyer Referral Services, which, as from time to time amended, shall be binding on lawyers. A lawyer shall not accept a referral from, or otherwise participate in, a lawyer referral service unless it complies with such Minimum Standards for Lawyer Referral Services.

(f) A lawyer shall not practice with or in the form of a nonprofit legal aid, mutual benefit or advocacy group if the nonprofit organization allows any third person* to interfere with the lawyer's independent professional judgment, or with the lawyer-client relationship, or allows or aids any person* to practice law in violation of these rules or the State Bar Act.

An asterisk (*) identifies a defined term in rule 1.0.1 of the Rules of Professional Conduct. For further discussion of a defined term, see chapter 2 of this Guide, Terminology.

A lawyer may not ethically accept any rebate, discount, commission, or referral fee from a non-lawyer or a lawyer not acting in a legal capacity. Even with full disclosure to the client and the client's consent, such arrangements involve "too great a risk of overreaching by the lawyer and the potential for actual or apparent abuse." ACTEC Commentaries on Model Rules Prof. Conduct, rule 1.5.

Acceptance of a referral fee from a non-lawyer may give rise to an impermissible conflict of interest. The State Bar of California Committee on Professional Responsibility and Conduct issued Formal Number Opinion 1997-148, finding that a lawyer who works in conjunction with a marketer of living trusts violates former rules 3-110 and 1-600(A) of the Rules of Professional Conduct. Such a relationship interferes with duty of loyalty to the client when the lawyer relies on the information supplied by the marketer, does not directly counsel the client regarding all the estate planning options and their advantages and disadvantages, and does not exercise independent judgment. For a further discussion, see chapter 3 of this Guide, Competence and Diligence, section 3.10.

Rule 7.2 of the Rules of Professional Conduct allows specific exceptions from the prohibition against a fee, promise, or other valuable consideration for recommending the services of a lawyer or a law firm. Those exceptions include the reasonable costs of advertising, the usual charges of a qualified lawyer referral service, and true gifts without an agreement or understanding of future benefit. For a detailed discussion of the ethical issues related to advertising of a lawyer's services, see chapter 10 of this Guide, Ethics and Technology, section 10.10. Referral fees otherwise permitted under the Rules of Professional Conduct and State Bar Act comply with a lawyer's ethical duties if the reciprocal fee arrangement is not exclusive, and if the client is informed of the existence and nature of the fee arrangement. Although not required by rule 7.2(b) of the Rules of Professional Conduct, a lawyer would prudently obtain the client's written consent after disclosures in accordance with rule 1.0.1(e) of the Rules of Professional Conduct.

Former California Rules of Professional Conduct, Rule 1-320 - Financial Arrangements with Non-Lawyers

> (A) Neither a member nor a law firm shall directly or indirectly share legal fees with a person who is not a lawyer, except that:
>
> > (1) An agreement between a member and a law firm, partner, or associate may provide for the payment of money after the member's death to the member's estate or to one or more specified persons over a reasonable period of time; or
> >
> > (2) A member or law firm undertaking to complete unfinished legal business of a deceased member may pay to the estate of the deceased member or other person legally entitled thereto that proportion of the total compensation which fairly represents the services rendered by the deceased member;
> >
> > (3) A member or law firm may include non-member employees in a compensation, profit-sharing, or retirement plan even though the plan is based in whole or in part on a profit-sharing arrangement, if such plan does not circumvent these rules or Business and Professions Code Section 6000 et seq.; or
> >
> > (4) A member may pay a prescribed registration, referral or participation fee to a lawyer referral service established, sponsored, and operated in accordance with the State Bar of California's Minimum Standards for a Lawyer Referral Service in California.
>
> (B) A member shall not compensate, give or promise anything of value to any person or entity for the purpose of recommending or securing employment of the member or the member's law firm by a client, or as a reward for having made a recommendation resulting in employment of the member or the member's law firm by a client. A member's offering of or giving a gift or gratuity to any person or entity having made a recommendation resulting in the employment of the member or the member's law firm shall not of itself violate this rule, provided that the gift or gratuity was not offered or given in consideration of any promise, agreement, or

understanding that such a gift or gratuity would be forthcoming or that referrals would be made or encouraged in the future.

(C) A member shall not compensate, give, or promise anything of value to any representative of the press, radio, television, or other communication medium in anticipation of or in return for publicity of the member, the law firm, or any other member as such in a news item, but the incidental provision of food or beverage shall not of itself violate this rule.

Case Study

Lawyer is considering signing up with an internet-based marketing company ("Company"). Company is a for-profit business and is not an approved lawyer referral service. Company's business model originally offered an online legal directory of lawyers that allowed clients, peers, and others to write reviews on listed lawyers. Company now offers a service that matches potential clients who need discrete and defined legal services with lawyers participating in Company's program. A lawyer who signs up with Company may offer only the services Company lists, although the lawyer may choose which of those listed services to offer.

The lawyer would provide services for a fixed fee that Company determines. To initiate a call by a Company lawyer, the consumer remits the entire amount of the fixed fee to Company. When services are completed, Company deducts and retains a so-called "marketing fee" and pays the fixed fee to the lawyer.

What ethical issues does participation in the described business model raise and how should Lawyer address them?

Rules 5.4 and 7.2 of the Rules of Professional Conduct preclude a lawyer from paying for cases, whether by a division of fees or as separate payment for a case. Likewise, Business and Professions Code section 6152 precludes the use of runners or cappers in the solicitation or procurement of business for a lawyer. Company's payment of a fee to Lawyer is a violation of rule 5.4(a)(4) of the Rules of Professional Conduct that limits such fees to a referral service that is established, sponsored and operated in accordance with the State Bar rules. Rule 5.4 prohibits a lawyer from dividing fees with a non-lawyer even with the client's consent, as cited in San Francisco County Bar Association Ethics Opinion Number 1981-1. San Diego County Bar Assn., Ethics opn. No. 2019-2.

The opinion also recites rule 1.8.6(c) of the Rules of Professional Conduct that a lawyer may not accept compensation for representing a client from one other than the client unless the lawyer obtains the client's informed written consent. Company's compensation business model requires a consumer to pay a flat fee without required disclosures or consent. Lawyer's failure to obtain informed written consent to this fee arrangement results in non-compliance with rule 1.8.6(c).

Ethics Opinions

Referral to a loan broker to obtain funds to pay legal fees is permissible provided the lawyer does not receive compensation for referral or have other business relationships with the broker. State Bar of Cal. Com. on Prof. Resp. and Conduct, formal opn. No. 2002-159.

A lawyer's arrangement with marketer of living trust packages may not interfere with the lawyer's independent judgment or involve fee-splitting with non-lawyers. State Bar of Cal. Com. on Prof. Resp. and Conduct, formal opn. No. 1997-148.

A lawyer may not directly or indirectly share compensation received as a result of soliciting engagements through non-lawyers, or compensate, give, or publish anything of value for the purpose of recommending or securing the lawyer's employment or as a reward for having made such a recommendation resulting in employment. State Bar of Cal. Com. on Prof. Resp. and Conduct, formal opn. No. 1995-142.

Non-lawyers involved with lawyers providing non-legal services may not share in the profits of the law practice. State Bar of Cal. Com. on Prof. Resp. and Conduct, formal opn. No. 1995-141.

A lawyer may ethically advise a client of an arrangement for shared compensation between a lawyer and a person such as insurance agent, provided full disclosure and the client's consent to the arrangement is made in writing, and the compensation shared is solely for the provision of non-legal services. State Bar of Cal. Com. on Prof. Resp. and Conduct, formal opn. No. 1995-140.

CHAPTER 9 ETHICS AND LITIGATION

California Rules of Professional Conduct, Rule 3.1 - Meritorious Claims and Contentions

(a) A lawyer shall not:

(1) bring or continue an action, conduct a defense, assert a position in litigation, or take an appeal, without probable cause and for the purpose of harassing or maliciously injuring any person;* or

(2) present a claim or defense in litigation that is not warranted under existing law, unless it can be supported by a good faith argument for an extension, modification, or reversal of the existing law.

(b) A lawyer for the defendant in a criminal proceeding, or the respondent in a proceeding that could result in incarceration, or involuntary commitment or confinement, may nevertheless defend the proceeding by requiring that every element of the case be established.

California Rules of Professional Conduct, Rule 3.2 - Delay of Litigation

In representing a client, a lawyer shall not use means that have no substantial* purpose other than to delay or prolong the proceeding or to cause needless expense.

An asterisk (*) identifies a defined term in rule 1.0.1 of the Rules of Professional Conduct. For further discussion of a defined term, see chapter 2 of this Guide, Terminology.

9.1 Introduction

A lawyer who litigates, arbitrates, or mediates trust, probate, conservatorship, and guardianship matters is subject to all ethical duties that generally bind all litigators. Those ethical duties have specific applications in the context of representing a litigating party and prosecuting or defending a litigated claim. These ethical duties imposed on the lawyer include the duty of candor to the court as provided in rule 3.3 of the Rules of Professional Conduct and the duty of truthfulness to all persons in rule 4.1 of the Rules of Professional Conduct.

Failure to observe these ethical rules may be grounds for sanctions against a lawyer for payment of costs, including fees pursuant to Code of Civil Procedure section 128.5, or other sanctions that the court may order pursuant to Code of Civil Procedure section 128.7. The court may order such sanctions pursuant to a motion by a party or on its own motion. Court-ordered sanctions under section 128.7 "shall be limited to what is sufficient to deter repetition of this conduct or comparable conduct by others similarly situated." An ethical litigation practice goes beyond the avoidance of sanctions and seeks a fair presentation of the evidence, with respect to the court, the client, an opposing lawyer or party, and all third parties connected with the litigation.

Cases

Sanctions were warranted against a lawyer who, because an appeal was so totally lacking in merit, had a professional obligation not to pursue it. A dispute about the views from a private residence was not an issue of public interest, and the appeal of the denial of a special motion to strike was frivolous. *Workman v. Colichman* (2019) 33 Cal.App.5th 1039.

California Rules of Court, rule 2.30(b) authorizing sanctions for "failure without good cause to comply with the applicable rules" applies to probate proceedings. The court cited rule 2.30(a), that specifically provides: "This sanctions rule applies to the rules in the California Rules of Court relating to general civil cases, unlawful detainer cases, *probate proceedings*, civil proceedings in the appellate division of the superior court, and small claims cases." (emphasis supplied). *In re Marriage of Bianco* (2013) 221 Cal.App.4th 826.

Disciplinary action was warranted for a respondent's continued assertions that the law governing loan modification services and fees was debatable, despite a court finding that the language of the statute and other applicable law was not ambiguous. The court concluded from persistent advocacy of baseless legal positions that the lawyer did not take ethical obligations seriously. "While [the lawyer] may freely urge any creative legal theory in good faith, he must 'accept responsibility for his acts and come to grips with his culpability.'" *In the Matter of Swazi Elkanzi Taylor* (Review Dept. 2012) 5 Cal. State Bar Ct. Rptr. 221, citing *In the Matter of Katz* (Review Dept. 1991) 1 Cal. State Bar Rptr. 502, 511.

9.2 Client Engagement and Scope of Representation

Under rule 1.2 of the Rules of Professional Conduct, the client directs the goals of the representation and the means of reaching those goals. The initial engagement letter in a litigated matter serves the dual purpose of defining the proceeding that is the subject of the representation and the specific approaches to reach settlement or adjudication of the client's interest—mediation or arbitration, discovery, pretrial motions, trial, and possible appeal.

The lawyer must defer to the client on all substantive decisions regarding the representation. Rules Prof. Conduct, rule 1.4. The lawyer must keep the client informed about significant developments relating to the litigation, including promptly complying with reasonable requests for information and copies of significant documents the client needs to make informed decisions. The engagement letter begins the process of informing the client of the scope of the litigation, and may discuss further the avenues the lawyer may recommend to prosecute or defend the client's interest and the estimated cost as each successive avenue is pursued.

The ethical duty of informed consent requires disclosure to the client of the potential risks of litigation. Rules Prof. Conduct, rule 1.0.1(e). For example, enforcement of a no-contest clause might cause a client to lose more than the client expected to risk. The lawyer can assure a client of best efforts in a litigated matter but cannot guarantee a result.

The initial engagement letter should specify the services that the lawyer will perform for the client, as well as any excluded services that the lawyer will not perform. If new matters arise in the course of representing the client, the lawyer should provide the client with a new or supplemental engagement letter and obtain the client's written consent to additional services. A detailed description of the initial litigated matter allows the lawyer to re-engage with the client before undertaking an appeal, or defending an unanticipated counter- or cross-claim.

9.3 Sample Engagement Letter – Representation in a Litigated Matter

The following form of engagement letter can be adapted for the representation of a single beneficiary who is not also the fiduciary in a litigated trust or estate matter. The form can be modified as needed for representation in other types of litigation. The lawyer should adapt it thoughtfully to the lawyer's customary practice and the needs of a particular client representation.

For sample disclosures and consents when engaging to represent more than one fiduciary or beneficiary client in a litigated matter, see section 9.5 of this chapter. For a sample engagement letter for a trustee in a trust administration which may be modified appropriately for litigation, arbitration, or mediation, see chapter 4 of this Guide, Identifying the Client and the Scope of Representation, section 4.7.

Dear [Client]:

Thank you for selecting ________________ (the "Firm") to represent you as a beneficiary of the [identify the trust, the will, or the probate].

Scope of the Engagement. We will counsel you on the legal and strategic aspects of the litigation and prepare, file, and serve on your behalf any required documents and pleadings. We will exert our best efforts on your behalf, but we cannot guarantee the outcome of the case. All communications we have with you or any other person concerning the anticipated outcome of the case are expressions of the Firm's opinion only, and it makes no promises or guarantees regarding the outcome of your case.

The Firm does not provide tax advice or prepare tax returns. We are happy to work with your accountant or other tax advisor to provide information needed to complete tax returns. The Firm does not provide investment advice, and you are not to rely on any informal expressions of opinion the Firm may give you regarding any particular investment.

This agreement does not include representation for any appeal that may be brought during the anticipated litigation. If an appeal is to be commenced, the representation will require a separate written fee agreement.

We will be pleased to perform additional services at your request that we specifically confirm in writing to you, and unless a new agreement is made, this fee agreement will also apply to those services. Nevertheless, we do reserve the right to review and modify our fee arrangements whenever the scope of our engagement is changed, and we may require a new fee agreement if additional or other services are required.

Fee and Costs. [See section 9.16 of this chapter for a sample compensation provision.]

Billing, Deposits. [See chapter 8 of this Guide, Compensation, sections 8.3 and 8.4.]

Court Reporters. The litigation that is the subject of this representation will be conducted in the ______________ Superior Court. Historically, court proceedings have been "on the record," that is, court reporters provided by the court attended and transcribed what lawyers and judges said at all hearings. A reporter's transcript can be important, because it can be referred to in order to resolve various disputes. The reporter's transcript is also an important part of an appeal. Currently, _____________ Superior Court no longer provides court reporters. Therefore, if any party desires to have a hearing reported, that party has the responsibility to retain and pay for the services of an independent court reporter.

Since some hearings are routine and deal with matters such as scheduling that are rarely material, we believe that it is most efficient to approach the decision whether to hire a court reporter on a hearing-by-hearing basis. While a failure to have a hearing reported can lead to the lack of a record for an important event in a case, paying for a reporter for every hearing can generate a significant expense for transcripts that will never be used. When we believe that it is necessary to have a hearing reported, we will retain a reporter. We will advance the reporter's fee on your behalf and it will be reflected on your bill. Since the reporting expenses and the appeal rights are fundamentally yours, you should feel free to discuss the reporting of hearings with us throughout the progress of the case. If you want every hearing reported, let us know and we will arrange a reporter for every hearing.

Alternatives to Litigation. Your case is a legal proceeding that is designed to lead to resolution by a judge's formal decision. We anticipate that your case will include appearances before the judge, sworn depositions, sworn declarations, and the filing of court papers known as pleadings. As we proceed toward trial, we will have opportunities to settle the case by private agreement rather than by a judicial decision. Opportunities for settlement arise through informal communications among the lawyers and their clients, and through more formal methods, including mediation and judicially sponsored settlement conferences. Prospects for a settlement are typically fluid and change with every new development in the case.

We will discuss alternatives to litigation with you during our representation and we will advise you immediately regarding any offers of possible settlement and mediation efforts. You should understand, though, that settlement requires voluntary action by all the parties. Undertaking litigation in anticipation of a settlement that may never happen is a mistake.

[NOTE ANY APPLICABLE STATUTORY OR LOCAL REQUIREMENT TO MAKE AN EFFORT TO MEDIATE.]

Lawyer-Client Privilege and Confidentiality. It is critical that you inform us of your actions and communications, past and present, regarding this matter, in order to permit us to best identify and protect your interests and to avoid any problems that might arise from a failure to communicate. It is also important for us to openly communicate our opinions, thoughts, and concerns to you.

To protect and encourage this vital communication between lawyer and client, California law imposes a duty of confidentiality on lawyers and grants you a lawyer-client privilege, both of which protect the confidentiality of our private communications. The duty of confidentiality prohibits us from sharing confidential information we receive from you with any third party without your permission. The lawyer-client privilege, which protects the privacy of our communications, is somewhat different, because it can be lost if the private communications are disclosed to third parties. Thus, you may lose the protection of the lawyer-client privilege if you disclose our communications to a third party. We recommend that you guard your lawyer-client privilege closely and consult with us before disclosing our confidential communications to anyone else.

You must carefully consider any communications you have with any third party regarding the case. Do not grant any interviews or give any statements to anyone on any pretext without first obtaining our consent. Avoid sending correspondence, especially texts and emails, regarding any part of the case or any person involved in the case, and do not post any information to social media websites regarding this matter.

Document Retention – Litigation Hold. Litigation includes a process known as discovery, during which the law requires that the parties exchange certain information, including documents. During the discovery process, you will almost certainly be required to produce "all documents" relevant to the case, or relevant to certain parts of the case. It is, therefore, extremely important that you refrain from destroying any document that has any relationship to this case or to any person involved in the case. In discovery the law defines the term "document" extremely broadly, and the definition includes duplicates and copies of documents. You must not destroy or alter paper documents or copies of paper documents. You must not destroy electronic documents or copies of electronic documents. Electronic documents include email messages, photographs, texts, and electronic records of all types.

File Retention. [See chapter 6 of this Guide, Confidentiality of Information, sections 6.15 and 6.16.]

Arbitration. Any dispute, claim, or controversy between you and the Firm arising out of or relating to this Agreement or its breach, including, without limitation, claims for breach of contract, professional negligence, breach of fiduciary duty, breach of statutory duty, misrepresentation, fraud and disputes regarding lawyer fees and/or costs charged under this Agreement, including the determination of the scope or applicability of this agreement to arbitrate, shall be determined by arbitration in __________ County, California, before one arbitrator. The arbitration shall be administered by ______________________ pursuant to its Rules and Procedures. Judgment on the award may be entered in any court having jurisdiction. This clause shall not preclude parties from seeking provisional remedies in aid of arbitration from a court of appropriate jurisdiction. This provision shall not apply to any ethics or disciplinary proceedings against the Firm. The parties shall bear their own legal fees and costs for all claims.

Termination of the Engagement. You may terminate this representation at any time, with or without cause, by notifying me. If you terminate the representation, we will return your file to you upon request. The Firm may make a copy of the file at its own expense. Your termination of the Firm's services will not affect your responsibility for payment for legal services rendered and out-of-pocket costs incurred before termination and in connection with an orderly transition of the matter.

The Firm, too, can terminate its representation by reasonable written notification to you. The California Rules of Professional Conduct identify conduct or circumstances that require or allow the Firm to withdraw from representing a client, including nonpayment of fees or costs; misrepresentation or failure to disclose material facts; action contrary to its advice; and conflict of interest with another client. If withdrawal ever becomes necessary, the Firm will give you written notice of its need to withdraw.

After termination of this representation, the Firm will have no obligation to keep you informed of subsequent changes in the law that may affect your rights or interest.

Consent to the Terms of the Engagement. Before we begin, you must consider the factors discussed in this letter and consent to the form of the representation. After you have considered this decision carefully, we ask that you please sign the statement that follows this letter to indicate your consent to the conditions of the representation. If, after considering this matter, you prefer a different form of representation, please let us know. Because any change in legal representation after we begin may result in an increase in the time and expense needed to complete the [subject matter of the engagement], for which you would be financially responsible, we urge you to give careful consideration to the structure of the representation before we begin. We have enclosed an extra copy of this letter to be signed and returned to us consenting to the conditions of the representation as described in this letter. The return of a copy of this letter signed by you will serve as authorization for us to proceed with the [subject matter of the engagement].

We enclose a stamped and addressed envelope for your convenience in returning the signed copy of this letter to us [and the required deposit]. If you have any questions about any of the terms of representation discussed in this letter, please call us. You should also feel free to contact a lawyer in another firm to discuss the effect of agreeing to the terms of the representation as outlined in this letter. We appreciate the opportunity to work with you on the [subject matter of the engagement], and we look forward to hearing from you soon.

Sincerely,

[Lawyer]

CONSENT

I accept the above terms and agree to be liable for fees and costs incurred by [Lawyer] under the terms of this agreement.

Date: ______________________ ______________________________
[Client]

9.4 Conflicts of Interest

Before accepting a representation in a litigated matter, the lawyer has an ethical duty to identify the client and any fiduciary, beneficiary, or other specific role the client may have that is related to the matter. The initial engagement letter should specify the client, the client's role if applicable, and the scope of the representation. Identifying the client and the scope of the representation in the engagement letter will assist the lawyer in analyzing the ethical duties that the lawyer owes to the client.

Conflicts of interest may arise in a litigated trust proceeding, for example:

1. The lawyer undertakes to represent an individual who has competing rights and duties, for example a trustee who is also a settlor or beneficiary of a trust;
2. The lawyer undertakes to represent an individual as a fiduciary, and that individual may also be exposed to personal liability for actions taken as a fiduciary; or
3. The lawyer undertakes a joint representation of multiple beneficiaries who are similarly situated.

For a detailed discussion of these adverse interests and the lawyer's related ethical duties, see chapter 5 of this Guide, Conflicts of Interest.

The engagement letter for a client-trustee would appropriately include a caution to obtain separate counsel should an issue of the trustee's personal liability arise in the course of the litigation. Independent representation should allow the client to assert the lawyer-client privilege when seeking advice on such issues, especially if the client pays for the advice with the client's own funds. For a detailed discussion of the lawyer-client privilege in fiduciary litigation, see chapter 6 of this Guide, Confidentiality of Information, section 6.13.

Advocating inconsistent legal positions in different courts on behalf of different clients is not a conflict of interest that requires a lawyer to obtain the informed written consent of the client, even if that position establishes a precedent contrary to the client's interest. Nevertheless, under rule 1.7(b) of the Rules of Professional Conduct, the lawyer must determine whether advocating an inconsistent legal position will materially limit the lawyer's effectiveness in representing a client in a different matter. The comment to rule 1.7 of the Rules of Professional Conduct sets out relevant factors in making that determination.

Trustee-Lawyer. A lawyer who also acts as a trustee in a trust litigation will need to balance the ethical duties of a lawyer with the fiduciary duties of a trustee. The court in *Wells Fargo Bank v. Superior Court (Boltwood Estate)* (2000) 22 Cal.4th 201 described the interrelation of the ethical duty of confidentiality with the trustee's fiduciary duties to the trust beneficiaries. There, the court confirmed that while the trustee has a duty to "keep the beneficiaries of the trust reasonably informed of the trust and its administration," that duty does not require the trustee to disclose lawyer-client communications between the trustee and a lawyer engaged to represent the trustee regarding the trust administration. *Id.* at p. 207 (quoting Prob. Code, sec. 16060). The issue arises when and to what extent the lawyer-trustee can assert the lawyer-client privilege when in effect self-communicating. While a trustee may waive confidentiality, the trustee has no obligation to do so. A limited waiver of the privilege, for example, disclosures of information regarding the trust administration as required by statute, does not compel a broad disclosure of privileged information. *Id.* at pp. 211-212; see also Rules Prof. Conduct, rule 3.7(a)(2).

Drafting Lawyer. A lawyer who drafted the instrument that is the subject of the litigation has specific ethical duties as a percipient witness. If that lawyer is retained to represent a client in litigation concerning the instrument, rule 3.7(a)(3) of the Rules of Professional Conduct requires the client's informed written consent to the representation. The client's consent is informed if the lawyer discloses the material risks and foreseeable adverse consequences of the representation. Rules Prof. Conduct, rule 1.0.1(e). The lawyer should disclose to the client the likelihood that the testimony will be contested, that the lawyer's personal conflict of interest will diminish the effectiveness of the testimony, and that the lawyer may be disqualified from acting as an advocate in the case. Best practice is to decline the representation in such a case. For a further discussion of the duties of a lawyer who may be a witness in a contested matter, see section 9.9 of this chapter.

Rule 1.7(c) of the Rules of Professional Conduct requires that an initial conflicts check include not only the possible adverse interests of prospective, current, or past clients, but also conflicts arising from personal relationships between and among persons interested in the case and the lawyer or another lawyer in the lawyer's firm. The lawyer's personal relationship with or responsibility for a party or a witness in the proposed litigation mandates written disclosure to the client. A lawyer, for example, may have a personal interest in appointment as fiduciary of an estate, or may seek to purchase assets from a trust. Such personal interest must be disclosed and the client's informed consent obtained before undertaking the representation. Rules Prof. Conduct, rule 1.0.1(e).

Poisoning the Well. A client or potential client—or perhaps even a lawyer who has been retained by a client—might purposefully communicate with lawyers or employees at several firms intending to provide them with confidential information to disqualify them or their firm in pending or planned litigation. While courts have shown increasing reluctance to disqualify a firm based on such communications, the best way for a lawyer or a firm to avoid being disqualified by any such attempt is to carefully limit the information provided by the prospective client in the initial communications. The lawyer or firm should ensure that the initial communications are designed to identify conflicts, not to deal with the substance of the matter. For a detailed discussion of communications with a prospective client and the related ethical duty of confidentiality, see chapter 6 of this Guide, Confidentiality of Information, section 6.18.

Comment on California Rules of Professional Conduct, Rule 1.7

> [6] Ordinarily paragraphs (a) and (b) will not require informed written consent* simply because a lawyer takes inconsistent legal positions in different tribunals* at different times on behalf of different clients. Advocating a legal position on behalf of a client that might create precedent adverse to the interests of another client represented by a lawyer in an unrelated matter is not sufficient, standing alone, to create a conflict of interest requiring informed written consent.* Informed written consent* may be required, however, if there is a significant risk that: (i) the lawyer may temper the lawyer's advocacy on behalf of one client out of concern about creating precedent adverse to the interest of another client; or (ii) the lawyer's action on behalf of one client will materially limit the lawyer's effectiveness in representing another client in a different case, for example, when a decision favoring one client will create a precedent likely to seriously weaken the position taken on behalf of the other client. Factors relevant in determining whether the clients' informed written consent* is required include: the courts and jurisdictions where the different cases are pending, whether a ruling in one case would have a precedential effect on the other case, whether the legal question is substantive or procedural, the temporal relationship between the matters, the significance of the legal question to the immediate and long-term interests of the clients involved, and the clients' reasonable* expectations in retaining the lawyer.

Cases

Successor trustees who petitioned, *in propria persona*, for instructions regarding trust interpretation did not engage in the unauthorized practice of law. The court distinguished a petition for instructions from other trust administration issues, when the trustees may have adverse interests to the rights of beneficiaries or other interested parties. *Donkin v. Donkin* (2020) 47 Cal.App.5th 469.

Former president and chief operating officer of the defendant was not disqualified from representing the plaintiff in wrongful termination claim against the defendant because the lawyer lacked confidential information relevant to the representation. The president and chief operating officer had not investigated or had any discussions with outside counsel regarding the plaintiff's claims. *Wu v. O'Gara Coach Co., LLC* (2019) 38 Cal.App.5th 1069, compare *O'Gara Coach Co., LLC v. Ra* (2019) 30 Cal.App.5th 1115 (former president and chief operating officer of the company and his law firm were disqualified from representing the company's former employees in a suit against the company as a prophylactic measure, even though the lawyer was not a lawyer when serving as president and chief operating officer. Such disqualification was based on a non-lawyer's fiduciary duties when receiving privileged communications and was necessary to protect the integrity of the judicial process).

A law firm represented two opposing parties concurrently for approximately ten years, without a written waiver of conflict of interest. Given this extensive time period, disqualification was inappropriate because the moving party had implicitly consented to the conflict and was estopped to raise it. *Antelope Valley Groundwater Cases* (2018) 30 Cal.App.5th 602.

A lawyer was disqualified from simultaneously representing a corporation and a related business associate who were both plaintiffs seeking damages from the same pool of money. The court found an obvious conflict because every dollar that one client-plaintiff obtains from the pool was a dollar not available to the other clients. *Bridgepoint Construction Services, Inc. v. Newton* (2018) 26 Cal.App.5th 966.

An advance waiver of conflicts of interest in an engagement letter was ineffective when the law firm had a current client with directly adverse interests, and the law firm did not tell either client of its representation of the other. The simultaneous representation of clients with adverse interests in violation of the rules of professional conduct rendered the engagement letter, including its arbitration clause, unenforceable as a matter of public policy. A successful motion for disqualification of a lawyer or firm may require disgorgement of fees. In this case, the court allowed the law firm to recover fees under a theory of quantum meruit. *Sheppard, Mullin, Richter & Hampton, LLP v. J-M Manufacturing Co., Inc.* (2018) 6 Cal.5th 59.

Counsel for the majority shareholder and the corporation were properly disqualified as to the corporation, but not the majority shareholder, in the minority shareholder's derivative lawsuit over the corporation and its assets. Counsel had a conflict because the claims gave rise to adverse interests between the corporation and the majority shareholder, and the majority shareholder could not waive the conflict on behalf of the corporation. *Ontiveros v. Constable* (2016) 245 Cal.App.4th 686.

A lawyer who had represented a company filed a cross-complaint on behalf of one of the shareholders against the company. Reversing the trial court, the Court of Appeal held that the lawyer was automatically disqualified because of the lawyer's concurrent representation of both the shareholder and the company. *M'Guinness v. Johnson* (2015) 243 Cal.App.4th 602.

A lawyer and a lawyer's wife sued a former firm and partner, asserting several claims arising from the lawyer's retirement. Holding that the lawyer lacked standing to seek disqualification of the defendants' counsel because the claims were not derivative, the Court of Appeal held that counsel representing the partner and the corporation did not have a conflict of interest. *Coldren v. Hart, King & Coldren, Inc.* (2015) 239 Cal.App.4th 237.

A law firm was not disqualified from representing an LLC, managing member, and another member in a dispute with two minority members involving an option agreement because no actual conflict or reasonable likelihood that a conflict might arise existed; the defendant minority members did not allege mismanagement or misuse of the LLC property. *Havasu Lakeshore Investments, LLC v. Fleming* (2013) 217 Cal.App.4th 770, accord, *Centex Homes v. St. Paul Fire and Marine Ins. Co.* (2018) 19 Cal.App.5th 789 (In an insurance coverage dispute, the court determined that independent counsel—paid by the insurer but taking direction from the insured—was unnecessary under former rule 3-310(c) of the Rules of Professional Conduct because the rule requiring independent counsel is only triggered "when there is a reasonable likelihood an actual conflict will arise.").

Ethics Opinions

A lawyer may not ethically assist one client in settling a matter when another client in the same matter reasonably believes that the settlement will materially adversely affect the second client's matter, even if the impact would be based purely on an anticipated change in the perception by the finder of fact. San Diego County Bar Assn., Ethics opn. No. 2017-2.

A client's blanket waiver of the right to disqualify a lawyer in any other matter based on alleged breach of the lawyer's duty of confidentiality or duty to avoid conflicts of interest is not of itself ethically improper, but such a waiver may not be enforceable depending upon the circumstances existing when the waiver was signed and when an actual conflict of interest develops. In any event, such a waiver may not be asserted as a defense to a disciplinary proceeding charging incompetent performance nor may such a waiver be used to limit a lawyer's civil liability for malpractice. State Bar of Cal. Com. on Prof. Resp. and Conduct, formal opn. No. 1989-115.

9.5 Sample Consent to Joint Representation

The following provisions would be adapted for inclusion in an engagement letter for joint representation of multiple clients in a litigated matter. The sample consent assumes that the prospective clients do not have directly adverse interests but that their interests may diverge during the course of the litigation, and it discusses specific instances when those diverging interests may make it impossible for the lawyer to represent both clients in accordance with ethical standards. The lawyer should adapt it thoughtfully to the lawyer's customary practice and the needs of a particular client representation.

> Dear [Clients]:
>
> This letter follows our discussion and your request that our law firm jointly represent each of your interests in the litigation you wish to file. This letter and proposed consent to concurrent joint representation is required by our ethical obligations as lawyers in the State of California.

When a lawyer represents multiple clients, the lawyer has an ethical obligation to consider whether there is a significant future risk that the lawyer's representation of a client could be limited by the lawyer's responsibilities to or relationships with another joint client or the lawyer's other current clients. Unless and until you or we know of facts creating an actual conflict, this concurrent representation is possible.

Actual conflicts of interest that may arise in this matter include you disagreeing whether one of you is entitled to a larger share of the trust estate or objecting to a distribution made to another of you. Likewise, in depositions or live testimony one of you may testify to facts that are adverse to the claims of any of the others. [Add other fact-specific conflicts that could arise based on specifics of the individual case.] As we have discussed with you, we do not see current actual conflicts that would preclude us from representing your interests collectively.

For us to represent your interests jointly, you each must recognize that as "joint clients" no confidentiality of communications or lawyer-client privilege exists between you. Although each communication between a joint client and the lawyer is protected from disclosure to third parties, absent very narrow circumstances, communications among and between lawyer and joint clients will not be confidential between them. By virtue of our representing each of your interests, each of you has the right to learn the substance of any communications we may have with the other. Our firm will be required to keep each client apprised as to significant developments in the matter and convey settlement offers to each client, whether individual settlement offers or global offers.

Because there are no privileged communications between you as joint clients, if an actual conflict arises in the future that requires us to withdraw from our representation of any one client, we need your consent to allow us to continue our involvement in the matter on behalf of the remaining clients. Absent that consent, a conflict with one client would cause us to have to withdraw on behalf of all clients.

When signed by [Joint Clients] this letter will confirm each client's consent, authorizing us to proceed on behalf of [Client 1] and [Client 2] jointly. By your signatures, you consent to this joint representation based on our discussions, terms, conditions, and disclosures set forth in this letter, and are consenting to our joint representation despite potential future actual conflicts which may arise.

Please read this letter carefully. If you have questions about this letter or our potential concurrent representation, we encourage you to consult with independent counsel to evaluate the risks and benefits of this proposed joint representation. We are available to answer questions you may have.

Sincerely,

[Lawyer]

CONSENT

My signature below confirms my consent to [Law Firm] undertaking representation of [Client 1] and [Client 2] despite the actual conflicts that could develop during the representation, and the possible disadvantages and adverse consequences set forth above. I have read, understand, and have either consulted with or have had sufficient time and opportunity to consult with independent counsel about the matters that are the subject of this consent.

Dated: ______ ______________________________
[CLIENT 1]

Dated: ______ ______________________________
[CLIENT 2]

9.6 Ethical Duties to the Court

California Rules of Professional Conduct, Rule 3.3 - Candor Toward the Tribunal*

(a) A lawyer shall not:

(1) knowingly make a false statement of fact or law to a tribunal* or fail to correct a false statement of material fact or law previously made to the tribunal* by the lawyer;

(2) fail to disclose to the tribunal* legal authority in the controlling jurisdiction known* to the lawyer to be directly adverse to the position of the client and not disclosed by opposing counsel, or knowingly misquote to a tribunal* the language of a book, statute, decision or other authority; or

(3) offer evidence that the lawyer knows* to be false. If a lawyer, the lawyer's client, or a witness called by the lawyer, has offered material evidence, and the lawyer comes to know* of its falsity, the lawyer shall take reasonable* remedial measures, including, if necessary, disclosure to the tribunal,* unless disclosure is prohibited by Business and Professions Code section 6068, subdivision (e) and rule 1.6. A lawyer may refuse to offer evidence, other than the testimony of a defendant in a criminal matter, that the lawyer reasonably believes* is false.

(b) A lawyer who represents a client in a proceeding before a tribunal* and who knows* that a person* intends to engage, is engaging or has engaged in criminal or fraudulent* conduct related to the proceeding shall take reasonable* remedial measures to the extent permitted by Business and Professions Code section 6068, subdivision (e) and rule 1.6.

(c) The duties stated in paragraphs (a) and (b) continue to the conclusion of the proceeding.

(d) In an ex parte proceeding where notice to the opposing party in the proceeding is not required or given and the opposing party is not present, a lawyer shall inform the tribunal* of all material facts known* to the lawyer that will enable the tribunal* to make an informed decision, whether or not the facts are adverse to the position of the client.

California Rules of Professional Conduct, Rule 1.2.1 - Advising or Assisting the Violation of Law

(a) A lawyer shall not counsel a client to engage, or assist a client in conduct that the lawyer knows* is criminal, fraudulent,* or a violation of any law, rule, or ruling of a tribunal.*

(b) Notwithstanding paragraph (a), a lawyer may:

(1) discuss the legal consequences of any proposed course of conduct with a client; and

(2) counsel or assist a client to make a good faith effort to determine the validity, scope, meaning, or application of a law, rule, or ruling of a tribunal.*

An asterisk (*) identifies a defined term in rule 1.0.1 of the Rules of Professional Conduct. For further discussion of a defined term, see chapter 2 of this Guide, Terminology.

Pursuant to California Business and Professions Code section 6068, subdivision (b), a lawyer has the ethical duty "[t]o maintain the respect due to the courts of justice and judicial officers." Decorum in the courtroom and deference to judges and other court staff is a positive ethical duty of a lawyer, not just an incidental addition to an effective trial practice.

Respect for the court includes respect for the orders that the court issues. A lawyer may not substitute the lawyer's judgment for the court's as to whether an order was properly entered or a case correctly decided. Pursuant to rule 1.2.1 of the Rules of Professional Conduct, however, a lawyer may ethically advise a client on procedures to determine the validity of a law, rule, or court order, and the possible consequences of disobedience to such a law, rule, or order that the lawyer concludes in good faith to be invalid.

The lawyer owes the court the ethical duty of a fair argument. In accordance with this duty, a lawyer must disclose authority that is directly adverse to the position that the client has determined to take, if not raised by an opposing lawyer.

Rules 3.3(a)(3) and (b) of the Rules of Professional Conduct prescribe the "reasonable remedial measures" a lawyer must take when a lawyer becomes aware that false evidence has been presented to the court, whether by the lawyer, the lawyer's client, or a witness called by the lawyer. In correcting false testimony from a client, the lawyer is nonetheless bound by the ethical duty to preserve confidential communications received from the client. For a discussion of the lawyer's ethical duties in withdrawing from representation of a client in the course of a litigated matter, see section 9.12 of this chapter.

The lawyer's ethical duty of candor to the tribunal may be implicated before litigation is actually commenced. In representing a client in a litigated matter, a lawyer has the ethical duty to advise the client that digital records are subject to discovery, and that those records cannot be destroyed. San Diego Bar Association Ethics Opinion Number 2012-1 holds that ethical competence requires that the lawyer instruct the client to issue a litigation hold as soon as there is a "reasonable anticipation of litigation." That anticipation can occur from a claim or a demand letter well before suit is filed. Ultimately, the litigation hold will allow the lawyer to comply with the ethical duty of candor when representing to the court that all relevant evidence has been disclosed in discovery. The litigation hold will also allow the lawyer to comply with the companion ethical rule not to conceal evidence or obstruct an opposing lawyer's access to such information. Rules Prof. Conduct, rules 3.3 and 3.4. For a sample disclosure of a litigation hold to be included in a client engagement letter, see section 9.3 of this chapter.

Comment on California Rules of Professional Conduct, Rule 1.2.1

> [1] There is a critical distinction under this rule between presenting an analysis of legal aspects of questionable conduct and recommending the means by which a crime or fraud* might be committed with impunity. The fact that a client uses a lawyer's advice in a course of action that is criminal or fraudulent* does not of itself make a lawyer a party to the course of action.
>
> [2] Paragraphs (a) and (b) apply whether or not the client's conduct has already begun and is continuing. In complying with this rule, a lawyer shall not violate the lawyer's duty under Business and Professions Code section 6068, subdivision (a) to uphold the Constitution and laws of the United States and California or the duty of confidentiality as provided in Business and Professions Code section 6068, subdivision (e)(1) and rule 1.6. In some cases, the lawyer's response is limited to the lawyer's right and, where appropriate, duty to resign or withdraw in accordance with rules 1.13 and 1.16.
>
> [3] Paragraph (b) authorizes a lawyer to advise a client in good faith regarding the validity, scope, meaning or application of a law, rule, or ruling of a tribunal* or of the meaning placed upon it by governmental authorities, and of potential consequences to disobedience of the law, rule, or ruling of a tribunal* that the lawyer concludes in good faith to be invalid, as well as legal procedures that may be invoked to obtain a determination of invalidity.
>
> [4] Paragraph (b) also authorizes a lawyer to advise a client on the consequences of violating a law, rule, or ruling of a tribunal* that the client does not contend is unenforceable or unjust in itself, as a means of protesting a law or policy the client finds objectionable. For example, a lawyer may properly advise a client about the consequences of blocking the entrance to a public building as a means of protesting a law or policy the client believes* to be unjust or invalid.

[5] If a lawyer comes to know* or reasonably should know* that a client expects assistance not permitted by these rules or other law or if the lawyer intends to act contrary to the client's instructions, the lawyer must advise the client regarding the limitations on the lawyer's conduct. (See rule 1.4(a)(4).)

[6] Paragraph (b) permits a lawyer to advise a client regarding the validity, scope, and meaning of California laws that might conflict with federal or tribal law. In the event of such a conflict, the lawyer may assist a client in drafting or administering, or interpreting or complying with, California laws, including statutes, regulations, orders, and other state or local provisions, even if the client's actions might violate the conflicting federal or tribal law. If California law conflicts with federal or tribal law, the lawyer must inform the client about related federal or tribal law and policy and under certain circumstances may also be required to provide legal advice to the client regarding the conflict (see rules 1.1 and 1.4).

Comment on California Rules of Professional Conduct, Rule 3.3

Remedial Measures

[5] Reasonable* remedial measures under paragraphs (a)(3) and (b) refer to measures that are available under these rules and the State Bar Act, and which a reasonable* lawyer would consider appropriate under the circumstances to comply with the lawyer's duty of candor to the tribunal.* (See, e.g., rules 1.2.1, 1.4(a)(4), 1.16(a), 8.4; Bus. & Prof. Code, sections 6068, subd. (d), 6128.) Remedial measures also include explaining to the client the lawyer's obligations under this rule and, where applicable, the reasons for the lawyer's decision to seek permission from the tribunal* to withdraw, and remonstrating further with the client to take corrective action that would eliminate the need for the lawyer to withdraw. If the client is an organization, the lawyer should also consider the provisions of rule 1.13. Remedial measures do not include disclosure of client confidential information, which the lawyer is required to protect under Business and Professions Code section 6068, subdivision (e) and rule 1.6.

Cases

Conduct of a lawyer manifested gender bias against female judicial officer, and thus was reportable to State Bar. Business and Professions Code section 6068, subdivision (b) imposes an ethical duty on lawyers to maintain the respect due to the courts of justice and judicial officers. *Martinez v. O'Hara* (2019) 32 Cal.App.5th 853.

A lawyer representing a workers' compensation applicant exhibited a pattern of unprofessional behavior warranting imposition of sanctions where counsel continually made wild, unsupported, and histrionic accusations with virtually no support and no reference to the record, which in turn forced the workers' compensation judge to shift the burden to the employer to address each of the applicant's accusations, regardless of how little evidence there was for any of it. *Smith v. Workers' Comp. Appeals Bd.* (2018) 2018 WL 2306656.

"An attorney is an officer of the court. He or she must respect and follow court orders whether they are right or wrong." *Osborne v. Todd Farm Service* (2016) 247 Cal.App.4th 43, 45 (citing Bus. & Prof. Code, sec. 6068, subd. (b)).

Lawyers are officers of the court and have an ethical obligation to advise the court of legal authority that is directly contrary to a claim being pressed. *Love v. State Dept. of Education* (2018) 29 Cal.App.5th 980; see also *In re Reno* (2012) 55 Cal.4th 428, 510-511.

"[T]o allow an attorney to engage in unprofessional conduct before the jury without a prompt and strong response from the court undermines the judicial process. If, without rebuke, an attorney does not show proper respect for the judge and the proceedings, how can a juror be expected to do so? If an attorney is permitted to flout a court's ruling, how can a juror be expected to adhere to the rule of law as instructed by the court? By mocking the court's authority, an attorney in effect sends a message to the jurors that they, too, may disregard the court's directives and ignore its authority. This type of attorney misconduct must be dealt with in the jury's presence in order to dispel any misperception regarding the credence that jurors must give the court's instructions. Furthermore, when an attorney engages in repetitious misconduct, it is too disruptive to the proceedings to repeatedly excuse the jury to admonish counsel. For these reasons, the court may act swiftly and strongly in the presence of the jury to admonish an attorney if necessary to preserve the integrity of the judicial process." *People v. Chong* (1999) 76 Cal.App.4th 232, 243–244.

"[D]efense counsel, however zealous in his client's behalf, has, as an officer of the court, a paramount obligation to the due and orderly administration of justice, and at all times should maintain a respectful attitude toward the court. A disavowal of intentional disrespect or wrongful intent is no defense to a contempt order." *Chula v. Super. Ct. in and for Orange County* (1952) 109 Cal.App.2d 24, 39.

9.7 Conduct of Litigation

California Rules of Professional Conduct, Rule 3.4 - Fairness to Opposing Party and Counsel

> A lawyer shall not:
>
> (a) unlawfully obstruct another party's access to evidence, including a witness, or unlawfully alter, destroy or conceal a document or other material having potential evidentiary value. A lawyer shall not counsel or assist another person* to do any such act;
>
> (b) suppress any evidence that the lawyer or the lawyer's client has a legal obligation to reveal or to produce;
>
> (c) falsify evidence, counsel or assist a witness to testify falsely, or offer an inducement to a witness that is prohibited by law;
>
> (d) directly or indirectly pay, offer to pay, or acquiesce in the payment of compensation to a witness contingent upon the content of the witness's testimony

or the outcome of the case. Except where prohibited by law, a lawyer may advance, guarantee, or acquiesce in the payment of:

(1) expenses reasonably* incurred by a witness in attending or testifying;

(2) reasonable* compensation to a witness for loss of time attending or testifying; or

(3) a reasonable* fee for the professional services of an expert witness;

(e) advise or directly or indirectly cause a person* to secrete himself or herself or to leave the jurisdiction of a tribunal* for the purpose of making that person* unavailable as a witness therein;

(f) knowingly* disobey an obligation under the rules of a tribunal* except for an open refusal based on an assertion that no valid obligation exists; or

(g) in trial, assert personal knowledge of facts in issue except when testifying as a witness, or state a personal opinion as to the guilt or innocence of an accused.

California Rules of Professional Conduct, Rule 4.4 - Duties Concerning Inadvertently Transmitted Writings*

Where it is reasonably* apparent to a lawyer who receives a writing* relating to a lawyer's representation of a client that the writing* was inadvertently sent or produced, and the lawyer knows* or reasonably should know* that the writing* is privileged or subject to the work product doctrine, the lawyer shall:

(a) refrain from examining the writing* any more than is necessary to determine that it is privileged or subject to the work product doctrine, and

(b) promptly notify the sender.

An asterisk (*) identifies a defined term in rule 1.0.1 of the Rules of Professional Conduct. For further discussion of a defined term, see chapter 2 of this Guide, Terminology.

Rule 3.4 of the Rules of Professional Conduct is not just a rule of civility. A lawyer has specific ethical obligations in the conduct of litigation, with specific regard to the production of evidence and witnesses.

The lawyer's ethical duties in the conduct of litigation are also informed by rule 4.1 of the Rules of Professional Conduct, requiring that a lawyer not make a false statement of material fact or law to any third person. The lawyer should consider this ethical duty in negotiating settlements. Rule 4.3 of the Rules of Professional Conduct prescribes ethical duties in communicating with unrepresented parties. A lawyer may not state or imply that the lawyer is disinterested, and may not give legal advice to an unrepresented party except to hire a lawyer. The lawyer may not seek to obtain privileged or confidential information. For a detailed discussion of the ethical duties regarding communication with third parties, see chapter 7 of this Guide, Communication, sections 7.2 to 7.4.

The Los Angeles County Bar Association, in its Ethics Opinion Number 531 (July 24, 2019), discusses a lawyer's ethical obligations when offered evidence from a former employee of the opposing party that reveals that relevant documents have been concealed from production. First, the lawyer must determine whether the former employee is lawfully in possession of the data. Rules 1.2.1 and 8.4 of the Rules of Professional Conduct prohibit a lawyer from engaging in, or advising or assisting others to engage in criminal conduct. The lawyer should consider consulting with a practitioner who is competent in criminal law and, if necessary, turn over the evidence to the court or other appropriate authority. Second, the lawyer must assess whether the data includes writings the lawyer knows or reasonably should know are subject to the lawyer-client communication, work product, or other privilege.

If access to this evidence is a significant development or leads to any relevant limitation on actions the client expects the lawyer to take, rule 1.4 of the Rules of Professional Conduct requires that the lawyer consult with the client and advise the client about limitations imposed on a lawyer's conduct by the Rules of Professional Conduct and the State Bar Act. A lawyer may not participate in, advise, or assist the client in gaining unlawful access to information that is confidential, privileged, or subject to work product protection.

Inadvertent Email. Rule 4.4 of the Rules of Professional Conduct codifies existing case law and ethics opinions regarding inadvertently received email. Pursuant to that rule, the receiving lawyer has two ethical duties: to refrain from examining the email and to notify the sender. The comment on rule 4.4 adds a third requirement to return the email to the sender or to seek a court order regarding its disposition.

Rule 4.4 of the Rules of Professional Conduct does not include a duty to destroy the inadvertently received email, and an affirmative representation that a digital record has been completely destroyed may not be feasible. The security of the email lies in the lawyer's ethical duty not to examine it or use its contents in the litigation. The lawyer should limit client disclosure, if at all, to the bare facts of receipt of the email and notification of the opposing lawyer. Further disclosure risks losing control of the email and violation of the lawyer's ethical duties in rule 4.4.

Connection Requests on Social Media. San Diego County Bar Association, Ethics Opinion Number 2011-2 discusses whether a connection or "friend" request sent by a lawyer on social media, using the lawyer's real name and profile, violates the ethical prohibition of lawyer contact with a known represented party, now set forth in rule 4.2 of the Rules of Professional Conduct. The opinion concludes that, at the very least, a connection request by a lawyer to a represented party is an ex parte communication under former rule 2-100(A) of the Rules of Professional Conduct. That the lawyer's connection request would not have arisen outside of the representation is sufficient to make a prohibited contact about the subject of representation. The opinion rejects a comparison to publicly available information, because information found on Facebook is not available until the profile owner gives permission. The opinion clarifies that lawyers are allowed to view and access the parts of a Facebook profile to which the profile owner does not restrict access.

Ethics Opinion Number 2011-2 also considers whether a lawyer who does not disclose the reason for the connection request has violated the statutory duty "to employ . . . those means only as are consistent with truth." Bus. & Prof. Code, sec. 6068, subd. (d). The reference in the opinion to the statutory duty is close kin to the lawyer's ethical duties to third parties in rule 4.1 of the Rules of Professional Conduct. Deception as to source of the connection request may also violate Business and Professions Code section 6128, which states that a lawyer commits a misdemeanor when the lawyer is guilty of any deceit or collusion intended to deceive the court or any party.

A lawyer should not send a connection request, or direct a third party to send such a request, to a person involved in a litigated matter without disclosing the lawyer's affiliation and the purpose for the request. Otherwise, the lawyer deceptively relies on the party accepting the request without recognizing the requester's name or their adversarial relationship.

Comment on California Rules of Professional Conduct, Rule 4.1, Truthfulness in Statements to Others

> [1] A lawyer is required to be truthful when dealing with others on a client's behalf, but generally has no affirmative duty to inform an opposing party of relevant facts. A misrepresentation can occur if the lawyer incorporates or affirms the truth of a statement of another person* that the lawyer knows* is false. However, in drafting an agreement or other document on behalf of a client, a lawyer does not necessarily affirm or vouch for the truthfulness of representations made by the client in the agreement or document. A nondisclosure can be the equivalent of a false statement of material fact or law under paragraph (a) where a lawyer makes a partially true but misleading material statement or material omission. In addition to this rule, lawyers remain bound by Business and Professions Code section 6106 and rule 8.4.
>
> [2] This rule refers to statements of fact. Whether a particular statement should be regarded as one of fact can depend on the circumstances. For example, in negotiation, certain types of statements ordinarily are not taken as statements of material fact. Estimates of price or value placed on the subject of a transaction and a party's intentions as to an acceptable settlement of a claim are ordinarily in this category, and so is the existence of an undisclosed principal except where nondisclosure of the principal would constitute fraud.*

Comment on California Rules of Professional Conduct, Rule 4.4, Duties Concerning Inadvertently Transmitted Writings

> [1] If a lawyer determines this rule applies to a transmitted writing,* the lawyer should return the writing* to the sender, seek to reach agreement with the sender regarding the disposition of the writing,* or seek guidance from a tribunal.* (See *Rico v. Mitsubishi* (2007) 42 Cal.4th 807, 817 [68 Cal.Rptr.3d 758].) In providing notice required by this rule, the lawyer shall comply with rule 4.2.

> [2] This rule does not address the legal duties of a lawyer who receives a writing* that the lawyer knows* or reasonably should know* may have been inappropriately disclosed by the sending person.* (See *Clark v. Superior Court* (2011) 196 Cal.App.4th 37 [125 Cal.Rptr.3d 361].)

Cases

"[A]s a general principle, a self-represented litigant who is not indigent 'must expect and receive the same treatment as if represented by an attorney—no different, no better, no worse.'" Nevertheless, the Court of Appeal overturned a dismissal when the trial court failed to clarify expansively for the self-represented litigant the deadline for filing an amended complaint in response to a demurrer and the consequences associated with a failure to file. *Nuno v. Cal. State U., Bakersfield* (2020) 47 Cal.App.5th 799.

Settlement offer that the lawyer for the LLC members proposed to the defendants, which referred to two well-known fraudulent schemes, did not violate rule of professional conduct prohibiting a lawyer from threatening criminal, administrative, or disciplinary charges to obtain advantage in civil dispute. The lawyer was threatening to expose alleged fraud in civil litigation, not through criminal charges, if parties did not settle. *J.B.B. Investment Partners Ltd. v. Fair* (2019) 37 Cal.App.5th 1.

"Substantial evidence supported trial court's findings that disqualification of defense attorney was necessary to prevent doubts about the integrity of the judicial process and to prevent future prejudice or harm to client from defense attorney's exploitation of contents of e-mail, which contained privileged attorney-client information and was inadvertently disclosed to third parties, and thus trial court did not abuse its discretion in disqualifying attorney in client's underlying legal malpractice action against one of those third parties; evidence showed that attorney thought it was permissible to use e-mail to oppose client's claims and that attorney's previous access to the e-mail would undermine public trust in the integrity of the adjudicatory process. Cal. Evid. Code section 954." *McDermott Will & Emery LLP v. Super. Ct. (Hausman)* (2017) 10 Cal.App.5th 1083.

A lawyer who receives lawyer-client material that was inadvertently provided by another must notify the sender. *Ardon v. City of L.A.* (2016) 62 Cal.4th 1176.

A lawyer who receives inadvertently produced documents during discovery has an ethical duty to refrain from unnecessary review of the documents, notify opposing counsel, and return the documents upon request. The inadvertent release of documents did not waive the lawyer-client privilege. *Newark Unified School Dist. v. Super. Ct.* (2015) 245 Cal.App.4th 887.

Ethics Opinions

Analogizing to rule 4.4 of the Rules of Professional Conduct and applicable case law governing inadvertently produced documents, the opinion discusses a lawyer's ethical duties once it is reasonably apparent to the lawyer that privileged documents of another party or documents entitled to work product protection have been obtained. The lawyer is ethically obligated to give notice to the privilege holder, the owner of the work product or their lawyer, and discontinue review of the material beyond the extent necessary to ascertain that it is entitled to protection from discovery. L.A. County Bar Assn., Ethics opn. No. 531 (July 24, 2019).

When a lawyer has engaged in no conduct or activity that induced an apparent material error by opposing counsel, the lawyer has no obligation to alert the opposing counsel of the apparent error. However, where the lawyer has made a material change in contract language in such a manner that the lawyer's conduct constitutes deceit, active concealment, or fraud, the failure of the lawyer to alert opposing counsel of the change would be a violation of the lawyer's ethical obligations. State Bar of Cal. Com. On Prof. Resp. and Conduct, formal opn. No. 2013-189.

If a lawyer receives transmission of an unsolicited communication between opposing counsel and opposing counsel's client or a third party reasonably suggesting that it is a confidential communication sent without the consent of its owner, the lawyer may not ethically read the communication, even if the crime-fraud exception might vitiate the privilege. The lawyer must notify opposing counsel as soon as possible that the lawyer has possession of the communication. The two lawyers should try to resolve the privilege issue or, if that fails, obtain the assistance of a court. A lawyer may not read, disseminate, or otherwise use the communication or its contents absent court approval or consent of its owner. State Bar of Cal. Com. On Prof. Resp. and Conduct, formal opn. No. 2013-188.

9.8 Conduct of Mediation

Representing a client in mediation implicates a lawyer's ethical duties regarding communication with represented parties and other persons. Notwithstanding the informal nature of mediation, the lawyer is nonetheless bound by the prohibition in rule 4.1 of the Rules of Professional Conduct against knowingly making a false or misleading statement to any person. Rule 4.1 and related ethics opinions distinguish statements of material fact from negotiating positions.

California law mandates specific disclosures to the client before entering into mediation. Under Evidence Code section 1129, a lawyer must provide written disclosure of the mediation privilege to the client "as soon as reasonably possible before client agrees to participate in mediation" or if after agreement to mediate, as soon as reasonably possible after retention. The lawyer must also obtain a signed acknowledgement that the client has read the disclosure and understands that the mediation privilege could limit the client's rights in a later dispute with the lawyer. A sample Mediation Disclosure Notification and Acknowledgment is appended to Evidence Code section 1129.

Rule 2.4 of the Rules of Professional Conduct prescribes the ethical duties of a lawyer acting as a mediator, including the duty to inform unrepresented parties that the lawyer does not represent them. Depending on the knowledge and sophistication of the parties to the mediation, rule 2.4 may require the lawyer-mediator to explain further and differentiate the role of a mediator from the role of a lawyer representing a client. A lawyer acting as a mediator is subject to the general ethical duty to avoid conflicts of interest and not to represent a party to the mediation concurrently as a client.

Statute

California Evidence Code section 1129

(a) Except in the case of a class or representative action, an attorney representing a client participating in a mediation or a mediation consultation shall, as soon as reasonably possible before the client agrees to participate in the mediation or mediation consultation, provide that client with a printed disclosure containing the confidentiality restrictions described in Section 1119 and obtain a printed acknowledgment signed by that client stating that he or she has read and understands the confidentiality restrictions.

(b) An attorney who is retained after an individual agrees to participate in the mediation or mediation consultation shall, as soon as reasonably possible after being retained, comply with the printed disclosure and acknowledgment requirements described in subdivision (a).

(c) The printed disclosure required by subdivision (a) shall:

(1) Be printed in the preferred language of the client in at least 12-point font.

(2) Be printed on a single page that is not attached to any other document provided to the client.

(3) Include the names of the attorney and the client and be signed and dated by the attorney and the client.

(d) If the requirements in subdivision (c) are met, the following disclosure shall be deemed to comply with the requirements of subdivision (a):

Mediation Disclosure Notification and Acknowledgment

To promote communication in mediation, California law generally makes mediation a confidential process. California's mediation confidentiality laws are laid out in Sections 703.5 and 1115 to 1129, inclusive, of the Evidence Code. Those laws establish the confidentiality of mediation and limit the disclosure, admissibility, and a court's consideration of communications, writings, and conduct in connection with a mediation. In general, those laws mean the following:

- All communications, negotiations, or settlement offers in the course of a mediation must remain confidential.
- Statements made and writings prepared in connection with a mediation are not admissible or subject to discovery or compelled disclosure in noncriminal proceedings.

• A mediator's report, opinion, recommendation, or finding about what occurred in a mediation may not be submitted to or considered by a court or another adjudicative body.
• A mediator cannot testify in any subsequent civil proceeding about any communication or conduct occurring at, or in connection with, a mediation.

California Rules of Professional Conduct, Rule 2.4 - Lawyer as Third-Party Neutral

(a) A lawyer serves as a third-party neutral when the lawyer assists two or more persons* who are not clients of the lawyer to reach a resolution of a dispute, or other matter, that has arisen between them. Service as a third-party neutral may include service as an arbitrator, a mediator or in such other capacity as will enable the lawyer to assist the parties to resolve the matter.

(b) A lawyer serving as a third-party neutral shall inform unrepresented parties that the lawyer is not representing them. When the lawyer knows* or reasonably should know* that a party does not understand the lawyer's role in the matter, the lawyer shall explain the difference between the lawyer's role as a third-party neutral and a lawyer's role as one who represents a client.

Comment on California Rules of Professional Conduct, Rule 2.4

[1] In serving as a third-party neutral, the lawyer may be subject to court rules or other laws that apply either to third-party neutrals generally or to lawyers serving as third-party neutrals. Lawyer neutrals may also be subject to various codes of ethics, such as the Judicial Council Standards for Mediators in Court Connected Mediation Programs or the Judicial Council Ethics Standards for Neutral Arbitrators in Contractual Arbitration.

[2] A lawyer who serves as a third-party neutral subsequently may be asked to serve as a lawyer representing a client in the same matter. The conflicts of interest that arise for both the individual lawyer and the lawyer's law firm* are addressed in rule 1.12.

Case

A lawyer's signature approving a settlement agreement as to form and content could demonstrate intent to be bound by its substantive provisions. The agreement included provisions imposing confidentiality on the parties and their counsel. The lawyer was bound by the terms of the agreement, and sufficient evidence showed that the lawyer violated its provisions by making public statements about the settlement. *Monster Energy Co. v. Schechter* (2019) 7 Cal.5th 781.

Ethics Opinion

Statements made by counsel during negotiations are subject to the ethical rules prohibiting a lawyer from engaging in dishonesty, deceit, or collusion. Thus, it is improper for a lawyer to make false statements of fact or implicit misrepresentations of material fact during negotiations. However, puffery and posturing, such as statements about a party's negotiating goals or willingness to compromise, are generally permissible because they are not considered statements of fact. State Bar of Cal. Com. on Prof. Resp. and Conduct, formal opn. No. 2015-194.

9.9 Lawyer as Percipient Witness

California Rules of Professional Conduct, Rule 3.7 - Lawyer as Witness

> (a) A lawyer shall not act as an advocate in a trial in which the lawyer is likely to be a witness unless:
>
> > (1) the lawyer's testimony relates to an uncontested issue or matter;
> >
> > (2) the lawyer's testimony relates to the nature and value of legal services rendered in the case; or
> >
> > (3) the lawyer has obtained informed written consent* from the client. If the lawyer represents the People or a governmental entity, the consent shall be obtained from the head of the office or a designee of the head of the office by which the lawyer is employed.
>
> (b) A lawyer may act as advocate in a trial in which another lawyer in the lawyer's firm* is likely to be called as a witness unless precluded from doing so by rule 1.7 or rule 1.9.

An asterisk (*) identifies a defined term in rule 1.0.1 of the Rules of Professional Conduct. For further discussion of a defined term, see chapter 2 of this Guide, Terminology.

Estate planning, trust, and probate lawyers are often percipient witnesses to contested proceedings, and the lawyer's testimony may be required in that proceeding. The lawyer may have prepared an estate plan that is now being contested, may have represented the decedent or the conservatee in a business transaction that is now in dispute, or may have represented a fiduciary whose acts are now being challenged.

Rule 3.7 of the Rules of Professional Conduct begins with a blanket prohibition on acting as both an advocate and witness in a contested proceeding, with limited exceptions. Rule 3.7(a)(3) prohibits the lawyer from acting as an advocate and a witness unless the lawyer obtains the informed written consent of the client. That consent itself may be insufficient. The comment on rule 3.7 states that the court has discretion to disqualify a lawyer, notwithstanding the informed written consent of the client, to avoid misleading the court or prejudicing a third party.

Rule 1.10 of the Rules of Professional Conduct imputes conflicts of interest to all members of a firm. However, rule 3.7(b) permits a lawyer to act as an advocate in a trial in which another lawyer in the law firm is likely to be called as a witness, unless rules 1.7 or 1.9 of the Rules of Professional Conduct regarding conflicts of interest preclude the lawyer from undertaking that representation.

Most of the difficulties inherent in a lawyer taking on the role of both advocate and witness are present regardless of whether the lawyer's testimony will be given in front of a jury or a judge. Although former rule 5-210 of the Rules of Professional Conduct only addressed jury trials, case law under that rule applied the prohibition to non-jury proceedings. *Kennedy v. Eldridge* (2011) 201 Cal.App.4th 1197 (a family law case that was heard before a judge). Rule 3.7 of the Rules of Professional Conduct does not limit the prohibition against a lawyer acting as a witness to jury trials.

The prohibition on acting as both advocate and witness may also implicate a personal conflict of interest with the drafting lawyer. For example, a potential malpractice claim arising from the drafting may come to light during the contested proceeding. Rule 1.7(c) of the Rules of Professional Conduct prohibits a lawyer and members of the lawyer's firm from representing a client when such a conflict with a lawyer's personal interest exists, without written disclosure to the client.

Comment on California Rules of Professional Conduct, Rule 3.7

> [1] This rule applies to a trial before a jury, judge, administrative law judge or arbitrator. This rule does not apply to other adversarial proceedings. This rule also does not apply in non-adversarial proceedings, as where a lawyer testifies on behalf of a client in a hearing before a legislative body.
>
> [2] A lawyer's obligation to obtain informed written consent* may be satisfied when the lawyer makes the required disclosure, and the client gives informed consent* on the record in court before a licensed court reporter or court recorder who prepares a transcript or recording of the disclosure and consent. See definition of "written" in rule 1.0.1(n).
>
> [3] Notwithstanding a client's informed written consent,* courts retain discretion to take action, up to and including disqualification of a lawyer who seeks to both testify and serve as an advocate, to protect the trier of fact from being misled or the opposing party from being prejudiced. (See, e.g., *Lyle v. Superior Court* (1981) 122 Cal.App.3d 470 [175 Cal.Rptr. 918]).

9.10 Protecting Confidentiality in Litigation

Los Angeles County Bar Association Ethics Opinion Number 529 (August 23, 2017) and San Diego County Bar Association Ethics Opinion Number 2012-1 discuss ethical duties when representing a client in litigation, when the client regularly transmits and stores information digitally. Those opinions address the intersection of ethics and technology, and the necessary steps to preserve the lawyer's duty of confidentiality and the client's right to assert the lawyer client-privilege. Consider the following common issues with practitioners in fiduciary litigation:

1. Communication with a client at a work email that is not private;
2. Breach of lawyer-client confidentiality by the "reply all" email;
3. Waiver of confidentiality when client forwards a lawyer's email to an accountant or other advisor; and
4. Client's inappropriate use of social media and the posting that is not taken the way it was intended.

These and similar communications may waive the lawyer-client privilege inadvertently, requiring that the lawyer disclose them in discovery or claw them back from opposing counsel.

The cited ethics opinions relate these issues not only to the lawyer's duty to preserve client confidences, but to the lawyer's duty of competence. Opinion Number 2012-1 defines competence to include understanding the client's technology: the number, types, and locations of computers currently in use and in use during the relevant period if no longer in use; the operating systems and application software the client uses; disc-or-tape-labeling conventions; backup and archival disc or tape inventories or schedules; the most likely locations of relevant electronic records; and electronic-records-management policies and procedures among others. For a further discussion of the ethical duty of confidentiality as applied to the use of technology, see chapter 10 of this Guide, Ethics and Technology, section 10.4.

Opinion Number 2017-529 warns lawyers to avoid unguarded disclosure of client information pursuant to an unauthorized connection or "friend" request as discussed in section 9.7 of this chapter. The failure to safeguard client internet communications and the lawyer's own work product could be detrimental to the prosecution or defense of the client's interests. As with other matters related to competent practice, managing and supervising lawyers have an ethical duty to ensure that staff members comply with the Rules of Professional Conduct to safeguard confidential information. For a further discussion of the duties of managerial and supervisory lawyers, see rule 5.1 of the Rules of Professional Conduct and chapter 2 of this Guide, Competence and Diligence, section 3.9.

Ethics Opinion

When a lawyer engaged by an insurance carrier to defend the interests of an insured obtains information that could provide a basis for the insurance carrier to deny coverage, the lawyer is ethically prohibited from disclosing that information to the insurance carrier. In such a situation, the lawyer must withdraw from the representation. L.A. County Bar Assn., Ethics opn. No. 528 (April 2017).

9.11 Competence in E-discovery

Formal Opinion Number 2015-193 issued by the State Bar of California Committee on Professional Responsibility and Conduct prescribes a litigation lawyer's ethical duty to be proficient with e-discovery. The lawyer's ethical duty of competence evolves as new technologies develop and become integrated with the practice of law. Professional competence related to litigation generally requires a basic understanding of, and facility with, issues relating to e-discovery, including the discovery of electronically stored information ("ESI"). The opinion acknowledges the current reality that almost every litigation could involve e-discovery.

A number of practical issues may arise in connection with e-discovery: redaction errors, incomplete search terms, and inadequacy of software. Inadequate software can impede the lawyer's production, use, and review of documents generated through e-discovery. Lawyers have an ethical duty to identify and hire skilled vendors who can properly discover, protect, and produce electronic records. Relying on the lawyer's own skills and knowledge in a field of complex and emerging technology is often a mistake. For a further discussion of the ethical duty of technology competence, see chapter 10 of this Guide, Ethics and Technology, section 10.2.

Opinion Number 2015-193 presents the fact pattern of a lawyer who represents a large company with an information technology department. The lawyer relies on a representation from a responsible officer that the client has provided the lawyer with all electronic data in hard copy form. The lawyer takes no further action to review the available data or to instruct the client or its IT staff about the search or the requirements of e-discovery. As directed by the lawyer, the client gives a vendor unsupervised direct access to its network. The opinion concludes that the lawyer violated the applicable ethical duties as follows:

1. By failing to make an e-discovery evaluation early, prior to the initial case management conference;
2. By making no assessment of the e-discovery needs of the case or of the lawyer's own capabilities;
3. By not consulting with another lawyer or an e-discovery expert prior to agreeing to an e-discovery plan at the initial case management conference and allowing that plan to become a court order;
4. By not fully understanding the danger of overbreadth in the agreed upon search terms;
5. By failing to instruct or supervise the client regarding the direct network search or discovery;
6. By failing to pre-test the agreed upon search terms or otherwise review the data before the network search; and
7. By taking no action to review the gathered data until opposing counsel asserted spoliation and threatened sanctions.

By negative inference, Opinion Number 2015-193 guides the litigating lawyer on proper compliance with the ethical duty of competence. Rule 1.1 of the Rules of Professional Conduct allows three options to a lawyer who lacks the required competence for e-discovery: (1) acquire sufficient learning and skill before performance is required; (2) associate with or consult technical consultants or competent counsel; or (3) decline the client representation. Competent handling of e-discovery may require an enhanced level of technical knowledge and ability, depending on the e-discovery issues involved in a matter, and the nature of the electronically stored information.

Rules 1.2 and 1.4 of the Rules of Professional Conduct require that the lawyer abide by the client's decisions as to the goals of the representation and consult with the client as to the means by which those goals are pursued. Ethics Opinion Number 2018-3 issued by the San Diego County Bar Association discusses client communication in the context of technology-assisted review of documents responding to a discovery request. The opinion states that such communication should include a discussion of the advantages and disadvantages of using a particular technological means or tool.

For example, advantages of technology-assisted review could include greater reliability, especially when that use is disclosed to an opposing party in advance. An opposing party who does not object or otherwise request modification of a technological approach may find it difficult to challenge the results when that approach is used.

Disadvantages of technology-assisted review could include controversies over the use of a technological approach, including the results generated. Even if the parties reach agreement, some financial benefit of technological efficiency may be lost in disputes with other counsel regarding the terms for searching, reviewing, and producing documents. In using technology-assisted review products to identify responsive documents for productions, a lawyer has an ethical duty to understand the products used and may not cede the lawyer's independent judgment.

Case

An inadequate privilege log did not waive the lawyer-client privilege and work product doctrine, but the privilege log failed to provide sufficient information for the trial court to evaluate objections based on the lawyer-client privilege and work product doctrine. *Catalina Island Yacht Club v. Super. Ct.* (2015) 242 Cal.App.4th 1116.

Ethics Opinions

While lawyers may use technology assisted review products to identify responsive documents for production, they should communicate with their clients about such use, must take care to understand the products they use, and may not cede their independent judgment. San Diego County Bar Assn., Ethics opn. No. 2018-3.

Ultimately, the lawyer will have to represent to the tribunal that the lawyer complied fully with the required discovery obligations. Even at the outset, however, when addressing e-discovery protocols, candor to the tribunal requires lawyers to represent fairly and accurately what they believe is necessary to accomplish the principal purpose of discovery: obtaining the facts necessary to evaluate, settle, or try the case. Exaggerated discovery demands may lead the court to believe that a lawyer has not fulfilled the lawyer's duty of candor to the tribunal. To the extent that the court sees through persistent, exaggerated demands, a lawyer's incompetence has, arguably, done irreparable injury to the client itself. San Diego County Bar Assn., Ethics opn. No.

2012-1. See also rule 3.3 of the Rules of Professional Conduct, Candor Toward the Tribunal, and section 9.6 of this chapter.

9.12 Withdrawal from Representation

California Rules of Professional Conduct, Rule 1.16 - Declining or Terminating Representation.

(a) Except as stated in paragraph (c), a lawyer shall not represent a client or, where representation has commenced, shall withdraw from the representation of a client if:

(1) the lawyer knows* or reasonably should know* that the client is bringing an action, conducting a defense, asserting a position in litigation, or taking an appeal, without probable cause and for the purpose of harassing or maliciously injuring any person;*

(2) the lawyer knows* or reasonably should know* that the representation will result in violation of these rules or of the State Bar Act;

(3) the lawyer's mental or physical condition renders it unreasonably difficult to carry out the representation effectively; or

(4) the client discharges the lawyer.

(b) Except as stated in paragraph (c), a lawyer may withdraw from representing a client if:

(1) the client insists upon presenting a claim or defense in litigation, or asserting a position or making a demand in a non-litigation matter, that is not warranted under existing law and cannot be supported by good faith argument for an extension, modification, or reversal of existing law;

(2) the client either seeks to pursue a criminal or fraudulent* course of conduct or has used the lawyer's services to advance a course of conduct that the lawyer reasonably believes* was a crime or fraud;*

(3) the client insists that the lawyer pursue a course of conduct that is criminal or fraudulent;*

(4) the client by other conduct renders it unreasonably difficult for the lawyer to carry out the representation effectively;

(5) the client breaches a material term of an agreement with, or obligation, to the lawyer relating to the representation, and the lawyer has given the client a reasonable* warning after the breach that the lawyer will withdraw unless the client fulfills the agreement or performs the obligation;

(6) the client knowingly* and freely assents to termination of the representation;

(7) the inability to work with co-counsel indicates that the best interests of the client likely will be served by withdrawal;

(8) the lawyer's mental or physical condition renders it difficult for the lawyer to carry out the representation effectively;

(9) a continuation of the representation is likely to result in a violation of these rules or the State Bar Act; or

(10) the lawyer believes* in good faith, in a proceeding pending before a tribunal,* that the tribunal* will find the existence of other good cause for withdrawal.

(c) If permission for termination of a representation is required by the rules of a tribunal,* a lawyer shall not terminate a representation before that tribunal* without its permission.

(d) A lawyer shall not terminate a representation until the lawyer has taken reasonable* steps to avoid reasonably* foreseeable prejudice to the rights of the client, such as giving the client sufficient notice to permit the client to retain other counsel, and complying with paragraph (e).

(e) Upon the termination of a representation for any reason:

(1) subject to any applicable protective order, non-disclosure agreement, statute or regulation, the lawyer promptly shall release to the client, at the request of the client, all client materials and property. "Client materials and property" includes correspondence, pleadings, deposition transcripts, experts' reports and other writings,* exhibits, and physical evidence, whether in tangible, electronic or other form, and other items reasonably* necessary to the client's representation, whether the client has paid for them or not; and

(2) the lawyer promptly shall refund any part of a fee or expense paid in advance that the lawyer has not earned or incurred. This provision is not applicable to a true retainer fee paid solely for the purpose of ensuring the availability of the lawyer for the matter.

An asterisk (*) identifies a defined term in rule 1.0.1 of the Rules of Professional Conduct. For further discussion of a defined term, see chapter 2 of this Guide, Terminology.

A lawyer who seeks to withdraw from representing a client must comply with the ethical duties in rule 1.16 of the Rules of Professional Conduct. Rule 1.16(a) sets forth the grounds for mandatory withdrawal; rule 1.16(b) sets forth the grounds for permissive withdrawal. The rule also prescribes the actions the lawyer must take after withdrawal to avoid prejudice to the rights of a client.

In a litigated matter, the client's insistence on an unsupported or frivolous legal position mandates the lawyer's withdrawal. Mandatory withdrawal in such a case acknowledges that the ethical duty of a lawyer to follow the directions of the client regarding the conduct of the litigation may conflict with the duty to advance only meritorious claims under rule 3.1 of the Rules of Professional Conduct, and the duty to avoid frivolous claims under rule 3.2 of the Rules of Professional Conduct. In a non-litigated matter, the client's insistence on such claims would be a ground for permissive withdrawal.

Withdrawal is also permitted under rule 1.16(b) if the lawyer, in good faith, believes that the court will find other good cause for withdrawal. Such permissive withdrawal would be based on the lawyer's subjective belief and not knowledge, actual or imputed, of objective facts and circumstances. The lawyer is nonetheless bound by local court rules regarding withdrawal, and must seek permission of the court to withdraw in accordance with those rules. A lawyer has an ethical duty to comply with any court order that denies permission to withdraw. *Osborne v. Todd Farm Service* (2016) 247 Cal.App.4th 43.

The ethical duty to preserve the client's confidential information continues through and beyond the process of withdrawal. State Bar of California Committee on Professional Responsibility and Conduct, Formal Opinion Number 2015-192 analyzes specific circumstances that may arise in seeking court permission to withdraw and the protection of the client's interests whether or not the court grants that permission.

The lawyer has specific ethical duties to a client after terminating the representation. Under rule 1.16(e) of the Rules of Professional Conduct, the release and return of a client's file upon request is mandatory, as is the refund of any unearned portion of a fee deposit. The return of client documents stored in electronic form is discussed in State Bar of California Committee on Professional Responsibility and Conduct, Formal Opinion Number 2007-174, interpreting former rule 3-700(D) of the Rules of Professional Conduct. Rule 1.16(e)(1) carries forward the requirement in the prior rule that the lawyer return all documents that are "reasonably necessary to the client's representation." The lawyer has the further ethical duty to review the returned documents and to remove any metadata that may include confidential information from another client.

Comment on California Rules of Professional Conduct, Rule 1.16

> [2] When a lawyer withdraws from the representation of a client in a particular matter under paragraph (a) or (b), the lawyer might not be obligated to withdraw from the representation of the same client in other matters. For example, a lawyer might be obligated under paragraph (a)(1) to withdraw from representing a client because the lawyer has a conflict of interest under rule 1.7, but that conflict might not arise in other representations of the client.
>
> ...
>
> [4] Lawyers must comply with their obligations to their clients under Business and Professions Code section 6068, subdivision (e) and rule 1.6, and to the courts under rule 3.3 when seeking permission to withdraw under paragraph (c). If a tribunal* denies a lawyer permission to withdraw, the lawyer is obligated to comply with the

tribunal's* order. (See Bus. & Prof. Code, sections 6068, subd. (b) and 6103.) This duty applies even if the lawyer sought permission to withdraw because of a conflict of interest. Regarding withdrawal from limited scope representations that involve court appearances, compliance with applicable California Rules of Court concerning limited scope representation satisfies paragraph (c).

Ethics Opinions

A lawyer may disclose to the court only as much as is reasonably necessary to demonstrate the lawyer's need to withdraw. Ordinarily, it will be sufficient to communicate to the court that ethical considerations require withdrawal or that there has been an irreconcilable breakdown in the lawyer-client relationship. In attempting to demonstrate to the court the need to withdraw, a lawyer may not disclose confidential client communications, either in open court or *in camera*. To the extent the court orders a lawyer to disclose confidential information, the lawyer faces the dilemma of not being able to comply with both the duty to maintain client confidences and the duty to obey court orders. Once a lawyer has exhausted reasonable avenues of appeal or other further review of such an order, the lawyer must evaluate the relevant legal authorities and the particular circumstances, including the potential prejudice to the client, and reach an independent conclusion on how to proceed. No categorical opinions can be made on whether it is acceptable to disclose client confidences even when faced with an order compelling disclosure. Whatever choice is made, the lawyer must take reasonable steps to minimize the impact of that choice on the client. State Bar of Cal. Com. on Prof. Resp. and Conduct, formal opn. No. 2015-192.

A lawyer is ethically obligated, upon termination of employment, promptly to release to a client, at the client's request: (1) an electronic version of email correspondence; (2) an electronic version of the pleadings; (3) an electronic version of discovery requests and responses; (4) an electronic deposition and exhibit database; and (5) an electronic version of transactional documents. The lawyer's ethical obligation to release any electronic items, however, does not require the lawyer to create such items if they do not exist or to change the application. Prior to release, the lawyer is ethically obligated to take reasonable steps to strip from each of these electronic items any metadata reflecting confidential information belonging to any other client. State Bar of Cal. Com. on Prof. Resp. and Conduct, formal opn. No. 2007-174.

9.13 Sample Withdrawal Letter

The following letter could be adapted for sending to joint clients whose directly adverse interests prevent the lawyer from effectively continuing the representation of both clients. For a further discussion of the ethical duty to avoid conflicts of interest, see Rules Prof. Conduct, rule 1.7 and chapter 5 of this Guide, Conflicts of Interest. A withdrawal letter should explain in detail any upcoming matters for which the client may need or want representation. Specific disclosures should be made regarding upcoming hearings, including the purpose of the hearing, the relation of the hearing to the overall conduct of the litigation, and all substantive or procedural deadlines.

The lawyer should adapt it thoughtfully to the lawyer's customary practice and the needs of a particular client representation. The letter could also be modified if the lawyer withdraws from representing one joint client and continues to represent the other.

Dear [Client 1] and [Client 2]:

You requested that our firm represent you both simultaneously in this matter in which you have a common interest. When we began this representation, we explained to both of you that if, during the course of the representation, either one of you should revoke your consent to the sharing of all confidential information that we consider relevant and material to the representation; or if other conflicts of interest should arise between you with respect to your respective interests in this matter that lead us to believe that our representation of either one of you would be adversely affected by our continued representation of the other of you, we would withdraw from the representation of both of you in this matter; and each of you would then have to obtain separate counsel.

[ALTERNATIVE 1: Noisy Withdrawal] We have become aware that [DESCRIBE NATURE OF THE CONFLICT.]. We believe that this represents a conflict that prevents us from representing and advising you both any further in this matter. Accordingly, we are hereby notifying both of you that we are withdrawing immediately from any further representation of either one of you in this matter. It will now be necessary for each of you to consider obtaining separate counsel.

[ALTERNATIVE 2: Silent Withdrawal] We have become aware of circumstances that we believe represent a conflict that prevents us from representing and advising you both any further in this matter. Accordingly, we are hereby notifying both of you that we are withdrawing immediately from any further representation of either one of you in this matter. It will now be necessary for each of you to consider obtaining separate counsel.

[IF THE MATTER INVOLVES LITIGATION AND COURT APPROVAL IS REQUIRED, DESCRIBE THE PROCESS.]

Please acknowledge receipt of a copy of this letter by dating, signing, and returning one copy of this letter to our office.

Sincerely,

[Lawyer]

Reprinted with permission from The American College of Trust and Estate Counsel.

9.14 Client with Diminished Capacity

The ethical rules that bind a lawyer practicing in trust and estate litigation allow no exception regarding the representation of a client with diminished capacity. The duty of diligent representation applies even if the client has difficulty understanding or retaining the lawyer's communications, articulating the client's wishes regarding the goals of the ongoing litigation, or the procedural steps that may be taken to accomplish those goals. The duties to the client are absolute, and the lawyer may not substitute the lawyer's judgment for the wishes of the client, however well intentioned. If difficulties in communication prevent effective representation of the client, the lawyer should consider withdrawing from the representation consistent with the procedures set forth in rule 1.16 of the Rules of Professional Conduct, and seek leave of the court as needed.

Business and Professions Code section 6068, subdivision (e) requires a lawyer to "maintain inviolate the confidence, and at every peril to himself or herself to preserve the secrets, of his or her client." The Supreme Court tracked this statutory provision in the revision of the Rules of Professional Conduct effective November 1, 2018, and declined to make any proposed change.

The statutory duty of confidentiality prohibits a lawyer from disclosing a client's diminished capacity and from actively taking any steps against the client's stated wishes. A lawyer who initiates conservatorship proceedings for a client without the client's consent discloses the client's "secrets" in violation that ethical duty and possibly discloses communications protected by the lawyer-client privilege. Evid. Code, sec. 952. In addition, a lawyer who seeks to initiate conservatorship proceedings for the client against the client's wishes and interest violates the duty of loyalty to the client. State Bar of Cal. Com. on Prof. Resp. and Conduct, formal opn. No. 1989-112. For a further discussion of the lawyer's ethical duty of confidentiality with regard to an incapacitated client, see Chapter 6 of this Guide, Confidentiality of Information, section 6.7.

The client is the holder of the lawyer-client privilege and the person authorized to assert that privilege to prevent the disclosure of evidence to the court or opposing parties. If a client is or becomes incapacitated, the privilege may be asserted by a conservator subject to the limitations regarding self-interest in Evidence Code section 953, subdivision (b). See chapter 6 of this Guide, Confidentiality of Information, section 6.13.

Deceased Client. Following a client's death, the lawyer has a continuing ethical duty to preserve the client's confidences. Nevertheless, an estate planning lawyer for a now deceased client may be authorized to make limited disclosures of communications with that client.

> In general, the lawyer's duty of confidentiality continues after the death of a client. Accordingly, a lawyer ordinarily should not disclose confidential information following a client's death. However, if consent is given by the client's personal representative, or if the decedent had expressly or impliedly authorized disclosure, the lawyer who represented the deceased client may provide an interested party, including a potential litigant, with information regarding a deceased client's dispositive instruments and intent, including prior instruments and communications relevant thereto. The personal representative or client may also authorize disclosure of other confidential information learned during the representation if there is a need for that information A lawyer may be impliedly authorized to make appropriate disclosure of client confidential information that would promote the client's estate plan, forestall litigation, preserve assets, and further family understanding of the

> decedent's intention. Disclosures should ordinarily be limited to information that the lawyer would be required to reveal as a witness.

ACTEC Commentaries on the Model Rules of Prof. Conduct, rule 1.6. As a witness, the lawyer would be required to testify as to confidential information relevant to the decedent's estate planning and specifically excepted from the lawyer-client privilege under the provisions of the Evidence Code.

The lawyer-client evidentiary privilege in court proceedings presents unique ethical issues if the client who initially held the privilege is deceased. The privilege may be waived by the client's successor in interest, typically though not always the client's personal representative. Disclosure may also be permitted when no person holds the privilege, for example when no personal representative is appointed for a deceased client.

The Evidence Code sets forth specific exceptions to the lawyer-client evidentiary privilege. Those exceptions cover multiple issues regarding the intention of the deceased client and the proper execution of testamentary documents. In the event of an actual dispute, the best practice may be to disclose information pursuant to these exceptions to all parties. A drafting lawyer who is asked for documents or for oral or written testimony should consider retaining independent counsel.

Statutes

California Evidence Code section 957

> There is no privilege under this article as to a communication relevant to an issue between parties all of whom claim through a deceased client, regardless of whether the claims are by testate or intestate succession, nonprobate transfer, or inter vivos transaction.

California Evidence Code section 959

> There is no privilege under this article as to a communication relevant to an issue concerning the intention or competence of a client executing an attested document of which the lawyer is an attesting witness, or concerning the execution or attestation of such a document.

California Evidence Code section 960

> There is no privilege under this article as to a communication relevant to an issue concerning the intention of a client, now deceased, with respect to a deed of conveyance, will, or other writing, executed by the client, purporting to affect an interest in property.

California Evidence Code section 961

> There is no privilege under this article as to a communication relevant to an issue concerning the validity of a deed of conveyance, will, or other writing, executed by a client, now deceased, purporting to affect an interest in property.

Cases

A minor in a juvenile proceeding, through his lawyer, petitioned the court for the appointment of a psychologist as a defense expert. The psychologist stated that she would respect the lawyer-client privilege and the lawyer's duty of confidentiality, and would not report client information concerning child abuse or neglect. The trial court denied the minor's petition, and the Court of Appeal reversed on a writ of mandate. The Court of Appeal held that a minor subject to a juvenile wardship petition has the right not only to counsel but also to necessary ancillary defense services, and the right to protect communications with both counsel and experts engaged to assist counsel from disclosure. The psychologist was willing to safeguard the confidentiality of the minor's communications at the risk of personal liability that communications to the minor's lawyer might not comply with the mandatory reporting requirements for child abuse and neglect. The lawyer was not a mandated reporter. *Elijah W. v. Super. Ct. of L.A.* (2013) 216 Cal.App.4th 140.

The lawyer-client privilege terminates when there is no person or personal representative to claim it. *HLC Properties, Ltd. v. Super. Ct.* (2005) 35 Cal.4th 54.

"The communication, as well as the relation between the attorney and his client, ceases to be confidential when it is clearly manifest that it is the intention of the client that the communication should be disclosed if any occasion therefor should be presented. The consent of the client to such disclosure … may be implied as well as express; and by requesting his attorney to draw his will the client impliedly asks him to do and say whatever may at any time and place be requisite for the purpose of establishing the integrity of the will." *In re Nelson's Estate* (1901) 132 Cal. 182, 188.

"It is [the client's] privilege to seal the lips of his attorney, or to permit him to make disclosures of confidential communications. When a testator has requested his attorney to become an attesting witness to his will, he thereby expressly waives the privilege." *In re Mullin's Estate* (1895) 110 Cal. 252, 254.

Ethics Opinion

A lawyer may properly petition the court for appointment of a new guardian ad litem, but may not disclose confidential information that the existing guardian ad litem requests remain confidential. San Diego County Bar Assn., Ethics opn. No. 2017-2.

Article

Rudolph & Hughes, *A Lawyer is a Lawyer is a Lawyer* (2019) 25 Cal. Trusts and Estates Q., Issue 1. The authors argue that a court-appointed lawyer owes the same duties of loyalty and confidentiality as to any other client, and is not an official such as a guardian ad litem who has a duty to report to the court.

9.15 Compensation Arrangements

Alternative financing of litigation fees and expenses is an increasingly common practice. Typically, but not always, the financing agency negotiates the loan directly with the client. The interest rate on such loans can be high. Such financing may implicate the duty of reasonable compensation and the ethical duties in rule 1.8.6 regarding the payment of a client's fees by a third party.

A lawyer may undertake to receive a contingent fee from a client who is a beneficiary contesting the terms of a will or a trust, that fee being secured by the beneficiary's interest in the trust. The lawyer should ensure that the security agreement with the client does not run afoul of a spendthrift clause prohibiting alienation of the beneficiary's interest. Such a contingent fee may violate the lawyer's ethical duty regarding compensation as set forth in rule 1.5.

A successful motion for disqualification of a lawyer or firm may require disgorgement of fees. *Sheppard, Mullin, Richter & Hampton, LLP v. J-M Manufacturing Co., Inc.* (2018) 6 Cal.5th 59. In this case simultaneous representation of clients with adverse interests in violation of the rules of professional conduct rendered the engagement letter unenforceable as a matter of public policy. Nevertheless, the court allowed the law firm to recover fees under a theory of quantum meruit.

Ethics Opinions

"If the lawyer has a material interest in the client obtaining funding, the lawyer must disclose that interest and seek the client's informed written consent prior to advising on the subject. In commercial funding arrangements, the funding agreement will likely be negotiated. If the client asks the lawyer to represent him or her in such negotiations, the lawyer should consider whether he has the experience or learning required as well as whether the lawyer has any personal interest that creates a conflict. If so, the lawyer must address those by a written disclosure that describes the relevant circumstances and material risks and then obtain the client's written consent. If the funder seeks client confidential information, the lawyer must advise the client of the risks of disclosure and obtain the client's informed consent to disclose confidential information to the funder. The lawyer should also take appropriate steps to limit the risks to the client that the disclosure of such information will effect a waiver of attorney-client privilege or work product protection which may include having the funder sign a nondisclosure agreement, appropriate labeling of shared materials as confidential or taking other steps to maintain the confidentiality of the shared materials." State Bar of Cal. Com. on Prof. Resp. and Conduct, formal opn. Interim No. 14-0002 (pending public comment and review).

Lawyers may refer clients to fee financing companies or brokers in which the lawyers have no ownership or other financial interests provided they comply with model rules 1.2(c), 1.4(b), 1.5(a) and (b), 1.6, 1.7(a)(2), and 1.9(a). If a lawyer refers clients to an entity in which the lawyer has or acquires an ownership or other financial interest, the lawyer would be entering into a business transaction with a client and would be required to comply with model rule 1.8(a). ABA Com. on Ethics and Prof. Resp., formal opn. No. 2018-484, A Lawyer's Obligations when Clients Use Companies or Brokers to Finance the Lawyer's Fee.

Note: Rule 1.8.1 of the California Rules of Professional Conduct is the parallel to ABA Model Rules of Professional Conduct, rule 1.8(a).

Articles

There are practical and ethical concerns regarding the use of third-party litigation funders. Ethically, there is an inherent potential conflict of interest between the litigation financer and the client with the lawyer placed in the middle. Also, there are concerns whether privileged and/or work product-protected information may be shared with outside litigation financing sources to obtain financing. Counsel must keep the client informed and discharge all duties in favor of the client, not the third-party providing financing. Miller, *Perils of Third-Party Funding* (Mar. 2017) L.A. Law.

Egan, *Other People's Money: Rise of Litigation Finance Companies Raises Legal and Ethical Concerns* (Dec. 2018) ABA J.

9.16 Sample Compensation Provision

The following provision would be included in an engagement letter that sets forth the terms of the representation for a new client in a litigation matter or a new matter with a current client. See section 9.2 of this chapter for a sample engagement letter. The lawyer should adapt it thoughtfully to the lawyer's customary practice and the needs of a particular client representation. For a detailed discussion of the ethical duties affecting compensation agreements, see chapter 8 of this Guide, Compensation.

> Dear [Client],
>
> Our fee in connection with the [subject matter of the engagement] will be the product of the time spent by our lawyers and other professionals multiplied by their respective hourly rates. The time for which we are to be paid includes not only normal office conferences, research, analysis, and advice associated with the [subject matter of the engagement], but also the time involved in telephone calls, faxes, e-mail, and other forms of communication. We will generally bill you for our services on a monthly basis. We adjust our hourly rates periodically. We consider the ability, experience, and reputation of our lawyers and paralegals when we set hourly rates. Changes are usually made each January 1, but sometimes they are made at other times. Any increase in rates will apply to all time beginning with the month when the rates are changed. Work done before that month will be billed at the hourly rates previously in effect. Different lawyers and paralegals in our firm may be involved in your work if that will result in lower fees, provide a specialized legal talent, or help us do your work more efficiently. We will try to assign lawyers and paralegals having the lowest hourly rates consistent with the skills, time demands, and other factors required for your work. We might not assign a lawyer or paralegal with the lowest hourly rate if, in our judgment, it may be in your best interests to assign a lawyer or paralegal with a higher hourly rate because of that

lawyer's or paralegal's skill and experience or because of the time constraints of the work. We record and bill our time in one-tenth hour (six-minute) units.

[INSERT CONTINGENT FEE ALTERNATIVE, IF APPLICABLE; CONSIDER ANY STATE STATUTE OR LAW THAT MAY APPLY; TAKE INTO ACCOUNT RESOLUTION BY SETTLEMENT AND THE POSSIBILITY OF APPEALS.]

You should note that there are certain limited circumstances in which there is a possibility that the opposing party's costs and/or fees could be awarded against you, for instance if [INSERT APPLICABLE ELEMENTS, FOR INSTANCE, "you are removed as a fiduciary or are found to have breached fiduciary duties, or if your suit is deemed to have been frivolous, vexatious, groundless or without substantial justification."] We will be discussing these issues with you from time to time during our representation, so you should not hesitate to ask about this if you have any concerns.

In addition to our legal fees, as described above, we will charge you for out-of-pocket expenses that we pay on your behalf and for our internal costs. Out-of-pocket expenses include items such as filing fees charged by government agencies, witness fees, transcription costs, and travel expenses. Our internal costs include items such as photocopying, long-distance telephone calls, fax transmissions, document scanning and electronic transmission, storage and retrieval, postage, overnight delivery, courier services, computer research charges, and complex document production. Rather than tracking precise costs for every single internal charge (which would ultimately result in higher hourly rates for our clients), we charge fixed costs for these types of expenses. Our charges for these internal costs may exceed the actual direct costs that we pay to outsiders (such as the telephone company or photocopying contractors).

Sometimes it is necessary to hire other persons to provide services for you, such as accounting or appraisal firms and other experts. Their work may have more confidentiality if we (rather than you) request their services, and so we may hire them. However, you will be responsible for paying their fees and expenses, whether paid directly to them or to us in reimbursement. We will seek your prior authorization to hire such persons if the anticipated expense will exceed $____. We have no obligation to incur or advance any expense exceeding $____ unless reimbursement is fully secured by an advance cost deposit.

Our bills are due when rendered. If a bill is not paid within 30 days after it is mailed to you, interest will accrue on the unpaid balance of that bill beginning on the thirty-first (31st) day and accruing thereafter at the rate of one percent (1%) per month. Interest charges will apply to specific monthly bills. Payments made on past-due accounts will be applied first to the oldest outstanding bill. If our bills are not paid reasonably soon after they are rendered, we reserve the right to stop work until your account is brought current and appropriate measures are taken to ensure prompt payment in the future. If we have to bring collection efforts for payment, you agree that you will pay the costs of collection procedures, including reasonable fees and costs incurred by us (whether paid to our firm or another firm retained by us).

We may require a retainer or advance fee deposit for your work. Unless you and we agree otherwise, the retainer or advance fee deposit will be applied to our final statement, and any unused portion will be returned to you. We may also request an advance cost deposit (in addition to the retainer or advance fee deposit) when we expect that we will incur substantial costs on your behalf. Each of you agrees that you will all be jointly and severally responsible for the payment of all amounts owed to us, and that we can seek payment in full from any one of you at our election. Any agreement among any of you to limit your responsibility for payment of amounts owed to us will not be binding upon us unless we agree in writing to those limits. Your joint and several responsibility for the payment of our fees and expenses includes the situation in which our representation is terminated for any reason prior to the completion of the [subject matter of the engagement].

It is understood that our fees and costs will be paid by you personally and will not be paid by or from the [trust/estate]. However, if the facts of this matter develop such that we believe that there is a basis for you to seek reimbursement from [the trust/estate/or other party] for some, or even all, of our fees and costs, then we will advise you accordingly.

In terms of how our fees and costs will be divided among you, [DESCRIBE BASIS FOR FEE DIVISION, SUCH AS EQUALLY, PROPORTIONATELY, ETC.; AND IF NOT EQUALLY, CONSIDER LISTING OF EACH CLIENT'S SHARE, AND ADDRESS WHETHER OR NOT THE CLIENTS ARE JOINTLY AND SEVERALLY RESPONSIBLE FOR THE FEES AND COSTS.]

Sincerely,

[Lawyer]

Reprinted with permission from The American College of Trust and Estate Counsel.

CHAPTER 10 ETHICS AND TECHNOLOGY

10.1 Introduction

New technologies are constantly emerging that improve a lawyer's ability to automate and deliver legal services. While these technologies offer many benefits that help increase efficiency, minimize mistakes, and decrease labor costs, there are also associated risks and pitfalls. As technology continues to evolve, so does the concept of a lawyer's duty of technology competence.

Recognizing the emergence of technology, its impact on the practice of law, and the importance of lawyers understanding technology, the ABA formed the Commission on Ethics 20/20 to study technology in law practice. Based on its findings, the ABA modified its model rules in 2012 to clarify that a lawyer's duty of competence includes both the substantive knowledge of the law and the competent use of technology. Comment 8 to model rule 1.1 provides: "To maintain the requisite knowledge and skill, a lawyer should keep abreast of changes in the law and its practice, *including the benefits and risks associated with relevant technology*...." (emphasis added). At the time of publication of this edition of the Guide, thirty-eight states have followed the ABA and adopted some version of comment 8 to model rule 1.1 imposing a duty of technology competence on lawyers. Florida and North Carolina currently require lawyers to complete a minimum number of hours of continuing legal education specifically on technology.

At the time of publication of this edition of the Guide, the State Bar of California proposed adding the following comment [1] to rule 1.1 of the Rules of Professional Conduct, Competence: "The duties set forth in this rule include the duty to keep abreast of the changes in the law and its practice, including the benefits and risks associated with relevant technology." This proposed comment highlights the importance of a lawyer's ethical obligations regarding technology.

In addition to the proposed comment [1] to rule 1.1 of the Rules of Professional Conduct, the duty of technology competence can be found embedded in various Rules of Professional Conduct. For example, rule 1.16(e) and comment 2 to rule 1.4 expressly permit a lawyer, upon request from a client after termination of a representation, to provide the client file by electronic mail. Also, the ethical responsibility of managerial and supervisory lawyers in rules 5.1 and 5.3 extends to ensuring that all lawyers and staff understand the technology used by the law firm and use it in compliance with a lawyer's ethical duties. Specific technology rules relate to the communication of lawyer services and advertising, including the use of websites and logos, as provided in rules 7.2 and 7.4, respectively.

Law schools now offer courses on the business of law, process management, and the use of data and technology to operate a law firm efficiently. For example, Suffolk University Law School in Boston offers an online Certificate in Legal Innovation and Technology, including courses such as process improvement and legal project management, design thinking for legal professionals, and the business of delivering legal services. This growing educational field shows that technology, automation, and artificial intelligence are changing how legal services are performed and delivered to clients, and how a law firm operates as a business.

The State Bar of California maintains an Ethics and Technology page on its publicly accessible website. On that page, the practitioner can find resources that analyze the ethical use of technology in a range of facts and circumstances. Those resources include original source ethics opinions, articles, and continuing education programs, with links to other State Bar pages and external links to local or specialty bar associations and other websites.

This chapter tracks the ethical duties discussed previously in this Guide: competence, confidentiality, securing client property, management and supervision, and communication. Each of those ethical duties is revisited with an eye on the specific implications of current technology. The chapter concludes with discussions on ethical advertising and artificial intelligence.

Article

Yokomoto, *Ethical Duty of Technology Competence* (2019) 61 Orange County Law., No. 10, p. 66.

10.2 Ethical Duty of Technology Competence

The duty of technology competence requires that lawyers have, at minimum, a baseline understanding of—and reasonable proficiency—in the technology that is currently being used and that is available. Specific competencies will vary among lawyers, law firms, practice areas, and types of client. To comply with the duty of technology competence, the lawyer has three choices: (1) sufficiently learn the necessary technology information and skills before undertaking the matter, (2) associate or consult with technical consultants or competent counsel, or (3) decline the representation. Rules Prof. Conduct, rule 1.1. Partners, associates, and staff may help, but a lawyer may not delegate the lawyer's baseline ethical duty to understand technology and use it competently.

In practice, a lawyer encounters widespread use of technology—with clients, opposing parties and counsel, courts, and witnesses. A lawyer may leverage technology such as automated document assembly, electronic court scheduling, and file sharing to deliver legal services. Internet-based searches and other research tools available online can assist in understanding the relevant facts or applicable law in a given case. Technology can also be used to present information or evidence in the courtroom. Technology competence includes an understanding of the technology that a lawyer currently uses in practice, the additional technology available, and the technology that a client or prospective client uses or owns. For example, if a lawyer is asked to represent a client in a matter involving data breaches, the lawyer needs to be versed in the specific software that the prospective client was using when the breach occurred.

For the trusts and estates practitioner, technology competence broadly covers two issues: the use of technology as a practice tool and the planning for the administration and distribution of digital assets. For the trust and probate litigation practitioner, the ethical duty may also include competence in electronic court filings and e-discovery.

Technology as a Practice Tool. Practitioners know that technology has superseded the days of secretarial shorthand, dictation, and typewriters; it has also superseded the days of stand-alone programs such MS Outlook, MS Word, and Time Slips. Technological platforms such as Clio and NetDocuments now offer integrated case management, contact management, document management, electronic mail management, client intake procedures, calendaring, time and expense tracking, billing, online payments, e-signatures, and other features in one software package. For firms with thousands of client files, transition to such a platform can be a costly investment, including migration of the firm's existing data to the new platform and then the ongoing monthly or annual cost of the technology itself. Nevertheless, with the rapid development of new programs and artificial intelligence, firms that do not transition may face higher costs later when implementation of certain platforms can no longer be ignored.

While this edition of the Guide was drafted and reviewed, the COVID-19 pandemic exploded around the world, highlighting the need for technological knowledge in the practice of law. In response to directives from the State of California, many law firms decided to shut down their physical offices temporarily. Law firms already working with cloud-based programs and shared files likely had an easier time making the transition than firms that needed to enable remote access into servers located at the office. Law firms set up for remote access through online programs, an internal department, or an offsite third-party company likely also had an easier transition. Functioning well away from the physical office was an adjustment. Telephones needed to be reprogrammed and mail scanned and emailed to the lawyers. Lawyers needed to learn how to communicate effectively with clients, partners, associates, and staff, and adequately supervise staff remotely.

The transition to working remotely shed new light on security and confidentiality issues. The use of Zoom, Skype, Go To Meeting, Microsoft Teams, and similar services increased dramatically. Privacy and security issues surfaced at a pace with increased use. While service providers quickly introduced encryption and security features for increased protection of data in transit and resistance to tampering, the initial security problems highlighted the lawyer's ethical duty to secure client information and keep it confidential. The COVID-19 pandemic put in stark relief the lawyer's ethical responsibility to remain current with technology, and to understand the risks of using technological devices and software in the lawyer's practice.

Lawyers who are not competent in the use of technology arguably put their clients at a disadvantage, and themselves at the risk of a malpractice claim. A violation of the ethical rule of technology competence does not by itself establish a breach of the standard of care in a malpractice action. Rules Prof. Conduct, rule 1.0(b). Nevertheless, a lawyer's violation of an ethical rule may be evidence of the breach of a professional or fiduciary duty on which a claim for damages could be based.

The incompetent use of technology when performing legal services can lead to inefficient work and unreasonably high fees. Rule 1.5 of the Rules of Professional Conduct prohibits a lawyer from collecting an unconscionable fee. A factor to be considered in determining unconscionability is the amount of the fee in proportion to the value of the services performed. Rules Prof. Conduct, rule 1.5(b)(3). Accordingly, the lack or improper use of technology could be a factor when an arbitrator or judge reviews an alleged violation of rule 1.5.

Planning for Digital Assets. Technology competence is also implicated for lawyers who practice estate planning and trust administration due to the growing presence, importance and value of digital assets. The lawyer must address two separate issues in planning for digital assets. First, the legal side—how to distribute the ownership of the digital assets, and second, the technology side—how to ensure access to the digital assets upon a user's death. Estate planners need to understand how both components relate to estate planning to explain the issues to a client competently so that the client can make informed decisions as to who will have access to the client's digital assets upon incapacity or death.

Estate planning for digital assets is different from planning for the distribution of a person's real property or business. Some digital assets may only be of a personal sentimental value, such as photos and journals, and some may have a monetary value, such as frequent flyer miles or a manuscript. Some digital assets may be protected by other duties of confidentiality, for example the patient records of a physician or psychiatrist. The planning area for digital assets was unclear for years. Because of privacy laws and other liability concerns, service providers often would not allow loved ones and other named fiduciaries to access the digital assets of a decedent. California's enactment of a variation of the Revised Uniform Fiduciary Access to Digital Assets Act has changed this planning area. Prob. Code, secs. 870-884.

The Revised Uniform Fiduciary Access to Digital Assets Act prescribes the methods an individual may use to direct the disclosure of digital assets upon death. First, a person may use a service provider's online tool. If one is not provided, then a person may give direction in a will, trust, or power of attorney. In the absence of both, a website's terms of service govern how to disclose information. As part of the estate planning discussion, the lawyer should advise the client regarding the importance of creating and maintaining an inventory of digital assets, listing where and how those assets are held, and including updated usernames, passwords, and answers to secret questions. In such an inventory the client should describe how the client wants to dispose of those assets. Then, the client needs to provide a named fiduciary with information on how to access the client's accounts and passwords.

A client may want to give heirs and beneficiaries access to digital assets that have monetary value, but not want a spouse or children to have access to all digital assets, such as private email accounts and photographs. Accordingly, estate planning lawyers must discuss with each client the options for limiting access to specific digital assets. Such discussions can be sensitive when planning for a married couple, if one spouse consents to the other spouse having access to that spouse's digital assets and the other one does not. A lawyer should consider whether different views on disclosure of digital assets give rise to a direct conflict of interest between spouses, or a significant risk to the joint representation of spouses in an estate planning matter, requiring either withdrawal or informed written consent to the continued representation. Rules Prof. Conduct, rule 1.7.

Digital assets include cryptocurrencies, such as the BitCoin, Eretheum, and Litcoin—digital currencies that use blockchain technology to create a decentralized, immutable, public ledger. Due to the potential value of such assets, an estate planning lawyer must understand how to plan for their valuation, and for their administration and disposition upon death. A critical part of cryptocurrencies is the private key or code that is the only way to recover those assets. The client may have a digital wallet with a cryptocurrency address or a private key. If a client dies without leaving information on how to access such a wallet or key, no financial institution or other authority exists to recover cryptocurrency, and its value may be lost permanently.

Electronic Court Filings and Virtual Court Appearances. California courts have moved towards electronic filing (e-filing) to enhance the efficiency of the judicial system. E-filing allows courts to process filings more efficiently with fewer clerks and less paper. Law firms and lawyers benefit from reduced costs by no longer requiring runners or clerks to be physically present at the courthouse to file papers. During the COVID-19 pandemic, courts in California began to require that judicial proceedings be conducted remotely, and that parties appear remotely for depositions by telephone or video conferencing technology. Even the Supreme Court of the United States began conducting oral arguments remotely in May 2020.

For a detailed discussion of the ethical use of technology to respond to discovery requests and the requirement to understand the client's use of such technology, see chapter 9 of this Guide, Ethics and Litigation, section 9.11.

ACTEC Commentaries on Model Rules of Professional Conduct, Model Rule 1.1

> *Competence with Technology*. A lawyer who uses technology to transmit or store client documents or communicates electronically with a client regarding the drafting of documents must be aware of the potential effects of such use of technology on client confidentiality and preservation of client information. A lawyer must stay reasonably informed about developments in technology used in client communications and document storage, including improvements, discoveries of risks and best practices.

Ethics Opinion

Before using a particular technology in the course of representing a client, a lawyer must take appropriate steps to evaluate: (1) the level of security attendant to the use of that technology, including whether reasonable precautions may be taken when using the technology to increase the level of security; (2) the legal ramifications to a third party who intercepts, accesses, or exceeds authorized use of the electronic information; (3) the degree of sensitivity of the information; (4) the possible impact on the client of an inadvertent disclosure of privileged or confidential information or work product; (5) the urgency of the situation; and (6) the client's instructions and circumstances, such as access by others to the client's devices and communications. State Bar of Cal. Com. on Prof. Resp. and Conduct, formal opn. No. 2010-179.

Articles

Wertlieb, Mohr & Burke Spencer, *Legal Ethics and the Coronavirus* (Apr. 3, 2020) Cal. Lawyers Assn.

Ambrogi, *At $1.2 Billion, 2019 Is a Record Year for Legal Tech Investments—And It's Only September!* (Sept. 16, 2019) Lawsites (The author surveys investment in law practice software with compelling statistics).

Streisand & Rees, *Cryptocurrencies and Trustees' Duty to Invest Prudently: Navigating Fiduciary Duties in the Age of Decentralization* (2018) 24 Cal. Trusts and Estates Q., Issue 3.

McEvoy, *Tips of the Trade: How to Help Client Avoid Taking Cryptocurrency to the Crypt* (2018) 24 Cal. Trusts and Estates Q., Issue 2.

Rosen-Prinz, *Planning for Digital Assets in California – Now with Less Uncertainty!* (2017) 23 Cal. Trusts and Estates Q., Issue 2.

10.3 Measuring Technology Competence

To measure compliance with the duty of technology competence, a practitioner may find the following questions helpful:

1. Are you comfortable using email and other electronic means to communicate with your clients?
2. Are you sending your client's confidential information in a secure manner that requires a password for access?
3. Are you scanning and saving your clients' estate plans to a secure storage site?
4. Are you comfortable using word processing and spreadsheet programs?
5. Can you use Adobe and redact confidential information from .pdf documents?
6. Does your firm maintain client information in a database that allows a thorough and quick conflicts check?
7. Is your firm's billing software up to date?
8. Has your firm established training and ongoing protocols for staff use of technology?
9. Are you comfortable using case management and document management software?
10. Do you know what technology your client uses and how that technology is incorporated into your client's business?
11. Do you understand how data security and e-discovery work and how your client, other lawyers, and courts are using them?

A lawyer informed and comfortable with technology can lead a firm into greater understanding of the related ethical duties. Analyzing the firm's needs and consulting with outside professionals can help a law firm select software and platforms that meet its current and anticipated practice needs. Monitoring and evaluating the regular updates of those programs can carry the practice into the foreseeable future.

To evaluate types of technology that a law firm might invest in and to determine its potential technological weaknesses, the practitioner may consider beginning with a list of all the firm's tasks. An outside technology consultant can help managerial and supervisory lawyers determine which programs will allow the firm to complete such tasks more efficiently.

1. *Conflicts Checks*. Many clients refer family members for estate planning or appoint family members as successor trustees and executors. Informed written consent may be required from each current, prospective, or former client by the rules 1.7 and 1.9 of the Rules of Professional Conduct. In a litigation context, before discussing a trust or probate challenge with a beneficiary, the lawyer must perform a conflicts check to determine if the lawyer drafted the subject documents or already represents the trustee or executor.

2. *Client Matters*. A firm can achieve significant time and cost savings by managing all email, documents, scans, billing, and invoices in one location. With a technological system incorporating all forms of firm communications, all information related to a client matter can be found at a single stroke.

3. *Digital Signatures*. Digital signature technology allows law firms and clients to sign documents securely. Law firms should consider an e-signature service provider that has a proven secure system, intuitive use, and access on mobile devices. Combining digital signatures with a system for engagement letters and online deposits can significantly decrease the time to engage a new client. Further advantages may include efficiency of sending documents to clients for signature and compiling completed agreements.

4. *Timekeeping*. Multiple timekeeping options are available including web-based, desktop, and mobile capabilities with calendar view and timers. Firms may also consider billing systems that accommodate fixed fee and hybrid timekeeping in addition to hourly. Client and matter entries should interface with Outlook, Google, or other online platforms the firm uses.

5. *Billing*. Software programs can track lawyer and paralegal time, as well as expenses and late fees. Pre-bills can be viewed online by the lawyers, and bills sent to the client electronically reduce the cost of mailing and may expedite payment.

6. *Client Trust Account*. Software can help the firm comply with the ethical duties related to a client trust account. That help ranges from accepting trust deposits, applying a deposit to billings, handling the associated trust accounting, paying an invoice from a trust account, all the way to reconciling a trust account.

7. *Reporting*. Software programs can create reports with time entry, expenses, trust transactions, and billing entries. Reports on the firm's timekeepers, originating lawyers on accounts receivable, work-in-progress, trial balances, and more may be invaluable in measuring the efficiency and profitability of the firm.

10.4 Use of Technology and the Duty of Confidentiality

A lawyer has the ethical duty to maintain inviolate the confidence, and at every peril preserve the secrets, of a client. Bus. & Prof. Code, sec. 6068, subd. (e). Existing and emerging technology places new imperatives on this familiar ethical duty. To comply with that duty, a lawyer must pay attention to such issues as password protection for client files held on a server or in the cloud, encryption of the email of the lawyer or the law firm, and ongoing monitoring of electronic files for phishing and ransomware.

The American Bar Association publishes commentary on its model rules. Comment 18 to model rule 1.6 (Acting Competently to Preserve Confidentiality) is instructive:

> Paragraph (c) [of Model Rule 1.6] requires a lawyer to act competently to safeguard information relating to the representation of a client against unauthorized access by third parties and against inadvertent or unauthorized disclosure by the lawyer or other persons who are participating in the representation of the client or who are subject to the lawyer's supervision. See Rules 1.1, 5.1 and 5.3. The unauthorized access to, or the inadvertent or unauthorized disclosure of, information relating to the representation of a client does not constitute a violation of paragraph (c) if the lawyer has made reasonable efforts to prevent the access or disclosure. Factors to be considered in determining the reasonableness of the lawyer's efforts include, but are not limited to, the sensitivity of the information, the likelihood of disclosure if additional safeguards are not employed, the cost of employing additional safeguards, the difficulty of implementing the safeguards, and the extent to which the safeguards adversely affect the lawyer's ability to represent clients (e.g., by making a device or important piece of software excessively difficult to use). A client may require the lawyer to implement special security measures not required by this Rule or may give informed consent to forgo security measures that would otherwise be required by this Rule.

In its Formal Opinion Number 2010-179, the State Bar of California Committee on Professional Responsibility and Conduct discusses specific examples of the duty of confidentiality applied to technology. The opinion concludes that a lawyer can use a laptop computer consistent with the duty of confidentiality if such use is limited to authorized individuals to perform required tasks, and that use is supported by training in the ethical duty of confidentiality. Depending on the sensitivity of the matter, a lawyer may need to avoid using a public wireless connection entirely or notify the client of possible risks. The loss or failure of the laptop computer and possible breach of client confidentiality and the lawyer-client privilege would be among those risks.

Texting has become more commonly used for communications between lawyers and clients since the issuance of Formal Opinion Number 2010-179. The ethical obligations of competence, security, and confidentiality in that opinion apply just as persuasively to different forms of communication technology as they emerge. The practitioner might consider technology platforms that are linked to lawyers' devices to comply with those obligations. Those platforms are designed to automatically retrieve email or text messages from lawyers' devices, store those messages, and relate them to a client file at the law firm. Technological retrieval and secure storage guard against loss of client data and defend against a claim of waiver of the lawyer-client privilege.

The ethical duty of confidentiality in an internet-based practice is the same as for a practice in a traditional office but requires specific diligence. The State Bar of California Committee on

Professional Responsibility and Conduct discusses the ethical duties related to a virtual law office in its Formal Opinion Number 2012-184. That opinion concludes that basic precautions would likely be sufficient to comply with ethical rules and protect confidentiality: client communications restricted to a secure internet portal created on the lawyer's website, storage and access to client information only through that portal that is password protected and encrypted, and assignment of a separate password to each client allowing access to information relating to that client's matter only. These requirements for a virtual law office suggest appropriate safeguards when a lawyer in a traditional office stores client information on the cloud. The technological base for a lawyer's practice does not change the lawyer's ethical duties, and will require investigation and understanding of the risks as well as the benefits of operating an internet-based practice.

Reliance on an internet service provider to store and protect client information raises specific ethical issues. Formal Opinion Number 2012-184 discusses the lawyer's ongoing duty to reassess systems periodically to confirm that they remain at the level for which the lawyer initially contracted, and that changes in the provider's business environment or management do not negatively affect their adequacy. In addition, the opinion suggests that the lawyer consider whether ethical duties require the client's consent to an outside internet service provider receiving and exclusively storing the client's confidential information.

The lawyer working remotely from the office is becoming increasingly common. During the COVID-19 pandemic and public health orders requiring social distancing, a broad spectrum of lawyers established offices in their homes with remote access to client files. If a lawyer's personal wireless system has been configured with appropriate security features, a lawyer would not violate the ethical duties of confidentiality and competence by working on a client's matter at home. Local security features available for use on individual computers include operating system firewalls, antivirus and antispam software, secure username and password combinations, and file permissions. Corresponding network safeguards that may be employed include network firewalls and network access controls such as virtual private networks inspection and monitoring. A home office without such security features is akin to an insecure public wireless connection, and a lawyer may need to seek informed consent from a client for its use. Cal. State Bar Com. on Prof. Resp. and Conduct, formal opn. No. 2010-179.

Advice to Clients. To inform the client and ensure protection of client communications and other information, the lawyer may discuss the following confidentiality issues as part of the initial engagement and regularly during the course of the representation:

1. Breach of confidentiality by the "reply all" email. Convenient clicks need to be thought through to avoid an inadvertent waiver of the ethical duty of confidentiality, or the lawyer-client privilege.
2. Client waiver of confidentiality by forwarding a lawyer's email to an accountant or other advisor. Evidence Code section 952 allows limited disclosures of confidential information to facilitate transmission of information or accomplishment of the purpose for which the lawyer is consulted. The lawyer and the client should make such disclosures jointly, deliberately, and sparingly.
3. Policies of client's employer regarding access to email stored on a company or firm server. If the employer reserves the right of access to employee emails, a lawyer and client should not use an office email to communicate about a represented matter.

4. Back-up of client communications and other data with a strong password and encryption.
5. Appointment of a custodian for digital assets and the preparation and maintenance of a list of digital assets and related passwords.
6. Amendment of estate planning documents to give a named fiduciary authority to access a client's digital files, including the contents of electronic communications to the lawyer.

Advice to Fiduciaries. A fiduciary client is nonetheless a client, and the lawyer should discuss the same issues regarding technological security of lawyer-client communications with a fiduciary client. A trust or estate administration raises specific ethical and administrative issues related to technology. To inform the client acting in a fiduciary capacity and to ensure protection of client communications and other information, the lawyer may discuss the following additional confidentiality issues with the fiduciary client:

1. Understanding the role of the lawyer for the fiduciary. When communicating with the beneficiaries, the fiduciary client can reinforce the lawyer's ethical duty to notify the beneficiaries that the fiduciary is the lawyer's only client, and that the lawyer does not represent the trust or estate as a whole or any beneficiary.
2. Maintenance of the trust records. Technology can assist the trustee in fulfilling the fiduciary duty to store, give access to, and produce accurate information regarding the activities of the trustee, and the income, expenses, assets, and liabilities of the trust administration. Digital records can also assist in the preparation of a final account, and fiduciary income and estate tax returns.
3. Response to requests for information from the beneficiaries. Maintaining the trust records in digital or electronic form can facilitate requests for a report and transparency of the trust administration. In a contentious administration, the trustee may consider allowing beneficiaries to access certain financial statements online.
4. Discussion of the interrelation of the lawyer-client privilege with the fiduciary duty to report trust information to the trust or estate beneficiaries and to disclose the trust records. That fiduciary duty to report does not require the disclosure of lawyer-client communications, if confidentiality is preserved.
5. Log of hours spent and services performed in the trust or estate administration. A regular and contemporaneous log will justify the trustee's fee and support a court petition for allowance of fees. In an estate administration, the executor or administrator may also need to show that hours spent performing extraordinary services are not disproportionate to those spent on ordinary services. *Estate of Trynin* (1989) 49 Cal.3d 868.
6. Segregated communications for issues of personal liability. A fiduciary client should maintain separate records and inform the lawyer of all activities that may implicate the fiduciary's personal liability. The lawyer can then advise the fiduciary client whether separate representation is necessary or advisable. For a further discussion of the related issues regarding the lawyer-client privilege, see chapter 6 of this Guide, Confidentiality of Information, sections 6.13 and 6.14.

Commentary on ABA Model Rules of Professional Conduct, Model Rule 1.6

> [19] When transmitting a communication that includes information relating to the representation of a client, the lawyer must take reasonable precautions to prevent the information from coming into the hands of unintended recipients. This duty, however, does not require that the lawyer use special security measures if the method of communication affords a reasonable expectation of privacy. Special circumstances, however, may warrant special precautions. Factors to be considered in determining the reasonableness of the lawyer's expectation of confidentiality include the sensitivity of the information and the extent to which the privacy of the communication is protected by law or by a confidentiality agreement. A client may require the lawyer to implement special security measures not required by this Rule or may give informed consent to the use of a means of communication that would otherwise be prohibited by this Rule. Whether a lawyer may be required to take additional steps in order to comply with other law, such as state and federal laws that govern data privacy, is beyond the scope of these Rules.

Ethics Opinions

A lawyer communicating with a client by email ordinarily must warn the client about the risk of sending or receiving electronic communications when there is a risk that a third party may gain access. A lawyer must use reasonable efforts to prevent inadvertent disclosure or unauthorized access. ABA Com. on Ethics and Prof. Resp., formal opn. No. 2011-459.

A lawyer may transmit information relating to the representation of a client by unencrypted email without violating the ethical duty of confidentiality because email affords a reasonable expectation of privacy from a technological and legal standpoint. Email poses no greater risk of interception or disclosure than other non-electronic forms of communication. Nevertheless, a lawyer should consult with the client and follow the client's instructions on how to transmit highly sensitive information relating to the clients' representation. ABA Com. on Ethics and Prof. Resp., formal opn. No. 1999-413.

As it pertains to the use of technology, the Business and Professions Code and the Rules of Professional Conduct do not impose greater or different duties upon a virtual law office (VLO) practitioner operating in the cloud than they do upon a lawyer practicing in a traditional law office. While a lawyer may maintain a VLO in the cloud where communications with the client, and storage of and access to all information about the client's matter, are conducted solely through the internet using a third-party's secure servers, the lawyer may be required to take additional steps to confirm compliance with a lawyer's ethical obligations due to distinct issues raised by the hypothetical VLO and its operation. Failure of the lawyer to comply with all ethical obligations relevant to these issues will preclude the operation of a VLO in the cloud. State Bar of Cal. Com. on Prof. Resp. and Conduct, formal opn. No. 2012-184.

In accepting credit card payments, a lawyer has the ethical duty to protect a client's personal data. Credit card issuers require a description on the credit card charge slip of the goods or services provided. In furnishing such a description, the lawyer may not disclose confidential information without the client's informed consent. State Bar of Cal. Com. on Prof. Resp. and Conduct, formal opn. No. 2007-172.

10.5 Use of Technology and the Duty to Secure Client Property

Lawyers save client and firm information in a variety of ways, including paper files, computer hard drives, a firm's dedicated server, or in the cloud. The lawyer's area of practice, size of the firm, and type of client may dictate the means that the lawyer uses to secure client property. Rule 1.16(e)(1) of the Rules of Professional Conduct defines "client materials and property" to include "correspondence, pleadings, deposition transcripts, experts' reports and other writings, exhibits, and physical evidence, whether in tangible, electronic or other form, and other items reasonably necessary to the client's representation, whether the client has paid for them or not." The lawyer must restore these materials and property to the client upon request when the representation ends, which necessarily includes the duty to secure that client property during the course of the representation.

Paper files can require a large amount of physical storage space and be easily subject to loss or destruction. Individual computer hard drives have space limitations and are subject to computer crashes.

Law firms commonly use a server for information storage. Other computers in the law firm must access the server to view, create, edit data, documents, and emails. While the server allows access to shared information with larger storage capacity than on individual computers, a failed or compromised server may leave all the firm files inaccessible.

Cloud computing uses a network of remote servers hosted in the internet to store, manage, and process data. Many available software programs and platforms use cloud computing. While storage and server breakdowns are not an issue with cloud-based programs, security continues to be a concern that lawyers and firms need to address.

ABA Formal Ethics Opinion Number 18-483 addresses a lawyer's obligation after an electronic data breach or a cyberattack has compromised digital files maintained in the lawyer's practice. The opinion defined a data breach as "a data event where material client confidential information is misappropriated, destroyed or otherwise compromised, or where a lawyer's ability to perform the legal services for which the lawyer is hired is significantly impaired by the episode." A lawyer who detects a data breach involving, or likely involving, confidential client information has an ethical duty to notify clients of the breach. The lawyer must take reasonable steps to mitigate the breach consistent with the Model Rules of Professional Conduct. Model rule 1.1, Competence, requires that the lawyer act promptly to stop a data breach and to alleviate further damage. Model rule 1.4, Communication, requires that the lawyer give reasonable notice to clients allowing time for employment of other counsel, and surrender papers and property to which clients are entitled. Lawyers would appropriately establish data destruction policies in accordance with these ethical duties. Further, an ethical violation may occur if a lawyer does not employ reasonable steps to "avoid data loss or to detect cyber-intrusion, and that lack of reasonable effort causes a breach."

ABA Formal Ethics Opinion Number 2018-482 discusses the ethical obligations of a lawyer when a disaster destroys client files. In such an event, a lawyer must comply with the ethical duty of communication in model rule 1.4 that requires the lawyer to keep clients reasonably apprised of the status of a representation. The same ethical duty applies in rule 1.4 of the Rules of Professional Conduct. A lawyer must evaluate available methods to maintain communication with clients while the disaster continues. The opinion suggests that lawyers keep electronic lists of current clients in a manner that is easily accessible.

If a disaster causes the loss of client files, lawyers must also consider their ethical duties under model rule 1.15 requiring lawyers to safeguard client property. The same ethical duty applies in rule 1.15 of the Rules of Professional Conduct. For current clients, lawyers should attempt first to reconstruct files from other sources. If reconstruction is not possible, the lawyer must notify clients of the loss of files or property. To prevent such losses, "lawyers should maintain an electronic copy of important documents in an off-site location that is updated regularly." ABA Formal Ethics Opns., formal opn. No. 2018-482, p. 9.

At the time of publication of this edition of the Guide, the State Bar of California Committee on Professional Responsibility and Conduct invited public comment on Formal Opinion Number 16-0002. That proposed opinion addresses the ethical duty of a lawyer or law firm to secure digital client information from unauthorized access and to advise clients of a data breach. The proposed opinion concludes that in the event of a breach, lawyers have an obligation to conduct a reasonable inquiry to determine the extent and consequences of the breach, and to notify any current client whose interests have a reasonable possibility of being negatively impacted by the breach. The proposed opinion does not opine on whether the lawyer or law firm is required to notify an affected *former* client.

Cyber Risk Insurance. Cyber risk insurance may compensate a law firm for disruption to services, cost of data recovery, or damage to the firm reputation from a data breach or cyberattack. The firm malpractice carrier may offer hacksurance to protect against cyberattacks and hacking, cyber theft and cyber fraud, and other criminal activities that result in lost or destroyed data. Computer data loss and restoration coverage may address losses when a computer is stolen or damaged and data cannot be restored or retrieved. Just as one significant estate plan or trust administration malpractice claim can injure a practice, so could one cyberattack that results in lost client information and the exposure of client confidential information.

Ethics Opinions

Lawyers need to evaluate "(1) the level of security attendant to the use of that technology, including whether reasonable precautions may be taken when using the technology to increase the level of security; (2) the legal ramifications to a third party who intercepts, accesses or exceeds authorized use of the electronic information; (3) the degree of sensitivity of the information; (4) the possible impact on the client of an inadvertent disclosure of privileged or confidential information or work product; (5) the urgency of the situation; and (6) the client's instructions and circumstances, such as access by others to the client's devices and communications." State Bar of Cal. Com. on Prof. Resp. and Conduct, formal opn. No. 2010-179.

Lawyers have ethical obligations to protect confidential client information when transmitting information relating to the representation over the internet. The opinion looks at advances in technology and ever-increasing cyber security threats, and provides guidance as to when enhanced security measures are appropriate. ABA Com. on Ethics and Prof. Resp., formal opn. No. 2017-477R.

10.6 Use of Technology and the Duty to Manage and Supervise

California Rules of Professional Conduct, Rule 5.1 - Responsibilities of Managerial and Supervisory Lawyers

> (a) A lawyer who individually or together with other lawyers possesses managerial authority in a law firm,* shall make reasonable* efforts to ensure that the firm* has in effect measures giving reasonable* assurance that all lawyers in the firm* comply with these rules and the State Bar Act.
>
> (b) A lawyer having direct supervisory authority over another lawyer, whether or not a member or employee of the same law firm,* shall make reasonable* efforts to ensure that the other lawyer complies with these rules and the State Bar Act.
>
> (c) A lawyer shall be responsible for another lawyer's violation of these rules and the State Bar Act if:
>
> > (1) the lawyer orders or, with knowledge of the relevant facts and of the specific conduct, ratifies the conduct involved; or
> >
> > (2) the lawyer, individually or together with other lawyers, possesses managerial authority in the law firm* in which the other lawyer practices, or has direct supervisory authority over the other lawyer, whether or not a member or employee of the same law firm,* and knows* of the conduct at a time when its consequences can be avoided or mitigated but fails to take reasonable* remedial action.

California Rules of Professional Conduct, Rule 5.3 - Responsibilities Regarding Nonlawyer Assistants

> With respect to a nonlawyer employed or retained by or associated with a lawyer:
>
> (a) a lawyer who individually or together with other lawyers possesses managerial authority in a law firm,* shall make reasonable* efforts to ensure that the firm* has in effect measures giving reasonable* assurance that the nonlawyer's conduct is compatible with the professional obligations of the lawyer;
>
> (b) a lawyer having direct supervisory authority over the nonlawyer, whether or not an employee of the same law firm,* shall make reasonable* efforts to ensure that the person's* conduct is compatible with the professional obligations of the lawyer; and

(c) a lawyer shall be responsible for conduct of such a person* that would be a violation of these rules or the State Bar Act if engaged in by a lawyer if:

(1) the lawyer orders or, with knowledge of the relevant facts and of the specific conduct, ratifies the conduct involved; or

(2) the lawyer, individually or together with other lawyers, possesses managerial authority in the law firm* in which the person* is employed, or has direct supervisory authority over the person,* whether or not an employee of the same law firm,* and knows* of the conduct at a time when its consequences can be avoided or mitigated but fails to take reasonable* remedial action.

An asterisk (*) identifies a defined term in rule 1.0.1 of the Rules of Professional Conduct. For further discussion of a defined term, see chapter 2 of this Guide, Terminology.

Rules 5.1 and 5.3 of the Rules of Professional Conduct require managerial and supervisory lawyers who delegate tasks to subordinates, whether junior lawyers or paralegals, to train and supervise them to ensure compliance with the ethical rules. The supervising lawyer needs to understand the technology enough to give clear direction, ask relevant questions, and determine that the tasks are completed properly and ethically. The duty of supervising lawyers to keep client information confidential includes training staff on the use of reasonably secure methods to transmit information to clients and third parties.

Many lawyers today use software to create revocable and irrevocable trusts, wills, and related estate planning documents. A supervising lawyer must understand how the software functions and train staff on the use of it, from inputting data to compiling the documents. Neither the lawyer nor the staff may cede independent judgment regarding the client's estate plan to a technological tool.

Managerial lawyers have a corresponding ethical duty to monitor the technology services that outside consultants perform for the lawyer or law firm. The managerial lawyer needs to frame the ethical issues for the consultant when technology is installed and monitor the technology for ongoing compliance.

Comment on California Rules of Professional Conduct, Rule 5.1

[1] Paragraph (a) requires lawyers with managerial authority within a law firm* to make reasonable* efforts to establish internal policies and procedures designed, for example, to detect and resolve conflicts of interest, identify dates by which actions must be taken in pending matters, account for client funds and property, and ensure that inexperienced lawyers are properly supervised.

[2] Whether particular measures or efforts satisfy the requirements of paragraph (a) might depend upon the law firm's structure and the nature of its practice, including the size of the law firm,* whether it has more than one office location or practices in more than one jurisdiction, or whether the firm* or its partners* engage in any ancillary business.

[3] A partner,* shareholder or other lawyer in a law firm* who has intermediate managerial responsibilities satisfies paragraph (a) if the law firm* has a designated managing lawyer charged with that responsibility, or a management committee or other body that has appropriate managerial authority and is charged with that responsibility. For example, the managing lawyer of an office of a multi-office law firm* would not necessarily be required to promulgate firm-wide policies intended to reasonably* assure that the law firm's lawyers comply with the rules or State Bar Act. However, a lawyer remains responsible to take corrective steps if the lawyer knows* or reasonably should know* that the delegated body or person* is not providing or implementing measures as required by this rule.

[4] Paragraph (a) also requires managerial lawyers to make reasonable* efforts to assure that other lawyers in an agency or department comply with these rules and the State Bar Act. This rule contemplates, for example, the creation and implementation of reasonable* guidelines relating to the assignment of cases and the distribution of workload among lawyers in a public sector legal agency or other legal department. e.g., State Bar of California, Guidelines on Indigent Defense Services Delivery Systems (2006).

Comment on California Rules of Professional Conduct, Rule 5.3

Lawyers often utilize nonlawyer personnel, including secretaries, investigators, law student interns, and paraprofessionals. Such assistants, whether employees or independent contractors, act for the lawyer in rendition of the lawyer's professional services. A lawyer must give such assistants appropriate instruction and supervision concerning all ethical aspects of their employment. The measures employed in instructing and supervising nonlawyers should take account of the fact that they might not have legal training.

Article

Wertlieb, Mohr & Burke Spencer, *Legal Ethics and the Coronavirus* (Apr. 3, 2020) Cal. Lawyers Assn. The authors discuss that the duty to preserve client property is a non-delegable duty.

10.7 Use of Technology and the Duty to Communicate

Rule 1.4 of the Rules of Professional Conduct defines the lawyer's ethical duty to communicate with a client. The client defines both the scope of representation and the means by which the goals of the representation are pursued. Consistent with that deference to the client, rule 1.4(a)(2) imposes on a lawyer the specific ethical duty to "reasonably consult with the client about the means to accomplish the client's objectives in the representation." Technology will be one of the means to accomplish those objectives.

The first step in complying with the ethical duty in rule 1.4 of the Rules of Professional Conduct is to establish the terms of ongoing communication between lawyer and client, and the specific issues that communication by email or social media may raise. A lawyer may transmit information to a client through an unencrypted email without violating the ethical duty of confidentiality because email affords a reasonable expectation of privacy from a technological and legal standpoint. ABA Com. on Ethics and Prof. Resp., formal opn. No. 1999-413. A lawyer must always follow the client's instructions regarding communication through technology.

A heightened ethical duty applies when the lawyer sends or receives substantive client communications by email or other electronic means, and potential third-party access to those communications is a significant risk. The lawyer has a duty to be aware of those risks and communicate them to the client. ABA Committee on Ethics and Professional Responsibility, Formal Opinion Number 2011-459 discusses communication with a client through the client's workplace computer or other employer-owned telecommunications device. Employers often have policies reserving a right of access to employees' email correspondence through the employer's email account, computers, or other devices. When the lawyer represents the employee in a matter, such policies compromise the client's ability to claim confidentiality. Third parties may possibly obtain access to an employee's electronic communications by issuing a subpoena to the employer. A sample disclosure on these communication issues to be included in an engagement letter is set forth in section 10.8 of this chapter.

A lawyer has a further ethical duty to maintain ongoing communication with the client in the event of a public emergency or catastrophic failure to the lawyer's own server or operating systems. ABA Com. on Ethics and Prof. Resp., formal opn. No. 2018-482. To be able to reach clients in such circumstances, lawyers should maintain, or be able to create on short notice, electronic or paper lists of current clients and their contact information. This information should be stored in a manner that is easily accessible. Clients will need to know whether the lawyer remains available to handle the client's matters, and what court appearances may be postponed. The opinion suggests that information about how to contact the lawyer in the event of an emergency may be provided in the engagement letter. Closures during the COVID-19 pandemic were a timely example of the need to alter the usual methods of communicating to clients to respond to changed circumstances, either internal or external to the lawyer's office.

San Diego County Bar Ethics Opinion Number 2018-3 provides guidance to a lawyer who may be considering a range of technological tools to pursue a client's case. That opinion poses the hypothetical of a lawyer litigating a matter regarding a complex series of investments that the client engaged in, and the financial and business performance of each investment. The document production in that litigation involved over 10 million documents. The lawyer in the hypothetical determined that hiring document reviewers would be cost prohibitive, and the lawyer could not supervise the work of the several hundred contract lawyers adequately. The lawyer chose instead to use technology assisted review to identify responsive documents. The lawyer had used the particular technology before, and used the recommended amount of seed sets to identify documents as responsive or not responsive. The opinion frames the ethical issues not just as a matter of competence but also as a matter of communication. The lawyer's ethical duty is to communicate with the client about the advantages and disadvantages of using a particular technology tool as part of the lawyer's duty to discuss with the client the means to pursue the goals of the representation. For a further discussion of this opinion, see chapter 9 of this Guide, Ethics and Litigation, Section 9.11.

10.8 Sample Disclosure in an Engagement Letter

The following provisions may be adapted for inclusion in an engagement letter to inform the client that communications may be sent and received electronically and to discuss the associated risks. The lawyer may also keep this client disclosure to present as evidence when making a breach of data claim to a professional liability carrier. The lawyer should adapt them thoughtfully to the lawyer's customary practice and the needs of a particular client representation.

> Dear [Client],
>
> In performing the legal services that are the subject of the representation set forth in this letter, we may send to you, or receive from you, communications transmitted through email or other electronic means. You should be aware of the risk that an unauthorized third party may access an unencrypted email, especially if you use a business-provided, borrowed, or public device or email address. Even if no data breach occurs, the use of an insecure connection may compromise your ability to claim the duty of confidentiality or the lawyer-client privilege to protect our communications from disclosure.
>
> By signing below, you consent to this firm sending you communication by email or other electronic means. Please notify us immediately, in writing, if you become aware of any hacking into your email account or other access by another person. Please also notify us, in writing, if you do not want us to send communications to you through email or other electronic means.
>
> Sincerely,
>
> [Lawyer]

10.9 Use of Technology and the Communication of Services

California Rules of Professional Conduct, Rule 7.1 - Communication Concerning a Lawyer's Services

> (a) A lawyer shall not make a false or misleading communication about the lawyer or the lawyer's services. A communication is false or misleading if it contains a material misrepresentation of fact or law, or omits a fact necessary to make the communication considered as a whole not materially misleading.
>
> (b) The Board of Trustees of the State Bar may formulate and adopt standards as to communications that will be presumed to violate rule 7.1, 7.2, 7.3, 7.4 or 7.5. The standards shall only be used as presumptions affecting the burden of proof in disciplinary proceedings involving alleged violations of these rules. "Presumption affecting the burden of proof" means that presumption defined in Evidence Code

sections 605 and 606. Such standards formulated and adopted by the Board, as from time to time amended, shall be effective and binding on all lawyers.

California Rules of Professional Conduct, Rule 7.4 - Communication of Fields of Practice and Specialization

(a) A lawyer shall not state that the lawyer is a certified specialist in a particular field of law, unless: (1) the lawyer is currently certified as a specialist by the Board of Legal Specialization, or any other entity accredited by the State Bar to designate specialists pursuant to standards adopted by the Board of Trustees; and (2) the name of the certifying organization is clearly identified in the communication.

(b) Notwithstanding paragraph (a), a lawyer may communicate the fact that the lawyer does or does not practice in particular fields of law. A lawyer may also communicate that his or her practice specializes in, is limited to, or is concentrated in a particular field of law, subject to the requirements of rule 7.1.

Rule 7.1 of the Rules of Professional Conduct is the companion to rule 4.1 and Business and Professions Code section 6157.1. Each cited authority prohibits the lawyer from making false or misleading statements, and rule 7.1 applies that ethical duty to communications about services to be provided to the client. The ethical prohibition applies not only to affirmative misrepresentations of fact, but also to omissions of fact that under the circumstances render a statement false or misleading. For a further discussion of the ethical duty of accurate communication to third parties, see chapter 7 of this Guide, Communication, section 7.2. Connection requests on social media are subject to the same duty prohibiting false and misleading statements, as discussed in chapter 9 of this Guide, Ethics and Litigation, section 9.7.

Rule 7.4 of the Rules of Professional Conduct codifies existing ethics authority prohibiting a lawyer from claiming to be a "specialist," "expert," or similar term unless certified by the California State Board of Specialization. The State Bar Legal Specialization Program was created pursuant to California Rules of Court, rule 9.35 and is maintained by the Board of Legal Specialization. The Board currently certifies specialists in the fields of Estate Planning, Trust and Probate Law and Taxation. Certification includes specific practice requirements in the field of specialization, an examination and application for initial certification, and re-certification every five years. A lawyer may use the logo on the law firm website and electronic mail, as well as print it on business cards and letterhead. A lawyer may not use the logo of the Board of Legal Specialization unless in good standing as a certified specialist with the State Bar of California.

STATE BAR OF CALIFORNIA
CBLS
CALIFORNIA BOARD OF LEGAL SPECIALIZATION

Comment on California Rules of Professional Conduct, Rule 7.1

[1] This rule governs all communications of any type whatsoever about the lawyer or the lawyer's services, including advertising permitted by rule 7.2. A communication includes any message or offer made by or on behalf of a lawyer concerning the availability for professional employment of a lawyer or a lawyer's law firm* directed to any person.*

[2] A communication that contains an express guarantee or warranty of the result of a particular representation is a false or misleading communication under this rule. (See also Bus. & Prof. Code, § 6157.2, subd. (a).)

[3] This rule prohibits truthful statements that are misleading. A truthful statement is misleading if it omits a fact necessary to make the lawyer's communication considered as a whole not materially misleading. A truthful statement is also misleading if it is presented in a manner that creates a substantial* likelihood that it will lead a reasonable* person* to formulate a specific conclusion about the lawyer or the lawyer's services for which there is no reasonable* factual foundation. Any communication that states or implies "no fee without recovery" is also misleading unless the communication also expressly discloses whether or not the client will be liable for costs.

[4] A communication that truthfully reports a lawyer's achievements on behalf of clients or former clients, or a testimonial about or endorsement of the lawyer, may be misleading if presented so as to lead a reasonable* person* to form an unjustified expectation that the same results could be obtained for other clients in similar matters without reference to the specific factual and legal circumstances of each client's case. Similarly, an unsubstantiated comparison of the lawyer's services or fees with the services or fees of other lawyers may be misleading if presented with such specificity as would lead a reasonable* person* to conclude that the comparison can be substantiated. An appropriate disclaimer or qualifying language often avoids creating unjustified expectations.

Statute

California Business and Professions Code section 6157.2, Advertisements – False, Misleading or Deceptive

> No advertisement shall contain any false, misleading, or deceptive statement or omit to state any fact necessary to make the statements made, in light of circumstances under which they are made, not false, misleading, or deceptive.

Ethics Opinion

A lawyer who provides a link to website visitors who are seeking legal services and advice, whether by email or some other form of electronic communication on the website, may effectively disclaim owing a duty of confidentiality to a visitor, but only if the disclaimer is in sufficiently plain terms to defeat the reasonable belief that the lawyer is consulting confidentially with the visitor. State Bar of Cal. Com. on Prof. Resp. and Conduct, formal opn. No. 2005-168.

Case Study

As part of an effort to recognize Law Day, a local radio station invites Lawyer to answer legal questions posed by the station's listeners. Lawyer agrees to appear without compensation to answer questions "live and on the air." The host of the radio program announces that callers should not expect their conversations with Lawyer to be held in confidence, and that the legal information provided "on the air" is not a substitute for callers hiring a lawyer to advise them about personal legal matters. Despite periodic announcements and confidentiality disclaimers during the course of the program, specific information about the caller's identity and legal issue is sometimes disclosed. During the show, a caller poses a question about a probate matter. Lawyer provides a generalized answer that, regrettably, is incorrect and misstates the law. During their conversation Lawyer cautions the caller that the question is outside Lawyer's area of expertise and suggests that the caller select and consult with a lawyer who practices in the area of probate law.

What ethical issues do public communications on a radio call-in show raise and how should Lawyer address them?

The context of a radio call-in show or similar format is unlikely to support a reasonable belief by the caller that the lawyer fielding questions agrees to act as the caller's lawyer or to assume any of the ethical duties that flow from a lawyer-client relationship. Nevertheless, Lawyer should keep in mind the limitations of the call-in format and Lawyer's own expertise. Because the purpose of the call-in show is to provide legal information to the public at large, Lawyer should avoid answering questions when unfamiliar with an area of law. State Bar of Cal. Com. on Prof. Resp. and Conduct, formal opn. No. 2003-164.

The opinion analyzes and bases its conclusion on California case law and former rules 3-110, 3-300, and 3-310 of the Rules of Professional Conduct. That analysis regarding a call-in radio show translates easily to a podcast, webinar with email link, or chat room.

Ethical duties to prospective clients are now set forth in rule 1.18 of the Rules of Professional Conduct. For a further discussion of the ethical duty of confidentiality to a prospective client, see chapter 6 of this Guide, Confidentiality of Information, section 6.18.

10.10 Use of Technology and Online Advertising

California Rules of Professional Conduct, Rule 7.2 - Advertising

> (a) Subject to the requirements of rules 7.1 and 7.3, a lawyer may advertise services through any written,* recorded or electronic means of communication, including public media.

(b) A lawyer shall not compensate, promise or give anything of value to a person* for the purpose of recommending or securing the services of the lawyer or the lawyer's law firm,* except that a lawyer may:

(1) pay the reasonable* costs of advertisements or communications permitted by this rule;

(2) pay the usual charges of a legal services plan or a qualified lawyer referral service. A qualified lawyer referral service is a lawyer referral service established, sponsored and operated in accordance with the State Bar of California's Minimum Standards for a Lawyer Referral Service in California;

(3) pay for a law practice in accordance with rule 1.17;

(4) refer clients to another lawyer or a nonlawyer professional pursuant to an arrangement not otherwise prohibited under these Rules or the State Bar Act that provides for the other person* to refer clients or customers to the lawyer, if: (i) the reciprocal referral arrangement is not exclusive; and (ii) the client is informed of the existence and nature of the arrangement;

(5) offer or give a gift or gratuity to a person* having made a recommendation resulting in the employment of the lawyer or the lawyer's law firm,* provided that the gift or gratuity was not offered or given in consideration of any promise, agreement, or understanding that such a gift or gratuity would be forthcoming or that referrals would be made or encouraged in the future.

(c) Any communication made pursuant to this rule shall include the name and address of at least one lawyer or law firm* responsible for its content.

California Rules of Professional Conduct, Rule 7.3 - Solicitation

(a) A lawyer shall not by in-person, live telephone or real-time electronic contact solicit professional employment when a significant motive for doing so is the lawyer's pecuniary gain, unless the person* contacted:

(1) is a lawyer; or

(2) has a family, close personal, or prior professional relationship with the lawyer.

(b) A lawyer shall not solicit professional employment by written,* recorded or electronic communication or by in-person, telephone or real-time electronic contact even when not otherwise prohibited by paragraph (a), if:

(1) the person* being solicited has made known* to the lawyer a desire not to be solicited by the lawyer; or

(2) the solicitation is transmitted in any manner which involves intrusion, coercion, duress or harassment.

(c) Every written,* recorded or electronic communication from a lawyer soliciting professional employment from any person* known* to be in need of legal services in a particular matter shall include the word "Advertisement" or words of similar import on the outside envelope, if any, and at the beginning and ending of any recorded or electronic communication, unless the recipient of the communication is a person* specified in paragraphs (a)(1) or (a)(2), or unless it is apparent from the context that the communication is an advertisement.

(d) Notwithstanding the prohibitions in paragraph (a), a lawyer may participate with a prepaid or group legal service plan operated by an organization not owned or directed by the lawyer that uses in-person, live telephone or real-time electronic contact to solicit memberships or subscriptions for the plan from persons* who are not known* to need legal services in a particular matter covered by the plan.

(e) As used in this rule, the terms "solicitation" and "solicit" refer to an oral or written* targeted communication initiated by or on behalf of the lawyer that is directed to a specific person* and that offers to provide, or can reasonably* be understood as offering to provide, legal services.

An asterisk (*) identifies a defined term in rule 1.0.1 of the Rules of Professional Conduct. For further discussion of a defined term, see chapter 2 of this Guide, Terminology.

Following the U.S. Supreme Court decision in *Bates v. State Bar of Arizona* (1977) 433 U.S. 350, California permitted advertising of lawyer services and enacted ethical rules in the State Bar Act and the Rules of Professional Conduct specifying what content constitutes advertising and prescribing how that content may be communicated. Rules 7.1 and 7.3 of the Rules of Professional Conduct preserve the distinction in the prior rules between the terms "communication" and "solicitation." A *communication* is a message or offer concerning availability for legal employment directed to a former, present, or prospective client, and includes unsolicited correspondence and internet postings to the general public. A *solicitation* is a targeted communication concerning the availability for legal services for pecuniary gain that is directed to a specific person or persons.

In its Formal Opinion Number 2001-155, the State Bar of California Committee on Professional Responsibility and Conduct discusses a lawyer's website providing information to the public about the lawyer's availability for professional employment. That opinion concludes that the website constitutes a "communication" under former rule 1-400(A) of the Rules of Professional Conduct and an "advertisement" under Business and Professions Code sections 6157 to 6158.3. Such a communication is subject to the applicable prohibitions on false, misleading, and deceptive messages. The content of the pages of the website, as well as the images and sounds that are part of the presentation, must comply with the ethical rules regarding advertising of services. The opinion further concludes, under the facts presented, that the website is not a "solicitation" even if it allows direct email communication to and from the lawyer.

To comply with rule 7.2(c) of the Rules of Professional Conduct, a website must include the name and address of one lawyer or law firm who is responsible for its content. This ethical responsibility rests with the named lawyer or firm and appears to be non-delegable to office staff.

Postings on the personal profile page of a social media website about a lawyer's professional practice may constitute communications subject to the ethical rules on advertising. Cal. State Bar Com. on Prof. Resp. and Conduct, formal opn. No. 2012-186. The ethical rules apply to such postings even though only individuals whom the lawyer has approved can view that personal page. The opinion distinguishes personal news from messages and offers concerning professional employment.

A website that allows visitors to submit legal questions raises unique ethical issues of confidentiality pursuant to the creation of a lawyer-client relationship, as set forth in rule 1.18 of the Rules of Professional Conduct. The lawyer offering to answer questions from the public may want to avoid ongoing ethical duties to visitors who take that offer but whom the lawyer elects not to accept as clients. A disclaimer may avoid ongoing duties to website visitors only if the disclaimer is in sufficiently plain terms to defeat the visitors' reasonable belief that the lawyer is consulting confidentially with the visitor. Cal. State Bar Com. on Prof. Resp. and Conduct, formal opn. No. 2005-168.

Client Testimonials. Favorable comments from a client who is pleased with a lawyer's services are natural additions to the website of the lawyer or the firm. The purpose of posting those comments would be to recommend the services of the lawyer or firm, and therefore they are advertisements subject to the limitations in rule 7.2 of the Rules of Professional Conduct. That rule prohibits a lawyer from paying a client for a positive review. Prohibited payments are defined as "anything of value" and could include a promise of continued representation.

The same analysis would apply to peer reviews of a lawyer on social media or third-party websites such as Avvo, Linkedin, or Google. For a discussion of the ethical rules that apply to referral fees and other financial arrangements with lawyers and non-lawyers, see chapter 8 of this Guide, Compensation, sections 8.8 and 8.9.

The comment on rule 7.1 of the Rules of Professional Conduct expressly targets guaranteed results from a lawyer's services as false and misleading communications. Comment 4 to that rule focuses on client testimonials that may create an "unjustified expectation" that the lawyer could obtain the same result for other clients without reference to the specific facts and law that apply to each client's case. To address this issue a lawyer might consider posting an appropriate disclaimer with the client testimonial: "This testimonial or endorsement does not constitute a guarantee, warranty, or prediction regarding the outcome of a current or prospective legal matter."

Before posting, a lawyer should review any testimonial to safeguard the client's confidential information. A posting implicates the ethical duty to preserve the client's confidences as provided in rule 1.6 of the Rules of Professional Conduct, and the duty not to use a current client's information to the disadvantage of the client as provided in rule 1.8.2 of the Rules of Professional Conduct. Obtaining the client's prior informed consent to the posting would comply with the ethical requirements in those rules.

A lawyer's potential response to a review on Yelp or a similar commercial website with which the lawyer has no financial tie presents similar ethical issues. The ethical duties of loyalty and confidentiality apply to a lawyer's response to such reviews, whether positive or negative. The San Francisco Bar Association considered whether a lawyer may respond to a negative online review by a former client alleging incompetence. S.F. Bar Assn., Ethics opn. No. 2014-1. The opinion concludes that details regarding the management of the case, the frequency and content of communications with the former client, and advice provided by the lawyer all fall within the definition of a "confidence," and therefore should not be ethically included in a publicly posted response to a negative online review. The opinion also discusses "secrets" that the former client would not likely want publicly disclosed. The opinion posits a hypothetical that the client matter was concluded, but also considered the analysis if it was not. The opinion suggests that the lawyer may be precluded from any substantive online response, even one that does not disclose confidential information, if the former client's action is ongoing.

The Los Angeles County Bar Association reaches a similar conclusion regarding responses to negative online reviews. L.A. County Bar Assn., Ethics opn. No. 525 (Dec. 6, 2012). That opinion adds the further requirement that the response to the negative online review be proportionate and restrained.

Departure from a Firm. A departing lawyer who has a "prior professional relationship" with a client or clients is ethically permitted to solicit those clients in accordance with rules 7.1 and 7.3 of the Rules of Professional Conduct and related statutes governing solicitation. Cal. State Bar Standing Com. on Prof. Resp. and Conduct, formal opn. No. 2020-201. Neither the departing lawyer nor the firm should pursue a client who makes known the desire not to be solicited or solicit a client in any "manner which involves intrusion, coercion, duress or harassment." Rules Prof. Conduct, rule 7.3(b). No lawyer should attempt to keep a client at a law firm by imposing conditions on how or when the client can leave the firm, transfer the client's matter, or receive a file. Both the departing lawyer and the firm have a duty to insure a smooth transition without prejudice to the client's interests.

Comment on California Rules of Professional Conduct, Rule 7.2

> [1] This rule permits public dissemination of accurate information concerning a lawyer and the lawyer's services, including for example, the lawyer's name or firm* name, the lawyer's contact information; the kinds of services the lawyer will undertake; the basis on which the lawyer's fees are determined, including prices for specific services and payment and credit arrangements; a lawyer's foreign language ability; names of references and, with their consent, names of clients regularly represented; and other information that might invite the attention of those seeking legal assistance. This rule, however, prohibits the dissemination of false or misleading information, for example, an advertisement that sets forth a specific fee or range of fees for a particular service where, in fact, the lawyer charges or intends to charge a greater fee than that stated in the advertisement.
>
> [2] Neither this rule nor rule 7.3 prohibits communications authorized by law, such as court-approved class action notices.

Comment on California Rules of Professional Conduct, Rule 7.3

[1] A lawyer's communication does not constitute a solicitation if it is directed to the general public, such as through a billboard, an internet banner advertisement, a website or a television commercial, or if it is in response to a request for information or is automatically generated in response to Internet searches.

[2] Paragraph (a) does not apply to situations in which the lawyer is motivated by considerations other than the lawyer's pecuniary gain. Therefore, paragraph (a) does not prohibit a lawyer from participating in constitutionally protected activities of bona fide public or charitable legal-service organizations, or bona fide political, social, civic, fraternal, employee or trade organizations whose purposes include providing or recommending legal services to its members or beneficiaries. (See, e.g., *In re Primus* (1978) 436 U.S. 412 [98 S.Ct. 1893].)

[3] This rule does not prohibit a lawyer from contacting representatives of organizations or groups that may be interested in establishing a bona fide group or prepaid legal plan for their members, insureds, beneficiaries or other third parties for the purpose of informing such entities of the availability of and details concerning the plan or arrangement which the lawyer or lawyer's firm* is willing to offer.

Former California Rules of Professional Conduct, Rule 1-400 - Advertising and Solicitation

(A) For purposes of this rule, "communication" means any message or offer made by or on behalf of a member concerning the availability for professional employment of a member or a law firm directed to any former, present, or prospective client, including but not limited to the following:

(1) Any use of firm name, trade name, fictitious name, or other professional designation of such member or law firm; or

(2) Any stationery, letterhead, business card, sign, brochure, or other comparable written material describing such member, law firm, or lawyers; or

(3) Any advertisement (regardless of medium) of such member or law firm directed to the general public or any substantial portion thereof; or

(4) Any unsolicited correspondence from a member or law firm directed to any person or entity.

(B) For purposes of this rule, a "solicitation" means any communication:

(1) Concerning the availability for professional employment of a member or a law firm in which a significant motive is pecuniary gain; and

(2) Which is: (a) delivered in person or by telephone, or (b) directed by any means to a person known to the sender to be represented by counsel in a matter which is a subject of the communication.

(C) A solicitation shall not be made by or on behalf of a member or law firm to a prospective client with whom the member or law firm has no family or prior professional relationship, unless the solicitation is protected from abridgment by the Constitution of the United States or by the Constitution of the State of California. A solicitation to a former or present client in the discharge of a member's or law firm's professional duties is not prohibited.

(D) A communication or a solicitation (as defined herein) shall not:

(1) Contain any untrue statement; or

(2) Contain any matter, or present or arrange any matter in a manner or format which is false, deceptive, or which tends to confuse, deceive, or mislead the public; or

(3) Omit to state any fact necessary to make the statements made, in the light of circumstances under which they are made, not misleading to the public; or

(4) Fail to indicate clearly, expressly, or by context, that it is a communication or solicitation, as the case may be; or

(5) Be transmitted in any manner which involves intrusion, coercion, duress, compulsion, intimidation, threats, or vexatious or harassing conduct.

(6) State that a member is a "certified specialist" unless the member holds a current certificate as a specialist issued by the Board of Legal Specialization, or any other entity accredited by the State Bar to designate specialists pursuant to standards adopted by the Board of Governors, and states the complete name of the entity which granted certification.

Paragraphs (E) and (F) of former rule 1-400 are redacted.

Statute

California Business and Professions Code section 6158. Electronic Media Advertisements; Compliance with Sections 6157.1 and 1657.2; Message May Not be False, Misleading or Deceptive; Message Must Be Factually Substantiated

In advertising by electronic media, to comply with Sections 6157.1 and 6157.2, the message as a whole may not be false, misleading, or deceptive, and the message as a whole must be factually substantiated. The message means the effect in combination of the spoken word, sound, background, action, symbols, visual image, or any other technique employed to create the message. Factually substantiated means capable of verification by a credible source.

Ethic Opinions

Lawyers who communicate about legal topics in public commentary must comply with the Model Rules of Professional Conduct, including the rules regarding confidentiality of information relating to the representation of a client. A violation of model rule 1.6(a) is not avoided by describing public commentary as a "hypothetical" if there is a reasonable likelihood that a third party may ascertain the identity or situation of the client from the facts set forth in the hypothetical. Significantly, information about a client's representation contained in a court order, although contained in a public document or record, is not exempt from the lawyer's duty of confidentiality under rule 1.6. ABA Com. on Ethics and Prof. Resp., formal opn. No. 2018-480.

A lawyer is not responsible for the content of a lawyer's profile on a professional online directory and rating website that a third party creates and maintains. However, if the lawyer chooses to exercise control over the profile's content by "adopting" the profile on the directory itself or otherwise using the profile to market the lawyer's practice, the lawyer becomes responsible for its content. The profile becomes a communication about the lawyer's services, and consequently the lawyer must comply with the rules for ethical advertising. The lawyer cannot post or induce another to post content that is false or misleading, and must undertake reasonable efforts to correct any such content. State Bar of Cal. Com. on Prof. Resp. and Conduct, formal opn. No. 2019-199.

Lawyers may use geographically targeted advertisements to market their legal services on general social media sites so long as the advertisements are truthful, and contain the information required in lawyer communications. San Diego County Bar Assn., Ethics opn. No. 2018-1.

A lawyer is not ethically barred from responding generally to an online review by a former client after the former client's matter has concluded. However, the duty of confidentiality prevents the lawyer from disclosing confidential information about the prior representation absent the former client's informed consent or waiver of confidentiality. S.F. County Bar Assn., Ethics opn. No. 2014-1.

A lawyer may publicly respond to disparaging comments by a former client, whether of malpractice or otherwise, provided that no client confidences are disclosed and the response does not injure the client's position in the previously represented matter. The opinion assumes that the client did not waive confidentiality by the client's comments. L.A. County Bar Assn., Ethics opn. No. 525 (Dec. 6, 2012).

Case Study

Lawyer is a member of a law firm focusing on tax law and litigation that maintains a firm website identifying the types of services the firm provides, the background and experience of the firm's lawyers, testimonials from firm clients, and other similar information. One page of the website, indistinguishable from the other pages in layout and features, is designated as a "blog," both on the page and in the related menus linking to it. The blog contains a series of articles written by Lawyer and the other lawyers of the firm on changes in tax law and other topics of potential interest to the firm's clients. Each post concludes with the statement: "For more information, contact [the author of the particular post]".

What ethical issues do public communications on a firm website and blog raise and how should Lawyer address them?

Blogging by a lawyer is a communication subject to the requirements of former rule 1-400 of the Rules of Professional Conduct and the State Bar Act relating to lawyer advertising, if the blog expresses the lawyer's availability for professional employment directly or indirectly through its description of the type and character of legal services offered by the lawyer, detailed descriptions of case results, or both. A blog that is an integrated part of a lawyer's or law firm's professional website will be a communication subject to the ethical rules on advertising and solicitation to the same extent as the website of which it is a part. In comparison, a stand-alone blog on legal issues unrelated to the lawyer's area of practice would not constitute advertising subject to ethical rules. State Bar of Cal. Comm. on Prof. Resp. and Conduct, formal opn. No. 2016-196.

10.11 Artificial Intelligence

Artificial intelligence (AI) is a branch of computer science that enables software to analyze a problem through predetermined rules and algorithms and to make decisions based upon that analysis. Lawyers frequently use AI or machine intelligence, for example through natural language legal research on Westlaw. AI can increase the efficiency and accuracy of legal analysis, enabling the lawyer to predict the outcome of a case based upon prior cases with similar facts that a programmed machine can speedily access. AI and other innovative technologies are rapidly expanding.

Implementing and using AI raises ethical issues similar to the technology related issues that lawyers already face. Lawyers must use AI consistent with the ethical duties of competence and diligence. A lawyer must not cede the lawyer's independent judgment to technology. The lawyer's duty to supervise and to ensure that delegated work is done competently applies when associates and staff use AI tools. Just as a lawyer's ethical duties are personal and cannot be delegated to staff, a lawyer must determine what legal work AI is not appropriate to handle.

As AI tools become more advanced and complex, lawyers will need to understand how they work and the limitations of specific AI applications. While lawyers would not be expected to understand the algorithm workings of AI systems, they need to have a basic understanding of how the machine processes information and the risks and benefits of using AI tools in each specific instance. This understanding may be harder to achieve as AI algorithms grow more advanced and machines begin to learn from their own information.

The ability of machines to research and analyze in ways that lawyers do for clients raises the question whether certain AI borders on the unauthorized practice of law, as codified in California Business & Professions Code section 6125. In response, the State Bar of California Board of Trustees formed a task force to review the consumer protection purposes of the prohibition on the unauthorized practice of law and to assess the impact of the definition in Business and Professions Code section 6125 on the use of AI. The task force completed its work and issued its Final Report and Recommendations on March 6, 2020. The State Bar of California Committee on Professional Responsibility and Conduct has already implemented one of those recommendations, inviting public comment on adding a comment to rule 1.1 of the Rules of

Professional Conduct that a lawyer's ethical duty of competence includes "a duty to keep abreast of the changes in the law and law practice, including the benefits and risks associated with relevant technology." Those recommendations also include establishing a working group to explore development of a "regulatory sandbox" as a means for evaluating changes to existing laws and rules that otherwise inhibit the development of innovative legal services delivery systems. The proposed regulatory sandbox would allow an applicant to propose a new delivery system of legal services and the opportunity to demonstrate that the benefits of anticipated access to legal services are likely to outweigh the potential risks of harm substantially.

This chapter only begins to touch upon the ways in which technology impacts the ethical duties of a lawyer or law firm. Many technology related ethics issues have unclear answers, or have answers that are overtaken by advances in technology and more widespread use of technology in the practice of law. Nevertheless, current and evolving ethics opinions, case law, and other authority are clear that lawyers cannot ignore the technology relevant to the practice of law, lawyers must use reasonable efforts to implement and use technology in a manner consistent with their ethical duties, and lawyers need to ensure that implemented technology is secure, monitored, and updated to avoid data and other breaches that may compromise confidential client information. Lawyers are encouraged to consult with technology consultants, read available resources on law firm security, undertake continuing legal education specifically on technology issues, and keep abreast and in compliance with the ethical use of technology in the practice of law.

Statute

California Business and Professions Code section 6125

> No person shall practice law in California unless the person is an active licensee of the State Bar.

Articles

Donahue, *A Primer on Using Artificial Intelligence in the Legal Profession* (Jan. 2018) Harvard J. of Law and Technology.

Garner, *Artificial Intelligence and Its Not-So-Artificial Ethical Implications* (2017) 59 Orange County Law., No. 10, p. 64.

TABLE OF CASES

TABLE OF ETHICS OPINIONS

CALIFORNIA STATE BAR STANDING COMMITTEE ON PROFESSIONAL LIABILITY AND CONDUCT, FORMAL OPINIONS

Los Angeles County Bar Association, Ethics Opinions

Orange County Bar Association, Ethics Opinions

San Diego County Bar Association, Ethics Opinions

San Francisco County Bar Association, Ethics Opinions

American Bar Association, Committee on Ethics and Professional Responsibility, Formal Opinions

INDEX TO DEFINED TERMS

References are to the Rule of Professional Conduct where the defined term is identified by an asterisk (*) in Administrative Order 2018-05-09 of the California Supreme Court.

Made in the USA
Las Vegas, NV
17 September 2026

54691885R00168